ALSO BY JOAN REARDON

M.F.K. Fisher, Julia Child, and Alice Waters:
Celebrating the Pleasures of the Table

Oysters:
A Culinary Celebration

Poetry by American Women, 1975–1989:
A Bibliography

Poetry by American Women, 1900–1975:
A Bibliography (with Kristine A. Thorsen)

Poet of the Appetites

Poet of the Appetites

THE LIVES AND LOVES

OF M.F.K. FISHER

Joan Reardon

NORTH POINT PRESS

A DIVISION OF FARRAR, STRAUS AND GIROUX

NEW YORK

North Point Press
A division of Farrar, Straus and Giroux
19 Union Square West, New York 10003

Grateful acknowledgment is made to the following:

Robert Lescher, for permission to reprint previously unpublished writing of M.F.K. Fisher, copyright © 2004 by Robert Lescher, as Trustee of The Literary Trust under the will of M.F.K. Fisher, deposited at the Arthur and Elizabeth Schlesinger Library, Radcliffe Institute for Advanced Study, Harvard University.

Julia Child, for permission to reprint unpublished letters from the Julia McWilliams Child Papers, 1953–1980, deposited at the Arthur and Elizabeth Schlesinger Library, Radcliffe Institute for Advanced Study, Harvard University.

Doubleday, a division of Random House, Inc., for permission to reprint excerpts from "I'm Here," copyright © 1956 by Theodore Roethke, and "The Far Field," copyright © 1962 by Beatrice Roethke, Administratrix of the Estate of Theodore Roethke, from *The Collected Poems of Theodore Roethke* by Theodore Roethke. Used by permission of Doubleday, a division of Random House, Inc.

Library of Congress Cataloging-in-Publication Data
Reardon, Joan, 1930–
    Poet of the appetites : the lives and loves of M.F.K. Fisher / Joan Reardon.— 1st ed.
        p.   cm.
    Includes bibliographical references and index.
    ISBN-13: 978-0-86547-562-5
    ISBN-10: 0-86547-562-8 (hc : alk. paper)
    1. Fisher, M.F.K. (Mary Frances Kennedy), 1908—Biography.
    2. Women food writers—United States—Biography.   I. Title.

TX649.F5R43 2004
641'.092—dc22

                                            2004006113

Designed by Jonathan D. Lippincott

www.fsgbooks.com

1   3   5   7   9   10   8   6   4   2

To John, whose loyalty and love have never faltered.
And to everyone who contributed to this book,
especially the elusive MFKF.

Contents

Who Was the Woman That Wrote That Page?[1]

Almost everyone can remember his or her introduction to M.F.K. Fisher. For me, it was "Two Kitchens in Provence," soon followed by a sampling from *The Art of Eating*, and then eventually the complete works. I liked the *way* she wrote, and imagined that it was exactly the way she spoke, with all those "ands" and "don't cares" and "things like that" popping off the page. Her descriptions forever etched my memory of the Deux Garçons café in Aix, where I had often observed the steady stream of tourists and students making their way along the cours Mirabeau, and the markets of Provence where I had shopped. She transcribed into the unforgettable language of ripeness and decay what I had always felt about the cherries, string beans, lettuces, and lamb chops that I had once purchased in Arles, St.-Rémy, and Cavaillon. She also wrote about Cain and Abel's potage and the trick of making a perfect oyster stew, about the Greeks' delicate cakes of sesame and honey and Carême's *pièces montées*, not with the seriousness of a culinary historian, but with every intention to seduce.

As a student in France in the early 1930s, Mary Frances read *The Physiology of Taste* by the gentleman gastronome Jean-Anthelme

Brillat-Savarin, a book without precedent in postclassical Western literature, mixing erudition, wit, and wisdom in a manner never before associated with food. Although she felt a special affinity with Brillat-Savarin, she was unaware of a limited number of American writers fast becoming arbiters of taste in matters of food and wine, like Theodore Child, who had written *Delicate Feasting*, and Frederick Stokes, who had published *Good Form: Dinners, Ceremonious and Unceremonious*. And Mary Frances had only a passing acquaintance with the twentieth-century works of George Rector, Joseph Wechsberg, Alexis Lichine, Julian Street, Lucius Beebe, A. J. Liebling, and Waverley Root. She came upon gastronomical writing whimsically, finding a treasure trove of amusing stories in old recipe books that instructed their users to "parboil the cock, flea him, and stamp him in a stone mortar," and add "cannel, cloves, mace, grains of parise, quibbles, and onions to Beef y-Stewed." She delighted in the offbeat and the familiar, and beginning with *Serve It Forth* in 1937, she seemed to write to share, amuse, and please those she loved.

With a willing suspension of disbelief, I followed her into an autobiographical world peopled with her grandparents, parents, siblings, neighbors "related by love alone," Laguna friends, public school and boarding school teachers, college roommates, university professors, husbands, lovers, landladies, waiters, and shopkeepers. So textured were her descriptions of her dyspeptic Grandmother Holbrook, awesome father Rex, statuesque mother Edith, and enigmatic sister Anne, that I would recognize them anywhere. She portrayed herself as a good girl who helped out in the kitchen, held her sister's hand on the way to school, surprised her mother with a decorated pudding and a notebook filled with stories she had written. But she was also the bad girl who deliberately chewed fresh tar, skipped classes to watch the circus practice, lied about spending her "missionary" money on a notebook, and deliberately tipped her baby brother out of his high chair.

As the years passed, she wrote about her one true love as well as the lesser loves in her life and about her travels with her daughters and her sister, and about living among the vineyards of Napa and Sonoma. I revisited Aix, Marseilles, and Dijon with her books in hand. Yet, although I loved reading her words and learning what she wanted

events that were stored in her memory. Her art was kaleidoscopic—
the same words telling different stories, the same story told with different words. She believed that she was a born writer, unlike her first
husband, Al Fisher, who was a writer manqué. "I write because I
must," she frequently said. And she constructed a mythology about
herself as a writer who couldn't read her work after it was published,
never paid attention to reviews, never went to press parties—a writer
who denigrated her writing.

At one time she fancied herself "the Dorothy Parker of the
kitchen" and the Katharine Hepburn of culinary arts and letters. Toward the end of her life, she clung to her self-image as a writer who
literally had to write to keep alive. She told her story in every imaginable way, through recipes and in memoirs. Like her beloved Georges
Simenon, she used autobiographical works and stories to give her
almost complete control over the interpretation of her past. She
scripted her biography by writing extensively about herself as she
wanted others to know her. And in so doing, she challenged those
who would try to resist the siren call of her words and tell her story as
it actually played out.

Although I may never *completely* know why she laughed, cried, seduced people, and then pushed them away, reread Simenon's books,
decorated her home with fertility symbols and her patio with gerani-
ums, I have come a long way toward discovering the reasons. The
central paradox of M.F.K. Fisher's life is that the woman who made
domestic life so sensual and intimate and made places come alive for
her readers was also a self-absorbed and, unfortunately, at times a destructive woman. Writing about her life, I have found much to praise
and much to blame. And it is all one.

When I visited her for the first time in 1987 and she invited me to
be her biographer, I declined the offer. But after I published *M.F.K.
Fisher, Julia Child, and Alice Waters: Celebrating the Pleasures of the
Table* in 1994, I felt that so much of Mary Frances's story was left un-
told that I should revisit her life and her works. I share what I found
with all those who, like me, have asked, Who was the woman that
wrote that page?

Poet of the Appetites

ONE

Born on the Third of July

(1908–1920)

Since the beginning of my talking years, my family has teasingly warned me and gullible listeners that I never spoil a story by sticking to the truth. This is a plain lie, because I do not lie. But I have never seen any reason to be dull, and since I was less than four I have enjoyed entertaining and occasionally startling anyone who may be listening.[1]   —M.F.K. Fisher

At the age of sixty-one, Mary Frances Kennedy Fisher could not resist the opportunity to enhance her entrance on the stage of the world into a drama of extraordinary derring-do:

I began in Albion, Michigan, and was born there on July 3, 1908, in a heat wave. I leapt forth only a few minutes before midnight, in a supreme effort from my mother, whose husband had assured her that I would be named Independencia if I arrived on the 4th . . . Father was not only editor and co-owner of the *Recorder*, with his brother Walter, but was a stalwart member of the volunteer fire brigade, and through his cohorts was able to keep our wooden house sprayed occasionally with a few good jets of hose water, to cool the air for Mother and me. This cost him a manly spree of ice cream and beer, later, in the back room of the firehouse.[2]

Unable to resist the lure of apocrypha, Mary Frances also introduced readers to an elderly neighbor, who, when she visited the

Kennedy newborn and saw her tiny hands open, said to Mary Frances's mother, "Poor child . . . can't last a week . . . no strength there," and expressed shock when she heard the baby's name: "Mary!!! My goodness, I'd have thought with your church upbringing you'd call her something from the *Bible!*"[3] Edith was speechless and sank deeper into her pillows.

Whatever the other circumstances of Mary Frances's birth, it occurred not minutes before midnight, but early enough in the day for its announcement comfortably to make page 3 of that day's edition of the *Albion Evening Recorder*: "Born to Mr. and Mrs. R.B. Kennedy, 202 Irwin Avenue,[4] July 3rd, 1908, a girl."[5] The big news of the day was the imminent selection of William Jennings Bryan as the Democrats' presidential candidate, and petitions for concrete sidewalks in the city. But then, this was a local paper that ran attention-grabbing sports headlines like "Finally Gets Even—Alma Man Carried Grudge for Nineteen Years at Last Took Revenge."[6]

Although she spent the first two and a half years of her life in Albion, Mary Frances was never tempted to return. The small Michigan town at the fork of the Kalamazoo River, however, was the setting of an important chapter in the lives of her parents, Rex Brenton Kennedy and Edith Oliver Holbrook, because it was their first home after a wedding that had had more obstacles than roses strewn in its path. They had met two years earlier, in 1902, when Rex had gone to work at a newspaper in Onawa, Iowa, and Evans Holbrook, a friend from the University of Chicago, introduced him to his sister Edith. It was spring, Edith was twenty-two, and they fell in love. Rex wooed her "in a nearby nut-grove, in several rendezvous arranged by her favorite brother,"[7] because he was not deemed worthy of the formal parlor of the town's only banker.

Edith's parents, Bernard David and Mary Frances Oliver Holbrook,[8] persisted in seeing the twenty-six-year-old newspaperman as insufficiently educated and socially inferior, and a rich uncle offered to send Edith off to Dresden to study music with a chaperone from one of her boarding schools. Determined and proud, Rex stayed in Onawa until "her Daisy Millerish stay was up."[9] When Edith returned eighteen months later, she went straight into Rex's arms. They were a handsome couple. Edith was over five feet eight and a dark-haired, stylish beauty; Rex was six-four with deep-set gray eyes, a slight wave in his brown hair, a prominent nose, and a deliberate slouch. Amid stiff upper lips and scarcely hidden frowns, they were married in September 1904. Then they left Onawa, journeying by rail across the fields of Iowa and stopping in Indianola, near Des Moines, for a day to visit Rex's parents, Clarence Klaude (CKK) and Luella Kennedy.[10] "Delighted to greet my first and (to date) only real live sister,"[11] wrote Rex's younger brother Ted, who was still living with his parents.

Three days later Rex and Edith reached Albion, where Rex was to join his older brother, Walter, at the helm of the *Albion Evening Recorder*. The Kennedy brothers had grown up helping their parents in a succession of weekly papers and had also worked at various newspaper jobs during and after their college days, so when Walter's boss at the University of Chicago Press offered to sell him the fledgling *Recorder*, Walter and Rex had purchased it, intending to assume the roles of manager and editor respectively. Rex and Edith moved into a house at 205 West Erie Street, where Walter and his bride, Agnes "Tim" Chambers, were already living in the second-floor apartment.

Years earlier, Rex had followed Walter to Simpson College in Indianola, where he played football as Walter had done, and on to the University of Chicago team. Although Rex did not have the tremendous strength and bulldog grit of his older brother and stayed at the university for only one quarter in 1901, he did go on to coach football for a season in North Dakota before becoming a newspaperman in Onawa. And when the Kennedy brothers began their professional and married lives together in 1904, they continued to share football as well, taking on the job of coaching the Albion College football team. While their husbands worked and coached together, Edith and her sister-in-law Tim joined the "Ladies Review," dedicated to the reading and discussion of good literature. Their friendship developed slowly, however, because the two women were very unlike. Tim was petite and, like her husband, outgoing; she loved to dance and go to parties.

Second-to-last of nine children, four of whom died in infancy, Edith was the favorite of her reclusive father. Educated at a young ladies' seminary in western Iowa and other boarding schools near Pittsburgh, and "finished" abroad, she played the piano and dressed elegantly in the clothes she acquired while traveling in Germany and France. She wore her long brown hair swept up and away from her face in the fashion of the day and was proud of her pinched waist. She also had a habit of tilting her chin up that could easily be interpreted as hauteur but proved to be shyness. Edith was not at ease with strangers, preferring solitary pastimes. She and Tim, however, shared a love of books, and they found ways to become a part of the Albion community of serious ministers, college students, and small industrialists. They also looked forward to bringing young Kennedys into the world.

Disappointment, however, attended Edith's first pregnancy, when a son was stillborn in January 1907. Nine months later Edith became pregnant again, and she gave birth to a healthy baby girl, notwithstanding the supposed prognostications of elderly neighbors. The baby was named Mary Frances, after Edith's mother. Family photographs picture a smiling Edith cradling her daughter in her arms, and another photo shows the six-month-old Mary Frances peeking at the camera over Rex's shoulder. In another may-have-happened story, Rex proudly introduced his baby daughter to neighbors and friends in the town's first automobile, owned and driven by the town's richest bachelor.[12]

Before Mary Frances's birth, Rex had purchased a rambling white clapboard two-storied house on the street of stately homes called Minister's Row. Located on the corner of Clinton and Irwin Streets, the house had a wraparound porch and spacious yard. Rex took charge of remodeling the interior, and during the most unsettling period of renovation, Edith took her ten-month-old daughter to Onawa to spend a few months with her parents.

Two months after their return, it was her parents' turn to visit. By this time their initial objections to Rex were substantially lessened. He was obviously doing well in the newspaper business, he had been able to purchase a decent house in a good location, and Edith was happy. Their precocious granddaughter was walking and winsome. The visit was the last time that Edith saw her father. He died the following year, leaving his indomitable wife a widow and casting a shadow over his daughter's third pregnancy.

When Edith Anne Kennedy ("Anne") was born on June 12, 1910, Mary Frances rushed to tell the two little Lane girls, who lived across the street, that she had a sister. During the next few days, the children spent hours sitting on the Kennedys' front steps waiting for a glimpse of the baby, who was very small, and, unlike her healthy older sister, plagued by digestive problems. Nursing was difficult, and finding the right formula took weeks. Edith watched helplessly as little Anne cried in discomfort and failed to gain weight, while Tim's daughter Nancy Jane, who was born the same year, flourished.

That winter was especially cold, and Edith began to question whether Albion was a good climate for the children. Rex had already started to think about a possible move to the West Coast. His younger brother Ted had a teaching position in Spokane and his mother and father, having also left Iowa, lived in Fairfield, twenty-five miles away. The prospect of owning either a fruit orchard or a citrus ranch appealed to Rex, and he had already shown an inclination not to remain in one place for very long. Although they had lived happily in Albion for seven years, in the early spring of 1911 Rex and Edith decided it was time to move on. In an amicable agreement, Rex sold Walter his share of the *Recorder* and, bolstered by about $10,000, made the sixty-hour train trip to Spokane.

It was Rex and Edith's first meeting with Ted's wife, Etta, and their eleven-month-old nephew. For that matter, it was only Edith's second meeting with any of her in-laws, and she did not feel at ease with the Kennedy clan. The senior Kennedys were Simpson College graduates, as were Ted and his wife, and their social contacts in Spokane were also Simpson alumni. Always a little disdainful of local colleges (her brothers had attended the University of Iowa, Northwestern, and Stanford), Edith considered herself both culturally and socially superior to her mother-in-law and sister-in-law. And she did not share the interest in journalism, football, and teaching that the Kennedys had in common. To make matters worse, Luella and CKK campaigned to make Rex's visit in Washington permanent. But their efforts to persuade him to invest in an apple orchard and settle nearby failed. He had already decided to bow to Edith's wishes to spend the summer months in a rented log cabin on Maury Island, across from Vashon Island in Puget Sound, where one of Edith's wealthy Holbrook uncles had a large and impressive home.

Mary Frances claimed that one of her earliest recollections of life on Maury Island was associated with the sandy shore: "I do have one clear memory of my life on Puget Sound, when I was down at the bottom of the beached rowboat pretending to save all our lives by dipping some of the bilge water out with a little tin cup . . . my sister Anne lay on her blanket. My mother always insisted that I could not possibly recall this too-early memory, but she was mistaken there. It is still clear and full to me."[13] After an idyllic summer on the beach, Rex and his family continued their travels in a new Model T. From Washington, they journeyed down the coast to southern California. In Ventura County Rex flirted with purchasing his long-dreamed-of orange ranch, and went so far as to take out an option on several acres, which he surrendered when he discovered that there was hardpan just below the surface. Discouraged, he returned to more familiar turf and purchased the *Oxnard Courier* in nearby Oxnard.[14] That venture lasted only a few months, however; Rex and his family then moved farther south to San Diego, where he obtained a position at the local newspaper. Independent as he was, Rex found working for others difficult, and his allergy to water fleas, which were indigenous to the area, literally made him ill. Finally, he decided to follow up on a notice about the sale of the *Whittier News*, which led to his purchasing a controlling interest in the paper in the fall of 1912.

At the end of the nineteenth century, California, with its promise of wealth and health, had drawn settlers from all over the nation. An area twenty-five miles inland from Los Angeles had caught the eye of Aquila Pickering, a wealthy railroad entrepreneur from Chicago, who had traveled west to seek out a place for a Quaker settlement in California. With several other Friends from Pasadena and Los Angeles, he purchased the land for $69,890 in 1887. "From the first," Pickering wrote, "we were favorably impressed with this beautiful situation: the high ground sloping away from the Puente Hills from which we could see the whole valley reaching toward the south and west until our eyes rested upon the coast, some 18 miles away."[15] A subdivision known as the Pickering Land and Water Company became the town of Whittier, honoring the Pennsylvania Quaker poet John Greenleaf Whittier, who was too old and infirm to visit the town that bore his name.

Although there were multi-acre plots available for ranches, the original town grid consisted of thirty-two blocks, with a sizable block in the center reserved for a park. When the lots established in this grid went on the market, many families from the East purchased land sight unseen. Most, but not all, were Quakers, as by charter "all fair-minded people" were invited to settle there.[16] The early economy was based on cattle raising; gradually the grazing lands were transformed into citrus and walnut ranches. A thriving fruit cannery followed, and the expansion of the Southern Pacific Railroad, including a spur connecting Whittier and Los Angeles, transported products and people between the East Coast and Los Angeles. However, it was the discovery of oil in the Puente Hills that brought the greatest influx of new residents. During the boom years from 1894 until 1904, the outlines of derricks mounted on the eastern slopes of the hills marked the profile of the town. Lots were sold and resold, water was brought to the expanding city at great cost by a sequence of flumes, permanent and more spacious homes were built around Central Park and fanned out from the affluent core of the city to the outskirts, and fine municipal buildings and schools were erected, including Whittier College.

By the time Rex invested in the *Whittier News*, Whittier had been incorporated as a sixth-class city with a population of over five thousand, the majority of whom were Friends. In addition to the Southern Pacific Railroad, the trolley cars of the Pacific Electric provided swift transportation within the community and to Los Angeles. Telephone service was available, and the first automobile agency flourished. There were shops for staples and fancy groceries, furniture and carpets, hardware and glass, as well as department stores and lumberyards. Saloons and the sale of liquor, however, had been outlawed practically since the town's inception.[17] Ten churches— Methodist, Baptist, Congregational, Episcopal, and Catholic, as well as Quaker—accommodated the town's various denominations. The *Whittier News*, one of three local and a few denominational papers, had six hundred subscribers and was published every day except Sunday.

A photo printed in the *News* two months after Rex took over depicts the entire staff—eighteen adults and seven newsboys—lined up in front of the building. Inside was a large workroom with a press and linotype machines in the back and editorial and business desks in the front. With the financial help of his mother-in-law, Mary Frances Holbrook, who had decided to come and live with her daughter and son-in-law, Rex purchased the former residence of a local department store owner, "a veritable palace,"[18] located in the center of Whittier, a block away from Philadelphia Street, the main thoroughfare.

Again there was renovating to be done, including the construction of an apartment on the first floor to accommodate Edith's mother. Only the kitchen, which Mary Frances remembered as "the nastiest room I had ever seen in my life,"[19] remained substantially unchanged from its late-nineteenth-century origins. "It was lit by one electric bulb hanging from the center of the ceiling directly above the kitchen table, with its two bins for flour and sugar underneath, and its chipped enamel top. The only natural light came from two high windows above the kitchen sink at one end of the room . . . the sink was very ugly, like everything else in the room."[20]

From the beginning of her residence there, Mary Frances claimed Whittier as her true home.[21] She loved the good air blowing "up the mild slopes of the hills from the flatlands between Whittier and the sea, where some dairy cattle grazed and where there was cultivation of the less soggy ground: potatoes, wheat. Then there was the ocean. Probably the air that reached us was blown for thousand of miles across waves and flowery islands . . . the Spaniards and Mexicans had been great ones for planting, and olive trees flourished in long avenues and hilly groves around the town."[22] Mary Frances also loved the "steady subtle odor" of the plentiful eucalyptus trees that attracted swarms of bees, and the great fields of wild mustard that grew in the hills and meadows, and the heady perfume of the orange groves on the outskirts of the city.

Yet indoors, there could hardly have been three more dissimilar adults living together under one roof. Edith, although less gregarious than her husband, recognized that she had a role to play as the wife of the editor of the *Whittier News*. She became an active member of the Women's Club and a supporter of the impressive town library. She exhibited her ardent love for all things British in everything she did and had, from singing in the choir of St. Matthias Episcopal Church to the British cretonnes and comfortable furniture that filled her home and the volumes of Dickens, Thackeray, and Scott that lined the bookcases in the living room.

Like her mother, she had hired help to do the domestic chores, and her daughters were always clean, well dressed, and well groomed. Edith insisted on politeness, especially at table, and the children knew to refrain from commenting on the food or bringing up disagreeable subjects. "Do you smell the jasmine?" was the conversation-stopping question she introduced whenever they got out of line or began a far-fetched story, and they knew that if she had to repeat the jasmine question, they were in trouble. Although she was known to bend the rules occasionally, there were a few—no chewing scraps of tar when Painter Avenue was being resurfaced, no sucking on ice chips that fell from the iceman's wagon—that would incur a few flicks of the switch on the legs or, worse, a spanking from Rex.

Reading was Edith's passion, and she indulged herself by "lying in state" on the living room couch, book in hand.[23] When things seemed overwhelming, she retreated to her room. Because Rex regarded illness of any kind with disfavor, she probably kept her migraine headaches from him with the same determination that she had concealed her morning sickness during her pregnancies.

While Rex had his newspaper, meetings of the Chamber of Commerce, Rotary Club, and Elks, and his barbershop pals to swap stories with, Whittier's Quaker reserve kept Edith rather isolated. Yet she struck up a friendship with Gwen Nettleship, the daughter of a neighboring family who was eight years younger than she and carried a trace of the accent of her native New Zealand. Soon "Aunt Gwen" was almost a second mother to Mary Frances and Anne, teaching them the delights of Joel Chandler Harris, milk toast, and long walks in the hills in back of the town reservoir.

A special bond also existed between Rex Kennedy and his older daughter. She looked like him except for his prominent nose, which she thought he had broken in a college football game. "When I was intelligent, generous, nicely behaved, I was told that I was just like him," she wrote in *Among Friends*, her memoir of these early years. "When I was impatient, rude, bitter-tongued, I was just like him too."[24] She liked to watch him shave while she and Anne soaked in the giant tub that he had brought from Albion. She also loved to go to the vacant offices of the *Whittier News* on Sundays to poke around in the pressroom and read *Nostrums and Quackeries*, a book of folk remedies, which she neatly slipped from Rex's bookcase. His expressions—"bushwah," "ridicklus," and "mazooma"—made their way into many of her later stories. His penchant for investing in orange groves (including smudge pots at fifty dollars a night whenever the temperature dropped) and his resistance to having a byline (although everyone in Whittier recognized "Heard in the Barber Shop" as his work) left their mark on her as well.

Mary Frances was to write at length about Rex, characterizing him as a would-be adventurer who settled for a newspaper career, but who never lost the "IDEA of a man leaving his own land and starting a new life in a new country alone."[25] He was "a wise Chanticleer [presiding] over his hennery, smoothing feathers with discretion and occasionally showing his spurs,"[26] and she questioned whether he was really predestined for the role of small-town editor, as his wife believed. She characterized his rescue missions on behalf of the vagabonds who landed in Whittier in the boxcars of the Southern Pacific as evidence of his "Lame Duck Syndrome"—a tendency she too would display. And her earliest memorable meals—along the roadside, at the dining room table in Whittier, or at the beach house—were shared with him.

Rex's presence dominated the house. The place overflowed with the magazines and newspapers he consumed, beginning at breakfast and ending at bedside. His schedule dictated everyone else's, from the cook's punctual serving of meals to the magical getaways to San Francisco and Los Angeles that were a part of his and Edith's relationship. He tooted around town in his Model T, and loved to drive devil-may-care on the scenic Turnbull Canyon Road with Edith proudly beside him in her duster and veil-draped hat, while Mary Frances and Anne giggled in the back seat.

Although he was a vestryman at St. Matthias Episcopal Church, Rex had abandoned the strict Methodist tenets of his parents' religion. The son of a writer who used his newspaper as a pulpit and vehemently denounced drinking, smoking, dancing, and gambling, Rex smoked cigarettes, two-stepped with the best of them, always had a decanter of port or sherry on the dining room sideboard, and enjoyed a daily glass of ginger beer or a highball with Edith when he came home from the *News* late in the afternoon. The loyalty and drive that he shared with his three brothers were Kennedy birthrights, but at times of stress there were also mood swings and bouts with depression, which he and his youngest brother, Burt, had inherited from their father.[27]

During the early years of his marriage, Rex had learned to avoid his wife's displeasure by keeping certain things—his rescues of the homeless and his longing for adventure—to himself. And he made it a point not to oppose Edith when she opened the doors of their home to Holbrook relatives and resolutely closed them to the close-knit Kennedys. Years later, Mary Frances's cousin Weare Holbrook disclosed to her his astonishment about the situation he had observed when he worked with Rex at the *News* for a few months one summer: "Another thing I remember (it made me feel rather *de trop*) was the way Holbrooks preponderd over Kennedys in your household. Pictures, letters, long-staying guests, were all heavily on the distaff side. Most of all, I recall your Kennedy grandparents: the bearded giant incredibly named Clarence Klaude, and *your* grandmother who was much prettier than *our* grandmother. They paid brief backdoor visits, not very often, and I never heard them quoted."[28]

Edith had bought into the notion that in-laws, especially mothers-in-law, were to be shunned, and only seemed comfortable with her own blood relatives. "It was a strange situation," Mary Frances wrote. "Now and then Rex rebelled, but Mother was really horrible about anyone not connected in some way with her own family. The only people she really liked were Walter and Tim Kennedy from Albion. Otherwise it was strangely hellish when Uncle Ted, for instance, came to see us. I soon caught on to some of this, of course, but by now I feel both cheated and embarrassed by some of Mother's compulsive snobberies."[29]

Rex threw his considerable energies into the expansion of the *Whittier News*, moving it into larger quarters nearby in 1915 and steadily increasing its circulation. His refuge was Laguna Beach, about forty miles south and west from Whittier, where the same year he acquired a lot near the Nettleships' summer campsite and built a simple redwood beach house for about a thousand dollars.[30] From it the Kennedys had a clear view of the blue waters of the ocean across the Pacific Coast Highway. And by climbing down the slopes that formed a natural breakwater, they had access to the vast stretch of sandy beaches.

After the paper went to press on Saturday afternoon, Rex and Edith packed the children and a few supplies into the car, and two and a half hours later they were in Laguna, where they were often joined by a group of St. Matthias regulars the next day. Edith seemed much freer and happier in Laguna than in Whittier. In the lean-to kitchen she stood for hours at the stove frying prairie oysters for family and guests. To accommodate them all and the food that the ladies had brought, the dining table often stretched from the kitchen into the living room. The Whittierites' laughter was louder in Laguna, and the men told jokes in the presence of the ladies, which was unheard of at home. In the evening they all drove back to Whittier.

Every summer from her seventh until her twelfth year, Mary Frances and Anne spent their vacation months there with Aunt Gwen, while Edith remained in Whittier with Rex and Grandmother Holbrook. The beach trio adopted a routine of simple outdoor meals, romps on the beach with pockets full of fried egg sandwiches, and suppers of freshly caught fish and farm-stand cucumbers and tomatoes. Sometimes Rex drove out on weekdays after the paper went to press, and then he and Gwen swam out to the rocks and gathered mussels, which Gwen steamed in seaweed for them all to feast on as the sun sank into the ocean. Gwen was their goddess, mentor, and pillar of strength, a steady presence in their lives who contrasted sharply with the more elusive figure of their mother, with whom every outing to Los Angeles to see a play or dine in a fine restaurant seemed like a favor bestowed.

Absent from the Laguna scene was Grandmother Holbrook—the third and perhaps most influential resident at 115 Painter Avenue. This proud woman, who had done her Christian duty by bringing nine children into the world, brought to the household her strong abhorrence of sensual pleasure—whether in food or drink or any other activity—and a commitment to Campbellite[31] doctrines of scriptural simplicity, baptism by immersion, and independent congregations. She attended religious conferences and services in various cities, visited family and friends in Pittsburgh, and sought relief for her tired body at Dr. Kellogg's sanitarium in Battle Creek, Michigan. Mary Frances thought of her as "a Rock of Gibraltar" and "a tree or a sheltering cover of some kind."[32] In another era and another place, perhaps, this undaunted woman, her gray hair heightened into an imposing pompadour and her body tightly corseted, could have managed a company. Unfortunately, the times dictated that she confine her energies to the role of matriarch. Her apartment, which consisted of a bedroom, a dressing room, and a bathroom, was a sanctuary, where Mary Frances read *The Imitation of Christ* and Bible stories to her and where she taught her granddaughters how to knit, lest idle thoughts and hands lead to mischief.

Her resolve to do battle with sensuality in all of its palpable forms and her adherence to the strictures of Dr. Kellogg's diet created a dichotomy in the meals at 115 Painter Avenue. When Grandmother Holbrook was home, seasoning was eschewed and meats and vegetables were cooked to a fare-thee-well. Grandmother's absences brought out the gourmand in Rex, who relished a rare steak or beef roast and a glass of "red ink." Edith was the dessert aficionado, her specialties the divinity fudge she'd learned to make in boarding school and the Lady Baltimore cake she baked for Rex's birthday. Laguna had its own culinary delights—real mayonnaise on salads and Aunt Gwen's fried onion rings. One menu taught Mary Frances what she didn't like to eat, the other awakened her palate and showed her how a meal enjoyed with loved ones became a feast. "Without my first eleven years of gastronomical awareness when Old Mrs. Holbrook was in residence I probably would still be swimming in unread iambics instead of puzzling over the relationship between food and love . . . I would not be this *me* but some other, without my first years in Grandmother's gastric presence."[33]

Anne was thriving on this regimen too, and with relief Edith watched as her younger daughter plumped into what Mary Frances called her "little brown sister." Only two years apart, Mary Frances and Anne were soul mates. Unable to pronounce "daughter," Rex's usual epithet for Mary Frances, Anne called her older sister Dote, and Anne more often than not answered to Sis. In bed, or perched on the toilet seat in the small bathroom on the porch outside the kitchen door, she listened to the stories Mary Frances concocted for her enjoyment. Together they sought out the various housekeepers to learn whittling or sing hymns. They constructed cities in the sandbox that Rex built for them in the yard, and invented their own language, "Margaret speak," a kind of private patois in imitation of one of their housekeepers, who had a cleft palate. They were partners in crime, smuggling the Nettleship dog into the back seat of the car on the family's Sunday afternoon drives in spite of Edith's aversion to four-legged friends. They slyly folded the funny papers provided by the children next door into their Sunday Bible stories, and wrote petitions to protest having cod liver oil mixed into their orange juice.

Yet there was an undercurrent of competitiveness to the relationship. Anne had her attention-getting strategies, such as the way she would play the invalid on the couch every Christmas after her annual raid on the holiday cookies had upset her stomach. Mary Frances shared her presents with Anne and entertained her, but she had her own way of proving that "I was there too."[34] Mary Frances learned to read when she was five and devoured the Kennedys' vast library of newspapers, magazines, and Frank Baum's Oz books as well as Bible stories and leather-bound classics. She loved to embellish the tales of adventure that she read and to concoct stories about the things she saw and heard on the way to school. She also sought to impress her teachers and peers with fictitious stories and fabricated tales about her grandmother's travels. While Anne was carving out an identity as the more dependent and affectionate child, Mary Frances was becoming both independent and precocious.

Mary Frances also realized that hanging around the kitchen and learning to cook was another way to be seen, and in her later books and stories, the habitués of the kitchen often figure as the real companions of her childhood. The black Cynthia, who could make a banquet out of hash, ruled the kitchen for six months before Grandmother Holbrook was in residence, but was hopelessly lonely in Whittier. Amimoto, the Asian student turned houseboy, delighted the two little girls by reading stories to them, but Edith was uncomfortable with the idea of a male servant, and he didn't last long. The four McLure sisters lived down the street, and at various times each of them took a turn at working for the Kennedys. Margaret, with her speech impairment, was Mary Frances's favorite. The giddy Spanish-speaking Anita, whom Rex brought into the house because a friend asked him to care for her, had a limited repertoire, but her total dedication to the preparation of chicken enchiladas or a superb flan endeared her to everyone except Edith. The proud, exotic Ora was one of the last housekeepers to serve the family before they moved down Painter Avenue, and her skill at knife-wielding caught Mary Frances's fancy.

From this amazing group of people Mary Frances learned to carve vegetables, dice and mince, mix a smooth white sauce, and make pie-dough cutouts. She took note of how a flaky crust could elevate an ordinary hash made from leftovers into a thing of beauty, and she learned the difference between overcooked vegetables and crisp ones. On the cook's night off, she helped Edith to prepare the evening meal, and on a rare occasion was responsible for making a simple supper for herself and her sister. She later wrote about "Hindu Eggs"[35] and the fiery results of exceeding a recipe's prescribed amount of curry powder, but she remained undaunted by the blisters her cooking raised in Anne's mouth and her own. Just as her exaggerated stories commanded the attention of those around her, she soon realized that experimenting with ingredients brought a heady kind of power that appealed to her. "I am the first to admit that one intoxicating angle of my early eagerness to substitute for the family cook on her day off was the extra attention it brought me. It made me feel creative and powerful, and that is possibly the truest reason for my continuing preoccupation with the art of eating."[36]

Because Mary Frances was already reading fluently, her mother did not think it necessary to enroll her in the Penn Street School until she was seven, a year older than most of the other students in her first-grade class. She idolized her teacher, Miss Newby, but she also felt much smarter than her classmates and was bored by their antics. Already very much the critical observer, she became fascinated by the dynamics between the young Quaker insiders and the non-Quaker outsiders like herself and her friend Margie Thayer. She remained aloof from the social machinations at recess, and when cliques formed without her, she claimed to be impervious to the exclusion.

The first kindergarten at the Penn Street School opened during the second half of Mary Frances's first year there, and Edith enrolled Anne in it. Mary Frances immediately became Anne's protector in the complex world of schoolyard intrigue. She insisted that Anne hold her hand while they walked the four blocks to school, and after a few months, when she felt her sister's dependence on her slipping away, she made up stories about haunted houses and witches lying in wait along their route to scare Anne into compliance. It was Anne, however, who introduced her older sister to what could only be called a "grand passion" the following year, when Anne fell in love with a little boy named Thomas. Recess after recess, the two youngsters would meet at the wire fence that separated the girls from the boys and press their hands together or kiss. Although the affair ended as quickly as it began, Mary Frances and her friends were never as oblivious to boys as they had been before the Anne and Thomas affair.

Mary Frances was selective in her friendships with other children. She observed, scrutinized, and, for the most part, dismissed her class-mates as either blind sheep following the leader of the day or parrots repeating the remarks of their parents. Occasionally, a fellow class-mate captured her attention, like Bertha, who wore a religious scapu-lar around her neck, and the maverick Gracie, who sported earrings, smelled of garlic, and cursed a little, but also "was so *common*."[37] Margie Thayer was her best friend, and on the Thayer ranch beyond the city limits, she and Mary Frances, along with Anne, acted out the plots of their favorite books in the barn or played with Margie's dog in the orange groves. But it was Anne who was her constant companion, Anne whose small hand Mary Frances would feel in hers on the way to and from school when the Quaker children turned to nasty taunt-ing—"What does your big fat mother do? What does your big skinny Irish father do?"[38]—another aspect of living in Whittier.

In May 1917, when Mary Frances was nine years old, a third daughter was born to Edith and Rex. From her frequent dipping into adult books, Mary Frances thought that she knew what had happened on the other side of the upstairs bedroom door about nine months earlier, and was ready to lend a hand with the new arrival. Anne, on the other hand, was seven and just coming out from under Mary

Frances's shadow. The arrival of Norah thrust her back into it again when Edith's attention was directed toward the new baby.[39] Because of the surgical removal of an abdominal growth before the birth, Edith's convalescence was lengthy and required the services of nurses along with the housekeeper. Edith luxuriated in her recuperation this time, and depended more and more on Aunt Gwen to look after Mary Frances and Anne. She also unconsciously placed more responsibility on her eldest daughter, who tried to please her mother with careful concoctions from *The Invalid's Cookery Book*, sometimes with unintended results. Not happy with the bland look of a cornstarch pudding that she had skillfully unmolded, Mary Frances garnished it with blackberries from a backyard bush to perk it up a bit. Hours later, Edith broke out in a painful rash. Fortunately it was short-lived, and that failure was balanced by successes like chipped beef in cream sauce and sponge cake.

Eight months later, with a nod from Edith, Rex invited his parents to join his family in Whittier. Luella's chronic cough had prompted the senior Kennedys to sell their home and newspaper in Fairfield and move south to California, where they believed the climate would be healthier than Washington's. Relying on Rex's advice and financial assistance, they purchased a five-acre orange ranch in La Puente, about four miles from Whittier, and began building a small house in the middle of it. While the construction of the residence was in progress, Grandfather Kennedy taught Mary Frances and Anne the intricate game of jackstraws and made up crossword puzzles to challenge them, and Mary Frances took her concerns about pierced ears to Grandmother Kennedy, who got along with her daughter-in-law this time without a riffle.

By the end of the following summer, as America plunged deeper into World War I, Rex was organizing war bond rallies. To Edith's dismay, he even thought of enlisting in the armed services. But when she became pregnant again in September, the forty-two-year-old Rex decided to remain editor of the *News* and concentrate on his growing family. After the armistice was signed, he raised enough money to purchase the six-acre citrus grove adjacent to his parents' property.

Smudge pots and crop yields became a part of Rex's daily conversation, and frequent visits to La Puente became a part of his daily routine. Often he took Mary Frances and Anne to stay overnight at their grandparents', where they snuggled under a feather comforter in the small bed they shared. Luella, an avid gardener, sent them home with fresh asparagus, lettuce, and other vegetables in season. But Edith began to fret over the overnights just as she was beginning to worry about her older daughters' attachment to Aunt Gwen. Their sense of distance from her was underscored by the birth of David Holbrook Kennedy the following May. "One more Kennedy boy for the world's needs,"[40] Luella wrote to Ted. At long last Rex had a son. Mary Frances and Anne became ballasts to the younger pair of Kennedys, and the first "batch" had little in common with the second. While the older girls accepted Edith's preoccupation with the younger children, increasingly they looked to their father for attention.

Rex's announcement, in October 1919, that he had purchased yet another plot of land—thirteen acres with a big white house and an orange grove on South Painter Avenue outside the city limits—delighted the entire family. The Ranch, as it would always be called, was adjacent to the Thayer property and familiar territory to Mary Frances and Anne, who frequently played there. The previous owner was an eccentric elderly woman who had planted magnificent fir trees in the front of the house as well as a great variety of subtropical shrubs and bushes that she had brought back from her travels. When Rex bought the property, part of it was a tangle of overgrown greenery and the house was in need of repair, but the ten-acre orange grove was flourishing. There was a separate guesthouse, a cook's house, several sheds and garages, and an old barn with chicken coops, rabbit hutches, and a pigeon roost. Inside the house there was ample space, and once again Rex decided to build a three-room suite for Grandmother Holbrook on the first floor, where there already were a living room, a dining room, and a large, airy kitchen. An expanse of lawn and many splendid trees ensured privacy for the family and space for the children to play. Edith, busy with a toddler and a baby, could gradually forgo Women's Club meetings and choir rehearsals in town, and Rex had at last found an idyllic mix of the rural living he had known in his youth and the legacy of print that was his birthright.

At one end of the barn Rex built a workroom, and Mary Frances,

Anne, and later Norah spent Sunday mornings watching him make repairs to his coops and hutches and tend to his chickens, rabbits, pigeons, and a cow, Jennie. Sometimes he put on his bee hat and gloves and inspected the hives while Mary Frances and Anne looked on from under the avocado tree. They learned to feed the animals and grew attached to them, especially to the dog that they were finally allowed to have. They gathered the flowers that seemed to grow everywhere, climbed trees and fences, and roamed through the roomy house with its wide, screened porches.

Now that they lived beyond the city limits, Mary Frances transferred from the Penn Street School to the East Whittier School, which was closer. But her real education continued to lie in the volumes that lined the living room, in the dictionary on the stand in the dining room, and in the answers to the many questions she raised with family members and friends. She also got an education of a different kind in the spring of 1921 when Grandmother Holbrook, who had been in the thrall of a nervous stomach for forty years, died after a brief illness. Because her grandmother was considered to have lived a good and dedicated life, Mary Frances thought she was in heaven and remained unmoved by her death. She had difficulty understanding why her mother wept so silently and for so long outside the closed door to the first-floor apartment, especially as Edith and Grandmother Holbrook had disagreed on so many things, from Edith's attending Episcopalian services—too Papist—to her refusal to terminate her difficult pregnancy with Norah. On balance, though, Grandmother Holbrook had not interfered with the way Edith and Rex lived and raised their children, and she had been generous to them financially. And they in turn had deferred to her and accommodated her, but they were not dominated by her.

"I believe with sadness," Mary Frances wrote decades later to her cousin Weare, "that we can blame practically all the faults of the current youth on the fact that they have no knowledge at all of living with older people, either their parents or more important their grandparents. I am slightly toc toc on this subject, and am truly thankful that Grandmother Holbrook had her own apartment in our house. She and mother plainly disliked and mistrusted each other, but never in the 11+ [sic] years we all lived together did either woman ever show anything but courtesy and real respect. And of course Grandmother and Rex really liked and admired each other."[41]

Now that their grandmother no longer dictated their schedule, Mary Frances and Anne saw no need to go to church on Sunday, and they wrote an elaborate petition to their parents to absolve them from the obligation. Attending church on special days like Christmas and Easter and even now and then was acceptable, but "we feel that staying home on Sunday mornings and working hard to help Father and perhaps helping with the laundry will bring us closer to God."[42] They won their case. In another reaction to their grandmother's absence, their meals became "heathenish." Milk, cream, and butter from the cow contributed to a rich diet of puddings and an orgy of baking. Their chickens produced fine eggs that they used for mayonnaise and other culinary delights. With fruit orchards and citrus groves, artichokes, asparagus, and a variety of other vegetables and salad greens, life was now filled with many new gastronomic experiences.

When Edith made cakes on Saturday mornings, Mary Frances measured sugar and flour. She also prepared afternoon tea for the ladies who occasionally visited Edith, and secretly prided herself on her mother's belief that Mary Frances's trimmed and thinly sliced nasturtium leaf sandwiches were second to none. At some point during those early years at the Ranch, she concluded that "the stove, the bins, the cupboards made an inviolable throne room." And, she wrote, "From them I ruled . . . and I loved that feeling."[43]

In the new liberation of the household, Mary Frances sensed "a communion of more than our bodies when bread is broken and wine drunk."[44] She and Anne could linger over after-dinner cupcakes, removing the lids and adding thick cream before they devoured the voluptuous dessert. A simple meal could end in a fabulous "white wine trip" that Rex and his daughters made to imaginary places they wished they could visit while they drank their water mixed with a little bit of wine. In such a climate, both the preparation of food and its consumption fed "the wilder, more insistent hungers."[45]

Somewhere in those post–Grandmother Holbrook years, Mary Frances also gradually realized that writing, like cooking, was not so much about the facts as it was about creating a certain kind of control over reality and power over the one who consumed. Whether at the stove or at the typewriter, spicing up a dish—blackberries on a bland pudding, extra curry in a stew—and embroidering a story would become her signature. And when she wrote about her Albion and Whittier years later in her life, she was especially "startling to anyone who may be listening."[46] She was not a fourth- or fifth-generation journalist, as she claimed, she simply followed her grandparents and father into a writing career. Clarence Klaude Kennedy's occasional physical disciplining of his sons for flagrantly disobeying his rules inspired her to draw an extreme portrait of her Kennedy grandfather as an abusive person and a religious fanatic reminiscent of Caligula. Comparing her Grandmother Kennedy's verses to Felicia Hemans's mild and sentimental poetry was also a stretch, because Luella's rhyming verses praised the blue skies of October, the smell of cookies baking, and the snow falling on Christmas Eve and were not in the tradition of "The boy stood on the burning deck." What Mary Frances took no notice of, and perhaps was not even aware of, were Luella's "Home Department" articles in the various papers that she and CKK published, which uncannily foreshadowed her own preoccupation with the pleasures of the table.

On other occasions Mary Frances made up grandiose stories about Edith on her premarital trip abroad shocking her parents back in Onawa with reports that she had clung to the gates of Buckingham Palace during a protest with Emmeline Pankhurst's sister suffragettes. Another exaggeration involved Edith's acquisition of a couturier gown at Maison Worth in Paris so she could be presented properly at the British royal court. And Rex, of course, was the unsubstantiated hero of many tales, like the one about his being hired as a young man, along with Walter, to protect the *Chicago Tribune*'s delivery boys from the Hearst newspaper thugs, thereby making himself William Randolph Hearst's enemy for life.

Mary Frances had inherited a Kennedy patrimony of journalistic prowess and family pride along with a Holbrook and Oliver legacy of escapism, snobbery, and unshakable belief. Bolstered by Rex's words—"Tell them who you are!"[47]—during her growing-up years, Mary Frances learned that being a Kennedy and the daughter of the *News*'s editor was a mark of distinction that trumped the moral superiority of the Quakers around her in Whittier.

Moving to the Ranch was both a continuation of her earlier years in the center of town and also an initiation into greater awareness. "I was still a very happy child," she would write of this time. "I stayed this way, excited and enraptured by everything and especially by the new life in 'the country,' for at least three or four more years."[48]

TWO

An Intolerable Waiting

(1921–1929)

So much of adolescence is an ill-defined dying,
An intolerable waiting,
A longing for another place and time,
Another condition.[1]   —Theodore Roethke

Rex took a strong hand in his son's education, but he left decisions about the education of his daughters to Edith. He could have done worse. A voracious reader as well as a product of boarding schools and tutoring abroad, she modeled her daughters' education on her own. Her careful courting of the head librarian in the public library eased the way for them to exceed the limits in withdrawing books. But her similar "queenly dismissal of the public school requirements as unimportant to us Kennedys"[2] paved the way for Mary Frances's frequent absences from grammar school and a lifelong tendency not to take formal study too seriously.

When Mary Frances was fourteen, she transferred to the newly built John Muir Junior High School in the center of town, "because I was the editor's daughter and I had to try anything new."[3] The change was not a welcome one. She disliked the longer ride into town, and was not thrilled to rejoin many of the classmates she had known at the Penn School. She was also unhappy about the fact that she was taller than the other girls in her class, and she daydreamed about escaping her fate by either joining her uncle Burt, who had gone to Uruguay as chief of Swift's beef division, or going back to Albion to stay with Aunt Tim.

For at least two years she had alternated between enjoying her role as the eldest Kennedy sibling and resenting the increased responsibilities that her mother gave her. And although she had endured her last spanking, when she was twelve, she could not forget the humiliation of that occasion. Told to release David from his high chair after the family and guests had left the dining room, she removed the tray and tipped her little brother onto the floor. Rex saw the incident and struck Mary Frances with such force that she flew across the room. Stung with pain and "embarrassment," she raced upstairs to her bedroom. The incident made such an indelible impression on her that years later she returned to it in "The Broken Chain,"[4] a story in which her mother describes the episode as the first time Rex had broken his vow never to strike one of his children in anger. That Mary Frances had provoked such a breach signaled the extent to which the role of dutiful daughter was beginning to irk her.

"I asked myself," she wrote, "why I was always the girl told to come home early from school when there were friends for tea. I knew that I could assemble the whole dainty farce better than anyone else. And mother *counted* on me . . . but why in Hell couldn't my younger siblings give up an afternoon now and then? Why in Hell didn't Mother train the current kitchen slavey to wheel in the tea-wagon?"[5] Her complaining put her at odds with Edith, who ultimately enlisted Rex's help in coping with their adolescent daughter. After Mary Frances celebrated her fifteenth birthday, he offered her the chance to spend the rest of the summer in the office of the *Whittier News*, pinch-hitting for the sports editor, the society columnist, or any other reporter who happened to be on vacation. Although the newspaper's circulation had grown to over three thousand and there were more than fifty employees on its payroll,[6] Rex and his reporters still worked together in the front office. They were a convivial group, and being among them was a pleasant change from being at home. Mary Frances quickly learned to get her copy onto the spindle on time, but back at the Ranch she continued to try Edith's patience by balking at kitchen and laundry duties until classes started at the Whittier Union High School in the fall.

As a freshman of the Class of 1927, Mary Frances's favorite class was English, and she devoted a considerable amount of time to writing romantic, highly derivative pieces. "I was always the English teacher's pet," she recalled, "wrote like mad for her, and assumed casually that I was a genius." "The Moon Maid," a story that she contributed to the annual Whittier High School yearbook, is an overwrought tale of a bejeweled tunic-clad youth walking the "hard, cool sand" when a flutter of light over the waves announces the coming of the Moon-maid Masne, who "crept into the hearts of lovers, poets, and children making them ready for the pure, searching moonlight which is kind only to the seekers of beauty." When the youth discovers that there are nine other rivals for the attention of Masne, a battle to the death occurs among the suitors. A distraught Masne then calls upon her mother, the Moon-goddess, who transforms each bloody corpse into a fluttering brown bird. Mary Frances concludes the tale with "Still on lonely, rocky beaches, the ten little, brown birds try to kiss the shadow of Masne, the Moon-maiden. Still, they sob piteously when the shadow disappears."[7] Undoubtedly she was influenced by her evening strolls on Laguna's beaches, with their rocky coves and rolling surf, and more than a little indebted to Walter Scott and Ovid's *Metamorphoses*, but the dialogue—with its "Thou'rt overbold with thy tongue, dog," and "What thou dost?"—was pure storybook. One phrase, however, does stand out: "His slender foot tapped impatiently on the sand." A foot tapping impatiently was a refrain that Mary Frances would use over and over again in her writing. Frequently it accompanied her description of Edith, who had a habit of tapping her foot under the dining table to show her displeasure, but the phrase also appears in the novel *Not Now But Now* (1947) and in other stories.

Mary Frances kept a diary during her first year of high school, perhaps in imitation of her mother, who regularly noted the day's happenings in a journal of sorts, and urged her daughters to follow her example. But already Mary Frances used her diary like a writer, jotting down lines of poems she was working on and recording the mood of the moment. As an adult, she concluded, "I must have been a very objectionable child—especially during my first year in high school—so serious, so sad and drudging in my pursuit after things. I can still see

myself, trying to look down my nose at popularity, and sex, and cheating—all in the same category, then."[8] But the truth was that she was
something of a snob, and for years had found many of her companions boring. "I was silently and really unconsciously supercilious
about most of my teachers," she wrote, "and all of my classmates."[9]

When fall approached and Anne was ready to enter high school,
Edith decided to enroll both girls in The Bishop's School in La Jolla,
an expense that the financial success of the *Whittier News* made possible. Founded in 1909 by the Right Reverend Joseph Horsefall Johnson, a friend of Rex's from college days, The Bishop's School offered
its students preparation for further academic work, cultural opportunities, and the essentials of Christian character. "Simplicity, Serenity,
and Sincerity" was its motto.

As boarders, Mary Frances and Anne drank gallons of milk from
the school's cows and ate delicious meals. Filipino waiters rushed hot
soup from the kitchen to the dining room and garnished platters with
radishes and celery sculpted into swirling ornaments. With their fellow boarders, the two sisters savored the local Torrey pine honey on
hot biscuits for breakfast, chives instead of cream sauce over the Friday fish entrees, and picnics of fried chicken and deviled eggs on the
La Jolla beach in celebration of the school's annual alumnae Old
Girls' Day. Mary Frances also learned the delight of secret indulgences. Permitted the purchase of one chocolate bar each day, she
frequently accumulated six or seven bars during the week. Then, alternating a bite of chocolate with a bite of saltine cracker, she would
savor all of the bars at one time while reclining on a pile of pillows in
her room.[10]

It was at the school's annual Christmas Party that she first tasted
raw oysters on the half shell. The sensation became one of the early
palate-refining experiences she recorded in *The Gastronomical Me*
(1943). In the chapter "The First Oyster," she also links the oyster
episode with her initiation into boarding school crushes and lesbian
relationships. She tells the story using her fellow students' actual
names, as was her custom, despite the sensitivity of the material. Sitting at the holiday party between the upperclassmen Inez (Moors-
head) and Olmsted (Allen), Mary Frances cannot bring herself to
swallow the raw oyster when she is asked to dance. "The oyster was

still in my mouth. I smiled with care, and stood up, reeling at the thought of dancing the first dance of the evening with the senior-class president. The oyster seemed larger. I knew I must down it, and was equally sure that I could not. Then as Olmsted put her thin hand on my shoulder blades, I swallowed once and felt light and attractive and daring, to know what I had done."[11] When the dance is over, Inez promises her a better dance than the one with Olmsted, and when Inez's arm tightens around her back, Mary Frances realizes that the junior has a crush on her. She flees the dance floor because she doesn't like Inez and then walks into the kitchen in search of another oyster, only to find the housekeeper tenderly feeding oysters to the school nurse. Mary Frances concludes her story by hoping "suddenly and violently, that I would never see one [oyster] again."[12]

When she went home for the Christmas holidays, Mary Frances sought an explanation from her mother for the same-sex relationships that she had seen at school, and she said that Edith gave her Radclyffe Hall's *The Well of Loneliness* to read.[13] What Mary Frances understood about lesbian affairs from her reading is unknown, but when she returned to school, she assumed a know-it-all attitude toward such relationships that manifested itself in her writings. In a short sketch called "Ridicklus,"[14] Mary Frances wrote about Anne's brief involvement in a secret guild of underclass girls who were a willing audience to the titillating antics of a few upperclassmen. Next to the room that Mary Frances shared with her sister, two senior girls, "Ivy, or Ina" (the Inez of the earlier oyster narrative) and her exquisite feminine roommate "gave a little show late every night on how men and women made love, with Ina/Ivy always on top."[15] Although Mary Frances said that she knew what was going on, she chose to focus on the reaction of the housemother when she learned of these activities, and the swift dismissal of the principal instigators. Because Anne was "always very female," Mary Frances assumed that she would brush off the experience. But she also linked adolescent sexuality to the androgynous oyster again, suggesting that at that age "we could go either way according to the tides."[16]

Mary Frances's own initiation into falling in love with another student was less dramatic and more nuanced than Anne's hijinks. It was never the subject of any of her boarding school tales, and she only wrote about it in detail while she was living in Lugano in 1959. The object of her "awkward, bewildered, confused"[17] love was Eda Lord, a day student and a motherless daughter whose father had enlisted the help of relatives to raise his only child. During this period of her life, Eda was living with an aunt in La Jolla and distinguishing herself at The Bishop's School in preparation for further studies at Stanford University. When Mary Frances arrived at the school in 1924, Eda was vice president of the junior class, a member of the debating club, an aspiring thespian, a player on the basketball, hockey, and baseball teams, and the editor in chief of the literary yearbook, called *El Miradero* after the tower on Bentham Hall. Unlike Mary Frances, who at that time wore her long hair in a single braid down her back, Eda had stylishly bobbed her hair, and it framed her face with an attractive dip over her left eyebrow. She exuded vitality and was one of the most popular girls on campus. Wanting to distance herself from Eda's other adorers, Mary Frances was infatuated but deliberately cool. "When I first met you I had already known more than my share of schoolgirl 'crushes' and their intricacies," she wrote in a statement titled "I Love You, Eda," which she drafted after visiting Eda and Sybille Bedford in Schaffhausen in 1959:

> I know that you are everything I recognized in you so long ago, tempered and refined and of course wearied by those processes. I had never felt one [a crush] myself, but there were *always* girls in love with me, and I admit that I felt sorry for them *always* and could not help despising them for weak fools. Usually if not *always* they were my inferiors physically or socially, and sometimes mentally.
>
> That is probably the main reason why, when I met you at Bishop's and began to sound to myself like all the emotional zanies I had been pushing around for so many years, it seemed clear to me that I myself must be completely inferior to you. If I believed, as indeed I did, that you were the most dazzling exciting human being I had ever met, it was because I was caught in one of the same mushy, ignominious, and disgusting "crushes" that so bored me in others. It was the only kind of love I had witnessed, except between parents and children and

siblings, and it is logical that I should think that I myself had been trapped by it.

I was horrified for fear I would annoy and repel you with my blind devotion, as I had been annoyed and repelled. I could not hide or deny that I thought you were the best, indeed the only, real thing in my world, but I tried hard not to act like the many other people who in their own ways felt more or less as I did. It seemed right and natural that girls would be swooning all over the damned silly neurotic hotbed for you, and I could only admit that I was as bad as any of them . . . You were the fashion at Bishop's, rather it was stylish to be in love with you. I was furious that I had to move with the crowd.[18]

But move she did. Not particularly interested in debating or the various team sports offered at the school, Mary Frances worked "like mad" for her very demanding English teacher, Helen M. Baker, and adopted the role of essayist and poet to attract Eda's attention. During her sophomore year, she published an imaginative poem consisting of a dialogue between a fairy and the limpid leaves "[who] whisper the secrets of the breezes to each other."[19] And she spent many hours in the office of *El Miradero*, reading galleys with Eda. Norah remembers, "Eda was a strong person, very important in MF's life. She really loved Mary Frances,"[20] and the feeling was mutual. When school was not in session, they corresponded with each other.

In the first semester of her junior year at Bishop's, the subject matter as well as the style of Mary Frances's writing changed. The fantastical themes and settings of her earlier work gave way to a highly impressionistic and sometimes foreboding brush with a less-than-benign spirit world. She wrote cinquains in the style of the American poet Adelaide Crapsey about the "beyond" and "ghosts not yet enough of Heaven." She also published in the school paper a short sketch called "Impressions," in which a snakelike woman dressed in little gold scales brushes against her in the theater and repels her: "All I know is that I felt—well as if nobody should touch me, not even myself. I didn't go to bed that night, because the sheets rubbed together with a soft, too-slippery sound."[21] The interest in supernatural phenomena, ghosts, and malevolent spirits would prove to be an enduring one.

These early publications were significant not only for the shift in subject matter, but also for the shift in audience: for the first time, she was writing to please someone other than herself. Praise from a demanding teacher for a piece well written may have, in fact, "put a germ somewhere about writing to please more people."[22] But getting the attention of Eda was a more compelling reason to write. "Once I told you that writing for me was (is?) a form of making love," she would remind her psychiatrist, Dr. George Frumkes, in 1953.[23] She was already well on her way to discovering that writing was a way to control reality, assume power, and, above all, please.

Although Mary Frances described herself as an indifferent student, her grades at Bishop's were consistently high—A and A– in English, B+ in Spanish, history, general science, and Bible. But in 1926, something—probably a severe attack of tonsillitis and a subsequent tonsillectomy—necessitated Mary Frances's withdrawal from Bishop's, and she finished her junior year back at Whittier Union High School, where she completed English, Latin, Spanish, and algebra courses begun at Bishop's. Living at home again, she spent more time with her younger sister and brother, helping them with homework and encouraging David, who spent much of his time up in the walnut tree with his imagined companion Tally.

When summer began, the whole family except Rex retreated to Laguna Beach, where they were joined by the many friends who also vacationed there. Recounting how Mary Frances and Anne went off to parties and dances at the beachfront pavilion where all the young people gathered, Norah remembered them as everything a nine-year-old little sister dreamed of becoming at sixteen. Both girls were "lookers," with stylish bobbed hair and attractive clothes, but Mary Frances was less beau-conscious than her sister. She wrote in her journal, "Sis always reduces or raises relations with my friends to a sex basis,"[24] and she often rued the fact that Anne was more interested in romance than companionship with the boys they knew in Laguna and Whittier. For her part, Mary Frances tended to treat them as older versions of her brother, David, and took their attentions lightly.

Instead of returning to The Bishop's School that fall, Mary Frances and Anne enrolled in Miss Harker's School, a preparatory boarding school adjacent to Stanford University in Palo Alto. Edith's

brother, Evans Holbrook, had begun a year of lecturing in law at Stanford while on sabbatical leave from the University of Michigan, and he might have convinced Edith that Miss Harker's School would be academically advantageous to his nieces. Or perhaps the fact that Eda was now a freshman at Stanford was a draw. If they were closer to Eda, however, they were farther from Whittier than they had ever been, and they alternated between homesickness and enjoying their newfound freedom. While classes were more challenging than they had been at Bishop's, nearby San Francisco soon began to exert its allure. They frequently ventured into the city on Saturday afternoons, buying corsages in Union Square and attending theater performances at the Geary or the Curran. Uncle Evans occasionally escorted them to Gump's luxury department store or to Chinatown. And they saw quite a bit of Edith, who on the slightest pretext came up to take them to lunch at the Garden Court.

Mary Frances soon began to write for the student yearbook. An essay from the time, titled "Mirrors and Salamanders" (eventually published in To Begin Again), explores dreams and their reality via dialogue between Mary Frances and Margie Thayer, who question Mary Frances's claim to be a salamander in her dreams. Mary Frances makes the case for the reality of the spirit world, saying that both and Anne "believe that to dream is to live—fully, completely . . . one dreams, one's body is useless, uninhabited—but how small of life is that weird machine called Body!"[25] Passionate swains for the hand of the Moon-maid and sighing leaves have given polemic in Mary Frances's writing, and real people, earnest q and answers, and a subject—the nature of dreams—would long preoccupation. The writer had begun to value the impo her own experiences, the people she knew, and the ideas ested her.

After Mary Frances's graduation in 1927, just one mor her nineteenth birthday, she and Anne joined their m beach house in Laguna while Norah and David wen nearby. When a local merchant needed someone to s while he was away, Mary Frances tended the shop, o Anne. And when Edith needed to return to town, or a lem necessitated picking up David at camp, or a n

transportation, they became willing chauffeurs. Usually, however, they relaxed in the lazy days of summer and roamed the shore with friends, including boys, in a casual companionship that Mary Frances described in her Laguna Journal: "Sis and Charles and I walked past Goff Island and back. We carried a lunch, laughed, shouted, leapt— three young fools. I love to spend a day like that—and end it hot from sunburn, tired as a dog, and very happy. A dog followed me all day: a lovely brown spaniel. Nothing flatters me more."[26] But there were also instances when Anne sought a more charged relationship, flirting with one of the young men whom her sister regarded only as a pal. "Perhaps she does it unconsciously—what does it matter?" Mary Frances reflected, adding, "Do I sound like a jealous, disappointed baby? God knows I'm disappointed—and in a purely selfish way I think—but I don't believe I'm jealous."[27]

The only really discordant note in an otherwise idyllic summer was the unanswered question of where Mary Frances would go to college. Norah remembered that "MF longed to go to Vassar but mother was scornful of anything except finishing schools."[28] When Edith did agree to consider UCLA, Aunt Maggie tried in vain to find a suitable room in Los Angeles for her. Eda, who was still studying at Stanford, held out the possibility of having Mary Frances join her at the University of London the following year. But Mary Frances's feelings for Eda seemed to make such a prospect less attractive rather than more so. Eda "annoys me intensely, stirs me a little—too much for comfort—and fills me with rather amused pity," Mary Frances wrote in her diary. "It would be a glorious adventure—with almost anyone else—Sis, perhaps."[29] But Anne had one more year at Miss Harker's, and separation from her sister was already part of Mary Frances's problem about "the whole college business." Despite their differences over boys, the "feeling as if I'll never be with her again"[30] was unbearable. While Mary Frances did not want to remain at the Ranch and attend Whittier College, a boardinghouse residence in Los Angeles and enrollment at UCLA was not tempting either. She was not even sure that she wanted to go to college, but she was certain that she did not want to go alone.

A visit from Uncle Walter helped to solve her problem. Walter's daughter Nancy was going to a small college in downstate Illinois for

a year before enrolling at the University of Chicago, and Rex and Edith thought it a perfect solution for their daughter as well. "Astounding! I am going to Illinois College—have escaped the Ranch!" Mary Frances wrote. "Half an hour after Uncle Walter arrived with the announcement that Nan is going there this winter, we decided, telegraphed, arranged, talked, and carefully avoided the fact that I will be gone nine months."[31] A shopping spree for a new fur coat, several dresses suitable for a much colder winter than she was used to, and black patent leather oxfords from Paris followed. When the family returned to the Ranch from Laguna, there were farewell dates with the young men she thought of as "dear boys." There were also farewells to her grandmother and grandfather Kennedy in La Puente, and more difficult goodbyes to her parents and siblings for their greatest separation to date.

Uncle Evans, a seasoned rail commuter between the West Coast and Ann Arbor, Michigan, where he taught law at the university, accompanied her east. His firsthand knowledge of the route, his enthusiasm for breakfast at the famous Harvey restaurants[32] along the way, and his acquaintance with the specialties of the dining car eased Mary Frances into her new role as a college student. The trip became part of her gastronomical education as well. Years later, she wrote two different versions of a memorable incident that occurred during that long and dusty trip to Chicago.

In *The Gastronomical Me* she relates the revelation of the dining car, where Uncle Evans gently suggests dishes like scallops and an avocado cocktail rather than the more familiar lamb chops. When they are joined in Chicago by Evans's son Bernard and are having dinner in the restaurant at Union Station, however, she forgets "all the ease that being with my uncle had brought me . . . and when my uncle asked me what I would like to eat, I mumbled stiffly, 'Oh, anything . . . anything, thank you.' " She instantly feels that her uncle "saw through all my *gaucherie*, my really painful wish to be sophisticated and polished before him and his brilliant son, that he was looking back at me with a cold speculative somewhat disgusted look in his brown eyes."[33] Then she inspects the menu carefully and orders an impressive meal to prove that his patience with her during the past five days has not been wasted.

Another version of the incident, written two years later, in 1945, appeared in *To Begin Again*. In this account, she and Uncle Evans are ordering a meal in the dining car when her uncle asks her if she would prefer a wild mushroom or wild asparagus omelet, and she responds by mumbling that she really doesn't care. At this point Uncle Evans puts down his menu and says sharply, "You should never say that again, dear girl. It is stupid, which you are not. It implies that the attentions of your host are basically wasted on you. So make up your mind before you open your mouth. Let him believe, even if it is a lie, that you would prefer the exotic wild asparagus to the banal mushrooms, or vice versa. Let him feel that it matters to you . . . and even that *he* does!"[34] Evidently this much advice is insufficient, and this version has him adding a final caveat: "All this may someday teach you about the art of seduction, as well as the more important art of knowing yourself." The added dialogue heightens the drama of the incident and elevates it above a schoolgirl's faux pas.

After spending a few days sightseeing in Chicago with her uncle and cousin, Mary Frances completed her journey to Illinois College in downstate Jacksonville. The trip was "long, hot, and sooty," and her first impression of Academy Hall was "worse." In this somewhat daunting setting, Mary Frances found her cousin already settled into a double room with her roommate, Rachel. But although Mary Frances really had not spent much time with Nancy since they were toddlers together in Albion, she liked the grown-up Nan immediately, and they established a long and trusting friendship.

The small, coeducational Presbyterian school had an enrollment of five hundred students, for the most part from Midwestern working-class backgrounds, and although Mary Frances wrote that she was lonesome for her family and missed her comfortable room at the Ranch, she found herself "interested in these people, their looks, conversation, everything."[35] Within a few weeks, she had made her single room into a cozy little alcove decorated with an Indian bedspread, pictures from home, and curtains that Aunt Tim had sent. But the steady diet of turnips and other root vegetables served in the cafeteria bored her, and Mary Frances, Nan, and Rachel frequently went to the College Boys' Café off campus for waffles and vegetable soup. Whenever a family member visited, the girls were treated to special dinners at the Colonial Inn. Most of the time, however, they spent their allowances on cream cheese, anchovy paste, French dressing, crackers, head lettuce, and ginger ale, which they consumed in their candle-lit dormitory rooms to the wail of blues on the Victrola. For Mary Frances this was a college version of the secret indulgences at Bishop's, and in *The Gastronomical Me* she credits the beautiful, expensive heads of lettuce as having "probably saved our lives."[36]

A longing for home lurks between the lines of her diary, which record her brief fascination with the lectures of her European history professor, her dates with scores of boys—especially with football-loving Cleary, "who divided his passion between football and James Branch Cabell [a popular American novelist]"[37]—and her fondness for her cousin. Homesickness prompted a trip back to Whittier at midsemester and probably played a role in a lingering bronchial infection that sent her to the Passavant Hospital in Chicago in November. On December 11 she wrote to her family, "About every ten minutes I have a partial stroke of paralysis at the thought that this time next week I'll be rolling home, and in three more days at home. Hope I exist until then."[38] She had not even contemplated the possibility of spending Christmas away from the family and the Ranch.

Trips home and other distractions, however, had an adverse effect on her grades. She had registered for sixteen hours of credit and managed to salvage only ten and a half. Faced with a final examination in biology, she wrote in her virtually blank test book, "To state and define the characteristics of protoplasm is a thing I should know how to do. Once I did know how—two or three months ago, perhaps. Now in the final examination, I do not know—and I do not care. I am losing five hours of credit. Too bad, isn't it?"[39]

Mary Frances returned to Whittier at the end of term aware that she had accomplished very little academically, but relieved to be leaving before the newness of her friendship with Nan wore off and Nan's roommate, Rachel, got on her nerves too much. Although she had enjoyed a weekend in Chicago with Uncle Walter, Aunt Tim, and Nan, and visits with Uncle Evans, the bitter-cold temperatures, icy walks, and sooty snow had turned her against the Midwest. As the train sped toward California, where warm weather, her own room, "clean air and no more pains in my chest—books, concerts, and plays," and family awaited her, she vowed that she would do nothing but read, eat, sleep, and look at the country until she arrived in California.

At the Ranch, Mary Frances luxuriated in the comfort of her grandmother's first-floor suite, which she and Anne had appropriated for themselves. After a few weeks she reluctantly registered for courses at Whittier College in order to gain sophomore standing wherever she enrolled in the fall. And it was not long before she was joined at the Ranch by Eda Lord, who had been expelled from Stanford in the spring of 1928, probably for poor grades or disciplinary infractions. More or less estranged from her father and aunt, Eda welcomed Edith's invitation to stay with them and take courses at Whittier until she left for London. Anne was away completing her senior year at Miss Harker's, so there was ample space to accommodate her, and Norah and David were enthusiastic about having another face at the dinner table. In later years, Mary Frances frequently referred to the fact that both of her parents and her siblings grew very fond of the girl whom she had first met and idolized at Bishop's. "I know better than ever, but have always known it and accepted it, that you are much more a part of my life than I am of yours," Mary Frances wrote after they saw each other in 1959. "I realized very strongly . . . how much a part you have been of what I suppose can be called 'the family': Edith and Rex knew and loved you *much* more than I understood then . . . today a note from Norah asks impatiently, 'What of Eda? How is she?' "[40]

At the beginning of the summer Mary Frances enrolled at UCLA to make up the rest of the credits she had lost during the first semester at Illinois College. While there, she met a young man named Alfred Young Fisher, who was vacationing in the Los Angeles area. Boyishly handsome, with brown wavy hair and blue eyes, Fisher was said to resemble the poet Percy Bysshe Shelley, a resemblance not lost on Mary Frances, who had just celebrated her twentieth birthday and felt she was marking time before something wonderful happened to her.

Born in Manhattan in 1902, Alfred Young Fisher was the second son in a family of three boys and a girl.[41] When he was nine years old, his father, a Presbyterian minister, accepted an appointment to the Third Presbyterian Church on Adams Street in Los Angeles and moved his family there. The Reverend Herbert H. Fisher was an exemplary shepherd of his congregation, and a strict father. His children started their day with prayers and readings from the Bible. His wife, Clara, was an accomplished pianist and passed on the love of good music to her children, who fell asleep at night to the melodies of Bach, Beethoven, and Chopin. Alfred Fisher learned to play the violin while he was still in grammar school, although by high school he had taken up less esoteric pursuits, playing football, selling newspapers, and working in the local drugstore. During summer vacations he dug potatoes in the San Fernando Valley and worked in the Kern County oil fields. The summer before his senior year, an on-the-job accident at a chemical plant where he was working slightly impaired his vision.

Following his graduation in 1920, Fisher enrolled at UCLA, but he balked at the discipline of the student ROTC program. His vision problems kept him from shooting with accuracy, and he disliked marching drill, the uniform, and what he considered the pompand posities of cadet training. While others advanced to captain, he remained a rear-rank private, and his colonel pronounced him one of the worst soldiers he had seen in forty years. He flunked out at the end of his freshman year.

After spending some time at Princeton's Preparatory School, he was admitted into the university itself (his father was an alum), where he excelled in the humanities and English. He had a full scholarship, and he earned spending money by proofreading for the *Daily Princetonian* and writing articles and reviews for the *Princeton Herald*. For three years he worked on a seventy-thousand-word essay on "The Function of Literary Criticism," only to destroy it when one of his readers criticized it. Taking on daunting writing projects only to abandon them if they were not considered outstanding proved to be a pattern, but he did produce poetry, corresponded with Robert Frost and A. E. Housman, and wrote an essay on Shelley that one of his professors praised as the best student paper he had ever read. At Princeton he made lasting friendships with a number of students who went on to become writers and professors.

After graduation, Al took a position as an English instructor at a boarding school in Wyoming to earn enough money to study abroad in preparation for a career as a literary scholar and poet. While at

Princeton he had had little time for a social life, and while teaching he was too busy with classes and keeping himself warm in a cabin where the supply of stove wood ran out too quickly and his inkwell often froze. But during the summer of 1928, he decided to vacation in Los Angeles, where Mary Frances's willowy good looks and soft voice caught his attention on the campus of UCLA. And when she told him she "would live in a piano box" if she "loved a man enough," the prospect "seemed to appeal to him, too. He wanted to get the hell out."[42] His attraction to Mary Frances was immediate and compelling, and when he returned to Wyoming in the fall he wooed her with sonnets and love letters.

That fall Anne was ready for college, and she and Mary Frances drove off in the Auburn roadster that Rex had bought for them to Occidental College, a small, coeducational Presbyterian school in Eagle Rock, about thirty-five miles northwest of the Ranch. Occidental's enrollment was about five hundred, and daily chapel was compulsory (although strains of "Jazz Me Baby" could be heard emanating from the fraternity and sorority houses on any given Friday night). "In the late 20s it was small and 'nice' for parents bewildered by suddenly strange children," Mary Frances told an interviewer years later,[43] and several of their friends attended the college along with Anne's latest beau, Bob Freeman. The sisters shared a little apartment in Erdman Hall but pledged different sororities and associated with different crowds. Anne went everywhere with Bob Freeman and frequently double-dated with her friend Fay Shoemaker and Lawrence Powell. Mary Frances wrote very little about Al Fisher's courtship, but she recalled later that she was not "really interested in dating because she had an off-campus romance well into gear."[44] Nevertheless, although she remembered working hard for an English professor she particularly admired, Mary Frances also spent a considerable amount of time trying to get a Gertrude Lawrence tan on the roof of Erdman Hall, and going to campus events with a student named Count Jones because he was an outstanding dancer. She even dated a sixteen-year-old freshman named Larry Bachmann, whose father was a producer at Paramount Studios. "I was brash yet eager to learn," Bachmann wrote years later. "I wanted serious discussions with someone with whom I empathized—Mary Frances Kennedy was the one who fitted that description . . . She understood my interest and sense of humor, which came from show business—something far beyond the knowledge of our classmates."[45]

Another student, Larry Powell, had become a big man on campus, with a reputation for both hijinks and his mastery of the saxophone and the piano. Because he chose to join the orchestra on the Dollar Line's four-month world tour during his junior year, he had not graduated with the Class of '28. So he spent his last year at Occidental dating the seventeen-year-old Fay and playing with jazz groups every weekend. Enamored of Robinson Jeffers (Occidental '05) and powerfully influenced by the school's eclectic English faculty, Powell and his close friends Ward Ritchie and Gordon Newell were determined to seek their future in literature and the arts, and to do it in concert. Mary Frances was aware of Powell, but more aware of his pursuit of Fay. After leaving Occidental, however, they were to become close friends.

Just before the Christmas holidays, Anne and Mary Frances made their society debuts at the Hacienda Country Club in North Whittier, where Rex had been instrumental in building up the membership and frequently played golf. In a novel based on his courtship of Fay Shoemaker, Larry Powell described the event: "The Callaghans [Kennedys] spent liberally on their daughter's dance. The entire country club was planted with flowers and shrubs. An entire Negro catering staff was moved in, and a ten-piece black band furnished music. There was plenty to eat, and a huge punch bowl that flowed. Few campus people were present, most of the dancers coming from Jane's [Anne's] finishing school and hometown connections. I kept all of the dances for Joy [Fay] and me, trading only one (out of courtesy) with Jane and Baby Face [Bob Freeman]." And he described Jane (Anne) as "dressed regally, a pearl tiara round her Madonna coiffure. She was big, but good to look at, always perfectly groomed and poised. Her brown, crinkly droopy eyes shone with ironical amusement."[46] Because Larry Powell was a senior and Fay Shoemaker only a freshman, Anne was protective of her, and Larry concentrated his narrative on that protectiveness to the exclusion of any mention of Mary Frances. Nevertheless, he portrayed the family as too "clannish," and disparagingly as "the aristocracy of Santa Ana [Whittier]."[47]

During her second semester, Mary Frances joined the staff of the college newspaper, the *Tawney Kat*, and put her *Whittier News* skills to good use. A piece called "Gertie at the Big Game or A Coed's Thoughts, If Any," was breezy, self-assured, and filled with the slang of the day: "If I ever write my self-confessions, I'll tell young damsels never to spend all but ten cents of next month's allowance on glad-tatters for the Big Game, the way I've done for the last three years. Take it from Diamond Lil, lassies, it ain't worth it, and I'll never do it again . . . Now I must devote myself to impressing the heavy swain with how much I know about football."[48] She affected the boy-crazy, clothes-conscious, clueless pose of a stereotypical coed even as she aspired to become the first female editor of the paper. But by the end of her sophomore year, Alfred Fisher wrote that he had applied for a Franco-American Field Service Scholarship to pursue an advanced degree from a French university the following year, and he asked her to join him.

Although Al could not provide for Mary Frances financially, he seemed to have been regarded as "Mr. Right" by Rex and Edith. He was well educated and he would introduce her to the sort of culture that Edith valued. It is not clear whether the Reverend Fisher disapproved of her wearing lipstick and stylish clothes, dancing, smoking, and reading risqué novels. But Mary Frances refused to accept Edith's negative attitude toward mothers-in-law, and from the beginning she made it a point to cultivate her relationship with Clara Young Fisher and to send her thoughtful gifts.

Mary Frances and Al had spent very little time together until the three months before their wedding, and that time was busy with preparations for the event and their departure to France. In her journal Mary Frances described this time as "a long series of faintly entertaining poses . . . entertaining to myself and slightly revolting."[49] Rex engaged a friend of the Kennedy family, the Hollywood photographer George Hurrell, to take pictures of the bridal party. Edith oversaw the stylish design of Mary Frances's gown, and Mary Frances went from fittings to rehearsals to the ceremony wondering what any of it had to do with her relationship with Al Fisher.

The wedding was held on the afternoon of September 5, at the Episcopal Church in San Gabriel; a reception for family and friends

followed. Grandmother Kennedy described the event in a letter to her
son Ted: "Great wedding! Everything more impressive than the bride-
groom. Mr. Alfred Fisher is a very agreeable & likable young man and
I think that he is very well-suited to be a satisfactory husband to M.F.
Time will have to tell how wide a swath he is to cut in the years to
come."[50] Luella may well have expressed what other family members
merely thought.

Although, as Mary Frances had said, they both wanted to "get the
hell out of California," the marriage of a Presbyterian minister's son to
a bored, underachieving Whittier debutante posed more questions
than answers.

THREE

The First Insouciant Spell

(1929–1932)

Dijon, délicieuse ville, mélancolique et douce.
—Victor Hugo

Describing her first ocean crossing in *The Gastronomical Me*, Mary Frances said that she was "shy, and surrounded with that special and inviolable naiveté of a new bride, so that Al and I walked about, and ate, and talked, almost without contact with the rest of the ship."[1] Although they were dimly aware of "one priest, one dancer, three medical students, and an incongruously proper middle-class plump Englishwoman"[2] who seemed to exhaust the selections on the ship's carte du jour at every meal, the Fishers often skipped formal meals, and instead nibbled on grapes and other edibles that had been sent to their cabin by well-wishing relatives before their departure. They seemed to be in love and discovering each other as lovers. "It doesn't seem possible that I've been married for so few days," Mary Frances wrote in her journal. "It seems that I've been living with him [Al] forever . . . all in my life that has any reality is connected with him. And that isn't exactly what I mean, because my years at home are very happy things to remember. It is more that my whole life, until I met Al, was a kind of searching for what I have now." Yet she added, revealing a kind of vulnerability that she seemed to associate with intimate relationships, "I hope it lasts . . . I can't help feeling a certain amount of amazed skepticism at my own existence. I think I'll always love Al, and I think he'll always love me, but I don't know that we'll always love each other."[3] Mary Frances also wrote about her personal sea change: "my smallest fingers and toes went numb a few hours after we sailed, and stayed so for several days after we landed."[4]

On the overcrowded boat train that sped the Fishers from Cherbourg to Paris, she ate a simple midday lunch that she later called her "most memorable meal." It consisted of the best bread she had ever eaten, a salad of fresh garden lettuces, Petits Suisses cheese, gnarled apples, good crude wine, and bitter coffee. "It sounds almost disrespectful to say it," she wrote, "but even the astonishing events of the past several weeks or so seemed but a logical preparation for this moment! Falling in love for the first time since I was nine,[5] being married for the first time, crossing the Atlantic for the first time . . . they all led irrevocably to 1:43 p.m., September 25, 1929, when I picked up a last delicious crust-crumb from the table, smiled dazedly at my love, peered incredulously at a great cathedral on the horizon, and recognized myself as a new-born sentient human being, ready at last to live . . ."[6]

"Paris was everything that I had dreamed . . . when we first went there. It should always be seen, the first time, with the eyes of childhood or of love," Mary Frances wrote. "I was wrapped in a passionate mist."[7] On their way from the train station to a small hotel on the Left Bank, near the quai Voltaire, they glimpsed the broad avenues, the impressive monuments, and the Seine flowing through the city. The next morning, while Mary Frances savored hot chocolate and croissants in bed, Al made his way to Sylvia Beach's bookshop, Shakespeare & Company, half expecting to meet James Joyce or Ernest Hemingway along the way. During the next few days they explored the city, drank aperitifs in the bars along the boulevard St.-Germain, and dined in small, inexpensive cafés with a few of Al's friends who were vacationing from British universities.

At week's end they journeyed south, as planned, with two of Edith's friends who were en route to Italy, where they planned to spend the winter months. Comfortably ensconced in a chauffeur-driven car, Al, Mary Frances, and the elderly ladies stopped for lunch in Avallon, along the Paris–Lyons route. Dining in the old post hotel, Mary Frances was served a potato soufflé as a separate course. "It was hot, light, with a brown crust, and probably chives and grated Parmesan cheese somewhere in it. But the great thing about it was that it was served alone . . . I felt a secret justification swell in me, a pride such as I've seldom known since, because all my life, it seemed, I had been wondering rebelliously about potatoes . . . I almost resented them, in fact . . . I felt that they *could* be good, if they were cooked respectfully . . . Here in the sunny courtyard of the first really French restaurant I had ever been in, I saw my theory proved. It was a fine moment."[8]

The following day, the Fishers were standing in the place d'Armes in the center of Dijon, the ancient capital of the Duchy of Burgundy. The smell of *pain d'épices* emanated from the various bakeries, and the Grey-Poupon shop flaunted faience display jars and mustard pots of various sizes. The market street was crowded with shoppers filling their bags with recently harvested apples and root vegetables, and pungent cheeses aged in marc de Bourgogne. "I do wish you could see this town," Mary Frances wrote to her brother. "I never did believe those illustrations in books like Grimm's fairy tales and so on, but I do now . . . All the houses are built right up to the edge of the sidewalks and are from two to five stories tall, and thin—perhaps only 2 rooms wide and a room thick. They are of stone and plaster, and in this town date from 1400 A.D."[9] There were broad cobbled streets like the rue de la Liberté with its modest Arc at the end of the tree-lined boulevard de Sévigné, which led to the train station. There were *places* named d'Arcy, François Rude, Wilson, and—the most impressive of them all—the place d'Armes, half-circling the Ducal Palace. Behind the palace was the outdoor market street and vantage point for viewing the fantastical Église Notre-Dame with its menacing gargoyles and great clock, Jacquemart, whose life-sized mechanical figures signaled the hours. As memorable as the colorful flags of the dukes of Burgundy waving along the rue Cardinale were the tiled roofs of green, yellow, black, and red.

The Fishers moved into the Hôtel Cloche, and Al immediately began an intensive one-month course at the University of Dijon to improve his French before going on to the University of Strasbourg to

now we're worse than the French, I think. Five francs seem outrageous for chocolate creams, and we think for weeks before we spend eighty cents on dinner."[19]

Their lodgings, enhanced by the small purchases she made, gradually became less spartan. She learned to use the hot plate to boil water for Al's shaves and also acquired a kettle to prepare tea for the young women she tutored. Returning to the rue du Petit-Potet at the end of the day, Al would sometimes present her with a perfect tomato that they would sprinkle with salt and eat as a special treat, or he would purchase a box of exquisite chocolates as a surprise. Pale pink roses from Al on their three-month anniversary, celebration dinners at Aux Trois Faisons, and Al's ritual gift of a fresh flower every Thursday all contributed to Mary Frances's conclusion that "everything's been too perfect to have standards of time applied to it."[20]

When they attended the Dijon Foire Gastronomique, which was held annually in November to showcase the country's food products and, especially, the wines of the Burgundian appellations, they became more convinced than ever that they were living in France's culinary capital. Although they were not invited to any of the official banquets, they could visit the tents, sample the pâtés, cheeses, and charcuterie, and taste the wines. With all the visitors in town for the event, prices skyrocketed and the restaurants were overcrowded. "We liked Dijon better in its normal state of mass-gourmandise," she wrote to Norah. And she described the tournedos Rossini at the first-class Buffet de la Gare, the good beer and wine and fresh oysters served at the Brasserie Miroir, the snails and tripes *à la mode de Caen* that made eating at the restaurant Crespin so enjoyable. Aux Trois Faisons, however, was her special place, and she wished that someday Norah could savor its food herself. It was dingy and plain on the outside, she said, but the French seemed to believe that a perfect sauce was more important than a velvet carpet. "After tasting the sauce you'd agree with them, I know. It's an art and religion, this French food, and I'm already an ardent follower of the faith."[21]

Mary Frances also wrote to Anne, urging her to come visit. She warned that there was no "dating," however, that young women wore oxfords and simple, dark woolen clothes, and that the French did not "spend money the way we do at home." But she added, "Darling,

you'll love it. It's thrilling, fascinating, marvelous—and it gets better
and better. Lamplighters and men who sing little songs to sell the
candy they carry in trays on their heads, and hot chestnuts on the
street corners, and wonderful doorways and cathedral windows, and
funny movies and revues and opera for almost nothing, and famous
restaurants and perfectly marvelous wines and liqueurs, and hundreds
of cafes where you sit on the pavement and watch the people or go inside and listen to music—and watch the people—you'll love it."[22]

Mary Frances and Al took weekend trips to see the Roman ruins
in Autun and nearby Cluny and visited Beaune to taste wines. There
were shorter excursions, too. "Yesterday we went for a walk in no special direction . . . just wandered in one part of the suburbs until we
found the mud too deep, and then did the same thing in another,"
Mary Frances wrote. "We saw lots of queer looking people . . . peasants with very baggy corduroy trousers and blue handkerchiefs around
their necks, and lots of children who like all French youngsters were
either very pallid or puny or simply bulging with blood and brawn.
It's still a wonder to me that any of them pull through the first six
years . . . the poorer ones, I mean. They are sent from their mothers'
arms to the gutters of the nearest alley, which is unspeakably filthy,
usually."[23] And there were other instances of child neglect that she
could not shrug off. "I am becoming a fanatic on the subject of children. I love them, and lately I have seen so much senseless, absolutely senseless, waste of decent human material, that all my ideas
have been strengthened a thousand times. If I can have children at
all, I'm going to do everything in my power to give them at least a decent start."[24] She was appalled at what seemed to her American sensibilities the "cruel ignorance of these French of the lower middle
class," and she could not reconcile the glories of French culture and
cuisine with the callous attitude toward children that she saw all too
frequently.

Although the Depression significantly curtailed the funds coming
from home, the Fishers still lived well compared to most Dijonnais.
When the Christmas holidays drew near, Mary Frances sent gifts
back to Whittier and wrote to Rex about the trip that she and Al were
planning. "I plan to draw out about fifty dollars for a vacation, because
I want to buy Al a cane for a present, and I also may see something I'll

want to buy in the South [Provence] . . . I seem to have inherited spend-thrift tendencies from someone."[25] Al was also extravagant with presents, and arranged to have some of his poems privately printed for gifts. As a Christmas surprise he gave Mary Frances No. 1 of the limited edition he titled *Occasional Verses*.

On December 16, the Fishers left Dijon to visit Avignon, Arles, and Les Baux before going on to Marseilles and the little fishing village of Cassis. There they strolled the deserted beaches, read books they had received from home, and attended a midnight Nativity service that was distinguished by the sounds of ancient Greek-Roman piping and drumming. The whole experience so gripped Mary Frances that she repeatedly returned to Cassis, and when she heard a recording of similar folkloric music almost sixty years later, she wrote, "I have returned there [Cassis] like a homing pigeon for countless years since that far-gone day—perhaps it is my 'spiritual home.' And the music is in my blood, from that first stupid open loving trial, in the little chapel in Cassis."[26] Al, on the other hand, "stood by his conviction, that if people know real happiness anywhere, they must never expect to find it there again."[27]

When classes resumed after New Year's, Mary Frances enrolled in a morning sculpture class at the Beaux-Arts. Having achieved some mastery of the language, she concentrated on French literature, from the Renaissance to the Symbolists, and took copious notes especially on the novels of Balzac and Hugo and the dramas of Molière, Corneille, and Racine. She also thoughtfully read and offered constructive suggestions on Al's various writing projects. "When Al asked with his usual courteous interest that I read his paper [on Progress] and tell him what I thought, I was suffused with a flattering flush . . . and at the same time, a skulking knowledge that that [being his reader] was exactly what I was meant to be, by my diabolic mate," she wrote in her journal. "The article is good, I think . . . clearly written in a style that seems to me to combine real profundity of thought with an air of ingenuous and naïve gaucherie. I don't know though . . . that's more or less my idea about the man himself, and it may be that I know him too intimately to disconnect him, now at least, from his work. Anyway, I was glad he wanted me to read the thing."[28]

Although she had made a few nuanced references to Al's "preconceived ideas of style and some remaining vestiges of his Presbyterian boyhood, and his persnickets [*sic*] and fussiness," she also knew that he was more single-minded and disciplined in his work than she was. On Valentine's Day she wrote to her mother, "I still think I got one of the two best men" (presumably Rex was the other). "He gets nicer and sweeter and funnier every day. That's good. It would be awful to be stuck here with a bore or a brute or an imbecile—or even an average man."[29] For her part, she noted that she was puttering along on a short story, but "it was terrible, I started it three times . . . but it all sounds like night work in a boiler factory."[30] She chided herself in her journal, and then shrugged off what she considered to be her lack of accomplishment.

At the end of April, the Ollagniers unexpectedly moved from 14 rue du Petit-Potet, and a new family, the Rigoulots,[31] took over the residence and its pensionnaires. Married for several years to a man who had wasted her substantial dowry, borrowed money shamelessly, drunk too much, and managed to alienate his three children, Mme Rigoulot had purchased the house on the rue du Petit-Potet in a last-ditch effort to avoid financial ruin. She neglected her person "because she gave every ounce of her time and energy to feeding [her pensionnaires]. She was bedraggled and shiny and often smelled. And what was even more distasteful, she was needlessly ailing."[32] Mary Frances initially avoided her gaze when she left for the Beaux-Arts each morning.

Mme Ollagnier's thrifty but delicious meals gave way to the face-saving extravagances of Mme Rigoulot. She served hot, creamy soups, roasted legs of lamb, the most expensive vegetables and bottles of wine. And when Mme Rigoulot's mother and father, a retired Alsatian confectioner, visited on Sunday, the multicourse dinner concluded with one of his apple tarts. Mme Rigoulot supervised the small kitchen and often did most of the cooking herself, offering to teach Mary Frances to make soufflés, pâtés, and truffled goose. Partly because she did not want to spend her time cooking, but more likely because she felt both pity and scorn for a woman who consoled herself with chocolate truffles and rich food despite her family's lack of funds, Mary Frances declined the offer. "I knew that she would drive me crazy, shatter all my carefully educated reserve and self-control, so don, and Glasgow. Al was gregarious, befriending a widow who was en route to join her relatives in Glasgow and exchanging paperback thrillers with the chief engineer even as he insisted that "the only thing he wanted in the world was complete solitude, time to *think*." Mary Frances saw further evidence of his self-delusion, and she predicted that the months ahead would be difficult, perhaps even disastrous for him. "I did all I could to convince him. But he loathed Occidental and his profession—or thought he did—and he remembered how happy he'd been in Dijon, young, in love, free. Tim [Dillwyn] and I, too, felt that it was terrible for a man as fine as Al to be so miserable as he felt he was, at Occidental. So—We all went to Switzerland."[65]

FIVE

Vin de Vevey

(1936–1939)

Once in Switzerland the songs of the vignerons made me feel lonely because I was unsure of what I was. I would stand listening to Jules,
singing in short harsh phrases as he took the back-basket up the vineyard
slopes. I would shudder for the world's pain, identifying my own with it.[1]
—M.F.K. Fisher

Having taken a train from Holland, Al and Mary Frances arrived in
Vevey at noon "inwardly very nervous: would T. [Dillwyn] be here,
would he still like us, would he want us to live with him when he saw
us?"[2] But Dillwyn was not there yet, so Mary Frances and Al went directly to the pension that would be their temporary home. By the time
Dillwyn arrived on the 6:10 train that evening, they had unpacked,
bathed, and dressed for dinner. Al saw that the broken man he had
accompanied to the Los Angeles train station eighteen months earlier
looked not only well physically but restored and vibrant. Mary
Frances hoped "to see months in a few seconds" in the casual greetings she and Dillwyn exchanged. "We were jittering for many more
reasons than could be written . . . We nibbled politely at dinner and
talked too fast, interrupting almost every sentence and laughing at
nothing," she wrote in her journal. "Later we went to a café, two
cafés, and drank rather a lot of *vin de Vevey* but not too much."[3] The
next day they drove to Le Paquis, where Al saw the "little meadow" for
the first time and Mary Frances revisited it, not in its spring splendor
but in the muted shades of fall. She found it even more beautiful this

time, and through the years, the impression of Le Paquis on that particular day never left her: "All those things . . . the fresh spouting water, the little brook under the willows, the old rich bending trees, the
grass so full of life there on the terraced wine-slopes laced by a thousand tiny vineyards . . . they were why when the peasants said Le
Paquis they meant The Dear Little Meadow, or The Sweet Cool Rest-
ing Place, or something like that but more so."[4] While the late October wind blew through the yellowing leaves that still clung to the
trees, they picnicked in the meadow, and Dillwyn sketched the outlines of the house he wanted to build. He planned to make the
vigneron's cottage, a two-storied stone dwelling with a well-worn granite staircase that seemed virtually indestructible, the center of the
new Le Paquis, adding rooms, French doors, and terraces that would
offer magnificent views of Lake Geneva and the French Alps beyond.
They talked about where and when they would plant vegetable and
flower gardens. Later that afternoon they visited the neighboring winery and tasted several bottles of Faverges 1934, a heady, ethereal wine
that seemed to be a distillation of all that they had seen and planned
that afternoon.

Plans for the house surrendered to the concerns of the moment.
Mary Frances began a journal "to tell us later a few of the early occurrences." Avoiding the personal, she described her entries as "a stiff
chronicle of vegetables bought, charwomen paid, meals consumed.
Or it will be pseudo-personal gossiping, skirting with timid words the
truly important relations and instead relaying small 'bright sayings'
and amusing anecdotes."[5] She wrote about how she, Al, and Dillwyn
went to Lausanne to buy a car, and signed a six-month lease for an
apartment in Vevey that would be more comfortable and spacious
than the pension where they were staying. They began to collect
kitchen items and secondhand furniture to furnish the apartment
and, eventually, Le Paquis. Mary Frances noted the acquisition of a
fine Valaisanne table with inlays and carved legs, described market
days and the small shops in Vevey, and wrote about the difficulties
Dillwyn had convincing the architect that they did not want a grand
manor house, but a home they could care for with a minimum of
help. When the first snows of the season whitened the Savoy Alps
across the lake and local women decorated the graves with chrysan-

themums for All Saints' Day, Mary Frances, Dillwyn, and Al moved into the Vevey apartment and set up house. They engaged a charwoman, shopped in the local markets, and made short trips to various vineyards to purchase wines for their table.

Beyond commenting on Dillwyn's early perception of her "sybaritic tendencies" and her own observation of his inconsistent extravagances, Mary Frances avoided any mention of their relationship in either her letters to Whittier or her journal. The threesome took short trips, enjoyed café hopping and fondue in the evening, went to plays and the cinema, and presumably at the end of the evening Mary Frances and Al retired to their room, Dillwyn to his. On the other side of the Atlantic, Rex and Edith read nothing into the arrangement; to them, it seemed little different from the Fishers' student days in France. In early November, Rex wrote to his brother Ted, "My David is running the academy newspaper at Lake Forest, playing end on the first team and enjoying his extra year in that institution. Norah is taking her second year's work at Wells College. Edith and I are sitting home and reading letters from them. Mary Frances and her husband have gone to Switzerland for a year. He studying, she writing."[6] Mary Frances had been as vague about the purpose of their being in Vevey together as she was about their future there.

That the three principals involved ever openly acknowledged the ambiguities of their arrangement even to each other was unlikely. Mary Frances seemed to believe that some greater agency would resolve these personal matters in the same way that the timely arrival of funds from Rex or Anne Parrish always smoothed out financial worries. She preferred to drift rather than to confront problems, and since childhood had abhorred scenes and arguments. When a moment became too tense, she tended to shift into a liminal role rather than betray her insecurity or discomfort openly.

Mary Frances had feared that Al would soon tire of their "prim, stuffy little commercial town, [being] no longer young, no longer passionate, isolated from any erudite colleagues,"[7] and that he would yearn for the attention of adoring students, faculty intrigues, and the occasional publication. Al did feel out of place, but not for the reasons Mary Frances stated. A sonnet dated November 29, 1936, reveals his sorrow not only for the loss of his father but also the impending loss of his beloved:

As when transfigured by great love one lives
In joy, and then, the vision fading, he
Sees only, once again, his grief, and grieves
Anew a parent dead, and all his friends see
Him who before was mild serenity
Bow his white face, while bitter sorrow thrives
In an untended heart, and utterly
His thoughts oppose what he believes:
Sorrow, for me, my dear love taking leave,
Despair sits holding mirrors to my eye
That I must watch my death instead of smile,
That I observe how well it suits to grieve,
That I present myself a constant lie,
That I absent me from my life a while.[8]

After construction began on Le Paquis in early January 1937, Al spent more hours watching the workmen digging the terraces and framing the house than he did in the apartment. Mary Frances rationalized his absences by suggesting that although he had routinely expressed his desire for solitude in order to write, his stronger need was to be surrounded by people. Yet Al later said that he increasingly felt like an outsider in the company of Mary Frances and Dillwyn. Although he helped Dillwyn plant a flower and vegetable garden and was genuinely interested in the progress of the house, he later told Larry Powell that he doubted that he would ever be part of the planned commune.[9] In April Al announced his desire to leave Vevey and seek a teaching position. Knowing that Edith and Rex would arrive in Paris in mid-May,[10] Mary Frances asked him to remain until their visit was over.

Describing this period of her life to her psychiatrist in 1950, Mary Frances indicated that she had naively thought that the arrangement in Switzerland would work. "It did not, of course. It was hell. We lived well, very graciously, very excitingly. I found that I was sleeping a great deal, a light peaceful sleep, to escape reality. My parents came to stay with us, while we were building a beautiful house in the vineyards above Vevey . . . I asked my husband to bear with me, to save them pain, and then to go."[11] She did not mention that she and Dillwyn were lovers, or that she was not able to tell her husband what he al-

ready knew, or to tell her parents what they did not know. Instead she
let the situation unfold slowly and often adopted a pose of indecision
or took refuge from her own role in ending the marriage by citing a list
of Al's failures. She also disavowed having left Al for Dillwyn. "It is
quite untrue," she told Larry Powell in 1938. "I have told Al that, and
I think he knows it, but no man likes to admit that a woman has left
him for any other reason than another man. If I had been going to
leave him, though, it would have been some six years ago (for Tim, or
any other man). It is true that I am with Tim now and will be as long
as he lives or wants me—but I would never have left Al for him. I am
sorry that Al won't admit that."[12]

Yet in the story "Stay Me, Oh Comfort Me," written in 1937, she
captures not only her confusion at Le Paquis but the trip she made to
Paris two days before Edith and Rex's arrival to seek her friend Eda
Lord's advice. She describes her emotional state in overwrought language: "I was tired. I wanted love, but I was tired of it, wearied by its
involutions, convolutions, its complex intraplexities. I had fled from it,
leaving there in Vevey the husk and the bud, the empty and the re-
filled, renewed, revived, recrucified . . . When I tried to write a letter
to tell my husband that I was well and happy, I knew that running
away had not helped us at all. I loved him too much to lie, although
not enough to live with him . . . and it was the same thing again: Stay
me with flagons, for I am tired, sick, tired, tired of love."[13] In Eda,
called Rina in the story, she expected to find solace. "She would be
like cool water . . . Rina knew everything about love. She knew so
much and for so long that she had left it all behind. I felt sure of that,
convinced of it."[14]

Arriving at Rina's apartment, however, she is saddened by her
friend's physical dissolution, then by her forced, affected, silly behavior. Seeing her repeatedly refill her glass, Mary Frances realizes that
her friend has become an alcoholic, and it is Rina who asks Mary
Frances if there is any help for her before her lover, Moira, enters the
room. The ensuing conversation is strained, feeble, and filled with
Rina's exaggerations about Mary Frances's social status. The three
women go to a neighborhood café for dinner, and heads turn in their
direction: "I saw their eyes slide with amazement over us: Moira so
cool and disdainful . . . Rina all puffed and bullish, like a monstrous

caricature of a creature neither man nor woman; and I so obviously
not a partner to either, I like a slim and modish cuckoo in this ex-
normal nest."[15]

It was a disastrous experience. Mary Frances found her former
confidante more needy than she, and incapable of offering help. The
following morning she exorcised the painful encounter by recording it
on yellow sheets of paper, which, she later told Larry, were lost somewhere in New York City. "Perhaps it is just as well . . . it was a painful
piece of writing, but one I had to do, willy-nilly. I'm very glad it was
not printed. If the copy that went to New York turns up I'll send it on,
and you can burn it for me after you've read it."[16] She then fortifies
her spirits with a double porto flip (two eggs beaten into a glass of
port) in an impersonal brasserie on the Champs-Élysées. She wandered the streets of Paris and visited the Tuileries, "getting used to
humanity again"; when she returned to the hotel she was "ready to
meet love alone again, not asking for another person's comfort, nevermore to thirst for any flagon but my own."[17] Her parents arrived late
that afternoon.

Mary Frances reserved accommodations for her parents on the
Right Bank, put flowers and fruit in their rooms, and arranged for
them to preview some of the exhibits of the Exposition scheduled to
open in June. It was Rex's first trip to Europe, and she wanted it to be
memorable. Years later, their pleasurable, leisurely lunches, enhanced
by caviar and champagne, and meandering walks in the gardens of the
Palais Royale were among her fondest memories and the subjects of
more than one of her stories. After a week in Paris she and her parents boarded the train bound for Vevey, where Mary Frances had also
planned every detail of their visit. Edith and Rex stayed at the Hôtel
des Trois Couronnes, an 1842 lakeside landmark that exuded echoes
of Newport and Saratoga. Within the next few days they toured Lake
Geneva aboard a steamer that stopped at the Château de Chillon and
Montreux. They then took the funicular railroad to the Hôtel Mirador
near the top of Mont Pelerin to view the lake, the Alps, and the countryside.

One evening Mary Frances planned a picnic at Le Paquis after the
workmen had gone home. Rex, Dillwyn, and Al picked the first peas
of the season from the garden, Edith shelled them, and Mary Frances

cooked them over a pinewood fire. Most of the people in the world she loved were there, the sky was filled with the glow of the setting sun, and smoke from the fire scented the air. Suddenly a neighboring cow from across the curve of the Lower Corniche began to shake her bell in a slow rhythm, creating a "kind of hymn." Listening to the mountain music, Rex lifted up his face and said passionately, "God, but I feel good!" Mary Frances wrote about the moment and the al fresco dinner set on a carpenter's table on the terrace at Le Paquis: "Small brown roasted chickens lay on every plate, the best ones I have ever eaten done for me that afternoon by Madame Doellenbach of the Vieux Vevey . . . There was a salad of mountain lettuces. There was honest bread. There was plenty of limpid wine, the kind Brillat-Savarin said was like rock-water. Later there was a cheese, an Emmenthaler and a smuggled [from Paris] Roblichon . . . But what really mattered, what piped the high unforgettable tune of perfection, were the peas, which came from their hot pot onto our thick china plates in a cloud, a kind of miasma, of everything that anyone could ever want from them, even in a dream." Her idea of heaven, she concluded the account, "that night and this night too, is fresh green garden peas, picked and shelled by my friends, to the sound of a cowbell."[18]

The Kennedys also dined at many of Mary Frances's favorite restaurants, like the Trois Couronnes in Vevey, the Hôtel des XIII Cantons in Châtel-St.-Denis, and the Hôtel de Ville et du Raison in Cully, near Lausanne. They hired a chauffeur to drive them into German Switzerland, stopping in the small village of Malters to eat the most perfect trout imaginable at the Gasthaus zum Kreuz. Accompanied by Dillwyn and Al, Rex went by rail to Milan before going on to his Rotary conference in Nice. He returned to Vevey and together with Edith left for England. Mary Frances concluded a letter to Larry Powell with the comment, "It was fun—Father's first sight of Europe went to his head like champagne, and we all caught his excitement."[19]

Thanking Mary Frances and Dillwyn for their birthday greetings the following January, Rex wrote vividly about the visit:

I sort of hate to have these birthdays arrive because it brings home to me that there is not much yarn left to wind on the ball. Some years I can look back and realize that I haven't wound much on the ball but just yarn, but that is not the case during this past year. The trip to Switzerland left a hump on the ball, and it will take several more birthdays before it is smoothed out again. Sweet Violets with Timmie [Dillwyn] on the streets of Milano; squabs and white wine on your terrace, not to say anything about the green peas; Swiss bell ringers swinging their tails in the moonlight high on the side of the mountains; the crack of a trout's skull on the edge of an ancient sideboard just three minutes before it was served with its blue eyes registering disapproval; new mountain peaks emerging from behind the clouds; barbecued pear trees, I mean barbered; simple little street shows surrounded by simple people getting a laugh from the stories unfolded by actors without scenery; Vevey with her board walk along the lake, her little shops and her markets and her hospitable people; these are some of the memories that have gone into the ball of yarn for 1937.[20]

There is not a hint of the emotional crises of their eldest daughter, or the mounting political crisis in Europe.

Al left Vevey in the middle of June 1937; despite the fact that Hitler was threatening Austria and Czechoslovakia, he went to Salzburg for the summer. "I stayed on, plainly the mistress," Mary Frances told her psychiatrist years later. "My first book, *Serve It Forth*, came out in America and England, in 1937, but I was so involved emotionally that I paid no attention to it, and indeed I have never felt anything but a kind of withdrawal and regret, at the publication of any book or story I have ever written since."[21] Her attitude of studied indifference to the reception of her work is echoed in letters to friends at the time. When writing to Larry Powell, she noted cavalierly, "I know very little of the book, but after reams of good reviews, and the enthusiastic letters from relatives who had been trying to get it for two weeks at Macy's or who had been told that Robinson's sold out three times, I was surprised *and* disappointed to get a letter from Harper's . . . quoting sales 22 copies one week, 34 another, and so on. *Someone* must have read the damned book—or is it what is called a *succès d'estime*? I want some money, that's what I want—to hell with esteem at the moment. Page Mr. Hearst. But I'm glad you like it, even if the public doesn't." She concluded with a neat coverup for Al's absence: "Please forgive my long silence, and Al's even longer one, and write to us."[22]

It is possible that the publication of *Serve It Forth* was a factor in Al's leaving. Except for a few revisions, he had not worked on *The Ghost in the Underblows* in four years. Nor had he succeeded in completing a novel to either his own or his colleagues' satisfaction. Despite Mary Frances's reservations about her book's reception, it had already created quite a stir before the June publication date, with excerpts appearing in the March and April issues of *Harper's Monthly*. The reviews were, for the most part, favorable. *The New York Times* hailed it as a delightful book: "It is erudite and witty and experienced and young. The truth is that it is stamped on every page with a highly individualized personality."[23] "Mrs. Fisher has written without pretentiousness and without the affectation of elegance which is probably the worst curse of public eating in America,"[24] Lucius Beebe wrote in *Books*. In the *Chicago Daily Tribune*, Fanny Butcher described the book as such "a delicate emulsion"[25] that it is difficult to tell whether it is the historical and literary references or the author's observations that are the book's basic flavor. Alfred Knopf sent a short note telling her he wished that he had published it, and Phil Townsend Hanna at *Westways* sent his congratulations.

There were, however, a few quibbles. Lewis Gannett labeled Mary Frances's observations about the American palate "an ignorant French fantasy about American culinary barbarism . . . That, of course, is mere superstition. Mrs. Fisher should come home and browse in Sheila Hibben's *National Cookbook* with its discriminating appreciation of indubitably great traditions . . . It is well enough for Mrs. Fisher to tilt at salads made to be photographed rather than eaten; but she should know better than to berate apple pie or titter at appreciation of good maple syrup. Such ignorance fits ill with her cosmopolitan gastronomic wit."[26] And *The Times Literary Supplement* (London) suggested, "The book is not entirely satisfactory; partly because the occasional desire to be shocking is really rather tiresome, and partly because one comes to suspect that her scholarship and experience are perhaps not quite so wide or thorough as she would like us to imagine."[27] Mary Frances paid little attention to either review, although Gannett's criticism would influence the subject of her next book. That friends and relatives liked *Serve It Forth* and sent her enthusiastic letters about the book pleased her more than the reviews. Yet while it was dedicated to Rex and Edith, Mary Frances felt that they took scant notice of it. In the Kennedy family writing was simply something one did with very little fanfare.

But Mary Frances was definitely charting new territory. She called it "humanistic-gastronomic writing,"[28] and it *was* "a delicate emulsion." In the short introduction she distinguishes among books about *eating*, books about *what to eat*, and books about *people who eat*. She intends "to fall between the three fires or straddle them all."[29] Ostensibly the book is about hunger, and the various ways people have, for the most part, dignified the satisfaction of hunger. The form she adopted for it is as immediate and lively as good conversation. It lightly mixes fact and fancy, incorporating vignettes of culinary history from the oldest extant cookbook, the *Hon-zo*, written in Egypt in 2800 B.C., and from cookbooks written by women in nineteenth-century England and America. Between the parable of Jacob (whom she characterizes as the first restaurateur) and Esau (the first gastronome) and the heady stories of Vatel and Lucullus, the author's own dining experiences—secret indulgences, restaurants revisited, and the subtle mysteries of time past and time present, the snobbery associated with certain kinds of foods, the rituals of preparation, her concept of an ideal kitchen—emerge unforgettably in a variety of landscapes and time frames. By juxtaposing the contemporary preparation of *escargots d'or* with Roman cookery, and the magical taste of a bite of chocolate followed by a bite of bread with the abstinence of medieval monks, she introduces readers to a style of culinary writing that avoids both the constraints of culinary history and the self-absorption of the memoirist, focusing her playful imagination and continuing attention on the pleasures of the table experienced in family kitchens or boardinghouses, in restaurants or on a hill in the Côte d'Or. She is the heroine of every tale: charming waiters, playing the perfect hostess or guest, complimenting her host in a pension dining room, and seducing her husband with the "kiss" of a toasted tangerine. Never dwelling on a subject for too long, her voice alternates between slightly humorous commentary and the celebration of appetite. Sometimes vexingly short on specifics, she nevertheless revels in telling a good story and is not shy about embellishments.

The fifteen months that followed the publication of her book were probably the happiest and most fulfilling in Mary Frances's life. As the mistress of Le Paquis, she created a distinctive ambience in the home that she shared with Dillwyn. The first floor of the five-hundred-year-old vigneron's cottage served as an office and reception area, with an imposing entrance door and two French doors opening onto a terrace overlooking Lake Geneva. The old granite steps led up to Mary Frances's combined bedroom and writing alcove. To the left of the reception area, a half flight of stairs led down to a large new salon with comfortable sofas and chairs, the dining table from Valais, a stone fireplace, and three pairs of French doors that also opened onto the terrace. Stores—solid metal curtains that closed like shutters, to cool the rooms in the summer and secure the property during the owner's absence—protected the doors. Dillwyn designed his studio-bedroom on the upper level above the salon, and behind the original dwelling and the new structure two garden rooms and baths had been built to accommodate family and guests. The kitchen was a few steps to the left of the salon. It had wide deep windows with ferns hanging in them. There were pictures on the walls, pewter serving pieces and cookbooks on the open shelves, and plates and silver arranged on top of an antique dresser. As planned, music and conversation flowed freely between the two rooms.

Mary Frances and Dillwyn had three cellars built: one to store jars of beans, tomatoes, vegetable juices, and brandied fruits and jams preserved from their garden and orchard; another equipped with bins and slatted shelves to store cabbages, apples, and root vegetables; and a third to keep local wines and favorite older wines brought from Burgundy. There were also bottles of eaux-de-vie distilled from the plums, pears, and apples they gathered from the orchard. Mary Frances praised the rich bounty the cellars contained: "When I went down into the coolness and saw all the things sitting there so richly quiet on the shelves, I had a special feeling of contentment. It was a reassurance of safety against hunger, very primitive and satisfying."[30]

During the summer months Mary Frances and Dillwyn worked

the garden, and sent surplus lettuces and other vegetables to a sanatorium for poor children nearby. They harvested onions, garlic, and
shallots, which Mary Frances braided into ropes and hung over the
rafters in the attic. She also learned to cook sweet peppers, eggplants,
and onions in their own juices, flavored with sweet butter or thick
olive oil from the Italian-Swiss villagers. Dillwyn fried tomatoes the
way his family's cooks prepared them in Delaware, and they harvested
corn that they had grown from seeds imported from the States. Their
gardening and cooking made them a source of curiosity to the villagers, who could not understand why there were no servants' quarters at Le Paquis and why people of their means depended only on
the services of part-time help from the village.

When alone they ate crisp salads and corn "oysters" (fritters),
freshly fried in butter, accompanied with bottles of beer cooled in the
fountain. In mild weather the terrace provided a natural dining area
for guests. Mary Frances usually served sherry, followed by dinners of
chilled soups and tureens of small garden vegetables, cooked sepa-
rately before they were tossed together with sweet butter. On special
occasions she ordered cheese pies or roasted birds from the village. In
cool or inclement weather they entertained in front of the fireplace
and invited their guests to serve themselves from a large casserole
simmering on the kitchen stove and from a bowl of fresh salad on the
sideboard. First-time visitors pleaded for the name of the cook and
were disbelieving when Mary Frances offered to give them her
recipes for the vegetable ragout and honey-baked pears. After the initial rumors in the village about the unmarried couple died down, the
number of their acquaintances grew. The owner of a small, luxurious
hotel in Montreux sang the praises of Mme Fisher's dishes. An elderly
Swiss judge and his wife mellowed in the glow of the salon's fireplace.
A fading Danish countess, whose husband was a patient in a private
hospital nearby, was also a guest at many of their dinners.

Whenever they could free themselves from the tyranny of the garden, Mary Frances and Dillwyn took short trips. Because Vevey was a
stop on the train route to Milan, they occasionally boarded the morning train to spend a day in Italy. They also escaped to Paris to visit
bookstores and art galleries and revisit the Voltaire, Brasserie Lipp,
and Café de la Paix. They tentatively planned to acquire a suite in an

old hotel on the rue Royale so they could leave books, clothing, and other necessities to facilitate their occasional visits to the city they both loved. But whether they ranged beyond the Swiss border or simply crossed the lake to dine and dance at the Casino in Évian, Le Paquis drew them back like a magnet. With a civil war already in progress in Spain and Europe readying for war, Le Paquis was a paradise of denial. They were too happy to take notice of any world beyond their "dear meadow."

It was all too perfect. The strain of the last months vanished in their togetherness, and Mary Frances was inspired to write again. In August 1937 she told Larry Powell that she had contacted Gene Saxton about writing a personal book because, she said, "my present life is a strange, complicated, interesting one . . . But my deep distrust—or is it timidity, cowardice even? of such self-revelations will, perhaps, prevent me from thus relieving myself." She commented that she was applying for a Guggenheim grant to help fund the writing of the book. "I think it's quite futile, as I'm already in the Happy Hunting Ground, supposedly, and never heard of a fellowship being granted to go *back* to America. However—it was good experience for filling out blanks."[31]

In September Al returned to the States and started to teach at Smith College, where he quickly distinguished himself as a popular teacher and poet. In a collection of poems by faculty members, he published a sonnet from his *Northampton Sequence: 1937*, written during either the summer or early fall:

> Since each, quite like a special, changing cell,
> changed in an individual and strange
> slow way, divergent from the parallel,
> those who once loved now suffer their love's change.
> Those who once loved, like transformations of
> themselves, as trees from seed or sounds to sound,
> slowly, with passing days, know that their love
> is foreigner, alien on native ground.
> Those who once loved have, by mutation, come
> to find themselves unrecognizable,
> and moving each in a same body's home,
> their purgatory now resembles hell.

Men need mercy. But pity those removed
From being merciful to those who loved.[32]

The poem expressed the finality of what he considered to be Mary
Frances's rejection of him and the deep personal pain it had caused
him. He seemed not to be able to address his loss in any other way.
He shied away from correspondence with his friends, and when directly questioned, he resolutely refused to speak "accusingly" of his
wife.[33]

Mary Frances's growing apprehension about what Al's family and
her own thought about their separation, and their friends' queries
about Al's move to Massachusetts, forced her to take action. In October she wrote to Larry Powell:

I'll see you in about six weeks! I planned to come home for
New Year's, but we [?] decided to come a month (or less) earlier. I want to see Al and do some work. I can see how our un-
explained actions might puzzle people, and I'm really terribly
sorry if I've caused you any embarrassment with conversations
and so on. As you know, I'm not much given to discussing either my own or other's people's business, and there must be
much that's puzzling . . . Yes, Al is teaching at Smith, a very
cushy job with plenty of time for his own work. He decided
suddenly to take the bid. It was a rather difficult decision, but
I suppose it's for the best. I'm staying here at Le Paquis, working hard on my book, and in my garden. I leave in about three
weeks, for New York and California and some even harder
work.[34]

Over Dillwyn's objection that returning to California was unnecessary when a letter could serve the purpose of telling her parents about
her plans to divorce Al Fisher, Mary Frances left for Cherbourg and
boarded a Dutch ship. "I must do it myself, a kind of castigation for
hurting good people," she wrote in *The Gastronomical Me*. "I was
prostrated . . . not seasick the way the stewardess wanted me to be,
but flattened, boneless, with despair at having gone away from
Chexbres [Dillwyn].[35] It was the strongest physical reaction I had

ever felt, and I was frightened and dazed."[36] Many of the passengers
on the ship were fleeing Europe, hoping to avoid conscription or
worse. Mary Frances couldn't wait to accomplish the business at
hand and return to Dillwyn and "neutral" Switzerland.

During the crossing Mary Frances wrote that she perfected the art
of eating alone, to the stewards' consternation requesting both a table
and a menu to herself. It was a way to keep loneliness and strangers
in search of companionship at bay. In New York she transferred to a
train bound for California, where family and friends—and the pain
that she would cause them—awaited. Whittier was still a small town
of more or less conventional people, and not only the failure of Mary
Frances's eight-year marriage but the circumstances leading to the
breakup would be embarrassing to Edith and Rex. Moreover, Al was
one of the family. Edith, especially, had warm feelings toward her son-
in-law, as did Norah, after all the time she'd spent with him in Dijon,
Strasbourg, and Cagnes. "To me, he was always remote, kind, beautiful," she wrote, "a man I was confident would eventually be acknowledged as a new Keats or Andrew Marvell."[37] To Mary Frances's great
relief, however, her family supported her decision. A short time after
her visit, Rex reassured her, "I am glad that you could come home
when you did, even though you did not receive any very definite advice as to how to solve your problem. My theory is that time will work
that out and that you will know what steps to take, before you are
forced to pick out the spot to plant your foot. In the meantime busy
yourself with writing and with your garden and know that right or
wrong I am behind you, ready if necessary to swear that wrong is
right. So, too, is Edith."[38] While in California, Mary Frances also visited Al's mother and sister, who were now residing in Pasadena, and
told them of her intention to make her separation from him final. Although California law required a year before a final decree could be
granted, she had made her decision and filed the necessary papers.

Before leaving Whittier, Mary Frances visited with Larry and Fay
Powell and made use of Larry's current position at the Los Angeles
Public Library to obtain more books about California at the turn of
the century. She said that she wanted to resume writing the novel
about life in early California, and particularly the founding of Whittier, that she had started in Eagle Rock. And while visiting Jake

Zeitlin's bookstore in Los Angeles, she accepted his offer to contribute a gastronomical bibliography for the local Wine and Food Society chapbook that he was editing. At about this time, she also
responded to a query that she had received from a literary agent
named Mary Leonard Pritchett. Although Pritchett marketed books
and plays primarily, she also specialized in placing material in quality magazines. The idea of having someone represent her and deal
with the vagaries of publishing appealed to Mary Frances, and she
signed on.

On January 10, 1938, Mary Frances sailed for Europe aboard the
Île de France, a ship that seemed cold and uninviting, particularly in
Second Class, and filled with dismaying, almost constant conversations about Laval, Blum, and the possible fall of France. During the
crossing, Mary Frances resolutely put the thought that Europe would
soon be engulfed in war out of her thoughts and continued her habit
of eating and drinking alone. This time, however, her aloofness and
savoir faire attracted the attention of a dashing young Norman named
Jacques. Playing the eternal naïf, she had cocktails and dinner with
him, told him the address of her hotel in Paris, met him and his
brothers for dinner while there, and then invited him to visit Le
Paquis whenever he traveled south. Reunited with Dillwyn, she casually told him about Jacques after she received a letter from him asking
her to accompany him on a trip. To Mary Frances's amazement, Dillwyn rebuked her for leading the poor chap on. It was only after the
frustrated Jacques had met Dillwyn and sized up the situation at Le
Paquis that she acknowledged that she had hurt the young man and
said a humbling goodbye. She vowed never again to be alone in a
restaurant or anywhere.[39]

Disappointed that she had missed most of the short, tranquil days
of winter at Le Paquis, which were ideal for reading and writing, she
nevertheless managed to complete the gastronomical bibliography, expand the entries in her journal, and return to the California/Whittier
novel before the days lengthened and the garden needed attention.
The letter to Jake Zeitlin accompanying the bibliography reiterated
her continued respect for books like "Mrs. Kander's oil-covered
masterpiece," *The Settlement Cookbook*, and "the greatest book on
gastronomy, Brillat-Savarin's *Physiologie du Goût*," as well as her pref-

erence for "a constantly shifting and permanently surprising library."
"I should keep it small," she said. "An important part of it would be
scrap-books; I am convinced that it should include information not
only about the physiology of taste, but of digestion: and one or two
good text-books on the human body in relation to food."[40]

She divided the bibliography into four sections: Gastronomy, Practical Cookery, Not Practical Cookery, and Wine. And she listed about
seventy-five books, at least half of which were French classics. The
primary standard she used for inclusion was literary style. "This arbitrary but well-proved criterion is perhaps but another indication of the
fine-nosed search for perfection of real gourmets, who know with all
their senses that a banquet must have the same harmony as a piece of
music, and a paragraph the balance and bouquet of a vintage wine."[41]
What Mary Frances had learned experientially by living in France and
Switzerland and by delving into culinary history at the Los Angeles
Public Library had served her well.

Only a few jottings remain of the Vevey journal, but an illuminat-
ing entry for February 7, 1938, noted that she had sent off some stories to Mary Leonard Pritchett and finished an introduction for
Zeitlin's bibliography. She also seemed to be doing some "vague mental nibbling at the Quaker story." Scribbled notes found among her papers indicated that she often kept pen and paper next to her bed "to
record my faint stirrings and flutterings," though read in the light of
day they often made little sense. Living with Dillwyn gave her more
leeway to be herself, to discover not only what she wanted to do but
also how to do it: "My whole existence has become more completely
physical than ever before in my life: I eat, sleep, listen, even cook and
read with an intensity and a fullness that I have never felt until now.
I am completely absorbed in myself—but myself as seen through
Timmy [Dillwyn]. It is a strange life, and one that cannot last long
probably. I am abandoned to it now."[42]

It is tempting to think that seeing herself "through Dillwyn" was
what led to their collaboration on a novel set in Vevey. They called it
Touch and Go, with its dual meanings of both a precarious state of affairs and quick action. Although Mary Frances said that they each
wrote alternating chapters, the dialogue, imagery, and voice suggest a
single writer.[43] Their choice of the pseudonym, Victoria Berne, also

hinted at female authorship, but they probably devised and developed the plot together. Published by Harper and Brothers in 1939, the novel was not unlike the kind of upper-middle-class fiction written by Dillwyn's sister Anne and a score of cosmopolitan women writers in the 1930s.

Touch and Go is a romance with very little passion and even less physical contact. The plot revolves around Anne Wilcox, a young widow who wants to become a mother because she believes that is the only way she can complete herself as a woman. Before Anne's search for a husband begins, the reader learns that her first marriage had been "a life of whisperings, of tiptoeing, of gentle reaching for things she couldn't comprehend. And when Edward died, it had been less dying than a quiet vanishing. Her mind could remember his name, recite his features, but he was not in her heart, nor could her body recall his touch any more than if he had never existed."[44]

The setting of *Touch and Go* is the luxury Pension Belle-Vu, in reality the Mirador Hotel, on Mont Pelerin, located above Vevey and accessible only by the funicular railroad. A collection of characters, including Anne Wilcox, accidentally gather there and their lives become intertwined. They converse knowingly and almost endlessly, frequently in awkward translations of French and German. And they become attached to each other and solicitous about their respective futures. Descriptions of Alpine scenery, the Vevey funicular with its stops at Corseaux, Chardonne, and Mont Pelerin, and the ever-changing, panoramic Lake Geneva re-create the landscape that surrounded the Edenic world inhabited by Mary Frances and Dillwyn. There are only hints that Europe is on the way to a devastating war. "Our book comes out in May—awful trash, but entertaining for hammock-trade—we hope it will make piles of dough,"[45] she wrote to Larry Powell.

Identifying Anne Wilcox with Mary Frances is irresistible; both were separated from their first husbands, although in Mary Frances's case it was by an impending divorce, not death. Mary Frances agreed with her mother that having children was a woman's destiny, and the novel expanded upon this idea. Driven by almost a Shavian "life force," Anne Wilcox meets a widower with two children, marries him, and becomes mother to another woman's children. Although Dillwyn was all that Mary Frances could have hoped for in a lover, she also knew that he could not father a child. The relevance of an adoption theme, suggested earlier in Mary Frances's life when she and Al considered having children, comes into play again and would be repeated in various guises in her fiction as well as in her personal life.

Meanwhile, during the spring of 1938, Le Paquis was serene, filled with budding vines, violets, primroses, and crocuses. The house was readied for visiting friends and relatives, who started to arrive at Easter time. One evening Dillwyn and Mary Frances left their current houseguest shortly after dinner for a rendezvous together, which became one of the "strangest meals" that Mary Frances writes about in *The Gastronomical Me*. Earlier in the day, Dillwyn has issued to her a written invitation, filled with scrolls and banners, to meet him in his studio at midnight for an Easter supper. Dressed in her best clothes, she joins him with a gift of beautifully painted eggs in a basket, and they feast on beluga caviar and "smooth potent gin" in a seductive setting of apple blossoms and candlelight. After the feast, she politely thanks him, says good night, and leaves her surprised seducer. Commenting on her action, she says: "I was unchaperoned, shy, flooded with a sense of propriety that had nothing to do with my real years, my real life with Chexbres [Dillwyn]. That is why I stood up and walked so primly past the upper part of the room, the part with the big bed and the clothes presses and such intimacies. That is why I said goodnight with such politeness to the only man in the world I knew. And that is why, long after I had lain me down in my small austere room, I heard from upstairs the sound of Chexbres' long gusts of laughter."[46]

The summer days passed quickly in a blur of entertaining and the comings and goings of guests. Anne Parrish and a friend, Mary Powers, spent June, July, and August there. David and Norah, enrolled in schools in Grenoble so that Norah could learn German before returning to the University of Michigan in the fall, visited often. In an unpublished novel called *The Theoretical Foot*, Mary Frances devoted a chapter to these four guests and a young couple who visit "La Prairie," a fictional Le Paquis. Also appearing in the novel is the local gravedigger François, who by this time was well established as a self-appointed manservant to Dillwyn and Mary Frances, busy running errands, shopping, and supervising the vineyard and gardens while his wife did the laundry and household tasks.

Mary Frances portrays Nan Temple, the fictional Anne Parrish, as a successful poet married to a Wall Street banker and who has been devoted to her brother Tim (Dillwyn) since his birth. She loves La Prairie and spends her time picking and arranging wildflowers. Her friend Lucy disapproves of her brother's lover, Sara Porter (Mary Frances), and she shows it in various ways. Daniel Tennant (David) idolizes his older sister Sara and is a companion to Honor (Norah), a sister only a year older than he. During the course of the summer he grows up and acquires a love of his own. Honor, on the other hand, makes Tim her confidant and has long talks with him about Sara's attitude about her siblings. She confesses that she always thinks, "What would Sara say?" before she makes a decision, and she is determined to free herself from her sister's influence. Tim patiently tries to explain the meaning of love and dependence to her. The novel revealed Mary Frances's uneasiness about how others perceived her relationship with Dillwyn as well as her concerns about Dillwyn's close relationship with his sister Anne. She also recognized the efforts of both David and Norah to free themselves from her influence.

During that summer, Dillwyn and Mary Frances discovered that the house and property were becoming increasingly expensive to maintain—so much more so than Dillwyn had anticipated that they could no longer afford to live there. Reluctantly he let it be known that it was available. Also, he must have felt that the actions of Italy and Germany in supporting Franco's fascist forces with aviators and "volunteers" in the Spanish Civil War in open defiance of a nonintervention treaty, signaled a broader conflict, as had Mussolini's support of Germany's annexation of Austria in the spring of 1938. Furthermore, the continuing German-Czech crisis, provoked by Hitler's demand for self-determination of the Sudetenland that summer, seemed only a prelude to German occupation of the region. Everywhere people were fleeing from what they perceived to be dangerous areas. Offered a good price for Le Paquis, Dillwyn sold it to a Dutch doctor, Kieviet de Jonge, agreeing to give him possession of the property in October.

On September 1, the morning after a celebratory dinner in which

Dillwyn danced exuberantly on the terrace of Le Paquis, David, Norah, Anne, Dillwyn, and Mary Frances drove to Bern for a holiday weekend. On the second day there, after purchasing theater tickets and arranging for dinner, Dillwyn experienced severe cramps in his left leg when he returned to the hotel. David tried to massage the leg and Mary Frances wrapped it in hot towels, but by seven-thirty the pain was excruciating. They called a doctor, who administered drugs and admitted Dillwyn to Viktoria Hospital the next morning. He was operated on for an embolism that had traveled from his ankle to the pelvic cavity. When the first operation did not relieve him of pain, he underwent another operation to remove several more clots from the thigh, but gangrene developed and the leg had to be amputated above the knee. While he was recuperating, Mary Frances reluctantly left his side, and with David and the loyal François moved the items she wanted to keep from Le Paquis into an apartment that they had rented in La Tour-de-Peilz, a few kilometers from Vevey.

Mary Frances then began her Bern journal,[47] narrating the painful story of Dillwyn's initial brush with death, his increasing reliance on Analgeticum and other drugs to ease pain, and their sojourn in both Bern and Adelboden searching for a cure. Although Mary Frances asked her mother and father to allow David and Norah to remain because she needed them, the American consul urged U.S. citizens to leave. They departed on September 30, the day the Munich Pact was signed. Dillwyn's sister Anne also left Bern with them because she had received word that Mrs. Parrish was gravely ill in Delaware. They traveled to Liverpool, and a week later were on a ship bound for New York. Meanwhile, the Swiss were growing increasingly uneasy about troop mobilization and fearful about the pact forged in Munich, which would soon prove to be a symbol of appeasement to Hitler's demands for occupation of the Sudetenland.

With only a Catholic sister as her mainstay, Mary Frances learned to give Dillwyn injections of various painkillers prescribed by his physician, and she was never very far from his side. After about a month, he had enough strength to leave the hospital on crutches to visit a café or restaurant for a special meal, but there were other times when the pain was so intense that he remained in bed. Toward the end of October, the doctors decided that the higher altitude of Adelboden might be better for him. After five days there, however, his temperature soared and the doctors diagnosed a bad case of phlebitis in the right groin and lower abdomen. With only drugs to relieve the pain and almost no appetite, he began to lose all desire to live. The doctors thought that Dillwyn's condition could be a paralysis of the walls of the veins, but they had never seen such symptoms in a man of Dillwyn's age. They advised no travel and at least six or more weeks of bed rest. Mary Frances moved in and out of his pain-filled days and nights like a shadow, recording her own confused anguish in her journal until her last entry on November 13, 1938.

In a letter to Larry Powell dated December 2, Mary Frances gave as a forwarding address 30 rue du Château, La Tour-de-Peilz, Vaud, Switzerland. She and Dillwyn moved into their apartment on Christmas Eve, and she wrote about celebrating the holiday there: "Once I lived in a beautiful modern apartment, very glassy Bauhaus, and there were broken pine boughs everywhere, and candle flames made countless by old mirrors, and we ate *pâté de Strasbourg* in a fine crust, and then heard Bach's *Passion According to Saint Matthew*, coming, I think, from Munich on the air. I was very happy, because I was so busy."[48] The change to a lower altitude, however, did not help Dillwyn's condition as they both had hoped.

After celebrating New Year's, they decided to return to the States. Aboard the *De Grasse* in early February, Mary Frances was the only woman among twenty other passengers, and although the captain and the chef were solicitous, she later wrote about the difficult trip: "I don't know how we ever got to New York. Chexbres [Dillwyn] was dying, really, and in revolt at the whole cruel web of clinics and specialists and injections and rays we had run away from in Europe, as if we knew that nothing could be worse than what was happening there to us. We were without nurses, for the first time in months. It was a very rough crossing, and I still wake up shaking sometimes to remember how I prepared hypodermics between rolls of the ship."[49]

Prior to sailing, Dillwyn had written to Dr. Springer in Wilmington, Delaware, informing him that the pain caused by phantom limb syndrome was steadily increasing, that virtually all the drugs except Analgeticum had ceased to be effective, and that the injections of various venoms had caused more pain than the embolism itself. When

Mary Frances and Dillwyn arrived in New York in mid-February, they went directly to Wilmington and registered at the Dupont Hotel under the names Victor and Victoria Berne. Then, after a series of consultations, more of Dillwyn's leg was amputated with the hope of mending nerve endings and perhaps achieving better healing. They kept the seriousness of his condition from his mother.

When Dillwyn was able to travel, he and Mary Frances went to California, first to the Ranch and then to Palm Springs, seeking comfort in the dry heat of the San Jacinto hills. As the climate seemed to provide relief for Dillwyn's continuing pain, they began to look for suitable property in the area and rented a small cottage in Moreno, near Riverside. Mary Frances thought of her one true love "in the dark opiate arms of Analgeticum" and realized that trying to duplicate Le Paquis in the San Jacinto hills would be close to impossible. Their needs and pleasures were totally different from those they had indulged during their Swiss idyll. Gone were the meals from their garden, the end-of-day glasses of sherry or vin de Vevey on the terrace. Gone was the rhythm of work and leisure.

As a sad reminder of Le Paquis and their Edenic existence there, *Touch and Go* was published in the spring of 1939. While it attracted very little attention in the publishing world, the reviews that did appear were unanimous in their appraisal of it as "fiction in a lighter vein." In *The New York Times*, Charlotte Dean wrote: "Miss Berne has an amusing little tale to tell, and she does it nicely. It is rather a pity that she expects you to be shocked at a few unconventional items—not too shocked, just surprised into a laugh once in a while. Aside from these Victorian notions of comic lack of restraint, which no one has been amused at for years now, the novel is light and gay."[50] Less tolerant was the *Saturday Review of Literature*'s critic: "There is very little touch and still less go about this self-consciously airy novel which at its best suggests G. B. Stern in one of her less matriarchal moods. The background is the Switzerland of the pension, of the ugly wallpaper and the potted begonias, of the idle uprooted exiles. The plot is the effort of a nice girl, rescued by his death from an insipid husband, to find herself another man . . . she succeeds with a German émigré. The most exciting event is an epidemic of measles."[51] Mary Frances cautioned Larry, "Our book's out—futile but entertaining . . . Don't waste 2 dollars on it. If I ever get a free copy I'll send it to you. I think ours went to Switzerland."[52]

Although almost totally preoccupied with Dillwyn's condition, Mary Frances could not help noticing that Rex had become more tense and brooding. Strained finances, Dillwyn's illness, the danger of war, and the first doubts of old age had begun to plague him in the fall of 1938 and warranted a letter from Edith to Ted Kennedy:

> I was quite concerned about him [Rex] for several weeks but he is a great deal better. It was just a combination of things, bad business conditions, too much political hurrah and worry about the children's being in Europe during the war scare. It just knocked him for a loop and he was as bad as Burt was that summer you were all here. He has developed the same phobia about his right hand, says he cannot hold a pen . . . It worries Rex that he cannot do for them [the children] as he had expected and that worries him to death. I can't get his point of view at all. I think they have had it pretty soft all their lives and they should be able to cut down on things . . . I always felt that he [Rex] was so much like Grandmother that he had missed out on that morose streak, but he certainly has it.[53]

Edith, moreover, had her own problems; she realized that her family needed her less. She tried to persuade Rex that giving their six-year-old grandson Sean a home at the Ranch would be good for him and Anne, who was struggling to care for her son while working full-time. There was also the disappointment of David's decision to leave Princeton and take art courses at Colorado State. Because Mary Frances and Dillwyn had advised him to pursue an artist's career, they now felt responsible for his choice and for the family's displeasure. These were added stresses at a time when Mary Frances was already burdened.

She and Dillwyn also knew that they had to make another trip to Switzerland before all of Europe was engulfed in war. They had to close the apartment in La Tour-de-Peilz and decide which personal belongings and furniture to sell or send to the States. Of greater importance was the need to obtain a supply of Analgeticum, not available in the States, which in the past months had provided Dillwyn with his only relief from pain. Grim as it seemed, he and Mary Frances carefully calculated how much of it they would need before more amputations were necessary, and then made arrangements to obtain it.

Before they left the States, however, Mary Frances and Dillwyn decided to legalize their arrangement. They were married in a civil ceremony in the Riverside city hall on May 12, 1939. The clerk, Selma Boylan, was the only witness. Thirteen days later, they set sail from New York on the *Normandie*. Mary Frances idealized the crossing and the return a short time later in *The Gastronomical Me*:

> We got up late, and went after bathings and shavings to the Lounge, where we sat in soft chairs by the glass wall and looked out past the people sunning themselves to the blue water. We drank Champagne, or sometimes beer, slowly and talked to each other because there was so much to say and so little time to say it . . . I have probably talked more to Chexbres [Dillwyn] and he to me, than to all the other people put together in both our lives. We often wondered about it: how could we talk so much and never bore each other. The wine served perhaps as a kind of delicate lubricant . . . but without it, it would have been the same.[54]

Meals were leisurely, movies a part of the trancelike voyage, and when New York loomed near, Mary Frances wrote that she felt "beautiful, witty, truly loved . . . the most fortunate of women, past sea change and with her hungers fed."[55]

On September 1, 1939, Hitler invaded Poland; two days later Britain and France declared war. Bombs raining down on Europe and the omnipresence of death were only the latest and the most dramatic instance of the world's pain seeping into their own.

SIX

Bareacres

(1940–1941)

I have never understood some (a lot of) taboos and it seems silly to me to make suicide one of them in our social life.[1]   —M.F.K. Fisher

In January 1940 Mary Frances and Dillwyn purchased ninety acres of untillable land in the San Jacinto hills southeast of Hemet, intending to renovate the pinewood cabin that stood on the property. "We're landed gentry again. God help us," Mary Frances wrote to Larry Powell. "We've put our last penny into 90 acres of rocks and rattlesnakes over near Hemet, on the hills by the Ramona Bowl. There's a very shack-y wooden house, which we'll have to live in 'as is' for a while, and there are several springs. We got the whole business, plus a lot of headaches and a great feeling of excitement and happiness, for $2750! We can't move until April or May. We have a dog, too . . . the funniest most irritating nicest one I've ever met, named Butch."[2]

For years people in the area believed that the cabin on the property was haunted, and not without reason. The first person who built a dwelling there, in the early 1900s, was known as "nigger Brown," and he sold kerosene to the townspeople and apparently made enemies while doing it. Rumor had it that his house burned to the ground in an act of revenge, and he perished in the kerosene-driven blaze. The next resident who built on the land in the 1920s also met a tragic fate. Known locally as the Squawman, the outlaw Indian trader Captain Hoffman migrated to the Hemet Valley from New Mexico with his Navajo bride, Gna Gli, for whom he built a squaw house north of his cabin in a grove of orange trees. A bullet hole through a south window of his pinewood cabin was the only remaining evidence of Captain Hoffman's suspected suicide or possible murder by either another Navajo or a member of the local Sobodan tribe who had vowed to revenge Gna Gli's defection. Over time, passersby had stolen Captain Hoffman's possessions and Indian artifacts but had not defaced the cabin in any way. Twenty years later, tales of suicide, murder, and revenge notwithstanding, the cabin looked "welcoming" and affordable to Mary Frances and Dillwyn, and they purchased it.

The town of Hemet stretched along the valley floor between the San Jacinto Mountains to the north and northeast and the barren ranges that separated the valley from the Pacific coastal lands to the west and southwest. Mount San Jacinto was clearly visible, and beyond it lay the desert and Palm Springs. To the south of the Parrishes' property, rocky hills rose to an elevation of more than 1,500 feet, and townspeople called the crest the Rim of the World or Gibbel Flat for the rancher who owned it. The Ramona Bowl, an open-air theater where a pageant commemorating Helen Hunt Jackson's tragic tale *Ramona* had been held every spring since 1923, was slightly beyond the western boundary of the property. After the Parrishes took up residence in the cabin in 1940, they greeted the galloping actors with cold bottles of beer after their climactic escape over the hills. A single road, Crest Drive, curved the length of the valley from west to east and led directly to the dirt road that crossed the riverbed and climbed over a thousand feet to the cabin, and beyond to the spring that provided water for the property. Rolling hills, giant boulders, and a canyon that split the ascent from Crest Drive to the Rim of the World distinguished the Parrishes' land from the lush apricot orchards on the valley floor.

An elderly couple had been squatting in the cabin but promised to move out by mid-March. Meanwhile Mary Frances and Dillwyn stayed in their rented house in Moreno, where they made plans to adapt the cabin to their needs. The five-room pine board house had been built in a U shape with the open space between the two wings facing southward toward the Rim of the World. It was bordered by a wall and terrace. The foundation of the house was built on rocks, and the floors of the porches along the northern side of the house were smooth concrete. A large stone fireplace dominated the main room.

When the house was finally vacated, Dillwyn and Mary Frances had walls shifted to enlarge space for Dillwyn's studio in one wing, and Mary Frances's study and a guest bedroom in the other wing. The porches were screened, one to serve as a bedroom and the other to extend Dillwyn's studio. Two baths were added and the kitchen, originally an old concrete-floored porch, was renovated, the floor covered with patterned linoleum, and a white porcelain sink, enameled stove, and icebox installed, as well as minimal counters, shelves, and bins. Mary Frances hung a mirror in an old mahogany frame over the vegetable bin so she could apply fresh lipstick and smooth her hair before she answered a knock on the door. Because five new pairs of French doors and the Dutch door from the kitchen opened directly onto the patio between the two wings of the house, Mary Frances and Dillwyn also planned to pave the area with flat stones when they could afford it. Whether they barbecued a steak or slept there at day's end, they wanted this open-air room to be "the heart of the place."

They christened the property Bareacres after an impoverished landowner in *Vanity Fair*. Mary Frances wrote, "We put so much of our lifeblood and our inner love and misery and strength into it [Le Paquis] that I felt sure I would never again be able to do it about any other place. And now . . . I am even happier about Bareacres, because I have no reservations about it."[3] Events in Europe, however, weighed heavily upon her and Dillwyn and brought great sadness. A friend had written to them from Vevey in January 1940, saying, "It is lucky that you left when you did and were able to get your things over for now it is hopeless."[4] Mme de Jonge, the present owner of Le Paquis, also reported that there was great anxiety about a possible invasion in the spring and that Swiss troops were mobilizing.[5] From France, Mme Rigoulot sent word of her father's death and the loss of her sensitive and poetic son Plume, who had been drafted into the army and died of pneumonia. When Paris surrendered to the Germans on June 13, Mary Frances and Dillwyn were devastated and feared for the lives of Georges Connes and his family as well as other friends in Dijon. Mary

Frances wrote, "Underneath everything we do or think, now, is the in-credible knowledge that Europe, the part we knew of it, is forever gone. The actual invasions and bombings are less final than what is dying in the people. They will go on, naturally, and will build a life that will soon seem natural to their children and to them. But a part of their spirit, and a part of ours, too, is dead."[6]

Dillwyn continually occupied himself with improving the cabin, by designing an ingenious scheme of movable canvas strips to protect the patio from sun and wind, making little doors for their new cat, Tawny, and her kittens to exit and enter the house, and designing a kennel for Butch. But he was never free of pain and frequently slept very little. Mary Frances urged him to consult Hal Bieler, a forward-thinking physician in Pasadena whom she had met earlier through Larry Powell. Although Dr. Bieler was unable to identify Dillwyn's medical condition specifically, he did believe that heavy smoking and malnutrition had caused it, and he prescribed a rigid regime that banned smoking, drinking, coffee, and spices. Mary Frances, how-ever, could not deny Dillwyn his long-accustomed pleasures. She ad-ministered injections of Analgeticum to him as needed day and night, his only relief from constant pain. Unspoken between them was the fact that they had secured only enough of the drug to last about four-teen months. Perhaps they both knew that by the time the supply of the painkiller was depleted, "the jig will pretty well be up anyway."[7]

The rhythm of their days and nights accelerated or slowed with Dillwyn's level of pain. If the cat or kittens or dog needed attention, Mary Frances and Dillwyn drove to the veterinarian in Riverside, but they avoided the trip unless it was an emergency. Mary Frances de-pended on the local library for her research, shopped locally, and saw very little of her neighbors, not wanting to leave Dillwyn alone for long. She cooked simply, and when they entertained, their guests were either family or close friends. On good days, Mary Frances told her psychiatrist years later, "Dillwyn painted like a possessed devil, which he was."[8] He completed *Les Fiançailles* (a still life of four Mex-ican dolls) and a series of fruit-and-vegetable paintings, as well as a series of portraits of local people who posed for him.[9]

Mary Frances finished writing *The Theoretical Foot*, begun earlier in Vevey, interspersing the chapters in which she tells the story of the guests at Le Paquis during the summer of 1938 with vignettes that trace the embolism Dillwyn suffered in Bern, the amputation of the gangrenous leg, and the onset of phantom limb syndrome (the "theoretical foot"). She ended the novel with Dillwyn's wild dance the night before they traveled to Bern. Mary Frances then sent the manuscript to Larry and Fay Powell and Anne Parrish for their suggestions. To her dismay, Anne not only objected strenuously to Mary Frances's portrayal of her friend Mary Powers as self-centered and domineering and to her own characterization as an obsessive sister, but also strongly suggested that there would be legal repercussions if Mary Frances attempted to publish it. Moreover, Anne took the opportunity to remind Mary Frances that by using actual people and events in her writing, she caused her friends pain. "I feel as though I had overheard confidences not meant for me, eavesdropping unwillingly on you and Dillwyn talking together," Anne wrote. "And it has turned what was, to me a beautiful time, into one of almost unbearably revealed suffering."[10] She cited, as another example of Mary Frances's insensitivity, the essay "The Social Status of a Vegetable," published in *Serve It Forth*, and called it an ungrateful, cruel portrayal of Mrs. Parrish as a snob, when, in fact, she had paid for Mary Frances's first-class trip to Europe. It was the first time that Mary Frances had been brought up short for her practice of using family, friends, and acquaintances in her pieces. Yet she could not or would not accept it as a criticism.

The day after she received Anne's letter, Mary Frances responded to Larry's letter, which highly praised the novel: "Your letters about my book were as manna to me, since only the day before they came I learned that it will be impossible to publish the thing, and furthermore that I had wrought irrevocable damage to one of the few friendships I care about. I was shocked and terribly surprised. But Tim [Dillwyn] has always said that I am basically naïve, and I suppose that was proof that he's correct. Anyway . . . it did me good to learn that you both thought the book had its good points. I'll put it away, and start soon on another one."[11] Two years later, in fact, Mary Frances would submit *The Theoretical Foot* to Sam Sloan, an editor at Duell, Sloan and Pearce, only to have it rejected.

In the meantime, she turned away from novel writing and began to cast about for an interesting culinary topic to explore. Mindful that some American critics had thought that *Serve It Forth* evidenced a bias against and neglect of native American gastronomy, Mary Frances considered writing a "fair, lively (if possible) journal of my own experiences in American restaurants."[12] And she began to think about what really distinguished an American restaurant from a Continental one and also about outstanding restaurants she had visited. She remembered reading about Anne Parrish's longtime friend, the journalist and raconteur Alexander Woollcott, who planned to operate an inn in Connecticut that would serve food as it should be served to a few choice bons vivants. In early February she wrote to Woollcott and asked him to elaborate on his plans: "If you have time and care to tell me what you think about this fairly fundamental desire in all good livers, I shall be grateful."[13]

She planned to use Woollcott's response, a section of Sinclair Lewis's novel *Work of Art*, and Dillwyn's stint as a restaurateur to write about those connoisseurs of the good life who had, at least at one time or another, thought of running the perfect restaurant or hostelry. As usual, she embellished and changed details of Dillwyn's culinary career to suit her project. Although his family had ridiculed his aspirations in the kitchen, Dillwyn had diligently cooked in Delaware and had made excellent sauces and cakes that, according to Mary Frances, commanded five times the going price at the local church bazaar. She wrote that later in Los Angeles, "He opened a small restaurant and turned it into what came dangerously near being a rendezvous for local *précieux*. He kept everything very simple. He always had one thing in the small window, which in spite of being very whimsical at times (a waffle with strawberries and thick cream . . . a folded yellow menu that gave recipes and unsolicited comments about the food listed) was watched avidly by not only the Los Angeles literati but the San Fernando truckers and the most devout disciples of Amy Semple MacPferson's [*sic*] nearby Temple. That was Dillwyn's ideal restaurant . . . What is your idea? What is mine?"[14] The book was not completed, but some years later, Mary Frances did publish portions of what she'd written in "If This Were My Place," a piece about running the mythical perfect restaurant.[15]

At this time Mary Frances also embarked on a separate project, writing to various people she knew and inquiring about the cookbooks in their personal collections. "Dearest Edie," she wrote to her mother, "This is a business letter. I am working on a series of articles which will probably turn into another *Serve It Forth*, but better, I hope, and am writing to several people who are known as gourmets and good cooks, to ask what they think about cookbooks."[16] And in a letter to the well-known hostess Mrs. Lewis Gannett, whose Thanksgiving dinner had been featured in *Life* magazine, she wrote, "I am especially interested in what good cooks consider their minimum kitchen libraries . . . if any, and whether they keep records of their standbys like Mrs. Simon Kander or Fannie Farmer and then a changing collection of less sturdy recipes."[17] Mary Frances also queried Gloria Stuart, her agent Mary Leonard Pritchett, and Dillwyn's friend Merle Armitage, chairman of the Los Angeles Light Opera Company, about their cookbook collections and their "most inspired recipes." The responses to her many letters were interesting, and, while there were endorsements of the familiar *Fanny Farmer Cookbook* and *The Settlement Cookbook*, there was little agreement about the effectiveness of newspaper recipes or even the merits of following a recipe literally. Gloria's answer was one of the few that differed from the others in originality and taste. "My favorite cookbooks are Mexican, Chinese, and Jewish, because they always give me an excuse to go to unknown sections of wherever I am looking for things like sour salt, goose fat, water ground corn meal, and oriental vermicelli." As one of her happier inspirations, Gloria playfully cited "a breakfast drink that I nicknamed 'Bieler Has Regurgitated,'[18] half unstrained grapefruit juice and half raw milk."[19] Unfortunately, Mary Frances did not pursue the subject further, although articles about cookbooks, some of them sparked by the exhibit of cookbooks in the French Pavilion at the 1939 World's Fair in New York City, were becoming increasingly popular in local papers.

Mary Frances did write a sequence of articles about her culinary experiences in Switzerland and urged her agent to place the pieces in well-paying magazines, because the purchase of and improvements on Bareacres had virtually depleted her and Dillwyn's savings. Although Anne Parrish subsidized them generously from time to time, her checks did not arrive in a predictable fashion, and it was difficult to pay bills and to budget. In a letter to Mary Frances dated Febru-

At the end of August 1940, Mary Frances sent off *Daniel Among the Women* to her agent. "I wish Pritchett would sell it to a slickie and make us some money, but the chances are slim. It is not an especially exciting novel. And she is not a very good agent," Mary Frances said peevishly and inaccurately, adding, "The times are bad, to put it obscenely."[28] At her urging, Dillwyn also voluntarily stopped taking injections of Analgeticum because they both realized that he was beginning to depend on stronger doses taken with greater frequency. Detoxification under Dr. Bieler's guidance was painful, and Mary Frances attended Dillwyn through sleepless nights, chills, and writhings. They adopted an even more stringent diet, dining lightly one day and eating only watermelon the next, and they frequently drove to the Soboba Hot Springs nearby, where swimming, massages, and a leisurely drink at the Ramada soothed their bodies and spirits. "Nevertheless, I have been filled, for several weeks now, with a terrible silent inward depression," Mary Frances wrote. "When T. goes to bed in the middle of the day and lies there quietly without even reading, I think, He'll never get up again. And when he is nauseated from a meal, which happens quite often, I think, He'll never eat again . . . I hate it. It follows me like my own shadow, and I wonder for how long."[29]

News from Delaware offered a welcome distraction. Two years earlier, Dillwyn's widowed sister Anne had remarried, and she and her husband Josiah Tizwell built an imposing home in Georgetown, Connecticut. After years of being doted upon by Anne, Mrs. Parrish now felt abandoned and lonely in Claymont, and in her letters to Dillwyn she complained that Anne was neglecting her. A wish to spend Christmas with his mother and to see Anne in Connecticut—and perhaps mend the rift between them—prompted Dillwyn to propose a trip to the East Coast for the holidays. Before they could travel that distance, however, they knew that they would have to replace their old car with a new one. In early September they put down a deposit on a gray-and-green 1941 Oldsmobile convertible. Dillwyn's obvious pleasure in being able to drive the demonstration hydromatic-drive car seemed worth the wild extravagance.

In mid-September Edith collapsed with angina pectoris and was hospitalized in Whittier. Mary Frances and Dillwyn drove to the

Ranch immediately. Rex flew home from Colorado Springs, where he was vacationing after having recently accompanied David there. During the next weeks Edith drifted in and out of consciousness, sometimes recognizing family members gathered around her, sometimes not. And because Norah was living at home and working at the *News*, she became the person in charge of things at the Ranch in her mother's absence. Within a very short time, the arrangement exposed some of the carefully hidden but very real antagonisms among family members. Without consulting Anne, Rex sent Sean away to Harding Military Academy in Glendora, arguably his prerogative because he was supporting his grandson and thought that the boy was a strain on Edith. But Anne was hurt. She also quarreled with Norah over household matters, like the kind of meals Norah was preparing or failing to prepare for Rex. And when Mary Frances tried to tell the housekeeper how to adjust to Edith's needs when she returned from the hospital, Norah openly resented what she considered to be Mary Frances's intrusion.

After Mary Frances returned to Bareacres, she wrote in her journal, "So it is plain that for the moment, at least, the family is at odds—and at a time when by all rules of sentiment we should be knit closely by our concern for Mother. It is a strange and disturbing thing to happen and quite unexpectedly, by me at least."[30] Rightly or wrongly, her sisters resented her. "I know, and none better, that too often I have felt obliged to step in, to boss, to direct, where perhaps it would have been better, and certainly easier, to let things go every which way rather than antagonize the younger ones of the family."[31] Her own anger manifested itself in second-guessing, hurt feelings, and wounding verbal exchanges. Norah stubbornly ignored the phone, and Mary Frances and Anne, who depended on her for information about their mother, called in vain. To complicate matters further, Norah announced her decision to leave home within a year in order to pursue her own career in journalism.

After more than three weeks at the Murphy Hospital, Edith returned to the Ranch. Rex installed a hospital bed in the first-floor bedroom suite and hired a nurse to care for her. When Mary Frances and Dillwyn visited, they found her dressed in a Chinese robe, looking rested and younger than she had in years. But ill will lingered under the surface, with Anne feeling hurt when Norah refused to go into Los Angeles to pick her up and drive her back to the Ranch, and Norah resenting the pull of her many responsibilities and her mother's needs. Mary Frances, torn between her various loyalties and her continuing care of Dillwyn, could not help but feel the "disintegration of my family as such."[32]

On December 3, the Parrishes left Bareacres and began the slow trip to Delaware in their Oldsmobile convertible. Because Dillwyn tired easily, they were forced to stop over for a day or two every three or four days along the southern route through Arizona, New Mexico, and Texas. When they were halfway across Louisiana, they decided to spend some time in New Orleans. Mary Frances wrote to Edith, "[It] reminds me of a mixture of salesmen's convention, the American Quarter in Paris in 1929 (full of shoddy bars and whiskey-voiced blonde divorcees), and the brothel district of Colon."[33] But after dining at Antoine's and other lesser-known establishments, she wanted to see more of the city on their return trip. From New Orleans they drove to Delaware, staying overnight in Wilmington before going on to Claymont. They found Mrs. Parrish better and livelier than she had been two years earlier. Although she was saddened by what she perceived to be Anne's neglect, Dillwyn's presence cheered her. Mary Frances and Dillwyn trimmed the tree on the morning of Christmas Eve, and, after a festive meal, they all exchanged presents in the evening.

Celebrating Christmas in Delaware and New Year's Day in Connecticut was bittersweet for Dillwyn, who realized only too clearly that it would be his last visit with his mother and sister. For her part, Mary Frances decided that the holidays were exhausting. She found Mrs. Parrish trying, although she liked her. Her relationship with Anne was more complicated. She resented Anne's lifelong intimacy with Dillwyn, their collaborative efforts as adults, and Dillwyn's financial reliance upon his sister. She also knew that Anne had harbored serious doubts about Dillwyn's marrying her, and much preferred Gigi as a sister-in-law. Although cordial and correct in her contacts with Mary Frances, Anne had never really accepted her into the family. Since their correspondence about *The Theoretical Foot*, Mary Frances felt Anne's deep disapproval more keenly than ever. For Dillwyn's sake, Anne entertained Mary Frances at her home, and then said goodbye. It was the last time the two women would see each other.

Before leaving the East Coast, Mary Frances and Dillwyn borrowed some of the canvases that Dillwyn had painted in Switzerland from his mother and sister and packed them in the trunk of their car. For some time Mary Frances had hoped that an exhibit of Dillwyn's work could be mounted through the efforts of Larry Powell, now employed as curator at UCLA's library, and she intended to press him on the project when they returned. As planned, they stopped for a few more days in New Orleans, where they ate delicious shellfish and good salads and drank the best coffee they had tasted since they left the city a month earlier. They also took time to rest in San Antonio, which was, according to Mary Frances, "to our surprise one of the loveliest cities we've found."[34] And then they stopped in Juárez, Mexico, across the border from El Paso, where Dillwyn did some quick sketches for future paintings.

By the end of January 1941 the Parrishes were back at Bareacres. Dillwyn supervised the paving of the patio, adding stairs from it to the second terrace, where Mary Frances had planted an assortment of succulents. He also practiced on the new piano they had impulsively purchased when they returned. It was a luxury that they could not afford, but knowing that it would give Dillwyn pleasure, Mary Frances urged him to buy it anyway. He was completing the paintings that he had sketched during their trip, and Mary Frances returned to writing, shifting focus once again, from American restaurants to oysters. She planned to write a book on this single subject, including not only the dishes she had dined on in New Orleans and on the East Coast, but also plebeian favorites like Po' Boy Loaves and Hangtown Frys, interspersing the recipes among descriptions of famous oyster bars and restaurants and the various legends and lore associated with the oyster. Mary Leonard Pritchett sold the manuscript to Duell, Sloan and Pearce, although Pearl Metzelthin, editor of the new magazine *Gourmet*, rejected three chapters from it.

In March the nerves in Dillwyn's good leg flared up, and he began experimenting with a series of cobra venom shots. Although the pain persisted, he painted as many hours as possible each day, only now with an added incentive. Larry Powell had arranged for a one-man show of Dillwyn's work at UCLA from March 31 to April 11, 1941. Ward Ritchie designed the program, with Dillwyn's words on the cover: "My aim is to find a picture language, a sort of highly personal shorthand set down with color and brush, which will catch, and convey with economy and emotional force, the *Spirit* rather than the literal likeness of the object painted."[35] There were 180 items on exhibit, including paintings, pencil drawings, watercolors, illustrations, and litho-pencil drawings with subjects ranging from landscapes to still lifes and portraits. The opening was a gay event attended by Gloria and Arthur Sheekman, Ward Ritchie, Larry and Fay Powell, and Kennedy family members. Dillwyn, aided by Larry and Mary Frances, resolutely walked the two flights of stairs to the gallery. The efforts involved in setting up the pieces had drained him, and his face that night more often than not reflected pain and sadness. Still, the exhibit was a validation of his work, and it greatly pleased him.

Not long after the show, Norah and David decided to go to Mexico for an extended stay. David had received a small grant to paint murals at Lake Chapala in west-central Mexico, and Norah intended to join him and write about her experiences in Lanikai, Honolulu, and Molokai the previous year. On June 20 they left Whittier with only a forwarding address of Wells Fargo in Mexico City. To Mary Frances's amazement, neither of them seemed much concerned with the need to be in contact with the family in case of an emergency. As she watched twenty-four-year-old Norah drive off with David, two years younger, looking like well-seasoned travelers in their brown cotton clothes, she thought that "physically they seemed too finely drawn to me for their ages: thin, pallid, with slender controlled hands, David's with curved nails, and both of them with tense lines at the corners of their mouths and smudges under their eyes . . . I pity them both, for they seem finished too soon. They need new blood in them."[36] What Mary Frances and the family did not know was that David intended to invite his girlfriend, Sarah Shearer, to join him in Mexico, and that they planned to marry there in late September.

By the first of July, Mary Frances began discouraging visitors at Bareacres. "Timmy has grown much worse in the last few weeks, and it's out of the question to have anyone here," she wrote to Larry. "He is increasingly weak, so that he can't walk at all unless I hold him . . . and his pain is terrible to think of . . . I never leave him anymore, so my contacts with the world consist of an occasional good morning with the Grocer-boy and the Indian who comes once a week to help me . . . We're well cared for, and lack nothing. I should be getting a lot of work done but I find it distasteful to me . . . I did a series of articles on gilt-edged gluttony (Diamond Jim et al) . . . And I plan to start on a very disagreeable novel, more to please Tim than myself."[37] Mary Frances was afraid that she did not have something that *must* be said. She also had deep reservations about the kind of novels that some women writers, specifically her sister-in-law, wrote. She later confided to a young writer, Leo Racicot, that books like Anne's *The Perennial Bachelor*, *Golden Wedding*, and *Methodist Faun* were "very lady-like. I'll always be sorry for her discretion, because she had a fine satirical eye. She was unwilling to write straight truth, and afraid to betray any animal pleasure."[38] Virginia Woolf and, especially, Colette were among the novelists whom Mary Frances admired, although she said on more than one occasion that she had to refrain from reading their books because she feared that she might imitate one or the other of these writers too closely.

Mary Frances celebrated her thirty-third birthday at Bareacres with Edith, Rex, and Dillwyn on July 3. The holiday weekend, festive with presents, highballs, and grilled steak, distracted her momentarily from the knowledge that it would probably be her last birthday with Dillwyn. Although his right leg looked normal, it collapsed when he tried to get out of bed, and the pain in his eyes began to signal despair. The doctors had forewarned them to expect a sequence of amputations on the remaining leg and, later on, the probable loss of Dillwyn's arms. Ominously, he no longer asked Mary Frances to hide the .22-caliber bullets for his gun in new places so he couldn't find them, as he had done on at least two previous occasions.

On August 6, while Mary Frances slept, Dillwyn left the cabin at dawn with his revolver and hobbled toward the Rim of the World. A single shot reverberated down the canyon and awakened her. Seeing the bed next to hers empty, she knew what had happened and phoned the police. She then called Rex, who immediately drove to Hemet with Edith and Anne. More than that she could not do, and she retreated to her room to mourn the loss of her one true love. Later that morning Rex identified the body for the authorities and notified Dillwyn's mother and sister. With the help of her family, Mary Frances arranged for the body to be cremated, as was Dillwyn's wish. The small tin box containing his ashes was buried under an overhanging rock near the Rim of the World. Reluctant to remain at Bareacres alone, Mary Frances returned to Whittier with her family, where she wrote a long and detailed letter to Dillwyn's sister, Anne, and responded as well as she could to Mrs. Parrish's initial hurt and bitter reaction to the suicide.

After their sojourn in Vevey, Rex and Edith had both grown closer to their son-in-law, and now they grieved his death. The loss was particularly traumatic for Rex because he had long maintained that suicide was a coward's act, and yet he felt that in Dillwyn's case it might have been justified. Edith wrote to Norah and David, who reacted to Dillwyn's death with a "terrible hurt."[39] The painter had become a kind of role model to David, who credited Dillwyn for giving him the encouragement he needed to pursue a career in art, and Norah had made him her confidant much as her sister had once done, sending him some of her stories from Hawaii. In one of her letters she had written, "Now, Godlike, Dillwyn-like, you are doing as much for me, and a pox on me if I can't write a book that I won't be ashamed to show you."[40] Sean's remembered reaction was perhaps the most poignant: "My first direct experience with death was in Santa Barbara during the summer of 1941, when I learned that Dillwyn Parrish had died. The news came in a letter from my mother, which I was reading aloud to Margaret [his stepmother] who was driving me to my swimming lesson. I remember trying to keep on reading while my eyes were overfilling with tears, and I finally had to stop. The precise circumstances of his death were kept from me, but I had been aware of his worsening illness and simply assumed he had died naturally. Years later, I learned he had taken his own life. By then I had a better understanding why."[41]

After Dillwyn's death, Mary Frances admitted, she thought seriously of suicide.[42] But she also wrote about her desire to work again and the need to learn to live her life alone: "It is four weeks and three days now . . . and I know even if the rest of the family does not that I must stop this ghastly life of compromise and get to work. It is bad for me, this drifting about and postponing the truth: I must live alone . . . I *am* alone, completely and unalterably, and living with other people or having them live with me can never make me any less so . . . I can't stand much more of the hopeless stupid life I've been leading since T. died."[43] But her nightmares persisted, and soon her only consolation was the gratitude she felt when she was able to sleep after eight o'clock without the sound of a gunshot startling the morning air. Even with her mother at the Ranch, or with Anne at Bareacres, she could not focus. She was unrecognizable to herself, and in her journal she wrote, "There are too many things that I can't write yet. They're in words in my head, but I am afraid of writing them. It is as if they might make a little crack in me and let out some of all the howling, hideous, frightful grief. It is difficult to know, certainly, how to live at all."[44]

The publication of *Consider the Oyster* within weeks of Dillwyn's death was simply a sorrowful reminder of the evenings she had spent reading it to him. With the book in hand, she wrote what she called "a sad little criticism" to her editor, Sam Sloan. "I wished that I'd been notified earlier when the book would be published, because neither Timmy nor I knew about it and I very mistakenly felt, for a few minutes anyway, that he might have put off dying, if he'd known the publication date. As it was he never saw the book, which was small and short. I dedicated the book to him, and I began to realize then that I must always write toward somebody I love, to make it seem real."[45]

The comic history of the oyster, written in a self-mocking authorial voice and peopled with bartenders, restaurateurs, and raconteurs, was designed to distract and delight Dillwyn with its tall tales and, in the chapter called "Love and Death Among the Molluscs," even a spoof of Virginia Woolf's androgyny-driven *Orlando*. Mary Frances wrote about the "indecisively sexed" life and ill-fated death of this mysterious bivalve, its aphrodisiac allure, and its ubiquitousness in ancient banquets. She also added recipes that were, in turn, comforting, exotic, and even purely fanciful. From speculation about the ingredients in Antoine's recipe for Oysters Rockefeller, she ranges to the Grand Central Oyster Bar in New York and the Old Port of Marseilles, from East Coast to West (Chincoteague to Olympia), and from the oyster stuffing she made at home to the creamed oysters served at the Hotel Pierre in New York. In a freewheeling way, she travels in time from the Sunday oyster stew suppers of her childhood to brief oyster-eating interludes in France, New York, the Delaware River Valley, and California. She blends oyster lore and personal experience with abandon, and shares her stories, her memories of stories told to her, and her recipes the same way she would share a tureen of oyster bisque, generously ladling out "a lusty bit of nourishment." The stories are as much about comfort, warmth, and love as they are about food.

In a restrospective review, critic Patricia Storace would write, "*Consider the Oyster* marks M.F.K. Fisher's emergence as a storyteller so confident that she can maneuver a reader through a narrative in which recipes enhance instead of interrupt the reader's attention to the tales . . . If eating sustains life biologically, storytelling sustains it culturally; a story gives a person a second, fourth, fifth life."[46] At the time, the reception was warm enough, if not so grand. E. L. Tinker called it "a gay, pleasant, and instructive book"[47] in *The New York Times*. And Clifton Fadiman praised the book in *The New Yorker*: "M.F.K. Fisher has now in her small treatise done full justice to the mild and modest mollusk . . . I commend especially the candid chapter entitled, 'Love Was the Pearl,' dealing with the powers of the oyster to promote more and better venery."[48] A clipping of the *Los Angeles Times* review prompted Mary Frances to tell Larry, "Thanks for the Time review . . . it is nice. Fadiman and luscious Lucius Beebe have both done well by me in NY, and otherwise I know nothing. I wish the book would sell like peanuts."[49]

Despite the attention the book received, Mary Frances spent the first months after Dillwyn's death in flight, often reaching the top of a hill breathless, or unconsciously walking into furniture as she hastened from room to room. She wrote, "People thought I was in a state of shock at the dying, but it was more one of relieved exhaustion after the last three years."[50] She decided, wisely or unwisely, to build a small house across the arroyo for a possible caretaker to live in, and she contemplated either a trip to New York City or part-time work in Los Angeles. She also advised Norah about marketing the stories she was writing in Mexico. In a letter written on October 14, she told her sister that she had arranged at least five of the stories into what she considered an appropriate sequence and airmailed them to Mary Leonard Pritchett for submission to *The New Yorker*. She then advised Norah, "my dear girl you must write and write and write. I mean that. You have a terrible eye: you see with the pitiless ironic eye of Atget's camera or of Zola. But you are crossed with a bit of K. Mansfield . . . as who is not and God help us all, I say. And you must write it out of you, and get beyond it, and get beyond Woolf and get beyond X and Y and F until you are terribly alone."[51] In late October, a distracted Mary Frances accidentally sideswiped a car in a parking lot. After that, Anne urged her to go to Mexico and visit Norah, David, and his new bride, Sarah. Anne even volunteered to arrange plane and hotel reservations and take care of her visa.

Because of fog and poor weather, instead of flying directly from Los Angeles to Guadalajara, Mary Frances's plane stopped overnight in Mazatlán. When a Mexican waiter served her some of the beans and tortillas that the help were eating in the kitchen, Mary Frances felt as though she were really tasting food for the first time since Dillwyn's death. After the short flight to Guadalajara the next morning, David and Norah met her at the airport and drove her to Chapala. The village, named after the lake, had lured David and Norah because of its proximity to Guadalajara, near-perfect climate, inexpensive standard of living, and reputation as an artists' colony. (D. H. Lawrence, his wife, Frieda, and the poet Witter Bynner had lived in the little village on the northern shore of the lake in the 1920s.)

Mary Frances was nervous about meeting Sarah, as were the newlyweds themselves, "wanting things to be easy and friendly long before we'd had the time to make them so. I was the oldest child, and David was the youngest, and between us there were years of dependence and resentment and love and ruthlessness, and now the knowledge that he had married sooner than we'd hoped for him, and in a far country, to an unknown girl. It was a cautious moment."[52] Sarah was a petite, blond, affable girl who looked very much like the sketch that David had shown Mary Frances and Dillwyn when they had visited him in Colorado Springs. "She had a true share of dignity. I liked that and her fine unlacquered fingernails and the sloping contours of her very quiet face."[53] After the introduction and a few pleasant words, Sarah tactfully decided to stroll by the lake while David and Mary

Frances, still uneasy with each other, toured the small house, where the whitewashed walls, tile floors, serapes, and minimal furnishings were enhanced by David's pictures on the walls. Mary Frances showered and put on lightweight clothing and the pair of Spanish *alpargatos* that they had purchased for her, then returned to the large living room on the first floor, where David had poured a drink for each of them and was sitting with his guitar on his knees. He looked taller and leaner than he had when he'd left Whittier seven months earlier, and his face seemed older. Avoiding any mention of Dillwyn's death, they talked about the short trip Rex had made to Chapala for the wedding and Edith's improved health. They also spoke about the possibility of war and what the German expatriates in the village predicted until a mariachi band strolled up and proceeded to play three or four songs in front of the house, silencing their speech.

That evening when they went to a bar on the lake for cocktails and heard the band again, Mary Frances sensed a mysterious connection between Juanito, the lead singer of the band, whose falsetto voice distinguished him from the others, and David. "The only thing that seemed to reach him [David], and then as a kind of reassurance, was the *mariachi* music . . . Juanito was a voice, passionate because David willed it so, singing to David for David,"[54] she wrote. And when she heard Juanito sing again after their dinner, she knew that the stooped, slender boy was a girl.

During the two weeks that followed, Mary Frances joined the others in painting murals at the municipal baths during the day, and dined with them in the evening. Once or twice they went to Guadalajara to shop in the markets. In the sparsely outfitted little kitchen, she washed lettuces, radishes, and tomatoes, boiled eggs for informal lunches, and on one occasion she concocted a sauce that they ate with tortillas. But her overriding impression of Chapala involved the strange young woman of the mariachi band and the mesmerizing effect she had on David. Mary Frances wrote that during David's months in Mexico "he was turned in upon himself with a concentration I had seldom seen, in a hard, furious devotion that was at once tragic and admirable. It was beyond selfishness, beyond cruelty, so that his marriage, his imperious gentleness with Sarah and his sisters, even the intensity of his eating and drinking had a remoteness about them impossible to assault."[55] He was totally oblivious of Juanito's obsessive, even tragic love for him. If he thought of her at all it was as an instrument that played music that pleased him and touched his soul in a satisfying way; her hungers had "gone unfed."

Toward the end of November 1941, when the murals they were painting were finished, they left Chapala and spent a few days in Guadalajara, where they heard Juanito sing for the last time. Mary Frances and Norah flew back to Los Angeles, and David and Sarah made the journey in their little car. The time in Mexico became a defining moment for all of them, especially for David, who was ill prepared for the events that would take place within weeks of their arrival home. Mary Frances captured the story of her flight, stop۰ ۰۰ ۰۰ Mazatlán, and arrival in Guadalajara—as well as the strange character of Juanito—in *The Gastronomical Me*.[56] No doubt Mary Frances drafted these two chapters during the three weeks she stayed with Norah, David, and Sarah in their little rented house in the fishing village along the shore of Lake Chapala.

Norah, David, and Sarah settled into life at the Ranch while Mary Frances divided her time between Bareacres and Anne's apartment in Beverly Hills. Anne and Sean had moved there when she took a job as an assistant to the Kennedy family friend and top Hollywood photographer George Hurrell, whose studio was on Rodeo Drive. On the morning of December 7, Mary Frances was staying with Anne and Sean, who was celebrating his birthday, when the news of the Japanese attack on Pearl Harbor came over the radio just before lunch and, as Sean said years later, "abruptly changed our lives in many different ways."[57]

Because it was widely thought that the Japanese would follow their attack by bombing the West Coast, southern California was immediately plunged into a state of war hysteria with nightly blackouts, sirens, searchlights, and antiaircraft fire. Air raid drills were practiced in schools and places of business, shopkeepers' shelves emptied, and the threat of Japanese submarines offshore was a constant fear. Mary Frances remembered only too well the system of complete blackouts in every Swiss village and city two years earlier, and the psychological blitzkrieg rampant across Europe whenever the Axis powers invaded another country. In the December 24 issue of the *Whittier News* she wrote about her experiences in Switzerland as Europe prepared for war. In the article she turned her attention to the things that the American housewife could do "to show her true colors of far-sightedness and calm and courage."[58] What followed was a detailed explanation for preparing one designated room as a shelter, what foods to have on hand, how to protect oneself in case of gas attacks, and how to achieve an absolute blackout. The three-column piece led to several more articles about living decently with shortages, rationing, and the other miseries associated with wartime. Mary Frances's fourth book, *How to Cook a Wolf*, was beginning to evolve quickly and surely.

Meanwhile, Rex wrote to his brother Ted, "My household is multiplied by the addition of a new daughter which David brought home. She is a fine girl and fits in very well. This Christmas we will all be home . . . David and his wife, Mary Frances, Anne and her boy and Norah. I am glad that we can be together. To hell with the Japs and the blackouts. David will probably get into the war in some capacity after Christmas. If his wife so elects we will be glad to have her with us. Here's hoping we don't have too Jappy a New Year."[59]

SEVEN

Hollywood Scenarios

(1941–1945)

To be happy you must have taken the measure of your powers, tasted the
fruits of your passion, and learned your place in the world.[1]

—George Santayana

Before the holidays in 1941, Mary Frances spent most of every day
in Dillwyn's studio writing *How to Cook a Wolf*, a book about survival,
both physical and spiritual, during the ghastly business of war. In reality, however, her own survival as well as her *wish* to survive drove the
book she had contracted to write during the first months of World
War II. "I was still in strong grief and was beyond any feeling of surprise; it seemed quite natural to do a good book exactly as I would do
a good report for Father's paper, to earn my living in the only way I
could. This was probably the first time I was aware of writing to pay
my way, and it may have helped to keep everything so clear and fast."[2]
With the upkeep of the home she and Dillwyn had shared together
and the many bills associated with his illness as well as her regular expenses, Mary Frances had a pressing need to support herself. After
the luxury of creating pleasing *amuse-gueules* and light fiction for
someone she loved, she now turned her attention to the privations of
wartime and to the basic fact that "since we must eat to live, we
might as well do it with both grace and gusto."[3]

Every chapter in *How to Cook a Wolf* was a "how to"—greet the spring, comfort sorrow, be cheerful though starving—all accompanied by appropriate recipes. There were also a few "how not to" chapters: how not to boil an egg, how not to eat unpalatable meals while spending time underground in bomb shelters or during blackouts, how not to starve. She described her memories of Edith's gingerbread, French food, and canned food, and then she arranged the anecdotes with recipes into traditional cookbook categories. She included soup recipes from Parisian Onion Soup to Minestrone in the chapter "How to Boil Water," and added her own recipe for Chinese Consommé, which consisted of a can of broth mixed with a can of tomato juice, enhanced by wine, vegetables, and judicious seasonings. The chapter "How to Carve a Wolf" collected various meat recipes, from Boeuf Tartare to Turkish Hash, as a gesture to all those Anglo-Saxon descendants who required some form of animal flesh every day for strength. She wrote about rice, polenta, breads, desserts, and wines. Taking her cue from those old standbys Isabella Beeton and Marion Harland, she also recommended tips to ensure the survival of household pets during wartime shortages in a chapter called "How to Have a Sleek Pelt." Mary Frances said that she wrote the book in little more than a month's time,[4] and that Larry Bachmann suggested the title. She and Bachmann had gravitated toward each other while at Occidental—Mary Frances because she enjoyed the braininess of the short, stocky collegian who didn't have many dates and was so deliciously critical of his professors; Bachmann because he admired Mary Frances's good looks, intelligence, and style. Now that Bachmann was a scriptwriter in Hollywood and Mary Frances was alone and lonely, they came together again, and Bachmann tried to help Mary Frances in every way he could. She dedicated *How to Cook a Wolf* to Lawrence Paul, omitting Bachmann's last name, and forwarded it to Duell, Sloan and Pearce, where Mary Pritchett had placed it. Sam Sloan recognized its timeliness and rushed it onto his 1942 spring list.

In early February, Mary Frances experienced severe stomach pains and was hospitalized for an appendectomy, which was performed by Dr. Hal Bieler in Pasadena. During the three weeks that she was recuperating in the hospital, she learned that Larry Powell had sent Dr. Bieler a copy of his novel about Dijon,[5] and she wrote to him,

Hal is more than enthusiastic about *Quintet*, and I hope very much that you will let me read it. I suppose one of the four [affairs] was Eda? I too am working on something[6] . . . I don't know whether it is a story or not . . . about her. Perhaps we should compare notes. I go out to Bareacres tomorrow, thank God. It is my real home . . . I know that now, more strongly than I have ever known it of any place . . . and I need to be back there . . . I plan to read myself sick, for the next two weeks . . . *War and Peace* again, *Kristin Lavransdatter* again, all of Proust again, several new books . . . Rebecca West's, V. Woolf's last, Scott Fitzgerald's last, and so on, until I'm really bilious. Then I'll stop for another year or so, and do some of my own work. I don't know what that will be yet.[7]

She maintained close contact with Powell, and she sought out friends like Gloria and Arthur Sheekman, who had recently returned to Hollywood from New York City and were living in the fabled apartment complex on Sunset Strip called the Garden of Allah, "the Algonquin of the West."[8] On weekends Gloria often brought bags of groceries to Hemet; with a glass of wine in hand, she and Mary Frances engaged in the kind of conversation that had always been easy between them. "We were Bohemians and proud of it since we first met in Laguna," Gloria said. "I had my acting and Mary Frances had her writing. It was always interesting."[9] Bachmann also became a regular visitor, and he encouraged Mary Frances to seek employment in Hollywood and not live alone at Bareacres.

World War II had created many openings at defense plants and in other industries for "Rosie the Riveters," while their husbands, brothers, and boyfriends volunteered to defend their country. It was transforming even the sleepy town of Hemet, where an aviation school was opened to train pilots, and the apricot groves and canneries began to give way to businesses and housing to accommodate the trainees. But when Mary Frances followed Bachmann's advice and sought work in Los Angeles, she found the city transformed in a different way by the war. Exiled from Europe, many screenwriters, artists, and musicians had sought refuge and gainful employment in Hollywood, and competition for jobs was fierce. Mary Frances felt discouraged about finding a position that would be satisfying as well as creative.

The publication of *How to Cook a Wolf* in May 1942, however, enhanced the reputation of M.F.K. Fisher as a different kind of cookbook author from the nutritionists who promoted balanced meals in many "home magazines." Mary Frances wrote about food as a necessity as well as a pleasure and was not too precise about recipes because she believed "no recipe in the world is independent of the tides, the moon, the physical and emotional temperatures surrounding its performance."[10] A short review in *The New York Times* praised *How to Cook a Wolf* as "lively, amusing and intelligent; and a real cook book, too."[11] And Clifton Fadiman wrote in *The New Yorker*, "Mrs. Fisher can be witty on the subject of boiling an egg, but she never allows the play of her mind to obscure her practical good sense. I commend her little book to all who are still intent on living most agreeably in a world full of an increasing number of disagreeable surprises . . . Any dull home-economics expert can tell you how to economize on food. Mrs. Fisher tells you how to economize and enjoy the result, which is quite another matter. When you finish this book you can hardly wait to get your teeth into a wolf."[12]

The general perception was that *How to Cook a Wolf* was not only entertaining but also practical, advocating a balanced daily menu rather than a balanced meal. Buttered toast for breakfast; an all-vegetable lunch of salad, casserole, or soup; steak or a cheese soufflé for dinner; and juice or fruit for a midmorning pickup might startle diners, but Mary Frances believed "palates will awaken to new pleasures, or remember old ones."[13] Her sage advice about menu planning, cooking, and baking, as well as the seventy-three recipes, demonstrated a dazzling command of culinary history as well as culinary savvy, which prompted Clifton Fadiman to conclude his review with the statement that "M.F.K. Fisher writes about food as others do about love, only better."[14] As the critic Walter Kendricks said, "Fisher thought well enough of both food and writing to perfect a hybrid genre, starting with *Consider the Oyster* and *How to Cook a Wolf*, that gently folded recipes into stories. But she never attributed to food a dignity or power that it cannot possess. Her highest praise for any dish, from bread and cheese to truffles, was to declare it good."[15]

The publicity photos by John Engstead that accompanied the book reviews of *How to Cook a Wolf* showed a radiant Mary Frances in a white apron cooking pasta at the stove and posing with Butch at a table on the patio of Bareacres. Rumors circulated that executives at Paramount Pictures, upon seeing the photos, sent a talent scout to sign her on as an actress. When she demurred, the studio offered her a position as a junior writer. More probably, Bachmann's friend Richard Halliday (Mary Martin's husband) pulled a few strings at Paramount to get her the job. The studio gave her a contract with a starting salary of $50 a week for nineteen weeks, beginning May 19 and ending September 30, 1942. The contract further guaranteed thirteen weeks in 1943 at $75 per week and five more years with time and salary increases, culminating in fifty-two weeks at $350 a week in the seventh year.[16] Mary Frances signed the contract on May 27, 1942, and started work immediately.

During the first year of the war, Paramount Pictures had produced *Beyond the Blue Horizon*, *The Major and the Minor*, *The Palm Beach Story*, *My Favorite Blonde*, *Sweater Girl*, *Take a Letter, Darling*, and *Road to Morocco*, starring luminaries like Bing Crosby, Bob Hope, Dorothy Lamour, Fred Astaire, Claudette Colbert, Mary Astor, Betty Hutton, Veronica Lake, and Rosalind Russell. Occasionally it released a war film like John Farrow's *Wake Island* (1942), but for the most part, the "Starred Mountain" opted for pure escapism. Mary Frances found herself in an unfamiliar world of glitz and glamour, populated not only by movie stars but also by writers Robert Benchley and Dorothy Parker, directors Billy Wilder and Preston Sturges, and lyricist Johnny Mercer, with such songs as "A Sweater, a Sarong, and a Peek-a-boo Bob" enlivening the soundtrack. As a junior writer she worked in tandem with one or two well-established writers on rewrites and even script proposals.

Because gas rationing limited travel between Hemet and Los Angeles, she leased a one-room apartment near the studio, not far from Anne, who was still employed as an assistant for George Hurrell. When she and Anne went out on the town together, Sean said, "MF spent many nights at our small apartment on Elm Drive. I remember because I would start out sleeping in my bed and then be moved to the living room couch later in the evening so she could have my bedroom."[17] The three of them drove to Bareacres together on weekends, leaving Beverly Hills on Friday afternoons after Anne returned home from work and stopping for dinner, frequently at a hamburger restaurant called Jarupa's, near March Field, where the cheeseburgers, pickles, and potato chips were excellent. The trips were often adventurous, especially when a blackout would force them off the road and they would have to sleep in the car until the all clear sounded. When not with her family at Bareacres or with her sister in Beverly Hills or at the de rigueur cocktail parties and dinners with Paramount associates, Mary Frances took steps to become her own best companion in the loneliness of her apartment. She devised suppers of Rye Krisp, a can of tomato soup, and a glass of sherry, and carefully purchased a few pieces of good china, a crystal glass or two, and a case of good wines for her solitary meals.

Gradually, instead of shopping in all-night groceries for canned foods, she marketed on the way to the studio, storing perishables in the water cooler outside her office. "I grew deliberately fastidious about eggs and butter; the biggest, brownest eggs were none too good, nor could any butter be too clover-fresh and sweet. I laid in a case or two of 'unpretentious but delightful little wines,'" she later wrote. "I was determined about the whole thing, which in itself is a great drawback emotionally. But I knew no alternative."[18] Noting that both Escoffier and the Chinese would be astonished by what she managed with a can of beef bouillon, a handful of watercress or a spoonful of soy, she described the progress of a leisurely evening meal served on a mixture of Woolworth and Spode. An aperitif of sherry or vermouth, followed by soup, poached eggs, toasted sourdough bread, a celery heart in browned butter, and a glass of wine became a feast in her walk-up, script-littered flat with the let-down bed. "If *One* [Dillwyn] could not be with me, 'feasting in silent sympathy,' then I was my best companion."[19]

Without the grounding that being Dillwyn's wife had given her and adrift after concentrating so much of her psychological and emotional energy caring for Dillwyn at Bareacres for so many months, a spiritually exhausted Mary Frances gradually divorced her private and vulnerable self from her public persona, choosing to submerge the one "in the remembrance of time past" and to throw herself into her image of a career woman for all the world to see. Hollywood was its backdrop, and the combined efforts of George Hurrell and John Engstead, photographers to many of the stars, made it happen.

The July 28, 1942, issue of *Look* magazine featured an article on M.F.K. Fisher, as the fourth in a series on American career women. Lavishly illustrated with full-page photographs by Engstead, the article pictured Mary Frances in Hollywood pin-up-girl style, hand-grinding coffee beans, doing her own shopping for ripe produce, growing grapes on her ranch, discussing a script with actor Joel Mc-Crea and director-writer Preston Sturges, and revising a manuscript in a kimono with a glass of sherry in hand. She was thirty-four years old, divorced and widowed, and, according to *Look*, one of America's successful career women: "She believes that the more charm and femininity a woman has, the better her chances for success."[20] Like more than half of America's career women in business, the professions, or the arts, M.F.K. Fisher had been married, the article reported. Like 76 percent of them, she had achieved success in one of five fields—writing, education, art, social work, or music. Like 63 percent of married career women, she owned her own home, but was more domestic than 60 percent of the women who do their own housekeeping because "she loves to cook, has a herb garden and a vineyard and works hard in them." She differed from more than half of the career women who had a statistical 2.5 children apiece, but, the article concluded, "[she] thinks that women with children are the happiest and feels career women make excellent mothers because they keep mentally alive and young."[21] Both the article and, especially, the photographs portrayed a woman who was strikingly glamorous, confident, and who, as Ted Gill wrote in the *San Francisco Chronicle*, "has a figure that protests her interest in food."[22]

The article prompted Rex to write to his brother Ted, "Did you see the spread of pictures in the July 28 issue of *Look* which Mary Frances drew. Four pages of pictures and ballyhoo. Her vineyard consists of six vines on a pergola and her herb garden of a flowerpot, but after all I suppose photographers must have some license, just the same as poets. Edith was amazed when she read in the article that her child had started cooking soon after she was able to hold a mixing spoon. Mary Frances has a fairly good job with Paramount Pictures and I believe will eventually draw down a salary many times the size of any I have ever considered. It doesn't seem to enlarge her head and that is all to the good."[23] If Rex did not congratulate his daughter on her accomplishments, he made no secret of them to others. In the same letter, Rex also said that David, in order to have an opportunity for officer's training, had volunteered for service rather than wait until he was drafted and expected to be inducted into the army within a week.

The event, however, was not to happen. The day before he was to report for service, David hanged himself in the Kennedy barn. He was twenty-three, and Sarah was pregnant with their first child. Rex identified the body for the authorities. The grief-stricken family gathered at the Ranch, with the exception of Mary Frances, who could not be reached, although Anne tried every means at her disposal to do so. "I remember my mother telling me on several occasions that the one time she needed to find Dote [Mary Frances] and could not, despite great efforts over an entire week-end, was when their brother David died," Sean said. " 'No one should ever be that completely out of touch,' was how my mother described it with considerable feeling. I was struck that she was for the first time in my life seriously criticizing Dote's behavior."[24] When Mary Frances did learn of David's death two days later, she canceled an appearance on the Bing Crosby radio show and joined her family. Thereafter David was a "closed subject" in family conversations, because, Mary Frances said, of the pain it would give Norah.

On July 25 Rex wrote to Ted, enclosing a clipping headed "Death Claims Whittier Boy" from the *Whittier News*. "I am too sore at heart to go into details. I feel sure that the boy must have justified himself in his mind, which had become twisted with too much thinking, but so far I haven't unraveled the reasoning, which he must have used. Edith and the rest of my family are standing the shock and keeping their chins up." "David's life and death was a sad short story," Mary Frances wrote years later.[25] "[He] was both charming and intelligent, and at both Lake Forest Academy and at Princeton showed that he might have made a very fine newspaperman, like his father and grandfather. It is possible that he might have become an equally fine social caricaturist because his drawings, although steadily more bitter and unhappy, were witty and interesting."[26] The war, undoubtedly, contributed to his cynicism, as did the increasing responsibilities of marriage and imminent parenthood. Perhaps an inherited Kennedy proclivity to introspection and melancholia also led to his suicide. In an interview toward the end of her life, Mary Frances said, "David and Norah were born in one batch and Anne and I in another. But Norah and I survived. One survived from each batch. David and I were very much alike. The youngest and the oldest, you see, were alike. He just couldn't and wouldn't take it. And I could and would."[27] Whether the "it" meant the vicissitudes of life or an inherited tendency toward depression or both, Mary Frances didn't say.

As had happened with Dillwyn's suicide, the circumstances of David's death were concealed from Sean, who learned of them from the cook's daughter when she showed the ten-year-old boy the place in the old barn where the event occurred. When he questioned his mother, Anne was unable to explain what had led David to commit such an act. Other family members were equally bewildered. Norah, who had always enjoyed a special bond with her younger brother, was devastated. Mary Frances despaired because she thought that Dillwyn's suicide slightly less than a year before had somehow given David permission to do the same. But Rex and Edith, undoubtedly, suffered the most. Mary Frances believed that the loss of their only son caused each of her parents to withdraw into a solitary world of grief that excluded her and her sisters.

David's daughter, Sarah Holbrook Kennedy, was born two weeks later, and David's widow returned to her parents' home on the East Coast with her child. Commenting on her sister-in-law, Mary Frances later wrote, "I think she was afraid of being with David alone, knowing that she had nothing for him, and he for her only one thing, the means to procreate. That accomplished, he died, like the bee who inseminates the queen. Sarah, seemingly bereft, has what she wanted."[28] After Sarah remarried a few years later, she maintained very little contact with the Kennedy family.

After her brother's death, Mary Frances worked on an original story classified as a war melodrama titled *O'Brien Had Four Wives* at Paramount. It was about a man who lives only for himself until, during the siege of Singapore, he learns that it is other people he really cares about. The script was never produced, but the work provided

Mary Frances with the distraction she needed from this latest loss. With Bareacres as her refuge, she slowly began to recover. Her siblings, too, began to move on. Having obtained a Red Cross scholarship, in the fall of 1942 Norah went to the University of Chicago to begin a master's program in medical sociology. Anne took a job as an occupational counselor at Plumb Tool Company near the Simi Valley, which paid better than the jobs she could get in Beverly Hills. She and Sean moved to a small house in Westlake Village near Thousand Oaks, and Sean was sent to the California Preparatory School for Boys in the Ojai Valley. Seeking to obliterate the memory of David's suicide at the Ranch, Rex had the barn torn down and built a garage in its place.

Mary Frances had written that it took months after Dillwyn's death to taste food again,[29] and it was even longer before she was able to open up emotionally. David's suicide affected her in much the same way. Nevertheless, she had more than one "good affair"[30] during her Hollywood career. In letters to friends and in interviews, she revealed that in addition to her affairs with Bachmann and San Francisco lawyer Harold Price, she had one or two shorter secret liaisons. In December 1942, after one such involvement, and before her lover went "off to war,"[31] Mary Frances discovered that she was pregnant. She promised her lover that she would never name him, and initially disclosed her condition to no one but Dr. Bieler. As was her habit throughout her life, Mary Frances kept her own counsel, revealing what she wished to make known, guarding her secrets. As her lifelong friend Gloria Stuart said, "MF kept many things to herself. She only told you what she wanted to tell you."[32]

Mary Frances returned for her second year at Paramount on January 4, 1943, and was immediately swept up in the wartime social milieu of the photographer Man Ray, directors Billy Wilder and Frank Capra, screenwriter Robert Riskin, and actors Franchot Tone and Groucho Marx. During those early months of 1943, she was also an occasional guest at Villa 12 at the bottom of the Garden of Allah, where Gloria and her husband were known for bringing together intellectuals from the East Coast, musicians, writers, and actors. Gloria's hostess book for January 30, 1943, noted as guests Groucho Marx, the Nunnally Johnsons, the Dalton Trumbos, and Mary Frances, dining on braised oxtails and dumplings, peas, carrots, and onions, and baked Alaska.[33] Later that year Mary Frances drew upon that dinner party to introduce a chapter on children's sensitive palates in *The Gastronomical Me*:

> I know a beautiful honey-colored actress who is a gourmande, in a pleasant way. She loves to cook rich hot lavish meals. She does it well, too. She is slender, fragile, with a mute other-worldly pathos in her large azure eyes, and she likes to invite a lot of oddly assorted and usually famous people to a long table crowded with flowers, glasses, dishes of nuts, bowls of Armenian jelly and Russian relishes and Indian chutney, and beer and wine and even water, and then bring in a huge bowl of oxtail stew with dumplings. She has spent days making it, with special spices she found in Bombay or Soho or Honolulu, and she sits watching happily while it disappears. Then she disappears herself, and in a few minutes staggers to the table with a baked Alaska as big as a washtub, a thing of beauty, and a joy for about fifteen minutes.
>
> But this star-eyed slender gourmande has a daughter about eight or nine, and the daughter hates her mother's sensuous dishes. In fact, she grows spindly on them. The only way to put meat on her bones is to send her to stay for a week or two with her grandmother, where she eats store ice cream for lunch, mashed potatoes for supper, hot white pap for breakfast.
>
> "My daughter!" the actress cries in despair and horror. I tell her there is still hope, with the passage of time. But she, perhaps because of her beauty, pretends Time is not.[34]

As she had done in the past, Mary Frances selected an anecdote about a friend's family upon which to weave an exaggerated tale, risking the displeasure of the friend to do so. "MF wrote about life as she *remembered* it—or as it suited her fancy. And fanciful she could be," Gloria wrote. "Sylvia did not 'hate my cooking' at all. And MF never had a meal at Mama's table, so how would she know what Sylvia ate there!"[35] Mary Frances was, indeed, beginning to take the "measure of her powers"—a phrase that appears throughout *The Gastronomical*

Me—and every experience, book read, childhood and adult memory recalled became grist for the mill of her storytelling prowess, with varying degrees of disrespect for the truth.

Meanwhile, 1943 was a good year for Paramount. Mary Martin, who became one of Mary Frances's friends, starred in *Happy Go Lucky* and *True to Life*. Cole Porter wrote the score for *Let's Face It*, showcasing the talents of Danny Kaye, Betty Hutton, and Bob Hope. And *For Whom the Bell Tolls* competed with *Casablanca* for Best Picture. While Mary Frances did not work on any of these pictures, during the thirteen weeks of her contractual arrangement with the studio she joined Waldo Salt, Val Burton, and Frank Tuttle in writing an original screenplay called *Yours with Love*. It was a World War I love story about a recovering Polish-American soldier and his correspondence with a shy, thwarted spinster who writes to him in defiance of her old-guard Boston background and risks all for a brief affair.

Mary Frances wrote Powell, "instead of waiting on the whims of an unpleasant producer, I have finally reconciled my ethics with my profession, and am working on my own stuff on company time."[36] Having seen an archived script based on the original 1856 autobiography of Peter Cartwright, an evangelical circuit rider in the nineteenth century whom Mary Frances admired because her great-grandfather Benjamin Kennedy had also been a circuit rider, she started editing Cartwright's story for possible publication.[37] She was also editing and annotating a book on food and wine by her friend Idwal Jones, a southern California writer and wine maven. It was largely through his efforts that Mary Frances, with her knowledge of French and Swiss wines, was invited to participate in wine tastings with notables like Angelo Pelligrini and Phil Townsend Hanna. In lieu of writing another gastronomical book herself, she hoped that editing Jones's book would placate Sam Sloan, who was eager for another success on the heels of *How to Cook a Wolf*.

By the end of March, just a few weeks before her stint at Paramount ended for 1943, Mary Frances again wrote to Powell and returned the first draft of his manuscript "Quintet," which she admired very much. She also hinted that she was about to embark on a very "hush-hush publicity job for the government."[38] She claimed to be unable to reveal any of the details about where she would be living or what she would be doing. She also told her family that she would probably go east on a government job. Rex wrote more specifically to his brother Ted, "MF working for Elmer Davis' Office of War Information . . . secret location."[39] With the exception of her sister Anne, who accidentally met the very pregnant Mary Frances on the street in Pasadena in June, her family did not even suspect that she was expecting her first child in August.

Meanwhile, *Esquire's* Arnold Gingrich had written to Mary Frances, offering her a contract to write a monthly article for the seven-year-old pocket-sized "high art" magazine *Coronet*. As editor for *Esquire*, Gingrich had inaugurated the magazine for the David Smart publishing empire, and he had advertised it with the slogan "Infinite riches in a small room." In 1943 Oscar Dystel was its editor, but Gingrich had an ongoing commitment to acquire good writers for *Esquire*, *Ken*, and *Coronet*. In the June 1943 issue Dystel introduced the "gastronomical publicist" M.F.K. Fisher, who "likes good food, wine, and company; and hates ration card complainers," as a contributor. Her first article was "Consider the Lunch-Box," and it echoed the "balance the whole day, rather than each meal" advice she had spelled out in *How to Cook a Wolf*. Ten consecutive articles in a series titled "The Pepper Pot" followed, each accompanied by a paragraph or two called "Do You Remember?" in which Mary Frances took on subjects like oysters at Delmonico's, a recipe for pickled capers, sludge, Southern cornbread, scrapple, and an old-fashioned Thanksgiving. Writing to Powell, Mary Frances said, "I'm a little ahead on the *Coronet* column, thank God. It's easy to write, but takes time trying to cut it to requirements. It pays me about a hundred a month, so who am I to quibble? I hope to God it keeps up, so I can stay at Bareacres for a few months after this job, and rest my soul in tranquility. I'll be through, come hell or high water, in August."[40]

Between the end of April and mid-August, instead of being on a secret government mission, Mary Frances lived incommunicado in a boardinghouse in Altadena near Dr. Bieler's office and home. During this period of reflection and introspection, she wrote *The Gastronomical Me*, which has come to be regarded as "the most vivid and sustained of her books."[41] "I'm working very hard, against a July 15 deadline . . . conceive and write a book in three months . . . less. I do about three or four thousand words a day on the job, too . . . fairly routine reports. Then I write on the book at night," she told Powell. "It's the first thing I've ever written, really, without Tim's cold judicial ear to listen. The *Wolf* doesn't count . . . it was mainly recipes. But this . . . I get scared and bewildered, wondering if it's good or bad, and not knowing. The book is autobiographical."[42] With chapters that spanned "the first thing [she] remembered tasting" as a four-year-old child to a reawakening of her appetite on a visit to Mexico in 1941, her book became a self-portrait, with food as its central paradigm.

The project can be seen as an effort to put the past into some kind of context before Mary Frances assumed the responsibilities of a single parent, an attempt to come to terms with her failed first marriage, her grief over the loss of her second husband and her brother, and her writing career. She drew the title for nearly half the stories, "The Measure of My Powers," from a quotation by the philosopher George Santayana: "To be happy you must have taken the measure of your powers, tasted the fruits of your passion, and learned your place in the world."

The stories in the collection tend to follow a pattern. From an interesting anecdote, Mary Frances draws a generalization, then turns to a tale from the past. For example, in "The Measure of My Powers 1919," after she relates the anecdote about Gloria's sensuous cooking and her daughter's rejection of it, she comments on children's eating habits, and then tells the story of her family's cook Ora, who not only knew how to please the Kennedy children's palates but also introduced cutouts on pie crusts and carved radishes into their daily meals. While Grandmother Holbrook looked on with disapproval, Mary Frances and Anne savored every dish Ora made until she disappeared one Sunday afternoon to murder her mother and commit suicide with one of her sharpened knives.

The characters in the book are the people "with me then, [with] their deeper needs for love and happiness:"[43] Grandmother Holbrook skimming froth from the kettle of strawberry jam, Father serving peach pie and thick cream to his two small daughters on their way home from their aunt's ranch, Al Fisher and Mary Frances celebrating their one-month anniversary at Racouchot's restaurant in Dijon, and Dillwyn Parrish and Mary Frances savoring the captain's dinner aboard the *Normandie* while Hitler marched across Europe. These tales reveal a more complex emotional terrain than she had explored in her first three books. They also fulfilled her desire to trace the evolution of her great love for Dillwyn, which she had refrained from writing about while living in Vevey. She prefaced the book by explaining that in taking hunger as her subject, "I am really writing about love and the hunger for it, and warmth and the love of it and the hunger for it . . . and then the warmth and richness and fine reality of hunger satisfied . . . and it is all one."[44]

In the book, taste experiences are always evocative and metaphoric. A young girl's gastronomical coming of age, symbolized by her eating an oyster for the first time at boarding school, leads to insights into the meaning of school crushes and curiosity about lesbianism. Mary Frances's intervention, at Mme Ollagnier's boardinghouse in Dijon, in an evening's adventure between a Czech girl and her German lover is an indictment of prewar politics symbolized by gastronomic and sexual perversity. "I knew," Mary Frances wrote, "that Klorr had been supping there, while Maritza lay naked on the bed and moaned for him. And I know that he had put the empty grape skins on her protesting flesh without ever touching her."[45] A young man drinking dark beer and eating enchiladas while listening to a mariachi bandleader sing "La Malagueña" in a Guadalajara beer hall is as much a foreshadowing of tragedy as it is an evolving scene of hunger unsatisfied.

The Gastronomical Me is M.F.K. Fisher's most personally revealing book, yet it is also the most oblique, telling a great deal indirectly but without resorting to the subterfuges of her later work. The sunny days of childhood and romantic days of honeymooning and studying in France mature into more complicated relationships and tragic events. The waiters, chefs, servants, innkeepers, and ship captains who all seem to fall in love with the author-heroine fade in and out of focus while attention centers on the ménage à trois at Le Paquis, on the idyllic year at Le Paquis after Al leaves, on Dillwyn's illness and death, and on David's inability to function normally in what he considered a mad world. Through the sequence of shared, happy, sad, and twisted events the author-heroine takes the measure of her powers and learns her place in the world.

In a letter to Powell written on July 16, Mary Frances described juggling her "secret" job with her concentrated effort to finish *The Gastronomical Me*. "The book was longer than I thought . . . 298 small-margined pages. It's an odd thing, and may bore the boys in NY. It's autobiographical all right . . . but neither True Confessions nor Leaves From My Kitchen Lovebook. I shudder to think what may happen to it. Oh well . . . I think it's a good job, and there are some stories in it I know you'll like. Then there are sections about Dijon, the Rigoulots, Miss Lyse, Jean Matrouchot . . . all that . . . that will interest you too. So it won't be time wasted."[46] Mary Frances mentioned that she would like to complete her work and return to Bareacres sometime in late August. "Maybe by then I'll find myself with one of the two children I am trying to adopt," she wrote. "It's a hell of a discouraging business . . . can't be done in California at all because legally I'm a spinster! Expensive, too."[47]

Amid all of this secrecy she gave birth to a daughter on August 15, 1943, and Dr. Bieler was the attending physician.[48] Mary Frances named the baby Anne Kennedy Parrish,[49] and on the birth certificate identified the father as the fictitious Michael Parrish, occupation serviceman. Two weeks later Mary Frances surfaced in Whittier, and, accompanied by her nephew Sean, whom she had picked up from his nearby summer school, stopped at Dr. Bieler's office. As prearranged, she called for her "adopted" daughter and drove to the Ranch. "I, of course, fell for the adoption line, not knowing any better at the age of ten," Sean recalled, "but wondered why my grandmother Edith burst into tears when she first saw Anna. Dote cried too. I remember thinking 'why is everyone being so emotional over an adopted child?' "[50] Pictures show Anna in Edith's arms with Rex as a proud grandfather at her side. If there were questions, they were not asked. Mary Frances brokered her explanations and carefully planned her strategy. Years later, she told Eda Lord, "In 1943 I had a daughter . . . rather complicated feat, as you can imagine, which I brought off to my own complete satisfaction."[51] That the truth of having a child out of wedlock could be so easily manipulated to serve her ends indicated to what extent Mary Frances had come to believe that reality was a flexible concept, in life as well as on the page. Subterfuge really worked, and in Hollywood there were many roles to play.

Mary Frances and Anna returned to Bareacres, where Dillwyn's studio had been converted into the baby's room. His pictures hung on the walls, among them *Angels of Birth and Tranquility* and the only one of his paintings of Mary Frances that had ever satisfied him, an impression with a bottle of wine, apples, and a white flower. In a letter dated November 3, Mary Frances told Powell that her "adopted" daughter was "right in every way. She is a healthy, impish little being with merry dark eyes. And now my life seems full and warm and rich again. I was out in the cold for a long time."[52] She hired as a housekeeper and nurse for Anna a widow named Elsa Purdy, who took up residence in the small cabin across the arroyo on the Hemet property.

In Hollywood rumors inevitably circulated, and in the close-knit world of screenwriters, there were people who knew the paternity of Mary Frances's child. Gloria Stuart intimated that she knew, and floated a rumor in her autobiography:

> Arthur and I were at a dinner party. The conversation came to a remark I could hardly believe I was hearing: "Did you know that MFK Fisher had a child by Val Burton?" Val Burton was a writer. A married man. I angrily reprimanded our host . . . The moment we got home, even though it was almost midnight, I called MF. She listened without exclamation or questions. I said, "MF, you have to do something about this. You can't have people saying this about you. Val Burton! It's dreadful!" Her reply was even-toned, unruffled. I was not to pay any attention to all this, she said. Gossip is gossip, or some such calming comment. I couldn't believe her lack of concern. Her indifference to a scandalmonger. And as long as I knew her, over sixty years, she never mentioned it again.[53]

Years later Mary Frances told her friend Marietta Voorhees, "It is wasteful to be secretive, furtive, shameful, all the things that are taught us by loving people who think they are right. I speak of some awareness of this two-edged sword, for I cannot and will not tell my older daughter of her father's true name . . . I feel no shame in any way, but instead a viciously strong sense of protection . . . not of myself, but of many other people."[54] To another correspondent, Mary

Frances indicated that if Edith and Rex knew the identity of Anna's father, they would have been very proud. But, truth to say, Mary Frances frequently told people what she thought they wanted to hear, often ignored the facts, and sometimes she said nothing at all. Over the years she introduced so much fiction into the facts of her life that it seemed futile to speculate about the identity of Anna's father.

On the other hand, there was nothing secretive about Mary Frances's affair with Bachmann. After Dillwyn's death, he was helpful and attentive and she was vulnerable. He was also very career-oriented, and during the war he volunteered to write and film documentaries for the Army Air Forces, usually at secret locations. His love letters to Mary Frances are filled with details about his work. At the same time they reveal his concern for her and her daughter's welfare and interest in her career, as well as his acknowledgment that Mary Frances might fall in love with another man while he is away: "I know what it means to you to be alone with the baby. I know that you are only half a woman when you are alone. That is because you have so much to give and that important part of you is not fulfilled if there is no one to take it and give you something in return. I also know that time is passing. And more than anything I know that I shall not be back for more than 6 months. And by all of this I'm trying in a most inarticulate manner to say that I fully expect you to remarry, or find someone else before I return. And I heartily approve—if such approval were necessary."[55] By the time this was written, Mary Frances had become involved with the San Francisco lawyer and wine enthusiast Harold Price, whose debonair good looks were similar to those of a younger Rex and whose admiring letters got Mary Frances's attention.

At the beginning of November 1943, Mary Frances told Powell that she awaited copies of *The Gastronomical Me* from Duell, Sloan and Pearce, who were apparently delighted with it. She hoped "it would sell like peanuts" so she wouldn't have to think about returning to Paramount until the beginning of the new year. Given the terms of her contract, her plan had been to work at the studio for a few months every year in order to earn enough money to retreat to Bareacres and do her own writing the rest of the time. Now she calculated the expense of a larger apartment and a nurse and felt that she could not cover both costs with her salary. "I shall simply plead Act of God or something," she told Powell, "if I'm accused of not following my contract."[56] Leaving Bareacres and the baby, even for a short time, seemed unthinkable; taking her daughter to Hollywood seemed impossible.

Favorable reviews of *The Gastronomical Me*, which appeared in leading newspapers and magazines from November into the new year, undoubtedly caused her to rethink her writing priorities. "There is deft and witty writing in this book—witty not in the sense of funny, but in the sense of sharply perceptive," S. I. Hayakawa wrote in *Book Week*. "There is also a prevailing sense of tragedy—death and the intimation of death against which one fortifies oneself by grasping at the sharp, sensuous joys of food and love."[57] Hayakawa's insightful praise was followed by favorable reviews in *The New York Times* and the *Saturday Review*. In the *Weekly Book Review*, Sheila Hibben wrote, "One may disagree with an occasional passage in *The Gastronomical Me*, but I can imagine no two opinions about Mrs. Fisher's style. The brilliance, the bite, the flexibleness that distinguished *Serve It Forth* are apparent in this latest work, which also marks an increase in the author's technical virtuosity."[58] And in *The New Yorker*, Clifton Fadiman described the book as "sadder, older, and less charming than *Serve It Forth*. It makes more evident than ever the fact that Mrs. Fisher was born to write novels and it's about time she did."[59]

Evaluating this pivotal work years later, the critic Patricia Storace wrote: "Here are meals as seductions, educations, diplomacies, communions. Unique among the classics of gastronomic writing, with its glamorous settings, its wartime drama and its powerful love story, [it] is a book about adult loss, survival, and love."[60] In his book *Material Dreams*, historian Kevin Starr advanced his thesis about how the experience of living in France changed the mind-set of the "Arroyo Seco" writers who had journeyed from southern California to Paris and Dijon, making them aware of a tradition and way of life more cosmopolitan than the California scene. As one of those writers, along with Lawrence Powell, and, in a minor way, Ward Ritchie, Mary Frances distinctively "melded eating and drinking, time and place, the hungers of heart and body with sex, love, security, strength, exhilaration, and identity."[61]

Bachmann wrote, urging Mary Frances to save the reviews and to change course as a writer: "I feel that you should start writing novels. I feel certain that you'll do damned well with them. I have some nebulous ideas. Mainly though I'd like to hear what you have to say on the subject and talk it over with you . . . Once you get rolling I think that will be all there is to it, and you won't have to worry about writing the sort of stuff you've been doing—you've done it and you've done it damned well—now it's time to move on to something bigger."[62] Although he had not yet received a copy of *The Gastronomical Me*, he had concluded that it was about food, the "sort of stuff" that he knew she had written about in the past and was contributing to *Coronet*.

As far as Mary Frances was concerned, her latest book was not that "sort of stuff." But she made no apologies for the assignments she took to support herself, her daughter, and their home. Like her heroine Colette, she wrote quickly and almost continuously. But she also aspired to more and listened when other voices—those of family, friends, and, most insistently, Bachmann—cautioned, "Please try not to write any more about food, if you can help it, in a book. And don't write any more about yourself. I am highly dubious and suspicious of people who do—dubious as to their growth as writers. Suspicious as to their imagination and ability to project their minds to other subjects. Look at Thomas Wolfe. He could really have been great were he able to get away from writing about himself . . . You can and do write about other things and do it well. So my mentioning it is groundless except I'd like to see you off in the other direction you will ultimately get to."[63]

Mary Frances tried to budget enough money from her work at Paramount and freelancing to keep out of debt and have time for the writing she wanted to do, and there were also a few unexpected windfalls. In December she entered into an informal arrangement with her father, who wanted to purchase ten acres of her land for a building site. There was no deed or exchange of title, but he paid his daughter $1,000 for it, and over the years he occupied himself with plans to build a small home on the property that he and especially Edith loved. As always during the holiday season, the family gathered at the Ranch, and Anna was christened on December 26, wearing a Welsh robe that Mary Frances borrowed from Idwal Jones. A photo of her in her long white gown sitting on Rex's lap shows a beautiful dark-eyed baby.

Early in 1944, after much thought, Mary Frances approached Paramount for a release from the remainder of her contract. She really did not like scriptwriting, and she couldn't imagine subjecting Anna to living in small quarters in Hollywood and commuting back and forth to Bareacres. The most compelling reason, however, was that she had fallen in love with Harold Price. The previous April, at his invitation, she had spoken about Burgundy wines at San Francisco's Bohemian Club. The morning after her presentation, despite gas rationing, a limousine was put at her disposal, and together with Price and a few other members of the San Francisco Wine Society, she drove north and saw the Napa Valley for the first time: "I was given a 'tour of the wine country' by some friends in San Francisco. We stopped in Napa at a dark old bar that out-of-towners have always found quaint, and then, warmed by our unaccustomed morning tipples, headed due north, up a true valley that gradually tapered to its end at the base of the great topless mountain, and I knew I would be back."[64] Northern California's vineyards and Price both made a deep impression on her.

Since that event, they corresponded, and he encouraged her to spend more time in San Francisco, perhaps even rent a house there. But her contract with Paramount stood in the way. Although in later years she characterized her split with the studio as a "Hollywood versus Fisher" epic battle, there is no evidence that her leaving was anything but amicable. Paramount might have objected to her breach of contract, and the Screenwriters' Guild also may have sided with her, but Gloria Stuart, whose husband was a charter member of the guild, could not remember Mary Frances even referring to a dispute with the studio. Nor was there any mention of a dispute in *Daily Variety*.[65]

Unquestionably Mary Frances took away a great deal from her Hollywood experience. She had made many friends, developed a lifelong interest in films, and gained fodder for her writing, in which this period of her life often figures, especially in *An Alphabet for Gourmets*. At the same time, she had honed her role-playing skills there, mastering the basics of the "center of the stage" persona that she cultivated throughout her life. She had learned how to enter a room and be noticed, she could command an audience, and she had developed a feel for the bon mot that was second to no one's.

In February she moved to San Francisco with Anna and Elsa. The three-story house that she rented had a large room on the third floor that looked west toward the Presidio and an adjacent park. Unusual for San Francisco at that time of year, the days were sunny, and Mary Frances was able to sit under the cherry trees in the garden with Anna. Through the intervention of Price, who was by that time her lover, the Wine Institute put a car with gas at her disposal, and the two of them took several trips to Napa and Sonoma, where they tasted excellent wines.

Always sensitive to people's food preferences and a keen observer of what she called "marital gastronomy," Mary Frances kept a journal that spring in which she noted the culinary idiosyncrasies of her family, friends, and lover, perhaps intending to publish it in some form. Commenting on Price's food preferences, she wrote:

> Very interesting to cook for. Has prejudices, but mostly classical ones, so that almost anything well prepared he can admire and enjoy. Wine is a prerequisite. Breakfast: plenty of fresh orange or grapefruit juice, well-strained, fresh coffee, thin crustless buttered toast. Light lunch—omelet or egg dish. Solid interesting dinner with two wines, no dessert, coffee. He eats salad before soup—salad or fairly substantial hors d'oeuvres. Many signs of years of "dining out," from coffee shops to Palm Court—but is tolerant in the main. Likes *cuisine classique des sauces*, but is appreciative of well-made, well-seasoned simplicity. Likes egg-dishes, potato-dishes, shellfish raw & cooked, plain salads, rare roast beef, good cheeses. Orders fancy desserts for women, but does not eat them. Would order food to accompany wine rather than the opposite. Likes Italian food for ordinary. French food for celebrating. Likes to cook, make salads, coffee, etc. Stimulating in the kitchen. Likes candlelight.[66]

Yet despite Price's centrality in her life at this point, Mary Frances wrote little else about him. Some of her anecdotes in the "B Is for

Bachelors" entry in *An Alphabet for Gourmets* probably refer to him, and he is her partner in a story called "War," posthumously published in *Last House*. In the latter, Mary Frances captures the highly charged emotional mood of San Francisco as a departure point for army and navy men who sail from the harbor into active duty. When she and her lover visit a few bars and a restaurant where they drink Gibsons, Château de Camensac 1923, and brandy, they are surrounded by soldiers, sailors, officers, and women ready to please. It was a familiar scenario of one last drink, one more kiss before loved ones and family were left behind. At the end of the evening, when the woman returns home alone, she finds her child and the child's nurse sleeping peacefully, and the furnace, which had recently gone out, supplying warmth to the house. Unlike the servicemen who will sail west into the fog and cold, she is thankful that she and her child are protected from the harsh reality of war in a house of love. But as the opening lines of the story suggest, there is an aura of unreality in her present situation: "Is it the woman I once knew? Is it a stranger walking in my shoes, accustoming herself to the unusual phases of this life?"[67] She seems to cast herself as both observer and participant in these scenes, infusing emotional ties with the temporary, contingent quality of war itself.

There are no letters to document the duration of Mary Frances's affair with Price (they remained friends after it ended), but there is a brief journal entry that refers to their deteriorating relationship at Easter time, probably due to the fact that she was not the only woman in his life. In an unsent letter Mary Frances described the months since February as a time filled with periods of ecstatic abandon and keen desperation. She tells Price that she welcomes his calls, but questions them in the light of his seeming intention to end the relationship. She hopes to see him and to comport herself with dignity, but believes herself to be not strong enough either physically or emotionally to endure another scene, because there have been too many of them. She concludes by saying, "I cannot bear quarrels. They are each one a cataclysm to me, and tear my roots. I love you more than anyone in the world, except maybe Anneli [Anna] in another way, but if life with you means even a shadow of the past week's torment, I'll flee it like the pox. I'm not fit for it—not adjusted to such pain. Some women can storm and weep and then recover, but not I. I love you, but such a life would be without honor for either of us."[68] Mary

Frances had leased the house in San Francisco until April 30, 1944, but she returned to Bareacres shortly before that date.

In a letter to Powell dated a month earlier, she had explained how difficult it had been to leave Bareacres and to move Anna, Elsa, and herself to San Francisco. "I've been both busy and lazy," she wrote, "leading a strange life of motherdom and giddy debauchery which has taken all my energy. I'm gradually coming into focus again . . . thank God, because I simply must tap out some more gastronomical nonsense to fill up a large hole in my bank book."[69] The contract with *Coronet* had come to an end, but she had recently negotiated an arrangement for a regular monthly column in *House Beautiful* for 1944–45. Seasonal and with catchy titles, the articles were totally unlike the "molded salad" school of food writing, and they broke new ground in culinary journalism. When the first of them premiered in June 1944, the editor of the magazine promised that "[M.F.K. Fisher] has the gift of creating moods around food as other writers create them about life and love. Her wisdom on the art of good living imbues even a recipe for apple pie with the fascination of a mystery novel."[70] A stunning photograph of M.F.K. Fisher taken by George Hurrell accompanied the introduction to the series.

Her menus for the *House Beautiful* articles included stuffed oysters, *coquilles aux crevettes*, and new potatoes *aux fines herbes*. While her recipes could hardly be called models of exactitude ("as for roast leg of lamb, the best thing to do is read a few books about it"),[71] most of them were clear and helpful and witty. She listed ingredients in the order of use and took the reader's intelligence for granted. The articles that she wrote to celebrate the Fourth of July, Thanksgiving, Christmas, Valentine's Day, and spring's arrival were filled with insights from her personal experience of the holidays at home and abroad. Her menus were always interesting, and she included suggestions on substituting ingredients, adapting recipes to personal preferences, and choosing appropriate wines.

What was amazing about the curious blend of sophistication and lighthearted banter that distinguished the *House Beautiful* series was that Mary Frances was so emotionally and physically drained during the months she worked on it. Although she left San Francisco on cordial terms with Price, the intensity of their affair had left her emotionally shaken. The loss of Dillwyn and David still weighed heavily upon her, as did the more recent death of Sam Sloan. Her mother's declining health also worried her. After one of Edith's visits at Bareacres, Mary Frances wrote in her journal: "Now mother with Aunt Petie talks on and on, mainly about her early days. That may be all right for very old women . . . but she's only 63! She is, as I've known for some time, deliberately escaping into her increasingly glamorous past because the present is painful and frightening and boring to her . . . but it is shocking to me to see such signs of real deterioration."[72]

Mary Frances's life was also complicated by her commitment as a member of the Writers' War Board to offer her services for war bond rallies. In the fall of 1944, she was summoned for a two-week period of service in October and another two-week period in December. The December date conflicted with the proposed opening of a posthumous exhibit of Dillwyn's paintings at UCLA. Writing to Powell, she asked for advice about postponing the exhibit until spring, and also voiced her concern about the duty itself. "For a person who hates crowds and planes and speeches and noise as much as I, it is a strange form of patriotism to have thrust upon me . . . But I feel it is the only thing I *can* do. I am in a kind of coma of fear at the thought of it."[73] Nearly everyone in Hollywood—actresses and actors, directors and writers—supported the war effort, and although she never wrote about it, Mary Frances did her part.

After the Christmas holidays at the Ranch, Mary Frances considered returning to Paramount, not to resume her scriptwriting career, but to revise the screenplay *Yours with Love* that she had worked on with Val Burton a year and a half earlier. The plans included using the existing screenplay as the plot of a novel that she would complete at the studio and publish with Duell, Sloan and Pearce. She would then give Paramount first option on the book for a film. In a long letter to Bernard Skadron, her accountant in Hollywood, she outlined the scheme and indicated her dismay over not having a current book under contract and not having enough time to work at Bareacres without interruptions from neighbors, the telephone, and Anna, who was now walking, talking, and singing to the moon. At the end of the day Mary Frances was tired and unable to write anything except "hack stuff" for magazines. The prospect of a private office at Paramount to go to every day made her more than willing to return to the Hollywood routine. The scheme, however, did not work out, and she did not complete the novel.

In mid-April, after experiencing anxiety attacks for about six weeks, Mary Frances decided that the past six and a half years had taken a more drastic toll on her physical and mental health than she realized. Strangely, after all her personal losses and trials, the death of President Franklin D. Roosevelt on April 12, 1945, was the final straw. Even in the context of the national mood of mourning, Mary Frances seemed more despondent than ever. Her friends advised a change of scene, and Dr. Bieler urged her to follow through on a plan to leave Bareacres for the summer.

Mary Frances sought refuge in New York City, where she planned to read, attend movies and concerts, walk, sleep, and even enjoy a river cruise. Gloria offered her the use of the Sheekman apartment at 165 East Forty-ninth Street and told her that the closet was stocked with vermouth. Taking Elsa and twenty-month-old Anna with her, Mary Frances boarded a train headed east, resolved to turn her back on M.F.K. Fisher until October.

EIGHT

The Refugee

(1945–1949)

I feel clearly that the reason I made such a foolhardy and in ways disastrous mistake in marrying DF was that for the first time I was not aggressive, not pursuant . . . I went to NY in a searching but quiescent, unbelligerent mood, sexually. I had achieved a child. I was alone, but although dissatisfied I was *satisfied*. And there was Donald, almost as soon as I arrived.[1]

—M.F.K. Fisher

Arriving in New York City, Mary Frances, Elsa, and Anna settled into the Sheekmans' vacant apartment next to a Third Avenue El stop in Manhattan. Creating the decor of the place, Gloria said, had been "like raising a dreadful child, and having it turn out better than could be expected."[2] In a burst of creative energy the winter before, she had laid the linoleum and hall carpeting herself, recovered chairs in black velvet, and stocked the closet with bottles of Noilly Prat and cans of the best olive oil, and she had filled the window boxes with box hedges. This last extravagance elicited Gloria's warning to Mary Frances, "Be careful of dripping water on passersby, they resent it, and complain to the landlord, and there's hell to pay."[3] It was the beginning of May, trees were in bloom, and the city was vibrant. When Germany surrendered unconditionally at Reims on May 7, and the ratification documents were signed in Berlin the next day, twenty-four-hour celebrations spontaneously erupted in Manhattan to mark the Allied victory in Europe. The habitués of Park Avenue drank champagne and breathed a sigh of relief, and in Times Square people partied, hugged anyone they could find in uniform, and cheered the bold V-E headlines carried by the morning papers.

Kyle Crichton, who was a friend of the Sheekmans and a contributing editor at *Collier's* magazine, invited Mary Frances to a dinner party the second night she was in the city, and it was there that she met Donald Friede again. Although Mary Frances had been introduced to him at a cocktail party in Hollywood during her stint at Paramount, she knew little more about him than that he had been associated with the Hollywood agent Myron Selznick and in a much earlier role had been half of the meteoric team of Covici-Friede, publishers of John Steinbeck and François Mauriac as well as controversial works like Radclyffe Hall's *Well of Loneliness* and Theodore Dreiser's *An American Tragedy*. Mary Frances also knew about his history of failed marriages and frequent career changes.

Intelligent, urbane, and cosmopolitan, Donald Friede was the sort of man whose company she enjoyed. And, Othello-like, he wooed her with tales of his past exploits, "the dangers I had pass'd." He was forty-four years old to her thirty-seven, American born, but raised in Europe because his father had been the Ford agent for all of Russia. He spent his freshman year at Yale in 1919 and his sophomore year at Princeton before he embarked on a succession of short-lived jobs at the American Express Company, American Tobacco Company, United Cigar Stores, Stern Brothers, Baldwin Locomotive Works, and the Message Exchange, a business founded by his half brother on the sound premise that people catching trains always thought of last-minute messages they had no time to deliver.

In 1924, after seeking the advice of a psychiatrist practicing in the new field of occupational therapy, Donald Friede went into publishing, first as a stockroom clerk at Knopf and then at Boni and Liveright. At the age of twenty-four, he used some of his paternal inheritance to purchase a half-interest in Liveright and became first vice president of the firm that boasted Theodore Dreiser, Sherwood Anderson, Ernest Hemingway, Ezra Pound, and Robinson Jeffers on its 1925 list. He also dabbled in the theater, promoting a New York production of Antheil's avant-garde *Ballet Mécanique*. After that money-losing venture, he joined forces with ex–Chicago bookman Pat Covici. For ten years they published distinguished American and European authors, were sued in New York and in Boston for publishing obscene books—*The Well of Loneliness* and *An American Tragedy*—

and then the Depression and a deflated book market forced them out of business. As a prototypical New Yorker during the roaring twenties, Donald traveled, wined, dined, gambled, and played with the best of the reluctant-to-grow-up generation. In the 1930s and early 1940s, as story editor for the A. & S. Lyons Agency, he lived for the most part in small hotels, drifted from Pierre's to the Ritz for client lunches, and was still paying alimony to the last of his four wives when he met Mary Frances at Crichton's apartment in the Village.

For two weeks he sent her flowers, dazzled her with conversation, and took her to expensive restaurants. After a memorable lunch that Mary Frances later wrote about in *An Alphabet for Gourmets*, she described dining-in-love: "I think of a lunch at the Lafayette in New York, in the front cafe with the glass pushed back and the May air flowing almost visibly over the marble tabletops, and a waiter named Pons, and a bottle of Louis Martini's *Folle Blanche* and *moules* more-or-less marinières but delicious, and then a walk in new black-heeled shoes with white stitching on them beside a man I had just met and a week later was to marry, in spite of my obdurate resolve never to marry again and my cynical recognition of his super-salesmanship."[4]

Mary Frances and Donald were married on May 19, 1945. On May 21, Mary Frances telegraphed the news to family and friends from Atlantic City: AM IN A DAZE OF AMUSEMENT EXCITEMENT HAPPINESS BECAUSE I ACCIDENTALLY GOT MARRIED SATURDAY TO DONALD FRIEDE.[5] After a few days the Friedes returned to New York, and for a time their "odd" honeymoon consisted of "Donald trotting back and forth to his hotel, catching fleeting sights of me between strung-up diapers and empty milk-bottles. But it doesn't seem to matter at all," she wrote to Powell. "He has much the *same* power Tim [Dillwyn] had, of making life very real for everyone. And he is fun. He's half German and half Russian, and has several marriages and an overfull life behind him. But so have I. We approve of this marriage and life."[6]

The Friedes sublet the screenwriter MacKinlay Kantor's duplex at 17 Bank Street in Greenwich Village for the months of June, July, and August. "It was fun, the summer of 1945 in New York," Mary Frances wrote. "To meet all the people of the various publishing sets as a callow Westerner . . . It was just after the war, a strange time indeed, and New York was filled with glittering bitter refugees. I promised to do a book for Pat Covici [now a senior editor at Viking] about a similar time in Switzerland when Geneva and all the little villages around the lake swarmed with brilliant refugees from France. Mme. Récamier and Mme. de Staël had their salons, then, and Brillat-Savarin flitted around the edges before he headed for the more golden shores of America."[7]

Much earlier, Mary Frances had escaped from Whittier with Al and had taken refuge in Dijon. Not too many years later, she fled the role of faculty wife in Eagle Rock and led an idyllic existence in Vevey with Dillwyn. During the summer of 1945, New York became her refuge, and the duplex on Bank Street her salon. As for Donald, her love of the moment, he was "a very subtle complex man . . . a great challenge to me."[8] Donald was flamboyant where Mary Frances was instinctively reserved, spendthrift where she was financially cautious. While Dillwyn had been her mentor and muse at the beginning of her writing career, Donald quite literally became her promoter, breaking her existing contracts and signing her with editor Pat Covici at Viking Press within weeks of their move to the Village. He also introduced her to Henry Volkening, a literary agent whom he thought could more advantageously represent her than Mary Leonard Pritchett.

The book she had contracted for with Viking was a collection of excerpts from past and present literature on the topic of feasting, man's fundamental need to celebrate the high points of life by eating and drinking. Almost every day, Mary Frances pored over indexes in the New York Public Library, gathering material from sources as ancient as the Bible and Chinese emperor Sung Nung's plant classifications and as modern as Marc Connelly's *Green Pastures* and Ernest Hemingway's *For Whom the Bell Tolls*. "I would work all day in the big reading room, with lunch often at exciting places and then a late afternoon glass of white wine in the gardens of the Museum of Modern Art while I waited for Donald," Mary Frances recalled. "We would walk or ride in the breathless summer twilight, to dine with people in their high apartments or down in the Village in the sidewalk restaurants. The whole long summer was a dream of hard work and hard play."[9]

Every day the newspapers announced new assaults on Japanese-held islands in the Pacific, and it seemed only a matter of time until the war would be over. Rationing would be a thing of the past, and travel restrictions would ease. In the midst of these momentous events, Mary Frances received a postcard from the owner of Le Paquis, Dr. Kieviet de Jonge. Desperate for money, he and his wife wanted to know if she was interested in repurchasing the property or if she knew anyone else who might want to buy it. Coincidentally, that very day Arnold Gingrich had called from Washington, D.C., inquiring if Mary Frances still owned Le Paquis and would consider selling it. Having been told by the authorities that he had to own property in Switzerland if he wanted to emigrate there, he immediately thought of M.F.K. Fisher and her home in Vevey. When she told him about the query from its present owners, he impulsively flew to New York and met her for a late lunch at the Lafayette Hotel. Gingrich recalled their meeting—the meal of *moules marinière* accompanied by crystal tulips of white wine,[10] Mary Frances's sketches of the floor plans of Le Paquis as well as her phone call to de Jonge, and his purchase of the property for twenty thousand dollars—in his memoir, *Toys of a Lifetime*.[11]

The summer was not all exciting lunches and stimulating parties, however. In early July, Donald was subpoenaed to return to California where his half brother Sidney and he were under indictment for misusing the U.S. mail, apparently to send pornographic materials.[12] Rather than ask his mother for funds, Donald used Mary Frances's savings of $3,500 for the trip, legal fees, and fine. Relieved that the matter could be resolved with dispatch, and more than a little grateful, Donald wrote: "Being away from you for what is after all the first real separation we have had since we met has increased my wonder at my fabulous good fortune. How was it possible I should have had this perfect thing happen to me—how is it possible for me to have your beautiful and fulfilling love. I feel very humble, and deeply touched, and gloriously happy, all at the same time."[13]

When Donald returned to New York later that month, however, he found that during his absence Mary Frances had had to hire a night nurse to stay with her because the anxiety attacks that had plagued her in California had returned. She had difficulty sleeping at night, and the midnight street noises frightened her. The last lines of a "Ballad" she presented to Donald in honor of his homecoming read:

So I sing now of that woman, hiding from her lonely bed.
Oh, do you, did you, know her?
Oh, did you, do you?[14]

The lines were strangely reminiscent of the beginning lines of the story "War" that she'd written about her months in San Francisco with Price, juxtaposing the *carpe diem* attitude of the departing servicemen at the beginning of the war with her own brief role as Price's mistress—"Is it the woman I once knew? Is it a stranger walking in my shoes, accustoming herself to the unusual phases of this life?"[15] Now, with the announcement of Japan's surrender imminent, Mary Frances found herself once again unmoored. She had just learned that she was pregnant, by a husband she barely knew, and who did not really seem to know her. Years later, when referring to this period of her life and her precipitous marriage to Donald, Mary Frances told her psychiatrist, "It seems very rash, as indeed it was. I felt that I was past the great passion of life, and so was he, and that we could build a very good companionship. It was a chancy thing, from the very first, and one of increasing strain and uncertainty for me."[16]

Another stress point was the realization that she and Donald would have to move when the Kantors returned to their apartment at the end of August. Unable to find anything suitable that they could afford in New York, and with their bank account dwindling, Donald suggested that they return to Bareacres. For many reasons, Mary Frances resisted the idea. By this time she was well aware of Donald's need to be in a constant whirl of professional and social activity, and she feared that the isolation and nonexistent social life of Hemet would prove to be disastrous. There must also have been some reluctance on her part to share the home where she and Dillwyn had spent the last two years of his life together. But under pressure, she reluctantly bowed to Donald's wishes, and they traveled west at the end of the summer.

Initially Donald welcomed the solitude of Bareacres and launched into a series of writing projects. He invited guests for long weekends and planned getaway lunches in Riverside and longer excursions to Beverly Hills. With family visits, friends stopping by, and their menagerie of dogs and cats, Mary Frances found that securing the zines but will not do either the typical 'love' stories or the kind of work I've been doing for the past years. That leaves a very limited field. Now, at least, I have made the final break with Mary Pritchett."[27] Summing up her present situation, she concluded that for better or worse the anthology would soon be out and she would finish her novel as soon as she could. If no studio bought the recently completed story line, she would send it to Volkening for his advice, and she planned to write an article on Southern cooking for a new magazine, which was temporarily titled Project X and slated for publication in 1947. The editor's offer was two hundred dollars, and they needed the money.

Shortly after her marriage to Donald in May 1945, Mary Frances had playfully challenged her sister Norah to follow her example and marry her fiancé John Barr, who at the time was serving in the army. Norah agreed, and became Mrs. John Barr in June. A year later, Norah and John, who had been recently discharged from the service, were living in the Kennedy house in La Puente, and John Barr, Jr., was born about six weeks after Kennedy.

With the number of her grandchildren now totaling five, Edith decided that a double christening would be a wonderful occasion to bring the family together. Mary Frances dreaded the fuss of getting baby food and other necessities together as well as the long drive. She also had her own "dead feelings about such religious rites,"[28] but she bowed to her mother's wishes. The family gathered at St. Matthias Church in Whittier on September 15. Mary Frances again borrowed Idwal Jones's little cotton peasant robe for Kennedy, as she had done for Anna's christening three years earlier. Feeling very mature for his thirteen years, Sean was both godfather to John Barr, Jr., and proxy godfather, for Pat Covici, to Kennedy. It was a gesture of Mary Frances's growing affection for her editor. A photograph taken at the Ranch afterward shows Mary Frances's sister Anne holding Kennedy, with John Barr, Jr., in the arms of Sean, and the rest of the family in festive poses. Under the surface of the celebration, however, were deep antagonisms that only worsened in the months to come. Donald disliked John Barr and Anne, and only thinly disguised his feelings. As far as Anne was concerned, she thought Donald was taking advantage of her sister and genuinely disliked him in return.

In her journal Mary Frances observed that Anne looked better

amount of time that she needed for writing was difficult and often impossible. Working against the clock, she completed the manuscript of Here Let Us Feast by January 1946, and almost immediately signed a new contract for a novel that both Donald and Covici urged her to write. "I said, 'But I am not a novelist. Some people are and some . . . I've been reading novels all my life, and I don't want to write one.' Obviously I had little chance to escape their professional and financial pressures, no matter how subtly or bluntly applied, so I sat down and wrote Not Now But Now. It was something I 'could and must do,' "[17] Mary Frances blandly wrote in an afterword to the novel. That she had already written two (unpublished) novels, collaborated on and published one, and revised another, was brushed aside, and the book jacket hailed Not Now But Now as "M.F.K. Fisher's only novel."

"I grow more tub-like and placid daily, but even so am working fast on the novel, and it is so easy and fun after that damned anthology that I feel almost guilty about it," she wrote to Powell. "When will we meet? There is still no plumbing . . . and as for me, I move cautiously from bed to kitchen to desk, and go to bed at 7:30 exhausted."[18] A blast of unusually cold weather in the valley had damaged water pipes from the pump to the house, and repairs in the bathrooms and kitchen were necessary. With a second child expected, Mary Frances proposed building a garage with a large room on the upper level so she and Donald would have a quiet place to work. Mary Frances also engaged a local couple, the Hearnsbergers, to live in the cottage, serving as caretakers of the property and fill-in babysitters whenever necessary because Elsa Purdy had returned to her own home.

On March 12, 1946, Dr. Bieler delivered Kennedy Friede.[19] Although Mary Frances's second daughter was a healthy baby, she was seven weeks premature, and as a precaution she remained in the Pasadena Lutheran Hospital for monitored care until April 24. During the months following Kennedy's birth, Mary Frances had difficulty concentrating on her writing, and she feared that the old wives' tale about reproduction dulling the female brain was true in her case. On July 3 she celebrated her thirty-eighth birthday with the observation, "We are in debt, which I hate as much as I always have. I refuse to feel grim about it, because I know that we can and will get out of it and meanwhile we are happy and healthy. What fine children we have! I know I'd seem dull and smug if anyone got me to talk about them, but that is how I feel . . . they are completely delightful and satisfying creatures, pleasant to look at, smell, touch, listen to, watch, kiss, feed, clean."[20] By this time, Donald had legally adopted Anna and given her his name.[21]

Mary Frances's photo albums as well as photographs taken by Man Ray picture happy days at Bareacres: Anna and Kennedy splashing around in the laundry tubs, Kennedy looking over Donald's shoulder the same way the baby Mary Frances had looked over Rex's, Man Ray cutting Anna's hair, Mary Frances comically grilling a hot dog with a cookbook in hand, and the four Friedes posed on the patio—all smiles. In a short piece Donald wrote, "On Being Married to M.F.K. Fisher," he described their simple meals, often one-dish ragouts of beef "simmering in the soup pot for a day or so, filling the house with a gentle and exciting aroma," and the grilled lamb chops and barbequed steaks, "thick and aged, marinated in soy sauce for hours, basted with chopped herbs, onions, melted butter and red wine." He also praised the "nameless dishes made of leftover peas and carrots or steak or rice or baked potato which come to the table twice as delicious, if that were possible, as they were in their original form. To my mind they are the perfect example of the triumph of an imaginative palate over the precise pages of a cookbook."[22] It was not only meals shared but hours spent in conversation about the current publishing scene, about their concerns, and about their hopes for their children, that, at least initially, held their marriage together.

During that summer of 1946, George Macy, publisher and president of the popular Limited Editions Club, offered Mary Frances a generous contract for a translation of Jean-Anthelme Brillat-Savarin's *Physiology of Taste*. Mixing erudition, wit, and wisdom in a way never before applied to gastronomy, Brillat-Savarin, a judge of the Court of Appeals in early nineteenth-century Paris, had combined philosophical meditations and linguistic (five modern languages plus Latin), scientific, physiological, and psychological analysis with personal observations, aphorisms, and anecdotes. He also broke new ground with his praise of bourgeois and provincial cookery.

First published in 1825, just a few short months before his death, Brillat-Savarin's book enjoyed more acclaim in France and England

than it did in the United States. Although there had been several French and other European-language editions of *La Physiologie du goût ou meditations de gastronomie transcendante* in the nineteenth and twentieth centuries, there were no English translations that reflected a mastery of the French language, a fluid prose style in English, and a grasp of gastronomy. Mary Frances had all three qualifications, plus a long-standing familiarity with the text. Macy offered her $1,500 for the first half of the translation and another $1,500 upon completion, welcome security in light of unpaid hospital bills and the cost of the new workroom-garage they planned to call Lulu's place.

In September, Mary Frances and Donald also worked out a story line that they hoped to sell to a major studio. Mary Frances dashed off a fifty-page synopsis in a few days, unthinkingly overtiring herself even though she felt heady about the project and revived by Donald's flattery about her contribution to their collaborative effort. When he returned from a quick trip to Hollywood a few days later, however, Donald found her barely able to cope with the children and a succession of visitors. "I had the curse, and was disturbed to find myself inwardly trembly and off balance, with lurking blacknesses in my thoughts for the first time in months,"[23] she wrote in her journal. When they were alone, she spoke to Donald about how deadlines were pressing on her and how necessary it was becoming to establish her own writing priorities. She also felt that he needed to begin *The Mechanical Angel*, his memoir about living in New York City during the twenties, a period he was determined to picture as he experienced it and not "in terms of raccoon coats, harmless hijinks, all that."[24] "I envy him for knowing what he wants to say, even if he hates his clumsiness in saying it," she had written in her journal, "because I myself have nothing at all to say."[25] She hastily decided to begin the Brillat-Savarin translation, "since I can ask for $1,500 when I consider it half done, and god knows we need the money,"[26] and try to complete *Not Now But Now* by November or December at the latest. She also retyped three unpublished stories she thought worth sending to Henry Volkening.

"I hope he is a good agent for me," Mary Frances wrote. "It is rather difficult to tell one that you are interested in writing for maga-

than she had for some time. Her years of night work at the defense
plant were over, and she had detached herself from the day-to-day
concerns at the Ranch. "I think it is very good for her morale to know
that I am overweight and that she looks slender and fit in slacks and
so on. That is all right, because I am still ahead."[29] At this point, the
fault lines in Mary Frances's marriage to Donald were still hidden,
and she was thrilled with her growing family. Her weight was another
issue and a lifelong preoccupation. After Kennedy's birth Dr. Bieler
had prescribed a diet of zucchini, yeast, and moderation in food and
alcohol for Mary Frances. But she was never as compliant as her doctor thought she was, and she justified her indulgences as fleeting
pleasures with Donald. To be sure, maternity had added a few more
inches to her measurements as well as some curves. But Man Ray's
photographs taken at this time show she was not obese, and mother-
hood had pleasantly softened her features.

Here Let Us Feast arrived a day before the Friedes went to the
Ranch for Thanksgiving. Mary Frances sent a copy to Powell and
thanked him for his help in procuring material for the collection. "I
have no feeling about it," she wrote, "except a profound relief that it's
done with. It was, for many unavoidable reasons, a tiring and even unpleasant task."[30] Nevertheless, the book was heralded as a "first," and
Kirkus Reviews predicted that readers would be delighted to find "almost more Fisher than selections."[31] Sheila Hibben's lengthy critique
in *Weekly Book Review* was an insightful assessment of an anthology
that avoided being the usual "lore of the table" kind of collection,
which either explained the origin of the word "sirloin" or described
the ordering of the Roman feast. "The present work," she said, "does
bring to the sentient reader an enduring sense of the significance of
food and drink so that one seems less to be reading a book than to be
engulfed in a tranquil memory (and maybe a promise) of good relations with the universe that might root us in deep enough to set us
growing again."[32] Reviews in *The New Yorker, San Francisco Chronicle,*
and *Los Angeles Times* were also positive.

In her broad sweep through the literature about feasting and
drinking in many lands and in many periods of time, Mary Frances
displayed a formidable command of the literature of gastronomy that
had been only hinted at in *Serve It Forth*. From the biblical story of

Eve and the apple, Charles Lamb's roasted pig, and Tobias Smollett's goose served with a sauce of pepper, lovage, coriander, mint, rue, anchovies, and oil, to Paul Bunyan's black duck dinner and *The Peterkin Papers* lady who put salt in her coffee, the selections are grace notes to the art of eating. What makes it especially pleasing is that it wears the prodigious research that went into it so lightly. Yet the depth of Mary Frances's understanding is evident throughout. In her extensive running commentary on the selections, she pays homage to the books that moved and influenced her since her childhood. It is M.F.K. Fisher's voice that the reader hears, and it is her deep feeling for the miracle of food and wine that transposes culinary history into personal narrative. Nevertheless, although Mary Frances thought the appearance of the book was attractive, after a hasty reading she said that she felt "sorry about this or that thing but in the main found it completely uninteresting . . . I hope it sells well . . . Certainly it is the last thing of its kind, the only one, that I shall ever do."[33]

That fall, the editors of *Glamour* magazine offered Mary Frances three hundred dollars for an article about Christmas parties that she described as "straight menu stuff," and although the money tempted her, she declined. "The main reason was not that I had gone against my firm resolve to stay clear of such tripe, but it was basically tactless of me to agree to so obviously disagreeable a job simply to make money while D [Donald] is not making it. I knew it depressed him. I was upset at my materialism, really."[34] In an effort to economize, she devised original Christmas gifts. Collecting Donald's old photographs, she organized them chronologically into an album, including the latest ones taken by Man Ray when he and his wife, Juliette, had visited them in October. Donald wanted the scrapbook to be his gift to Kennedy and Anna so that in later years they would appreciate his colorful life.

Mary Frances also planned to give edible gifts of cookies, "nice smelly ones like Pffernussen [sic]," to neighbors, friends, and family. What she did not mention in her journals were Donald's escapes from the communal baking sprees. As Norah mixed the cookie dough, Mary Frances whisked pans in and out of the oven, and the babies and Anna played on the kitchen floor, Donald's view of a domesticated Bareacres was the one reflected in his rearview mirror as he fled. Hollywood had become his refuge, and Mary Frances preferred not to dwell on his frequent trips there. At the same time, she bowed to family pressures to keep up appearances. This year Mary Frances had really wanted to avoid the usual tensions and spend Christmas at Bareacres with Donald, the children, the animals, and a little twinkling tree with a fire going in the fireplace and some champagne. But when Christmas Eve arrived, she simply could not refuse to be a part of the traditional celebration at the Ranch, and they drove to Whittier.

After the holidays were over, Mary Frances sent her novel to Covici, again questioning the value of her work. She also wrote one of her "not sent" letters to Rex, calling his attention to the fact that he had never acknowledged her latest book. The omission was typical, but nonetheless hurt her deeply. "I sent you and Mother the book almost two months ago, but you have never indicated in any way that you have seen it or even that it exists. This hurts me. I don't want you to say that you like it . . . but it would make me happy and encourage me to go on working if you would say, through Mother, or Norah or Sis, that you are proud of me for having finished a job against real difficulties. I have always felt that you considered me a little lazy or careless, and all the time I was slugging away to finish this last book I kept thinking how much it would please you to know that I could do what I set out to. What you think of me is one of the most important parts of my existence." As a postscript she wrote, "This letter obviously was not sent, but I keep it because it is part of the picture of my resentment of the basic fact that Father because of David's death has withdrawn from his other three children . . . It is a sad thing. He has no joy in us, and we in our turn find our love and respect turning to a sour mockery of respect and affection and the companionship we want, all of which could so well solace him, in part at least, for the abrupt break in a glass that might otherwise have stayed flawed and fearful for a long time."[35] It was the first time she acknowledged so openly that David's suicide had not only sent Edith into the seclusion of her room, where her health remained fragile, but had also alienated Rex from the rest of his family.

The next night Mary Frances had a dream that she retold in great detail in her journal. It was about a spontaneous visit from Edith, who was in finer form than either Mary Frances or Donald had ever seen her. They were all drinking white wine together, chatting gaily, and Edith was showing great interest in the memoir that Donald was writing. In the dream her mother's visit was so thoroughly delightful that Mary Frances kept telling herself "that this was a kind of summing-up of everything good and lovable in Mother, a sort of synthesis of all that I remembered with happiness in my whole life with her. I felt an actual physical sensation, a kind of glowing and throbbing, of happiness, and of thankfulness that Donald had had this chance to see her for what I basically love in her, beneath the old age and weakness and timidity of the present . . . and I thought it was wonderful that Donald could now see that Mother, in spite of her taciturn attitude toward our writing, was really very pleased about it."[36] At the end of the dream, Edith returned to Whittier, and a phone call from the Ranch brought news of her death. Oddly enough, Mary Frances said, she did not experience grief in the dream, but a kind of gratitude that her mother's gay living spirit had escaped from its wracked shell after validating their life and work. There might have been some connection between the dream and Mary Frances's suspense over the reception of her novel at Viking. The tension cannot have been eased by the fact that Houghton Mifflin had shied away from Donald's memoir. But Mary Frances's preoccupation with what she perceived to be her parents' disregard of her work predated her involvement with him, as did her longing for her parents' approval.

In mid-February, Mary Frances told Powell that she was working on the translation of Brillat-Savarin and continued to be astonished that all the gossips of the period were so close-mouthed about him. In her introduction she intended to speculate about why he didn't marry, what attracted him to his constant companion, Dr. Richerand, and why he kept his book a secret for so many years. "I'm getting really steamed up about the period, damn it, and may find myself caught in some sort of book about it."[37] The mystery surrounding Brillat-Savarin's career as a lawyer and the professorial persona that he adopted in his work interested her, as did his cousin by marriage, Juliette Récamier, whom he clearly admired and with whom he shared what Mary Frances coined "a refugee-mentality." During the Reign of Terror he was forced to flee from Belley to Switzerland, and then to America, where he earned a living playing in the orchestra of a New

York theater and giving violin lessons until the fall of Robespierre allowed him to return to France. His cousin, too, was banished from Paris by Napoleon and sought refuge on the shores of Lake Geneva in the salon of her friend Madame de Staël. Brillat-Savarin was a favorite guest at Juliette Récamier's soirees, suppers, and dinners, but in the crush of crowned heads and assorted political and social lions, he caused very little stir. All the while, however, he clearly thought his own thoughts about everything from the proper preparation of food to the subtle distinction between the pleasure of eating and the pleasures of the table.

Living with his thoughts and words, Mary Frances came to admire what she called his "stylish mind." "His teasing of priests, and his underplayed pleasure in them when they were good men of any cloth; his tenderness and irony toward pretty women, and his full enjoyment of them; his lusty delight in hunting, in a good row, in a cock-snoot at disaster . . . and the way he made all this plain to me, in a prose perhaps more straightforward than any that has come down to us from this verbose flighty period in French literature,"[38] justified all of her efforts. She firmly believed that his book was meant to live for more than a century, and her translation and glosses would contribute to that end.

Just as the original was written in what Mary Frances described as "straightforward prose," the glosses she wrote to accompany the text are well researched yet conversational, witty, and engaging. She was bold about taking on the extravagances of the Regency period and on the character of Brillat-Savarin's friends: "In my opinion there are too few ancients like Dr. Dubois," she wrote, "or perhaps that is but a sentimentalized theory of mine which would totter if I had to spend my days with some lip-smacking patriarch."[39] And when the professor launches into a discussion about fish, Mary Frances quotes a Japanese haiku in response, as the most meditative statement about fish that she has ever read.

To read the finished translation is to be aware of the continual distillation process in Mary Frances's writing. Many of Brillat-Savarin's ideas, distinctions, and even words reappear in her works. Some of the early articles she sketched out for the alphabet sequence in *Gourmet* also find their inspiration in his *Physiology of Taste*. Later

when she contemplated articles and even a book on the most important men in her life, she put Brillat-Savarin high on her list. And his
belief that "animals feed themselves; men eat: but only wise men
know the art of eating,"[40] gave her the title of her most critically ac-
claimed collection.

By mid-February, Covici returned her novel with a few suggestions
and much praise. She agreed to make final changes and send it back
to him as soon as possible. In her journal she noted her appreciation
for the publisher's apparent enthusiasm: "[It] pleases me in a rather
grudging un-reassuring way. I can't believe any book I could ever write
is as good as they say this is, and I keep thinking of the far day when
I may perhaps write something I myself will feel satisfied about and
nobody will like it but me."[41] Donald and Covici had pushed her into
writing the novel, and she herself hoped that a major studio would
purchase it, but the more compelling motive to turn from culinary
prose to fiction was probably Powell's "Quintet," a novel conceived as
the literary equivalent of a composition for five instruments or voices.
Its main character, a student at the University of Dijon, tells of his liaisons with five women: a fellow student, a friend of a friend, an older
woman visiting the university town, a woman he met in Cagnes-
sur-Mer, and a young British woman engaged to his cousin. What
connects the five parts of the book is the *train bleu*, the swift and legendary train that departs from Paris's Gare de Lyon for the south of
France and in the novel symbolizes the hero's inevitable leave-takings
over the period of his studies in Dijon. Powell had written the novel in
1941, and intended to use a letter from Henry Miller praising the
book as an afterword. Fay, however, objected to the publication of her
husband's youthful amours, and Powell, deferring to his wife's wishes,
withdrew it. Mary Frances admired the novel, "so honest, so straightforward, so good and reassuring as writing,"[42] although some of the
memories it brought back carried more pain than pleasure for her.
She advised Larry to put it aside if he must, but encouraged him to
publish it someday. She had never been too fond of Fay, and now
thought that she was doing an injustice to her husband. The novel
was eventually published as *The Blue Train*, but not until 1977.

There is no doubt that Powell's narrative strategy, a group of stories
tied together by a central character, a dominating symbol, and a merg-

ing of time past and time present, influenced Mary Frances. But unlike Powell's hero, Mary Frances's heroine herself moves through time and a series of conquests that leave her essentially unfulfilled. *Not Now But Now* begins and ends in the present, when four characters are introduced who have had encounters with Jennie in the past, each of which is explored in the four episodes that follow. Paul is Jennie's lover in Part I, competing with his father for Jennie's attentions in the superficial, bourgeois Lausanne of 1938. Part II begins in 1847, on the eve of France's Second Republic, when a penniless Jennie falls ill on a train bound for London and is rescued by the aristocratic Julia Collingworth, who employs her as a servant only to be betrayed by Jennie's theft and her consequent seduction of the butler. Part III takes place in 1927, in a small Ohio college town where the youthful Barbara becomes infatuated with Jennie, a visiting older woman of the world, to the despair of Barbara's boyfriend and father. And Sir Harry, who in Part IV is Jennie's paramour in post–Gold Rush San Francisco, 1882, is the wily horse breeder who callously shares his "filly" with several other men about town. Each of the four parts begins with a journey by rail, repeats the theme of seduction and betrayal, and reveals little more about the heroine than her capacity to subjugate and exploit. Although Jennie is called "our private Circe" by her four guests in the opening and closing scenes that frame the novel, she eventually slips away from them. As a symbol of the freedom Jennie seeks but cannot find, Paul, one of the quartet of fawning characters, introduces the four words "not now but *now*," which allow a parachutist the necessary second and a half to clear the plane before pulling the ripcord. Jennie never quite achieves liberty, and instead goes from one entanglement to another.[43]

When the novel was published at the end of July 1947, reviews were mixed at best. "Mrs. Fisher is an authority on cooking and eating," wrote John Farrelly in *The New Republic*. "This is her recipe for a novel: to a generous helping of ham and corn, add artificial color and artificial flavor. Beat the whole into a light fluff. Half bake."[44] In a gentler vein, J. W. Chase wrote in *The New York Times*, "It is not easy to convey the ironic charm with which Mrs. Fisher presents her stories. She has the sophistication to write simply with a minimum of affection. Her mockery is not jaundiced; she laughs with you at

Jennie but is careful to make you keep your distance. The dialogue
has a natural sparkle rarely found in a first novel. Mrs. Fisher loves
the flow of dresses, the intimacies of food. In the midst of such
praise, it is perhaps boorish to add that this novel is not without a serious blemish. The third tale, set in an Ohio college town, seems definitely out of place. Here Mrs. Fisher loses her sureness of touch, and
her characters bog down in a mire of unconvincing detail."[45] Part III,
the section of the book that had shocked, outraged, and upset some
of the people who were familiar with the manuscript, came in for the
most criticism. But as Hamilton Basso pointed out in his *New Yorker*
review, even if evil is ageless and some women like Jennie are its per-
sonification, there is nothing particularly novel in that concept. "And
since all that Mrs. Fisher brings to her treatment of it is a sort of brit-
tle preciousness, I think we can dismiss the whole thing. Quirk-
ishly."[46] Although there were the inevitable comparisons to Virginia
Woolf's *Orlando*, critics were also quick to point out that *Not Now
But Now* did not offer the same aesthetic and intellectual satisfaction.

If the newspaper and magazine reviews were not encouraging,
Covici and Donald, who hoped to sell the movie rights, supported her
effort. In answer to Powell's query about how much of herself she had
revealed in the novel, Mary Frances wrote:

> I don't reveal myself in this book any more than . . . I do in an
> article for *Harper's Bazaar*. Or in a page of translating Brillat-
> Savarin. And you can say that is completely. Or not at all. But
> whatever it is, it is naked. I'm glad you as *un vrai amateur* ap-
> preciated my occasional "betrayals" of my sex . . . Some day I'll
> write better, and you'll like it better. As for KA Porter and VW
> . . . they can and have and will and *ad eternitas* write rings
> around and around me. You know that, I want to be good, but I
> also want children and love and stress and panic and in the end
> I am too tired to write with the nun-like ascetic self-denial and
> concentration it takes. If I live to be fifty . . . ah, that is my song
> . . . if I live to be fifty, I'll know how to write a good book.[47]

But in her private journal she questioned, "can I write, should I write,
dare I write?"[48] Years later she dismissed the novel she had dedicated
to Donald as "a potboiler."[49]

In the meantime, Donald had sold one chapter of *The Mechanical Angel*, about the flop of "Antheil's *Ballet Mécanique*," to *Esquire*, and he was still sending the book to various publishers. Mary Frances was supporting their family with more than a little help from Rex. Increasingly unhappy about the situation, Donald began negotiations in late June for the position of story editor with the Ralph Blum Agency in Beverly Hills and sought to be released from his obligations to A. & S. Lyons. He was hired; shortly thereafter, he received the added fillip of a contract from Knopf for his memoir. In a flurry of activity, he commuted back and forth from Beverly Hills to Bareacres, and took longer trips to New York to line up his stable of writers for Blum. "While he is away," Mary Frances wrote to Powell, "I, loyal wife-and-mother, go up to Hollywood and try to find a house big enough for the four of us, Butch, all the manuscripts Donald will have to read and the authors he will entertain . . . and M.F.K. Fisher! What a rat-race!"[50] They planned to keep Bareacres open to escape the social whirl of Hollywood on weekends and spend time with the children.

With at least ten more weeks of hard work to complete the translation, and a book about Juliette Récamier in mind that she had not even mentioned to Volkening, Mary Frances dreaded the upheaval of the move to Hollywood. Yet she took the time to go through her journals and papers in preparation for the move, and destroyed the majority of them, saving only the Bern journals and a diary dated from the purchase of the Hemet property until Dillwyn's death in 1941. Reading over at least twenty-four years of entries and jottings, she questioned whether she made too much of aches and pains and whether her ramblings about her family relationships might give Anne, Norah, and her mother pain if they ever saw them. But the decision to destroy her papers had a deeper motivation. "I felt that my life as I had tried to live it up to that time was over . . . everything I had learned from Dillwyn and other good people must be put aside . . . I must readjust my ways of eating and drinking and feeling and behaving and thinking and judging . . . It is a wonder I did not sell Bareacres and have my hair dyed and give up M.F.K. Fisher and so on to make a completer change . . . So into the fire . . . Possibly I destroyed what might a hundred years from now make an absorbing story."[51] With deep misgivings, she borrowed a thousand dollars from Rex, although his finances were stretched because late that summer Edith had suffered a heart attack, and her hospital bills were considerable. With the money she rented a house in Cheviot Hills, near all the major studios, and purchased a new station wagon to facilitate moving their belongings from Hemet.

In every way, the six months that the Friedes lived in Cheviot Hills were a terrible mistake. Ralph Blum was a shrewd, successful, and in many ways unscrupulous businessman, who, although he offered Donald a handsome salary, also exacted long hours and total commitment. Donald's penchant for lavish entertaining, maids and nannies, and expensive getaways quickly strained their budget. Always a gracious hostess, Mary Frances was torn between arranging parties and dinners and trying to earn more money by writing for magazines. During September and October she was near collapse, but did not seek help because she did not want to make Donald's lot any worse than it was. Edith's health was also a concern. After almost two months in the hospital, she was home with an oxygen mask and two full-time nurses in residence at the Ranch. Norah, living in La Puente with her husband and son, bore most of the burden of keeping things going in Whittier until her second son, David, was born in November. Mary Frances tried to pick up the slack and visited her mother as often as she could. She also began to write a short, chatty letter to her mother every day, one aspect of his daughter's output that Rex was able to acknowledge: "I realize that you are aware that Edith reads your letters to me and I want you to know that . . . your daily letter to Edith has done much to convince her that she is still needed and desired by her family and I am inclined to believe has done more for her than the doctor's pills."[52] A welcome relief, but also another demand upon her time, was Georges Connes, who was a guest professor at the University of Buffalo that year and an occasional visitor.

Besieged by all of these disruptions, Mary Frances was still able to complete the Brillat-Savarin translation by the end of January 1948. "Here is a carbon of my foreword and afterword to the translation, which I think you might like to see," she wrote to Powell. "We are in turmoil, which I'll tell you about soon . . . are trying to figure *how* we can escape from this place to Bareacres, and still keep ourselves and the children even meagerly fed. We hate this town, most of the people in it, what it does to the few good ones including ourselves, what the climate does to our bodies, what the life does to *our* life, all very destructive . . . So . . . Turmoil. One thing: Donald is definitely out of the agency business, thanks to fantastic things, which you'll also hear from us. One thing about Life With Friede, there's never a dull moment!"[53]

Whether because of a single incident or a series of differences, Blum had fired Donald after the first of the year, and the Friedes frantically tried to sublet and vacate their Cheviot Hills house and return to Bareacres. By March 1, they loaded up the station wagon for the last time and escaped from the whole Beverly Hills scene, having lost more than $8,000 on the venture. Donald sold more articles to *Esquire*, and Mary Frances, through the efforts of Volkening, agreed to do an abecedary for twenty-four consecutive issues of *Gourmet*, beginning with the November 1948 issue. To add to their problems, the Hearnsbergers decided to leave the cottage at Bareacres and return to Arkansas. Mary Frances tried to juggle writing the *Gourmet* articles along with cooking, laundry, babies, and Donald's "falling to pieces." His condition was, she believed, the result of bad studio-commissary lunches, the Blum Agency disaster, and the return to Bareacres. When the Bielers visited them at the beginning of April, Donald's health was so precarious that Dr. Bieler took him back to the hospital in Pasadena when he and his wife left Hemet. Feeling too tired and jittery to remain at Bareacres alone with the children, Mary Frances drove to Whittier and stayed at the Ranch during the four weeks that Donald was hospitalized.

The months that followed were difficult. As Donald made a slow recovery, their debts mounted, and Mary Frances frantically tried to churn out the *Gourmet* articles. A dispute broke out with Macy over the Brillat-Savarin translation, which he had planned to publish in late 1948 or early 1949, accompanied by Sylvain Sauvage's handsome illustrations. But when Macy discovered that Mary Leonard Pritchett had arranged for two long excerpts and glosses from the book to be published in *Gourmet* at around that time, he threatened to halt publication. Ultimately, excerpts from the translation, without Mary Frances's accompanying glosses, were published in the August and September 1948 issues of the magazine, and the breach of contract dispute was resolved, but the squabble heightened the tension between Mary Frances and Pritchett, and the unpleasant exchange of letters with Macy exacerbated the stress Mary Frances was under.

Nevertheless, Mary Frances completed the *Gourmet* magazine ABC series in August. Almost immediately she began to revise and enlarge the articles for possible publication as a book, all the while despairing that hack stuff was her lot. She had written the series under great pressure, telling Covici, "The more hastily and more carelessly I write stuff for magazines, the more quickly it is snapped up and paid for. This does not add to my respect for the present state of The Western Word."[54] When Covici visited Bareacres for the first time later that month, he suggested another novel, but Mary Frances rejected the idea, and decided to pursue the biography of Juliette Récamier instead. "I am going to write my own peculiar version of Madame Récamier! No American woman has ever done it, as far as I know . . . and that proud beauty was such a sexual and intellectual enigma that I'd love to put my own questions up to her . . . Did she or *didn't* she with everyone from Napoleon to . . . to . . . to . . . ? If not, why and how not? It means a hideous lot of work . . . all those refugees wrote letters like mad . . . Madame de Staël and so on."[55] Covici liked the idea.

Although the advance that Viking offered for the biography was unusually generous, Mary Frances applied for a Guggenheim Foundation grant as well. In the application she listed her achievements and stated that she "had established [herself] in a limited, and, fortunately for [her] a sparsely inhabited field of upper-class comment on the pleasures of the table."[56] She set forth her plan to do a "highly personal portrait" of Récamier as the "archetype of intellectual-cum-sexual refugee," comparing it with the refugee mentality of the current postwar world. She wanted to turn away from obligations, forget contracts and commitments and descriptions of "perfect buffet-luncheons"; more to the point, she wanted some ease from the tyranny of her checkbook balance.

During the fall of 1948, Mary Frances took up her journal again. Influenced by the "deep-shadowed aspect of autumn" on the hills, she noted that during the months of August, September, and even October she seemed to undergo

an annual period of inner restlessness and often of outer chaos. Last year it was the Blum affaire, with all its dreadful danger-

ous futility and waste, and me powerless to do anything. Then
there was the mounting tragedy of Dillwyn's end, so long ago,
in August, and my own senseless flight to Mexico, all that. Before then there was Anne's birth . . . I mean, going backwards
. . . looking from here to then . . . and our moving from NY to
God knows what kind of life Donald would find in Bareacres
. . . then ten years ago yesterday, that September in Berne
when the Munich Pact was signed, Dillwyn pinned to a bed by
the stump of his little leg . . . and two years after that (what
confusion I can make with a calendar, but in my mind it is
clear) the hunt through southern California for a place to hide,
and the sight of this hillside where I would like to spend most
of my remaining days, then to die here. Yes this time of year is
the heaviest for me upon my soul.[57]

In a candid letter to Covici, Mary Frances spelled out her situation at Bareacres. A local couple were now living in the cottage, so
she had babysitting and some household chores taken care of for five
and a half days a week. Donald, recently recovered from his latest
bout with gastric pain, was growing increasingly restless, and New
York beckoned as the only place where he might find employment. Although it seemed that their present situation could not continue
much longer, a move to New York, where it cost a fortune to live and
to educate and clothe the children, seemed financially irresponsible
to her, and she objected. On October 25, 1948, Donald was again admitted into the hospital in Pasadena. This time Dr. Bieler was not op-
timistic about his condition, which he was beginning to fear was more
psychological than physical. Mary Frances could send only partial
payment for Bieler's continued services. She scrambled to send pieces
off to *House Beautiful* and even spent two days researching an article
on a new kind of sanatorium for young women with mental problems
that had opened near Whittier. She had neither the time nor the energy for any serious work on the Récamier biography.
    Somehow they managed to get through the holidays, but after the
first of the year Donald decided to go to New York for a change of
scene and to scout out possible jobs in publishing. He returned after
little more than a month, disillusioned and bored with the people he

hospitals, rest-homes, and honor system booby-hatches—and you really have cause for crises.[62]

The letter was a litany of all the troubles he had brought to Mary Frances, not least a problem with erectile dysfunction that she had suspected before they married. The admission was sincere, but at this point, too late.

Donald left the Ranch to seek further treatment in New York and implied to Covici and their other friends that Mary Frances and the children would soon join him. "No, it doesn't sound strange that you thought the children and I might come east," Mary Frances wrote to Covici. "But we can't, for a long time I imagine . . . although I know it would be good for me, as a writer and a person too, to be able to talk with you and one or two other people. This is a peaceful place, and one I love, and I can rest and lick my wounds here (after four years of pretty destructive and active combat!) . . . I want to work hard on Récamier this autumn and winter . . . I am oppressed by how much I owe Viking, and once I have paid it off I'll never allow myself to accept such large advances again . . . I like the Bileck illustration on the very nice little excerpt from the Alphabet . . . and thank you for letting me see the *Kirkus* review, which sounded fine."[63]

An Alphabet for Gourmets was released in July 1949, handsomely illustrated with Marvin Bileck's drawings. Mary Frances dedicated it to Hal Bieler, "who has taught me more than he meant to about the pleasures of the table." This wonderful abecedary offered a kaleidoscopic view of the experiences and influences that dominated Mary Frances's life in the mid-1940s. From "A Is for Dining Alone" (a replay of living in Hollywood) to "Z Is for Zakuski," which draws on the memories of "a man [Donald Friede] I know, who spent his boyhood in St. Petersburg," meals, recipes, and bits of Brillat-Savarin's sage advice cunningly come together.

Kirkus Reviews hailed it as "a merry, sometimes biting, often passionate defense of a lover's approach to food—any kind of food,"[64] and a philosophical chat about eating and drinking. The *San Francisco Chronicle* observed that it was "no cookbook in spite of the recipes it contains"; instead, it was a book filled with "shrewd observations and luscious memories."[65] And probably to Mary Frances's delight, because she read and reread his books, the *New York Times* reviewer, Rex Stout, wrote: "Since Mrs. Fisher wrote it, naturally it is witty, pungent and highly civilized, but also it has a special charm. It tells of the bad as well as the good. It tells how to scramble eggs with love and wisdom, and it also tells how to scramble them with ignorance and rancor. It describes the finest meal the author ever ate, and it also describes the most ghastly one. It not only guides and titillates; it warns."[66] But there were also danger signals. In *Commonweal*, Kappo Phelan reviewed the book with the caution: "Mrs. Fisher's present volume will seem somewhat disappointing, I think, to her long-term public, but it is surely intriguing enough to send any new reader back to the more substantial books."[67] And in a brief comment, *The New Yorker* noted that "in spite of an aura of not really unpleasant smugness about the book, it is an entertaining and knowledgeable one, well written whenever the author is not self-consciously turning out a beautiful paragraph."[68]

In mid-July, with her advance on the Récamier biography spent, her application for a Guggenheim grant rejected, and more than $24,000 in debt, Mary Frances wrote to Covici that she could not possibly set even a tentative date for the completion of the biography. She simply did not have the peace of mind or the time to write the kind of book that she felt it must be. She noted that she had written four long-overdue articles for *House Beautiful* in five days, and that the editor had responded that he wanted six more as soon as possible. Magazine writing kept food on the table. Meanwhile, with the recent departure of the latest caretakers from Bareacres, she was again temporarily without relief from household duties.

In August, Donald checked himself into the Harkness Pavilion in New York. By September, Mary Frances was very near a nervous breakdown herself. Dr. Bieler suggested she see a psychiatrist immediately. She spoke to one of Donald's doctors, who referred her to a Los Angeles psychiatrist named Dr. George Frumkes. In late September she wrote, "I had three interviews with Dr. Frumkes. He feels, and I agree with him, that an analysis would do me a great deal of good. I have decided, however, that unless I grow much worse, it will be best for me to put off this long, expensive, and absorbing task for several months."[69] She also thought that Dr. Frumkes' plan to see her every week was too difficult to consider and that the drive to Los Angeles and back (300 miles) was prohibitive. Between short periods of depression and physical trembling, she entertained the idea of moving from Hemet to San Francisco in order to put the children into better public schools and to be able to work without the demands of Bareacres. If she did this, she would arrange for psychiatric care there. In a subsequent visit to Dr. Frumkes, she told him that she had even interviewed with George Cukor about returning to Hollywood as a scriptwriter. After a few more sessions with Dr. Frumkes, Mary Frances invited Rex and her sister Anne to Bareacres for the weekend and explored the possibility of moving to the Ranch, where she could help Rex manage the household, put the children in good schools, and be able to see Dr. Frumkes on a regular basis. She also sought Gloria and Arthur Sheekman's advice about moving back to Whittier to care for her father. As Gloria remembered it, they were unanimous in saying that she had no choice, that she must do it for him and for herself.[70]

Meanwhile, Donald could not face the reality of his separation from Mary Frances. He again proposed that she and the children move to New York, or that he return to Whittier and live with Rex, or that he return to Bareacres, but by this time Mary Frances had arrived at a decision with Dr. Frumkes' help. When she wrote to Donald on October 17, her letter was a point-by-point answer to the many solutions that Donald had raised, and a rejection of all of them. It also was a frank statement of the problems inherent in their marriage from the beginning. "I am in a state very much like combat fatigue," she said:

> The symptoms began a few days after our marriage, when you told me that you could not and would not make love in "normal ways." (That was your first great mistake, not to tell me that, and not to make love at all, until we were legally married. Did you perhaps think I was too naive ever to realize it?) Your arrest, about a month after our marriage, and your bland acceptance of my savings to buy you out, so that your mother did not need to be disturbed, added to my desperation. The first week we were married I almost walked out the door in Atlantic City,

but I was too proud and too conscious of all the people who had begged me not to be foolhardy enough to marry you. The fourth week I almost walked out of the window. But I was still proud, and too conscious of how much further I could hurt people I loved.[71]

They had good moments together, she conceded, but she simply could not cope with his compulsive escapes from Bareacres, from unpaid bills, from responsibilities, and from reality. For the first time she mentioned a divorce. She was seriously considering the possibility that she could make a decent home for Rex and could give the children a father figure whom they already thought "holds up the sky" if she went to live at the Ranch.

On November 7, Mary Frances informed Donald, "I have decided to move for a time to the Ranch . . . I'll put Anna in the school I went to, a very good rich country school whose bus stops at the gate. I'll put Kennedy, two or three mornings a week, in an excellent pre-school in Whittier . . . I feel that within a month I'll have time to work . . . and that's what I want to do."[72] Three days later, Mary Frances began her first "trek" westward with the children and some of their belongings.

With her third marriage coming to an end, Mary Frances managed some time in UCLA's Clark Library, where she tried to advance her research on the Récamier biography, and during November she spent Sunday mornings there proofreading her translation of Brillat-Savarin without interruption. There she saw Powell, whose marriage to Fay was under strain because of his numerous infidelities. The two friends, who had known each other since their student days, found each other in a new and unexpected way. As Powell described it in his "MF: A Reminiscence," "Our relationship was of giving, not taking. No demands were made; everything was freely given. We were spared the destructive emotions that often trouble relationships as close as ours."[73] The "magical Autumn" that Powell occasionally referred to in letters was fleeting and commemorated simply in a framed print called *The Venus of Cyrene* that he gave Mary Frances after their one night together in the fall of 1949.

Some of Mary Frances's letters directly or indirectly refer to their brief affair, and for a time her epistolary closing, "Love to you all," changed to "Love." In her more romantic moments, she entertained the idea of spending the month of November at Bareacres with Powell, and wrote, "I would give much, and when I use that word, I mean it, to have the month happen . . . a kind of completion, a full swing of the planets. But I do not see it in actuality."[74] Except for luncheon dates when both were at the library, and Powell's occasional visits to the Ranch for dinner with Mary Frances, Rex, Anna, and Kennedy, he and Mary Frances never spent an extended period of time together. Instead they continued to correspond as they had always done, never resuming the intimacy they had shared during that "magical Autumn."

In December, Mary Frances wrote to her uncle Ted that she and the children were "in residence at the Ranch." During the past month, she had fired the hired help because she suspected that the housekeeper was operating a brothel in the cookhouse, and had engaged responsible people to clean and cook. Repairmen were brought in to make some necessary changes and repairs. Nourished by her cooking, Rex had gained several pounds. In a sense she had traded the care of one man for the care of another, a "frail, brave, stubborn man dying of fibrosis of the lungs," but it was an exchange she resolutely made.

NINE

Now an Orphan

(1949–1953)

I'm truly sorry about your father . . . not for him so much as for you. Are
you now an orphan? I think so. And I know that it has nothing to do with
being old or young. The feeling of being alone in the world without anyone to hang on to the way one does with a mother or father is odd indeed, and quite indescribable.[1]   —M.F.K. Fisher

Living in Whittier again meant that Mary Frances was not only returning to her youngest years, but also depending upon two little children and an aged father for companionship and, as she put it,
"whatever love she would get."[2] Moving to the Ranch also distanced
her from the home she and Dillwyn had created together, the place
where the spirits, and literally the ashes, of her "one true love" and of
her brother and mother dwelled, and the setting of the last troubled
months of her failed third marriage. Whittier, by contrast, resonated
with memories of Rex, Anne, and Norah, and the life she had left
twenty years earlier. "For a long time I did not realize that I was here,
really. Then I began to protest, and gave myself a rough year or so,
filled with black moments of panic and despair."[3]

In her various letters to family and friends during those early
weeks at the Ranch, Mary Frances omitted mentioning that she was
experiencing anxiety attacks and physical symptoms like sweating,
nausea, and dizziness. Instead, she focused on the "housekeeper,
nurse, chauffeur" role she played more or less convincingly. "I have no
rosy feeling of filial nobility about this," she wrote to Donald. "There

are many benefits to me . . . but the main thing is that I can see that Rex lives the winter with the dignity and decency he wants and Edith wanted for him . . . It will be good to be near Norah, too, and perhaps help her a little with the pregnancy."[4] In a surge of enthusiasm she wrote about refurbishing the interior of the now run-down family home and adapting it to the needs of her father, daughters, and herself. Rex moved into the two-room suite on the first floor that Edith had occupied during her long illness. Six-year-old Anna and three-year-old Kennedy inherited the upstairs master bedroom as a playroom and bedroom. Mary Frances decorated the second-floor North Room in shades of hunter green and used it as a combined bedroom-office. She straddled rolls of wallpaper and balanced paint buckets, made new curtains, decorated the porches with plants, and even spruced up the guesthouse. She was able to hire women to cook, do laundry, and clean, and eventually she found a couple to care for the house and garden.

Hoping to dispel some of Rex's loneliness, she entertained his friends and invited her own to the Ranch. It pleased her to see her father eat with interest and even gusto again. She had long observed the difference between what she called "matrimonial gastronomy"—that is, the dinners of meat, potatoes, vegetables, dessert, and coffee that Rex usually ate at home to please Edith—and the way he ate away from home or when he was at Bareacres. And while his breakfast ritual of grapefruit juice (made by pouring boiling water over chopped fruit and letting it stand all night), one egg with ham or bacon, two slices of toast with marmalade, and two cups of coffee never varied, Mary Frances teased his palate with curries, game, stuffed fowl, and casseroles.

Donald was conspicuously absent from the Thanksgiving table that year. He had recently established himself in San Francisco, and although he had assured Mary Frances that he was completely well and eager to earn his living by reading manuscripts for a fee, she had resolutely refused his request to resume their life together either in New York, at Bareacres, or in San Francisco until he was financially able to support them. For several months, despite an occasional visit, the relationship hung in limbo, with Donald repeatedly professing his love for Mary Frances and the children and his wish to be a reliable husband and provider, and Mary Frances torn between guilt over denying her children a father and her conviction that Donald's track record of irresponsibility would persist. Their letters to each other, often referred to by Donald as an "Alphonse and Gaston act," devolved from polite inquiries, earnest promises, and professed love to a bitter sequence of accusations, rebuttals, and reminders of past failures. "This is NOT Alphonse and Gaston, Chub," she wrote. "I'm NOT being polite and noble and so on. I am not a wife to you in any sense of the word, at this point, nor are you a husband to me. If the situation is for any reason too distasteful to you, or actively impossible, you have only to say so, for I have told you frankly that I think it is much more likely to prove so to you than to me."[5] Having decided against his request for an extended visit at Christmas, Mary Frances set her preconditions for a reconciliation: Donald would have to remain both physically and mentally healthy and draw a salary that would support herself and the children for a year. Both knew that Donald's ability to meet her demands was unlikely.

In response to Donald's offer to live in Whittier and "share her burdens," Mary Frances wrote: "In return for steady and conscientious (and loving) attention to the welfare of this Ranch I am getting rent and good board for three people." She received a hundred dollars a month from her mother's estate, which did not quite cover the upkeep of Bareacres and insurance. Extras like clothing, excursions with Anna and Kennedy, and incidentals were entirely dependent on royalties and fees from the articles she sold. She had to borrow from Rex to pay for doctors' bills and unexpected expenditures. But she thought the present situation was preferable to the increasing indebtedness she experienced during her marriage to Donald and his dismissal of what he considered to be her "bourgeois" preoccupation with bills. "When we married," she wrote to him, "I had about $4000 in my checking account, over $5000 in bonds, about $2000 in stocks, and no debts. In the four years of our marriage I earned quite a lot, here and there . . . large royalties, good sales to magazines, all that. I also signed notes to my parents for almost $20,000, and borrowed from Viking. We also borrowed over $2000 from your mother for your last illness . . . that is I borrowed that: I don't know how much more she advanced you. All this is gone."[6]

She concluded, "Do you think that because I spend some 18 hours a day caring for two rapidly developing and strong willed little girls and an old and crotchety man who spits and clicks his dentures I am not lonely? Do you ever imagine that at times I don't envy you your snug little map-lined room, the freedom of your prowlings, the insouciance of your social life, your mental life, your gastronomical life? Let's get this straight."[7] She was referring to Donald's well-established pattern of renting a comfortable room in a small hotel, furnishing it according to his taste, and taking his meals in carefully selected restaurants where the head waiters knew his preferences in tables, food, and wines. By the time this letter was written in January 1950, Donald had already settled into a residential hotel in San Francisco and had engaged in several discussions with the *San Francisco Chronicle* book critic Joseph Henry Jackson and authors like Lewis Mumford about starting his own literary agency. He was even exploring the possibility of a book review television show on KRON, a local station.

While Donald's letters exuded enthusiasm over his restored health—"I am to-day, a healthier and more alert man than I have ever been in my life—and in every way, including mental health. I am capable of anything which should be attempted by a man of my age [forty-eight], and of many things which most men of my age could not attempt, and I look good, too"[8]—Mary Frances was less forthright about her present condition:

> Physically I am full of energy and a fairly constant sense of well-being. I have lost about 22–25 pounds, which I badly needed to do. I eat as simply as possible, drink just as simply, smoke about three cigarettes a week, and sleep with comparative ease. Emotionally I am for the most part stable, with now and then a very faint hint of fluttery nerves if I become upset or over tired. My last period of shakiness, with absolutely no morbid compulsions, was the week preceding my move up here. It was partly because of that move and my basic unwillingness to make it, but mostly because of the engagement I had made to be star-speaker at the Shakespeare Club in Pasadena. So much had happened to my strength of will or

mind or whatever you'd call it, that I was in a real funk, completely unsure of myself. It went off beautifully.[9]

Another boost to her professional self-esteem was the publication of *The Physiology of Taste*. The deluxe slipcased edition of Brillat-Savarin's masterpiece, which cost twenty-five dollars, was sent to 1,500 members of the Limited Editions Club on Christmas Eve, 1949. It was widely hailed as the first translation of the gastronomical classic published in America in the twentieth century, and it was widely praised. Craig Claiborne in *The New York Times* said Fisher's prose perfectly captured the wit and gaiety of the book and lauded the hundreds of marginal glosses that M.F.K. Fisher added to elucidate the text. The Heritage Club, part of the same ownership, followed up with a five-dollar edition, less elegantly bound and without slipcase, available to its members in January. Macy promised bookstore sales in the spring of 1950.

Revisiting *The Physiology of Taste* in 1988, Mary Frances wrote, "It seems odd that I continue to speak of it with such apparent conceit as the best translation available in the English language, but I know without any cavil that this is true. I'm equally aware that before long my translation will sound as odd and archaic as does the original French, and that a newer and better one will come along. This is as it should be. It pleases me that whoever has the next try at this will have my translation to refer to than any others I have read. They are scholarly enough, but sadly inadequate."[10]

Early in January, Mary Frances began to see Dr. Frumkes on a regular basis. At his request she wrote up her family and clinical history, in which she outlined her three marriages and publishing record. The account was straightforward as far as it went, but the omissions, especially about her love affairs, and her relationships with her parents and sisters, were significant. She said that she had been "a very easy-minded child . . . but given to emotional reactions to family upheavals, usually in the form of throat aches . . . after about my 15th year I was moody and miserable, and when I was about 18 I developed severe monthly headaches, which the family doctor dosed with strong medicines, instead of trying to cure the constipation which had afflicted me since about my fifth or sixth year."[11] When she and Al returned to Laguna in the early 1930s, she recounted, she had experienced fluctuating moods and "a mild form of discontent," and had confided to Powell she feared she might lose her mind. It was after Dillwyn's suicide, however, that she had felt a frantic desire to shoot herself for about a year and then briefly again just before Anna was born.

She told Dr. Frumkes that before going to New York City in 1945, she "literally went to pieces, perhaps from boredom . . . I shook, and sobbed, and wanted to sleep all the time. In New York I was all right, very solid emotionally, until Donald was arrested and sent to California to testify, when I realized that I was frightened of being near windows in tall buildings, frightened of being alone in the apartment with the baby. I got a night nurse while he was gone. Things went quite well until after Kennedy was born, when I spent many moments of desperate depression . . . not suicidal, just hopeless." There were a few recurrences, fairly fleeting, she said, of the wish to escape.[12] Since June 1949, however, she confessed that she had lived very precariously, never knowing when a wave of nausea, trembling, and panic would seize her. Her mother's decline over a period of seven years, Donald's hospitalizations and breakdown over the past two years, and her still-vivid memories of Dillwyn's three years of suffering had brought on physical symptoms that she could neither cope with nor explain. She was forty-one years old, and she had simply seen and felt too much pain.

At first, discussions about her separation from Donald and her panic attacks dominated the sessions. She talked about her reluctance to tell Donald of her intention to divorce him, and said that although she really did not think that he was suicidal, she herself could not possibly face the end of a third marriage. Probing deeper, she began to admit that her unwillingness to say what she wanted was probably another instance of her "vanity," her wish to appear good and unselfish and sparing of other people. She thought that if she were childless, she might try to make a good life with Donald again, but now she saw more clearly than ever that he "warred" against the children for her attention, "for my protective and constructive love as well as my unwearied sexual energies." If a choice had to be made between the well-being of the children she loved and her partnership with Donald, she knew she must put the children first. Dr. Frumkes repeatedly cautioned her about Donald's ability to play on her vulnerabilities, and she adopted his take on this and on many other issues. Typically after an appointment with him, she drove back to Whittier reviewing the session in her mind, and frequently she wrote letters to him relating the thoughts and reactions that a particular visit set in motion. If and when he answered at all, his letters were brief and professional, and he consistently declined to accept her invitations to visit Bareacres or socialize in any way.

Mary Frances entered some of her reactions to sessions with Dr. Frumkes in her journal, along with notes on everyday occurrences. She also outlined her strategies to avoid waking up in a panic. She said that she played music, took long baths, and calmed herself with a whiskey and water. "If I have trouble in the night I may make myself get up and write it away, for a new trick," she said. "The other night Anna said when I put her to bed, 'Work tonight, Dote . . . I love to hear the machine going . . .' And I thought about how when she was three or maybe four days old I carried her in a basket across the great gray house in Altadena and typed for a long time with her on the floor beside me."[13] Through her long struggle with panic attacks, nightmares, unreasonable fears, and self-doubt, the compulsion to write, whether in her journal or letters or for publication, never eluded her for long.

On February 9, 1950, Julia Louise Friede died, leaving her son a considerable inheritance. Donald's newfound solvency, along with a firm commitment to host a TV show called *The Book*, caused him to press more vigorously for a reconciliation. In March he arrived at the Ranch for a "fiesta" weekend, bearing fans from Chinatown for the children and his mother's mink coat and pearls for Mary Frances. "It was a difficult weekend . . . the poor devil landed neck-deep in the worst possible situation here, in many ways," she wrote to Covici. "He is emotionally and perhaps constitutionally unfitted to family brouhaha, and my cook quit and my very pregnant sister [Norah] arrived with two small unruly sons, and her husband, loathed publicly by Donald as only Donald can loathe publicly, came later."[14] Somehow they all behaved civilly, and during the four days of Donald's visit he and Mary Frances actually arrived at the point of discussing how to divorce as quietly and cheaply as possible. Mary Frances would not request alimony, and Donald would establish trust funds for the children's care and education. Donald, however, had not really given up his cause, and was determined to wear down what he considered to be Mary Frances's stubbornness and unreasonableness. He was also reluctant to abandon his role of paterfamilias. In his own way he took pride in his children; he collected their drawings, and loved showing them off at the ice cream parlor and the circus.

At the Ranch, the children seemed somewhat insulated from their parents' problems. Unlike Bareacres, where there was a threat of a snake under every rock, the Ranch offered freedom and a great shaded yard, a cookhouse and guesthouse to play in, and fences to climb. Anna, with a kitten clinging to each shoulder, would often peer into the pigpen to find her favorite piglet. Although Anna usually played the princess, Kennedy the big bad wolf, the girls were easy in each other's company.[15] When Donald visited, he slept in the bedroom at the end of the corridor, and the girls would wake him up in the morning by jumping into his bed. If their mother experienced bouts of nausea or panic, they were unaware of them. And if they broached an indelicate topic at table or engaged in tattletale chatter, they heard the same words their mother had heard during the years of her growing up. "Do you smell the jasmine?"

"I love those little people,"[16] Mary Frances wrote, and reproached herself for being irritable with them or for talking to Anna as if she were older than she was. As for Kennedy, she had redeemed the terrible mistake of Mary Frances's marriage to Donald. "I solace myself with the wonderful knowledge of Kennedy's existence," she told Covici. "She is as solid as marble, or steel, or whatever's solid. I'll keep her that way, through hell itself, and not let her be spoiled by money, nor pampered. She already has a true sense of reality."[17]

In late March, Norah moved her family to the Ranch from their home in La Puente before her third son, Matthew, was born. During Norah's hospitalization in Pasadena, Mary Frances drove Rex and Norah's children to Bareacres for a weekend, but Rex's fatigue and worsening lung congestion made their holiday there difficult, as did the discovery that several things of value were missing from the house. The evidence pointed to the overseer Mary Frances had hired, and the theft reinforced the impracticality of maintaining the property from Whittier. Up to this point, Mary Frances had resisted making any decisions about Bareacres, to which she imagined retreating when the children were grown. Now she took steps to store some of her things and began to think seriously about renting the main house, reserving the upper floor of the garage and the cottage for her own use.

In the early days of summer, Mary Frances wrote an article on San Francisco restaurants for the *San Francisco Chronicle*. She also decided to revise *How to Cook a Wolf*, writing a new peacetime or Cold War introduction and adding marginal notes, footnotes, and a section of additional recipes. She thought that the revision would take about a month to six weeks of intensive work. Explaining her decision to Covici, she wrote, "The truth about my current revision of the *Wolf* is that I am incapable of any other kind of work at this point. It can be done in snatches. Even if I felt ready to do a sustained piece of thinking-and-writing, which I do not, it would be impossible here, with the present domestic set up."[18] She could not summon either the energy or the desire to come to grips with the Juliette Récamier biography.

Her bracketed notes to *How to Cook a Wolf* turn it into a kind of conversation with herself and counterpoint the wry humor of the first, "wartime" edition. Revisiting the goodness of soup, she adds, "As a matter of fact, soup is even better, in my gastronomy, than it was nine years ago. This is due partly to my increased knowledge of its ever-changing structure, and partly to my own increased age. A good hot broth is more welcome now, and will be more so in yet another decade . . . or two or three!"[19] She added a recipe for *petits pois à la française*, acknowledging the classic version and emphasizing that she fit the ways to the means by using mediocre frozen peas and, with silent resignation, a head of tasteless "Alaska" lettuce and salted instead of sweet butter if more convenient, and the results always pleased her. Perhaps the most enlightening "noggins" of wisdom found in the revised text were related to her own experience as a mother teaching her children "to eat with thought." "I feel, even more strongly than I did in 1942," she wrote, "that one of the most important things about a child's gastronomical present, in relation to his future, gastronomical and otherwise, is a good *respect* for food. It horrifies me to see contemporary mothers numbly cooking and then throwing away uneaten lamb chops, beans, toast; mussed but un-savored puddings; deliberately spilled or bedabbled milk. I think children should be given small portions of food, according to their natures, and allowed to cope with them at their own speeds, but fin-ish them, before more is trotted out in the currently fashionable pedi-atric pattern . . . They learn their capacities. They learn good manners. Above all, they learn to respect the food so many other chil-dren cry for."[20]

Interjected asides like "Do I really know?," "Is it important?," and "How arbitrary can you be?" convey the impression that she is think-ing about the matter, revisiting her original observation or recipe, and permitting the reader to overhear her solitary musings. Her new "Conclusion" repeats a familiar theme, that "since we must eat to live, we might as well do it with both grace and gusto."[21] The enduring message of *How to Cook a Wolf* is the will to survive, whether in wartime or in the battle with old age or in a *crise de nerfs*. At a time when Mary Frances was desperately seeking ways to find both physi-cal and mental stability herself, the revision of the book kept M.F.K. Fisher in print.

Although she still experienced panic attacks, under Dr. Frumkes' guidance she gradually learned to read the danger signals and adopt ways to talk herself out of her black moments. If they occurred while driving, she turned in at the nearest gas station and distracted herself by buying gas. If she felt that being alone at the Ranch would be dangerous, she kept Kennedy home from preschool and reassured herself by patting her little girl's cheek and playing games with her. "Physically I notice, as I go to the kitchen for apple-juice for Mary [Kennedy], that my knees feel wobbly, and that my cheeks are flushed," she told Dr. Frumkes. "I drank a glass of Vermouth while I was writing this letter to you . . . It is whistling in the dark, all right . . . I *will not* think of future trouble . . . I *will* touch Mary's solid lit-tle cheek to reassure and give me courage . . . I *will* be fine again by noon, and make a pleasant lunch for her and Rex . . . I can be strong like that as long as I am not in the clutches of one of these horrible *physical* manifestations of whatever it is that is troubling me. Then I am, almost but not quite helpless. And it is the fear of suddenly being *really* helpless that apparently haunts me."[22]

Her sessions with Dr. Frumkes progressed from dealing with her ongoing issues with Donald to her compulsion to write, her self-doubts, and her former relationship with Dillwyn. Possibly reflecting Dr. Frumkes' 1950s-era psychoanalytic bent, she concluded, "Dillwyn was life for me. Life is sex, and sex life. Now Dillwyn is dead. Therefore sex, which is also life, is dead or at least means death. I want Dillwyn, but cannot have him. I want sex, since I am still alive. But if sex means death to me, at times I want death."[23] She told Frumkes that she would welcome death, but her sense of responsibility to her children was too keen and would always prevent a self-destructive act on her part. She entertained other insights into her relationship with Dillwyn, including the possibility that she may have actually hated him without knowing it. Although she had always felt that he had been a completely satisfying lover, he had been sterile and unable to give her a child. For the first time, she considered that he had been everything to her and yet "in the most primitive way, *nothing*."

Mary Frances doubted whether passing affairs could be a viable choice in her present circumstances. On one occasion, she had asked Rex if he minded her entertaining Harold Price at the Ranch, and he had told her in no uncertain terms that as a still-married woman he thought she was "being completely indiscreet, stupid, and a little maniacal to think of such a thing . . . It made me feel like the cook being dressed down by the butler, which is perhaps what he intended."[24] She also expressed distaste for the hurried, furtive, and unsatisfying gropings that went on whenever "the Librarian," Larry Powell, visited. She also confessed to Dr. Frumkes that Powell's failure to see her before his recent departure for a year abroad had hurt her more than she cared to admit. She longed for the attention of educated, intelligent men and their witty, urbane conversation, and lovemaking that expressed connoisseurship. "I honestly would rather have *nothing* than a hectic taste."[25]

Sensing her vulnerability, Donald, now the successful host of his own TV show, wrote glowingly about a small house he had discovered for sale on Nob Hill that would be perfect for the four of them plus a full-time maid. He repeatedly invited Mary Frances to visit him in San Francisco and sought ways to see her and the children at the Ranch, while at the same time managing to elude Mary Frances's lawyer when he tried to go over details of the divorce settlement. Conveniently, when Rex was rushed to the hospital with pneumonia at the end of July, Donald was spending a weekend at the Ranch and was a great help. Mary Frances found herself reconsidering her course of action, until she reminded herself that "I distill the same poison for him that he does for me."[26] She and her lawyer appeared before a judge on August 8, 1950, and an interlocutory decree of divorce was granted, to become final a year later.

Having resolved at least that issue gave Mary Frances new strength. She took a short "sabbatical" from her sessions with Dr. Frumkes, and experienced an intense desire to work again. But when Covici invited her to visit him and his family in New York, she regretfully declined. She told him that she felt more confident and energetic than she had for some time, although she added, "Often I feel bitterly lonely, and now and then I feel frightened at being 42 and flat broke, and occasionally I feel dismayed at the sorry state of my professional standing, and once in a while, in fact very often, I feel bored as hell to be doing nothing but household chores and baby-tending and father-tending instead of traveling-theatre-parties."[27] When the school year began, she was committed to four daily half-hour trips taking the children to and from school. Anna, who had attended nine different preschools, kindergartens, and grammar schools during the past three years, was finally happy at a small, country Quaker school which was in session from 8:30 a.m. until 5:00 p.m. during the week. Mary Frances enrolled Kennedy in the afternoon session of the lab kindergarten at Whittier College, which meant driving her to school at 12:45, returning to have lunch with Rex, and then picking her up at 3:30. From nine in the morning until noon, Mary Frances kept the twelve-room house as decent as possible. Even if she managed to get help with cleaning, laundering, gardening, and cooking, the lockstep schedule of school-marketing-managing monopolized her time and energy. She concluded her letter to Covici by saying, "I cannot and will not allow myself to grow nervous or over-tired and resultingly cross and inadequate as a mother. Right now the children are more important than Modern American Literature, at least to me!"[28]

In October, the realization that she had made a mistake in hiring her latest caretakers, who proved to be incompetent, and the strain of maintaining her daily schedule caused a relapse. She told Dr. Frumkes that she was almost as apprehensive, insecure, and depressed as she had been at her low point a year earlier, and she had no one to talk to but him. Anne was in the midst of a romantic entanglement and was not particularly responsive to Mary Frances's problems. Norah had decided to leave La Puente and rent a small house in Sunset Beach for three months while she made up her mind to either reconcile with or divorce her husband. To compound her problems, when Donald visited for a few days at the beginning of November, he launched a personal attack, saying that she was absolutely finished as M.F.K. Fisher and could never hope to recoup her professional standing. He also said she "had lost her looks" because of the insensate life she insisted on living in Whittier, when she could be a rich, beautiful woman living with him. The next morning when he said that he regretted the "schism" that seemed to exist between them, Mary Frances icily said it was fully justified in light of what he had said the night before. His answer was that she managed "to distort every truth into an insanely vain reflection on [her] own goodness and nobility and magnanimity."[29] Mary Frances reacted to the visit with a severe panic attack, and wrote to Dr. Frumkes for an appointment. If necessary, she would consider hiring a taxi service to take the children to school.

If Donald's words about the demise of M.F.K. Fisher's career and his unkind remarks about her "lost looks" were hurtful, his letters from San Francisco several weeks later, after a visit to New York, caused more pain. His words were clipped, noncommittal, dutiful but distant. She suspected that he finally accepted their divorce and had really left her to go on with his life. She subsequently learned that while he had been in New York, he had made the acquaintance of Eleanor Kask, who was in charge of publicity and advertising at Funk and Wagnall's. Kask had invited him, in his role as television host, to attend a publicity party, and the two were "drawn deeply to each other." Kask was a beauty who was nineteen years younger than he, and she had just left her second husband and was planning to divorce him in Reno. Donald told Mary Frances that he intended to stay with her there while the divorce was being processed, flying back to San Francisco for his show each week. At the end of that time he believed they would know if they were truly in love.

"Donald's final and (so far as I know him) complete leaving was something I had arranged for, insisted on, hoped for, expected," Mary Frances told Dr. Frumkes. "But when it suddenly happened I felt great regret. I felt desolate. Above all my pride was wounded for in some cruel way I had obviously wanted him to go on being miserably lost without me. I was affronted to discover what I thought I'd hoped for, that he would give up waiting for me to return to him. This school-girl attitude, which did not last very long, reminded me of my childish pique when a man I had thought found me essential to him was able to leave for a year in Europe without seeing me."[30] Until she met Donald, Mary Frances had acknowledged being the pursuer in most of her relationships. Five years earlier, she had noted in her journal, "I for the first time since perhaps my ninth year could sit back, welcoming the unfamiliar assault after so long a period of wooing my mates."[31] But now she knew that the determined aggressor who proposed to her a few days after she had arrived in New York was completely capable of seeking out another talented and beautiful woman, and that he had done so.

By mid-December her loneliness manifested itself not in panic, but in a kind of numbness. She didn't care about the ten pounds she had gained or about her inability to shrug off petty complaints and little boredoms or about her many attempts to put something down on paper that was not carping, somber, or unpleasant. She did care passionately that she had "absolutely nobody to say anything to" except her children, who could not respond like adults and were often bewildered, and her father, who all too often turned off his hearing aid because he was tired and knew the familiar exchanges of their household routine. More than ever, Mary Frances missed Dillwyn, with whom she had shared "an easy vocabulary," and Donald, who "spoke parts of it with me." Norah, with whom she had always been able to communicate in a substantive and satisfying way, was deeply immersed in her own problems, as was her sister Anne, and Larry was in Europe. She wished she could see Dr. Frumkes twice a week and then rebuked herself that she had arrived at a point where she had to pay someone to listen to her.

Between making pongee robes for both of her sisters and collecting gifts for the children, Mary Frances planned an elaborate Christmas at Bareacres at Rex's request. She invited Walter Kennedy, who was visiting his daughter Nan in Los Angeles, Norah and her boys, and Sean Kelly and his friend Michel Le Gouis (the nephew of Georges Connes), who was studying at San Francisco College with Sean; most of them would stay at a nearby hotel. She also planned an extensive menu, with roast suckling pig as the centerpiece. A few days before Christmas, Mary Frances, the children, and Michel Le Gouis drove to Bareacres and started to prepare for the holiday. Perhaps it was being back at Bareacres that lifted her spirits, or perhaps it was the presence of the handsome young Frenchman, who was the sort of conversationalist she especially enjoyed, but in any event *le reveillon* 1950 was a holiday to remember.

During the first weeks of 1951, Mary Frances told Dr. Frumkes that although she felt she did not need immediate help, she nevertheless wanted to continue writing to him and anticipated seeing him "to make myself solider."[32] She had sailed through the holidays, and when they were over, she felt like writing again. To that end she had hired a neighbor to come in six mornings a week to care for Kennedy and take charge of household tasks. The project she had in mind was a novel "which formed in my mind and/or heart the previous week. I am determined to write it, for my own good. It will be the story of a love affair that *almost* happened to me during the Christmas holidays. I plan to consummate it on paper! (An aging female's dream!) So . . . I'll put off a little longer what I honestly hope and want to do . . . see you regularly."[33]

During an extended holiday weekend trip to San Francisco with Rex and Norah in January, they dined with Harold Price, "pleasantly it turned out, to my father who has never seen him but has been suspicious of him for many years."[34] She filled in for Rex at a Philharmonic board meeting and wrote it up for the *News*, which also added to her feeling of strength. But her real coup was devising a plan to celebrate her father's seventy-fourth birthday on January 25 by giving a party for about a hundred people. It was something that she would not have contemplated a year ago, when it had been a struggle to invite one person to dinner. She prepared most of the food, including seventy-four chicken drumsticks, herself, and except for physical fatigue after the event, the party was a success. "I think I have let myself grow rather self-indulgent . . . so I say 'Next Monday . . . mañana . . . after the party . . . and so on,' " she told Dr. Frumkes. "My work goes very slowly, but I do not fret about that."[35]

Seemingly, the only situations that she could not handle very well involved Donald. On January 25 he and Eleanor Kask had embarked on a long après-divorce motor trip, and because he wanted Eleanor to meet the children he suggested that they visit the Ranch en route from Palm Springs. They arrived for what Mary Frances said was a "terribly gay and sophisticated and civilized" lunch on February 2. She had arranged for Rex to have his meal in Whittier because she felt that it was consummate bad taste to have her father host a luncheon for his daughter's ex-husband and the ex-husband's current mistress. And she had ignored Donald's request that she keep the children home from school for the day.

The luncheon was cordial enough, but Mary Frances sensed that Donald was ill at ease, glib, and somewhat sad. At one point while he retrieved something from the car, Eleanor thanked Mary Frances for allowing her to come. She was understandably uncomfortable, and she respected Mary Frances as a writer and wanted to make a good impression. After Donald took Eleanor to the airport for her return flight to New York, he returned to the Ranch to visit the children and spend the night before returning to San Francisco the next day. At four o'clock in the morning, Mary Frances woke to her first panic attack in several months. Dry mouth, thudding heart, wet palms, violently shaking legs and jaws, and a feeling of pressure against the inner ears—all of the familiar symptoms were present as well as an uncontrollable fear that Anna and Kennedy might be subjected to the horrors of an atom bomb attack that she had dreamed about. The hallucinatory experience lasted two hours and left her shaky until midmorning.

She immediately wrote to Dr. Frumkes, saying that her relapse was undoubtedly due to the tension and fatigue associated with the party for her father and to the "ridiculous" luncheon with Donald and his girlfriend the day before. Though it went off smoothly, she said, "I found Donald silly and boring and unattractive physically. Or so I thought. But before I went to bed on the night before the attack, I was caught up by a strong wave of sexual hunger, very rare for me. I did not want any specific man, but just a good lover. It did not last long, but I was surprised by it. I imagine my unaccustomed and lengthy celibacy is beginning to catch up with me."[36] Afraid to risk any more tension, and more than a little apprehensive about placing herself in a social situation, Mary Frances excused herself from the party Gloria Stuart had arranged for her husband's fiftieth birthday the next evening, even though Anna had wanted to wear her new dress, and Mary Frances had wanted her daughter to see her hobnobbing with movie stars and celebrities as in the past.

She visited Dr. Frumkes several times over the next six months, prompted by the sheer strain of caring for her father, tensions with her sisters (Anne spent a month at the Ranch after terminating a romantic relationship, and Norah's divorce was in progress), troubling dreams about Dillwyn, and, most unsettling of all, Donald's refusal to relinquish the role of husband and father. He had given up his television show in order to join Eleanor in New York, and for appearances' sake, they made up a story about being married in Mexico at the beginning of March,[37] but Donald still pressed for a reconciliation with Mary Frances.

Unlike the Donald Friede of a year ago, he was in a position to offer her financial security. And although he had not found a position in publishing in New York City, he was confident that one was forthcoming. He was also willing to return to either Los Angeles or San Francisco to work. He told Mary Frances that Eleanor fully understood that he still loved Mary Frances and their two daughters and wanted to be united with them, but the day would come when he would either have to commit to Eleanor by marrying her or risk losing her. What he could not tolerate, he told Mary Frances, was eventually not having either her or Eleanor. "You are the damnedest combination of patsy and mule-like stubbornness I have ever known—or could ever imagine," he told Mary Frances. "You are also—by the very fact that you are one of the most truly creative people I have ever known—utterly unable to see fact as fact. 'Never spoil a story by sticking to the truth' may be—and is—a fine motto—but not if it is applied to human relationships at all times."[38] Having said that, he claimed that she had taught him how to love and how to be a completely fulfilled human being, and he wanted her back.

As Dr. Frumkes had warned Mary Frances, Donald understood

both her vanity and her loyalty, and he played on both. And she, either consciously or subconsciously, encouraged him with lengthy letters filled with charming anecdotes about the children and life in Whittier. But when he insistently asked her to marry him again in both April and July of 1951, she refused. In what she considered a retaliatory move, he moved into Eleanor's house on West Twelfth Street in Greenwich Village that he and Mary Frances had admired but had been unable to afford in 1945, and planned to make a home with Eleanor there.

Meanwhile day-to-day living with Rex was becoming more difficult. If Mary Frances saw the telltale traces of his spittle in the kitchen sink, it threw her into an inner tirade about his increasingly unsavory personal habits. Only a year before, she had started to write what she intended to be a story about him, in which the information that she had discovered and collected about old people would come together in celebration of the man who was now old and trusting of her. "I went in after he had turned his lights off and put the glasses beside his bed, and his face turned up to me like a child's when I leaned to kiss him," she wrote. "My heart turned over."[39] A year later, in "Rex—II," written sometime in 1951 and published posthumously, she vented the anger and hatred she felt when she had to rub his smelly feet, hear his long "masturbatory belchings," and wipe up dribbles of his urine on the floor by the toilet. "Tonight I could not really *look* at Rex, because I was so angry at him for spitting in the sink: I knew he would see my anger. Perhaps that would have been a good thing. But I do not love him that way, and am not able to have good rousing battles with him. So I hide my bile. I don't think it really hurts me at all—except that I am clumsy enough to vent some of it on the two people I love best, my innocent children."[40] "Rex—II" should probably never have been published, but it did reveal Mary Frances's deep disappointment at seeing a sentimentalized Rex I be inexorably succeeded by an increasingly unappealing Rex II.

Yet even now her feelings about him were complex, and she saw that the relationship was not simply one of dependency:

I think that perhaps we are so close, in spite of our antagonisms, that some of his own inner anxiety may have seeped into me, and I wish I could tell him to count on me, to lean on me, to trust me. He cannot. He does not. He is too tired, and for too many years he has isolated himself, in order to escape himself. I must not forget this, for I too could be as he is, helpless before himself. The trouble is that I would indeed, or *could* indeed, be helpless, whereas he has, at god knows what expense to himself and to others, never quite been so. He has survived. His strength has been instinctive, and at times murderous . . . quite beyond his control. I know a little of what he did, unwittingly to Mother . . . to David . . . to Ted.[41]

It was not a relationship that she explored in any depth with Dr. Frumkes, her excuse being that she would simply go over and over the too-familiar question of how to walk out on an old man who was now dependent on her physically, however much he still held himself apart emotionally.

Caught between the needs of her father and her daughters, Mary Frances once again found it difficult to summon the energy to write. Furthermore, "the old days of having editors beating at my doors are gone," she wrote to Dr. Frumkes.[42] That she was destroying herself professionally haunted her just as she was convinced that she was harming herself physically by gaining too much weight and drinking too much sherry and vermouth. In early July she decided to send Anna and Kennedy to summer school for three weeks in order to do some serious work. When they departed, she found that she no longer had an excuse to avoid writing, but she found that she dreaded it. Goaded on by her father, who told her that she could write a story at least as good as the one he had just read in *The Saturday Evening Post* (and, he hoped, not as embarrassing as the "filthy" novel she had published a few years before), she began a story about a seriously disturbed boarding school girl. So involved did she become that she eventually had to limit her time on it lest she spend the whole night writing it in her head. Before the children returned on July 31, she had completed the novella-length "Legend of Love."

The story concerns two children, not sisters but friends, who, not surprisingly, closely resemble the sensitive, slender Anna and the robust, lovable Kennedy. When the colorless Mrs. Palmer, recently widowed, joins the teaching staff at Miss Abel's boarding school, her seven-year-old daughter, Janet, becomes the best friend of Nini, the little girl who "was destined, foreordained, to be the final victim. She had everything that was needed, all the requisite virtues of a murderee—or so it seemed for a time."[43] The potential murderer is Nan, one of the "Old Girls," who slowly terrorizes the school first by killing the turtle Janet brings to school and then by wringing the neck of a dove and placing it on the breast of the sleeping music teacher. Nan's malicious streak continues when she grasps the hands of some of the younger girls and swirls them around and around by a pigpen, where their screams excite the resident pig to kill her newborn piglets. After discovering that Nan has exhibited a similar pattern of behavior at previous schools, Miss Abel sends her home, but not before Nan hangs Miss Abel's spaniel when her plan to lure Nini into the barn to harm her fails. That evening, after Nan is safely gone, her malevolence is exorcised during the annual Christmas program, when hymns are sung, Gospel stories are read, and innocence is restored.

The source of the plot may have been a newspaper account of juvenile malevolence, but the story also betrays Mary Frances's own plan to teach French at the University of Southern California after her father's passing. It betrays as well some of the characteristic weaknesses of her fiction. The ending, especially, borders on the sentimental, and the dialogue is stilted and improbably suited to the characters: a new teacher says, "I still feel scared, being here . . . that conditioned reflex," and a handyman replies, "I'm Swiss myself. Had a girl once from the Canton of Vaud."[44] The geriatric music teacher, the indomitable principal, and the limp widow who speaks in adult fashion to her seven-year-old daughter are straight out of central casting. Nevertheless, completing the story was a breakthrough for her, and Volkening quickly sold it to the *Ladies' Home Journal* for publication as a complete-in-one-issue condensed novel.

Donald congratulated Mary Frances on the sale of her story, while informing her that he would marry Eleanor immediately after their divorce became final in August. "I have always felt that you are a deeply rich and untapped well of wonderful fiction," he wrote, "and if you can keep yourself away from the hot literary stove for a while, you will be wise to do it. It is quite obvious, in reading magazines, looking at the publishers' lists, checking the book-stores, that the for-sale professionals have taken over the field that you almost pioneered."[45] In response, Mary Frances repeated some of the conclusions that she had reached with Dr. Frumkes' help. "I discovered an odd thing about writing that story. It was the first thing I've ever written simply to *write*. Always before, without any exception, I've written for *someone*. That explains my almost abnormal disinterest in reputation and 'public' and so on. I imagine all I've ever wanted was the approval and encouragement and interest of a *person*. Well . . . I can't indulge in writing to please myself; the children are still too young to be an audience. So, I think I must putz along on hack stuff."[46]

Unable to travel to Beverly Hills four times a week for psychoanalysis while maintaining her daily routine at the Ranch, but believing herself to be in need of more regular help, Mary Frances set up a schedule of weekly appointments with Dr. Frumkes. She felt she needed to explore more thoroughly her growing resentment over the responsibilities with which she was saddled, and her consequent sense of entrapment. Also of utmost importance to her was her increasing difficulty in writing anything more than letters to Norah, to her father, and to her psychiatrist—many of which were unsent. She told Norah:

> I have decided that at this stage of my life I am as obviously a letter-writer as other people may be alcoholics or benzedrine-boys. The need to use words and direct them toward a chosen person is almost physically urgent to me, especially in the mornings. I have always liked it. When I was very young, I wrote every Sunday to Uncle Park, I can remember writing postcards and such like to you and Dave, from boarding-school and boats and France. I wrote to Al as I thought he most wanted me to write. Then to Dillwyn I wrote without restraints. Increasingly I wrote chatty letters to Edith, trying deliberately to please and amuse her . . . I had got into the daily habit of a daily note to Edith, but because of Donald's illnesses and absences could keep up a kind of imitation of my habit: he is fun to write to, for we share the same tricks of vocabulary, as do you and I. But now *that* avenue is blocked . . . that leaves

you. I find myself wondering what my wordy brain will do if and when you too withdraw from the field . . . I look up at this lengthy mumble and doubt very much that I send it to you.[47]

As a child she had felt the heady power of cooking—"from the stove, I ruled"[48]—and as an adult she had seduced people with her singular style of preparing and presenting food. Whether it was a stew or a story made little difference; "I see more clearly all the time that I have used my good but small talent to impress other people."[49] But, she asked Dr. Frumkes, was it vulgar to let the general public read what was clearly intended for one person? Was it what the police called "indecent exposure"? Did she, in fact, outrage her sense of modesty by figuratively playing with herself in public? If she did not write, what would she do? "My peculiar combination of a fairly good style and self-exposure has given pleasure to many people . . . And people I admire profess to admire me . . . as a writer, I mean. But am I admirable? Or am I simply a skillful exhibitionist who can use words?"[50]

When the "walls began to break down" during her weekly sessions with Dr. Frumkes, she understood what he meant when he told her to write in a freer or even incoherent way. Taking his comments about her unflagging composure and abhorrence of seeming to be out of control a step further, she wondered if her "occasional foolhardy and passionate gambles with men had been a way of showing myself that I am not always the correct and coherent woman, turning the neat and sometimes witty phrase with God-Damned Poise? Perhaps now I should have a wild affair with a *book*, since there's no man around to fasten my hungry mind-and-body onto?"[51] After this particular session, Mary Frances left the office shaken. She wrote to Dr. Frumkes the next day: "I feel too ready to weep, to unlock the fetters, unlace the strait-jacket . . . At this moment I could lie on the floor and bawl my silly soul out."[52] Given her reaction to the ongoing therapy, she realized that it was simply too complicated to go further. "Could I keep up my present passive and even tranquil routine?" she asked Dr. Frumkes. "It seems important to me to do so."[53] They both decided it was time for a sabbatical, and Mary Frances asked him to file away the following question that she would like to explore when her sabbatical ended: "Why am I so afraid of being *undignified?* I use it in a deliberately childish and naïve way, and by it I mean a thousand things like ugly, formless, messy, graceless, incoherent, undisciplined."[54]

When Rex's health stabilized during the fall of 1951, he visited his brother Ted in Spokane and from there went to Albion to spend a few weeks with Walter. He also decided to go on a pheasant hunt with his golf partners in early November. Mary Frances seized the opportunity and, together with Norah, took the children to Ensenada, in Baja California, for a three-day holiday. Their accommodations were luxurious, with a well-stocked kitchen for breakfasts and lunches. They took their dinners in a simple, friendly place in town. Mary Frances wrote that she felt happier than she had in many years, with equally happy children. They spent their days walking along the shore, watching the fishermen, and looking for rock crabs at low tide. No radio, no telephone, and no urgent duties spoiled the serenity of the moment.

A week before Christmas, Rex was taken to the hospital, where he was told by his doctor to stop his regular schedule of work at the *News* for a month or else. He chose "or else," but did rest at the Ranch during the holidays. In February 1952, largely because he had not heeded the doctor's warning, Rex's health deteriorated further and he was hospitalized again. In what Mary Frances in her lighter moments labeled an amusing fait accompli and in rebellious moods referred to as "getting sucked in," she was hired by her father to handle his mail and take over his desk six mornings a week. With both girls in school, it seemed workable, but she had a nagging feeling that they would soon resent her lack of attention to them. Writing to Dr. Frumkes seven weeks later, she referred to being "enthroned as The Boss's Daughter," writing a couple of features and a column each week and pinch-hitting for the society editor when needed. "By now I simply accept it as one more unexpected phase of my present life. I have tried countless ways to make it clear, not only to Rex but to the rest of the family, that I am doing this *only while he needs me,* and that I am not considering taking over the *News* for the benefit of my sisters and of course myself. This is for REX."[55] Still, Mary Frances had to admit that once she hit her stride, the whole experience was good for her. "I seem to *fit* my new skin, morally or however you might say it,"

she wrote in a letter to Dr. Frumkes. "I feel at ease, calm, tolerant . . .
I enjoy being me, most of the time, even though I am not living at all
the kind of life I think I would choose."[56]

Ending up with the job at the *News* was, as Dr. Frumkes described
it, as inevitable as boy meets girl, and, contrary to what Mary Frances
feared, the job did not result in nocturnal panic attacks. She slept
more peacefully than she had in years. Taking the "measure of her
powers," she found herself going back to her early days in Whittier,
possibly to make the present more acceptable to herself. She wrote in
her journal:

> In the wheelchair of my enforced presence here I run like a
> colt down the unpaved streets; I skin my knees once more and
> with an even sharper pain, with even brighter blood, upon the
> sidewalks we had to skate on, almost forty years ago. I scoot
> down the grassy hills in an orange crate for a sled, where prim
> villas crowd now, and I fight and sing and tumble with a gang
> of children who are gone or dead or bald long since. Now and
> then I see one of them hereabouts, and I feel a kind of mirth,
> to hold the mirror of them up to my own tired eyes and graying
> hair. It has happened, I say. It has actually happened to *us*. And
> then I am in the top of the apricot tree in Aunt Gwen's or-
> chard, where Gerrard's Market and a filling station now hum
> with business, and one limb below me Garland and Talbert
> boast about riding sixty miles an hour last Sunday in Doc
> Moorehead's new Maxwell, and on the drying weeds under the
> tree my little fat sister Anne watches two bees get drunk on
> rotten fruit . . . Anne now so smartly haggard, and so smart, the
> boys now so prosperous and paunchy.[57]

If she was becoming fatigued (always hazardous) or resentful of
her added duties, her letters written during odd moments at the *News*
did not reflect it. "Have done a couple of things for Etta Mae [society
editor] . . . one dreadfully pompous and badly written thing which to
my surprise had been written by the literary duchess of Whittier, Miss
Fink . . . teddibly, teddibly solemn conference schedules by the
Council of Church Women," she wrote to Norah. "I did the best I

could with it and was amused when I handed my re-write to Etta Mae to have her remark quietly, 'Do Gooders. Burp.' "[58] These multipage letters to Norah, who had recently moved to Atascadero, paint a picture of a daughter trying to persuade her father to buy a deep-freezer, or drive to Bareacres for the weekend, or board a train to visit Norah in her new home more than two hundred miles away. Some of them also expressed anger, hurt, and frustration with her role as "innkeeper" and peacekeeper. Letters to Dr. Frumkes establish a different scenario of valiant efforts to avert slipping back into physical and mental pain. Given her demanding schedule at the *News* and virtual isolation at the Ranch, these busy, often hilarious letters were her mainstay, her therapy, and her link to what she now considered her former life. She lacked writing projects of her own, with the exception of a book on California wines initiated by the San Francisco Wine and Food Society and under contract to the University of California Press, and a few introductions to other people's books. Letters were her five-finger exercises, and she made them an art form.

Through letters she also reestablished connections with people she had lost contact with through the years. Eda Lord, whom she had last seen in Paris in 1937, wrote about the changes in her life since surviving the war in France. Mary Frances responded in kind with her own "condensation of a saga," bringing her up to date and telling her of distant plans that included introducing her daughters to England and France. When Arnold Gingrich sent word that he was marrying again, she congratulated him. And when Larry Powell returned from Europe, he and Mary Frances resumed their friendship and correspondence.

During the spring and summer of 1952, Mary Frances's role at the *News* expanded considerably. Although Rex continued to write "Heard in the Barber Shop," Mary Frances moved into editorials in addition to features, book reviews, and home and garden articles. She attended Press Club meetings and worked out suggestions to integrate the paper more fully into the life of Whittier, and she even devised a plan to turn the vacant building next door into a coffee shop for the editorial staff and pressmen. As she herself admitted, she was too good at her job, and Rex came to know that his daughter was a newspaperwoman after all. But in July, she virtually collapsed at the office and had to be driven home. Her internist diagnosed her condition as extreme fatigue and prescribed Danatol and complete rest. She left her job at the *News*, but reassured Rex that she would continue as his assistant and take care of his personal finances and correspondence.

By September, Mary Frances had resumed many of the duties she had given up in July, and was considerably unhappier about the situation in which she found herself. Her father's assumption that she would "step in" at the *News* was particularly galling because he had excluded her from the paper when she had always wanted it and at times actually needed it, especially when she and Al had returned from France. Now that Rex had lost his only son and was no longer able to go on alone, he was pushing her to carry on the Kennedy newspapering legacy.

Rex still maintained control of the paper, however, even though he was ceding control in other ways. Cashing in on a postwar boom that extended Whittier's city limits with row after row of small cottages, he sold his orange grove to the developers who were already bulldozing the trees on neighboring properties, retaining the Ranch house and a few acres surrounding it. During the next weeks, when the noise of chainsaws filled the house, Rex saw much of his past life obliterated in the dust. But he declined Mary Frances's offer to move them all into a home in town or at least to escape the felling of the trees by taking a vacation for a week or two. When Ted visited in November, he found his older brother holding his own, and his admiration for the care his niece provided her father was unbounded. In a thank-you letter to Mary Frances he wrote, "The Kennedys are all loath to betray or acknowledge any emotionalism. One comes by the knowledge of their inner feelings circuitously if at all. But doubt not that Rex has a deep sense of gratitude and appreciation."[59]

There were the usual Thanksgiving and Christmas holiday family reunions, perhaps more poignant because Rex's steady decline was so evident. At times he dozed off when the children were noisily playing nearby. At other times he had wrenching coughing spells. He rallied if he had a Rotary Club luncheon, and he still drove his fifteen-year-old roadster, taking a few more liberties with traffic regulations than ever. But when Walter visited after the New Year, Mary Frances knew that there was much discussion between them about trust funds. Although she did not think that Rex's death was imminent, she wondered how much longer she could tolerate living at the Ranch. With the local schools growing more crowded, she worried that her girls' education was being compromised. She hated the rapidly changing neighborhood, the sounds of other people's phones ringing, the play of headlights through the fences Rex had installed around the Ranch. Early in 1953, she asked her father to consider a year's leave of absence from the paper so they could all travel north and live in the Napa Valley. If he was unwilling to do that, she proposed buying an old house in the center of Whittier and taking an official position at the *News*. Rex vetoed both ideas.

While her cousin Nan was visiting in April, Mary Frances experienced the old symptoms of panic and apprehension. Nan promptly called Anne in San Francisco, who was between jobs and more than willing to stay with her father in Whittier while her sister and the children went to Bareacres for two weeks. On their return, Mary Frances had the impulse to take Rex and the girls to San Francisco for a long weekend. It would prove to be his final trip to the city.

In May, Rex spent three weeks in the hospital, returning home, at his insistence, with three nurses and an oxygen tank. He instructed Mary Frances to promote his assistant editor to the position of managing editor because he wanted her home with him. Mary Frances told her uncle Ted "he either does not know or does not care to admit that things have changed a bit since he bounced back from several cases of lobar pneumonia."[60] Over the next few weeks, in what she described as a kind of slowing down, Rex drifted off into two or three periods of coma, from which he'd awake with increasing confusion. At the end, he became openly hateful toward and fearful of his daughter, which would have been impossible to bear were it not for a very kind nurse and the comfort of the same elderly Quaker doctor who had been with Mary Frances during Edith's last hours.

Rex Kennedy died on June 2, 1953. Services were held in the Episcopal church two days later. At his request, a blanket of deep red roses, which always reminded him of Edith, adorned his casket. After the ceremony, Mary Frances, Anne, and Norah took his ashes to Bareacres to mingle with Edith's, David's, and Dillwyn's in that place of peace. As Rex had predicted, after his death there was a "kind of

Roman Holiday" with everyone from the governor to the janitor at the *News* stopping at the Ranch to pay their respects to a man who had become a Whittier institution. The state legislature passed "House Resolution No. 179," which expressed "heartfelt sympathy and sorrow to the family of Rex B. Kennedy"[61] in recognition of his great contribution to the city of Whittier and state of California.

He had made his eldest daughter executor of his estate and one of the heirs to the *News*. He also left her with a complex emotional legacy. Mary Frances disapproved of his imperiousness and self-centeredness, and resented the emotional distance that he had maintained from her, her mother, and her sisters, especially after David's death. She was hurt by his repeated failure to acknowledge her professional success, and she despised his failure to pursue his own fondest dreams. Yet he had supported her at crucial moments, notably in her decision to divorce Al Fisher and in receiving Anna as part of the family, probably knowing that she was in fact his biological grandchild. She had inherited not only his forehead, determined chin, and intense green eyes but his sense of family and of humor. With his death she was an orphan, and she felt it keenly.

TEN

Californienne

(1953–1956)

Here I play too many parts, often because I enjoy them or find them challenging. When I am in France I am more truly real to myself.[1]
—M.F.K. Fisher

During the month after Rex's death Mary Frances took Anna and Kennedy to Morro Bay for a week's vacation. In "Another Love Story," a fictionalized account of her escape from Whittier published in *The New Yorker* almost thirty years later, Mary Frances wrote, "The old man was out of his long sadness and final struggle, and they were out of the hollow house, and the early spring air was winier by the mile."[2] In the story, after driving two hundred miles north along the Pacific coast, the mother and her two daughters seek refuge in a weathered beachfront motel in a slightly down-at-the-heels seashore community that seems to come alive only on weekends when tourists check in. The residents are mostly commercial abalone fishermen and old men who fish from the long pier and pay scant attention to little girls, who rent fishing poles and become adept at landing bass. The girls befriend a boat operator named Mr. Henshaw, who takes them and their mother on tours of the inlets and coves around the bay. Thanks to the children's vigorous plotting (they are actually trawling for a husband for their mother), Mr. Henshaw proposes marriage to the woman because he wants to "see to it that they [the children] learn what they are meant to do with their lives . . . you could live anywhere you wanted to, and I would never bother you except to be your friend."³ The mother concludes that Mr. Henshaw has really fallen in love with the children, not her, and the story ends with their departure for home early the next day.

In Mary Frances's letters to friends like Bachmann and Powell she simply mentioned that she took her daughters to Morro Bay for a week, but in other letters, she also hinted that both Anna and Kennedy were "apprehensive about whether I could make a true family by myself, and they wanted me to marry at once, *anybody*, the service-station boy or the 76-year-old gardener."⁴ Although their naive campaign to find a husband for their mother had begun sometime before Rex's death (most likely when they learned of Donald's marriage to Eleanor), the loss of their grandfather undoubtedly contributed a sense of urgency to finding another man for the family. The episode with the boat owner may or may not have happened, the girls may have been quick learners as fishermen or not, Mary Frances may or may not have had a "near death" experience when the owner of the boat steered it in the "churning currents and choppy swells . . . and she felt trapped, doomed."⁵ But the plot more or less mirrors what happened in Morro Bay that week.

After their vacation, Mary Frances left Anna and Kennedy with Norah in Atascadero while she flew to Salt Lake City for the annual writers' conference at the University of Utah, to which she'd been invited a few months before Rex's death. It was the first time in many years that Mary Frances had felt stable enough to travel alone. Although she had flown to Mexico to stay with Norah and David, she had developed a real dislike for flying, and she never knew when a panic attack would occur. This time, however, her initial jitters dissipated, and when she looked through the plane's window, she noted with increasing pleasure the richness of the Sacramento Valley, and farther east, the ghostly mountains and pewter lakes of Utah. When she landed in Salt Lake City, a driver from the university whisked her off to the campus, where she spent her first night in a dreadful little room in a sorority house, and then moved into a much larger room vacated by the novelist Vardis Fisher the next morning.

She was unaccustomed to the contrast between the handsome facades and crumbling interiors of campus buildings, and between the well-appointed public rooms and the shoddy student quarters with their poor lighting, wobbly furniture, and cracked plaster. Even more disconcerting were the strange rituals of communal living, which brought the faculty together from early-morning breakfasts to much-earlier-morning nightcaps. She kept a detailed journal for Covici during her week there, noting what she thought of colleagues like Malcolm Cowley and his wife, Muriel, Stephen Spender, Vardis Fisher, and Caroline Gordon. She soon discovered that the attendees had signed up basically to find out the answer to only one question: Why doesn't *The Saturday Evening Post* take my first article or poem for $5,000, or $500? To her chagrin, their interest seemed to have nothing to do with work or with a love of words. She found the workshops difficult to manage, as many of the attendees, bent on simply getting a secret formula for a successful essay or article, didn't even bother to submit pieces for group criticism.

Yet she was fascinated by her fellow writers, and stimulated by the chance to spend time in their company. "It was a complete change for me," she wrote to Covici, "after so long with an old deaf man and two small children, to breakfast-lunch-dine and walk and drink with highly practiced *talkers*. SS [Stephen Spender] delivered lectures on the smallest pretext—Caroline Gordon rambled outrageously about Suhthahn [Southern] hospitality and so on—Malcolm Cowley bumbled on in the Old-School-tie tradition. But they were articulate people, all of them, and it was good for me to have to conform to the strange boarding-school routine of our lodgings, and listen and occasionally say something over the weak coffee, limp toast, crucified eggs. I felt shy and clumsy."[6] She was particularly struck by the focus of the other writers, whose deep knowledge of their particular fields seemed to highlight the eclectic pattern of her own reading—mystery novels, sociology, philosophy, anything from Ayn Rand to Georges Simenon.

She decided to return to California a day before the formal end of the conference, earlier than planned. The Cowleys and Stephen Spender, who had made the whole affair worthwhile for her, had already left. Spender, especially, had strongly affected her: "It's as if a very rare beautiful bird had flown swiftly through the room of my life, singing a music I would always hear but never find the words to. Or it is as if my life were a walk, from dawn to dusk, a journey I must take on foot, and suddenly at a turn in the road a stallion with great wings stood there for a minute, and neighed and looked at me, and then vanished. He is a giant, in his spirit as well as his mind and heart and body, and I cannot now conceive what effect this week of peculiar intimacy will have on the rest of my life, but I feel very happy about it."[7]

Returning to Atascadero, Mary Frances stopped at Norah's home, picked up Anna and Kennedy, and drove to Whittier, where the vacant house offered little by way of welcome. Her first priority was settling the details of Rex's estate. She, Anne, and Norah shared equally in the inheritance, and together the sisters decided to give up the family's controlling interest in the *News*. Mary Frances had ruled out the possibility of following in Rex's footsteps, with considerable misgivings; her letters to Norah during the brief time that she substituted for Rex at the paper make it clear that she had really enjoyed batting out columns and doing rewrites. "It has been quite a thing for me to decide," she told Dr. Frumkes, "for I love newspapers. If I did not have the children I quite possibly would become a hard-faced cold lonely 'woman editor' . . . and try to run things to suit myself (and my sisters). But I refused to raise my girls down there . . . I would have to give at least ¾ of myself to the paper, with very little left over for them, two refugees in the smog. No."[8] She explained to her uncle Ted that neither she nor her sisters were willing to live in Whittier and hold the *News* together as a "Kennedy" paper. Until ownership changed, however, it was up to her to see to the smooth running of the paper, and the business of attending board meetings, hiring and firing employees, and balancing the books fell to her.

Mary Frances and her two sisters also decided the fate of the Ranch. The area around it had changed dramatically. The city's population had swelled to 200,000, the pace of life had accelerated, the surrounding hills had been recklessly gouged for building sites, native plants like poppies, lupine, and sage had been uprooted forever, even the quality of the air was poorer. Renovating the dilapidated house would have cost in excess of $4,000. Rather than try to keep up a "white elephant," they decided to donate the house and two acres of land to the city for a children's park in honor of Rex's memory. Even though the house would be leveled, the beautiful trees would be saved, and they hoped that something of Rex's spirit would remain as well. "The park idea for children is more wonderful as you think about it," Ted said. "I like to think of a long, loosely clothed, somewhat gaunt figure sitting there under the big trees, a cool drink by his side, quietly smoking a cigarette while he looks out across the newly arranged space with the children at play."[9]

It was Mary Frances's intention to leave the Ranch intact until after the Fourth of July weekend. With great care she planned a final fling that also included the celebration of her forty-fifth birthday. Nan and her family came from Los Angeles, as did Mary Frances's friend June Eddy. Norah and her sons arrived from Atascadero, and Anne was also present, as were loyal *News* staffers and neighbors. After the party, Mary Frances planned to begin a new life in a new place surrounded by all of Dillwyn's paintings, her books and records, and treasures like her mother's teacups and her grandfather's revolving bookcase. On July 6, the furnishings and family mementos were divided among the family members. A few weeks later, the packers and movers took over, and Mary Frances and the children traveled north.

Since the day she had driven through the Napa Valley during the gas-rationing years of World War II and "smelled the pure sweet air," Mary Frances had known that she wanted to live there someday. Now, it was only a short time before she found a perfect house a few miles southwest of St. Helena. The Red Cottage, as the Bourne property was called, was old and comfortable, with vineyards on three sides and a sloping forest of nut trees, redwoods, and pines ascending into the Mayacama Range on the fourth. To the south, toward Napa, the valley floor was "an almost unspoiled carpet of grapevines, half-buried in blazing golden mustard in early spring, brilliant as a Turkish rug when the leaves turn in October."[10] To the north, Route 29 led directly into the two-block commercial center of St. Helena and beyond to the springs and town of Calistoga.

Mary Frances took her time in beginning a household again, putting up temporary bookcases, unpacking books, and making curtains. For the most part, Anna and Kennedy seemed to adjust well to yet another change in their young lives, and soon were so comfortable with their new surroundings that the idea of a helpmate for their mother faded. In September they went to the public school in St. Helena, and seemed "gay and busy," Mary Frances told Eda Lord. "The people are mostly fifth and sixth generation wine-growers, Swiss and Italian and French, and their children are a good change from the bewildered harried kids in the subdivisions in Southern California."[11]

Through the girls and their activities, she began to meet other adults—Yolande and James Beard,[12] Tony and Elsine Ten Broeck. Marietta Voorhees, a teacher, became a friend, as did winemakers and people associated with the vineyards, like the wine connoisseur Paco Gould and his wife, Romie. "They were hardworking people with a fine capacity for other serious activities like eating, drinking, and talking,"[13] Mary Frances said of them. Friends from San Francisco and farther away came to visit too. While on business in San Francisco, Volkening and his wife drove up to St. Helena in late October. Mary Frances had not met with her agent for more than eight years, and during the course of his four-day visit, they discussed how and when she would resume writing. Volkening urged her to think seriously of another novel. He also told her that Donald, who had joined Eleanor Kask as an editor at World Publishing, was working out a handsome deal to bring out a plush omnibus edition of five of M.F.K. Fisher's earlier gastronomical books, under the title *The Art of Eating*, and he wanted her to do an introduction. She told Volkening that she was not quite prepared to work yet. The biography of Juliette Récamier was still in limbo. The "old-age project" that had been on the back burner for several years now had gained a certain immediacy from Rex's illness and death, but she had already turned down a good offer for it because she wanted to do it her own way and in her own time. Echoing her earlier reflections to Dr. Frumkes, she told Volkening that for her, writing a book was a form of love, and she had no one to make love to. She could not make up a lover the way the children made up imaginary playmates. Whether this was part of the M.F.K. Fisher myth, as her oft-repeated reluctance to read her own material was, or a rationalization for not writing, or a genuine fear that she could never again be the M.F.K. Fisher of *The Art of Eating*, she had decided the time was not quite right to take on anything more demanding than a few articles.

Norah had taken a leave of absence from her USO Traveler's Aid job in Paso Robles, and she and her three sons had rented a cottage across a neighboring vineyard for the fall. Anne, who now resided in Sausalito, was also a frequent visitor. Despite her busy job as a corporate librarian at Bethlehem Steel in South San Francisco, she was lonely because Sean had joined the air force, and she had no lover. The relationship between Mary Frances and Anne teetered, as always, between friendship and a subtle competition to be thinnest, most married, and most visible. But Anne had a strong interest in Anna and Kennedy, who looked forward to stopovers with their aunt on the way to San Francisco, when they had the honor of walking her poodle, Pepe, and the privilege of sampling their aunt's favorite hors d'oeuvre, beef tartare balls rolled in dried parsley. Anne rarely prepared a meal, but was lavish with gin and vermouth and seemed to subsist on a combination of liquor and pills.[14]

The scenario of their first Thanksgiving celebration up-valley was a tale of feasting that Mary Frances told and often reconfigured in articles about observing that quintessential holiday: "Down the table marched breadbaskets and ripe grapes on their flat bright leaves and the wine bottles . . . all from the valley where we stayed so thankfully; Charles Krug and Louis Martini had made the whites, and Inglenook, Beaulieu and Krug again the reds,"[15] Mary Frances wrote in "One Way to Give Thanks." Although the details of the feast would change, the tapestry of red-leaved vines, of trees that shimmered golden in the November sunshine, and the decaying perfume of discarded grape skins and forgotten raisins remained the constant in those evocative narratives, as did the happy children carrying prepared dishes from one cottage to the other.

"I seem to have hit another level of behavior or existence," she wrote to Dr. Frumkes.

I have learned a lot about myself, thanks largely to you I believe. Physically I have changed a lot too: I am plainly in the middle-years, and walk-sit-eat, sleep-breathe differently, with a different rhythm and necessity. I continue to be very *nice*, and my "God Damned poise" is still there, but I waste a lot less time on a great many things, which used to bother me. My relations with the children are good for the most part . . . I occasionally feel completely bored with them, and am rather short-spoken. I am also unfairly "mature" with Anna, the older, who reminds me too much of many of my worse sides when I was young . . . I grow sarcastic and carping with her, for she seems much more than ten years old. But in the main I think both girls are very balanced and keen about life. Kennedy asks now and then about Donald, but Anna does not . . . I suppose I can't keep up this dual role forever, but right now it is no burden to be mother-father.[16]

By now, Anna knew that Donald was not her father. For a while she believed the story that Mary Frances told her, that her father had died in the war. Over time, Anna discovered that this was not the case, but that Mary Frances would not reveal who her father was.

Monthly board meetings necessitated overnight trips back to Whittier, where Mary Frances often acted as a "blotter," absorbing the anxieties of the staff about their continued employment at the *News*. The delay in finding a buyer for the newspaper also reopened her inner debate about signing it away. But in January 1954, after much negotiating, Mary Frances and her sisters sold the *Whittier News* to Leo Owens, a fourth-generation newspaperman who had restructured the *St. Louis Post-Dispatch* before retiring and who currently owned the *Richmond Independent*. He planned to bring in an editor-publisher and retain the rest of the Whittier staff.

"By the time we get taxes paid and lawyers and so on, we'll each (my two sisters and I) have a fairly nice sum[17] to be paid over the next five years . . . I am in a state of secondary shock which may well last my life-time," Mary Frances told Larry Powell. "It was the only possible choice . . . and the only possible way I can soothe my obviously psychosomatic gut-aches and doldrums is to dream, fairly constantly, of the small town weekly that awaits me."[18] And she spelled out a scheme that she and Norah intended to pursue over the next two to five years. They planned to inaugurate a paper in the Napa Valley and then merge it with a well-established weekly. To this end, Norah intended to go to night school to perfect her camera work, and Mary Frances thought about enrolling in a trade school to study typography and layout. The plan was aborted when Norah decided to accept a position as a school guidance counselor in Berkeley, where she and her boys moved in January.

Although in her letters Mary Frances was glowing in praise of her new life, she was still casting about for other options. She entertained the idea of getting a small apartment in San Francisco so Anna could go to a professional ballet school, and keeping the Napa house as a weekend retreat. She also contemplated pursuing her earlier dream about taking the girls to France. Never one to bank money for some indeterminate future, she felt that her inheritance from her father's estate would be much more valuable to her daughters if spent during the course of their growing-up years. During their Easter-break ortho- dontal exam, Mary Frances introduced the possibility that she might take them to France for the school year after next. But the doctor's as- sessment of the girls' teeth and the bracework that would be neces- sary in the future led him to suggest that the coming fall would be a preferable time for such a sojourn. Mary Frances seized the moment, and almost immediately began inquiring about transportation and liv- ing arrangements. Under the terms of her custody agreement, she felt obliged to enlist Donald's approval of the venture, and she wrote to him, outlining her plans to visit Man and Juliet Ray in Paris and re- new her friendship with Michel Le Gouis. She assured Donald that Georges Connes would be a great resource in helping her to select a town or village to live in as well as in advising her about schools and tutors for the children. She even dreamed of the possibility that No- rah would join them with her boys. They could all rent a chalet in the Swiss Alps during the summer months, à la Heidi. She also wrote to Volkening about securing a magazine contract for an article on the Foire Gastronomique in Dijon.

Everyone endorsed her plan except Anne, who tried to convince the children that they wouldn't be accepted by their St. Helena friends when they returned home and accused Mary Frances of "try- ing to recapture the old glamour" of her former life. Mary Frances vented her dismay to Norah, and expressed her own worries about Anne, who she felt needed medical and psychiatric help to remedy the ravages of pills and alcohol, and to help her regain the stability that had been threatened by the loss of her parents, the Ranch, and the proposed yearlong absence of her elder sister. As for recapturing the "old glamour" of her former life, Mary Frances said that was neither possible nor desirable.

The exchange underscored Mary Frances's ongoing sense of responsibility for her younger sisters, especially Anne. "Well, hell . . . if it would do any good I'd ask her to come right along with the children and me," she wrote.

> But it wouldn't . . . any more than it has helped her much to come up here quite a lot and try to live here exactly as she thinks she should continue to live *everywhere*. The Spoiled Adolescent . . . stamp the pretty foot, snarl and heckle at the children, order any available man around like a bar-room flunky, accept every service from me . . . It is a pattern which is senseless, and which I feel she intuitively hates but cannot break for herself . . . But I do worry about her. I have for many years. Now I do more than ever. And I am up against this bitter silent antagonism because I am going to do something I feel is very wise and exciting and beneficent, and it becomes in my mind a part of my general feeling that there is something that must be done to help her and that I am only accentuating her loneliness and need for help.[19]

Mary Frances did, in fact, ask Anne to join them on the trip, but Anne's idea of staying in luxury hotels and visiting exotic casinos and spas was not really compatible with Mary Frances's plans to board the girls and stay in out-of-the-way pensions herself.

Mary Frances's first itinerary included a flight to New York City, where she planned to see Volkening and Covici as well as have the girls spend some time with Donald and Eleanor before they sailed to France on the *Liberté* in late August 1954. But instead they were able to secure reservations on the small Dutch freighter MS *Diemerdyk*, which departed from Oakland earlier in August. "This is a nice little ship . . . mostly cargo, everything from canned pineapple to surgical cotton, with crew and officers of around 85, and 61 passengers. Except for the Captain and the Chief and the Chief Steward, the former are young healthy intelligent boys, between about 15 and 24, in training for the Dutch Navy and/or Merchant Marine," Mary Frances wrote to her uncle Ted. "Things are quite different since the war . . .

the old days of extravagance are gone . . . no more wasteful buffet-suppers, with half-finished bowls of caviar, and so on! The passengers are for the most part elderly single females, with about five husbands of well over 70 . . . one bachelor of 75, who hides behind a monocle and a permanent scotch-and-soda. There are 9 children aboard, to everyone's surprise, and they are really nice kids (Thank God). My girls are having a rare old time . . . they swim two or three times a day in the little canvas pool, and sleep like puppies. So do I . . . I'm still not used to being so carefree . . . no dishes-marketing-telephones-beds-&&&&&&."[20]

A snapshot of Anna and Kennedy next to a life preserver shows two happy youngsters—one eleven years old, one eight—still cosseted from the uncertainties of adolescence. Acutely aware of how fleeting this period of "Lady Rowena one minute and Tom Sawyer the next" was, Mary Frances made the most of being with her daughters during the leisurely voyage. She shared their excitement when they fell in love with their "monkey-like waiter" or each adopted a different old lady, whom they identified by a necklace of small pearls or an ill-fitting set of dentures, and whose fortunes they followed throughout the course of the trip.

When the ship docked at Antwerp, Mary Frances and the girls were among the last to leave the ship, and they accidentally got caught up in the death of an elderly woman who was en route to England with her sister. The bizarre tale of the woman's collapse at the customs table, Mary Frances's frantic communications with the ship's doctor, and the surviving sister's panic became the story "The Weather Within," which she wrote in Aix that fall and sent to Norah to read. In it she describes at length her ambivalence about making arrangements for the cremation of the body and changing her own plans to sightsee in Antwerp with her daughters because she was entrusted with aiding the surviving sister. She did not want the role, which was cast upon her by the simple circumstance of having been one of the last passengers to disembark. Nevertheless, she did help the surviving sister to inform the proper authorities, and invited her to check into the same hotel where she and the girls were staying. The next morning she found a few bills in payment for the meal they had shared the evening before and a thank-you note slipped under her door.

After less than twenty-four hours in Antwerp, Mary Frances and the girls went by canal boat to Bruges and then by train to Paris, where they changed stations and went directly to Aix-en-Provence and the refuge of the Hôtel Roi René. The town, which had been founded by Roman invaders on the ruins of a much older site more than two thousand years earlier, had been recommended to Mary Frances by Georges Connes because the weather in either Arles or Avignon, her initial choices, would be too harsh with the mistral blowing. Built on a sedimentary basin and surrounded on three sides by ranges, ridges, and mountains, Aix had a milder climate. Connes also felt that the historical, educational, and cultural opportunities offered by the old capital of Provence would greatly benefit Mary Frances and her daughters.

The first day in Aix, Mary Frances and her children walked through the dry, bright, August streets along the boulevard du Roi René and the rue d'Italie. "I did not know what direction I was taking," she wrote some years later in *Map of Another Town*. "We came upon the benign fountain of King René, with the green tunnel of the Cours stretching westward, and it was more like a flashing vision of promise than any I had yet seen."[21] Anna and Kennedy ordered lemonade and Mary Frances drank beer on the terrace of the Deux Garçons, and then they strolled westward along the cours, toward the impressive circular expanse of the fountain in the Rotonde and then to the Glacier, in a little park called the place Jeanne d'Arc. It was in the Glacier that Anna and Kennedy had their first lunch, a *jambon*, in Aix. Even more delightful than the ten-inch baguette spread with sweet butter and filled with ham was the fancy server that contained pots of pink, hot, cool, brown, and yellow mustard. Although they were not particularly fond of mustard, the possibilities seemed limitless, as did the attentions of Ange, who soon became their favorite waiter.

From the expensive Roi René, Mary Frances and her daughters moved into the small Hôtel de France, and Mary Frances pursued her plan to submerge her daughters in the language. Through the network of Connes's friends and associates in Dijon, Mary Frances contacted Mme Wytenhove, a respectable Aixois widow with three children of her own, who was willing to board the children with her family for a few months in her home on the place de l' Archevêché. When the school term began in late September, the Dominican nuns at the École Ste.-Catherine accepted Anna as a day student, but they thought it advisable for Kennedy to wait two months before attending classes. During that time Mme Wytenhove tutored her at home.

On November 8 Mary Frances went to Dijon for the first of two weekends at the Foire Gastronomique.[22] Since her first visit to the fair in 1929, when it was held in a long canvas shelter along the cours du Parc, the annual food-and-wine celebration had been moved into impressive permanent quarters. Pennants displaying the insignia of Burgundy hung from all the lampposts leading to it, and buses shuttled visitors from the railroad station to the gates. Inside the main entrance, a twenty-foot revolving Table of Lucullus captured everyone's attention with its stunning glassware, silver, and linens and its glorious array of prepared dishes, artfully arranged bunches of grapes, and local delicacies—all of which changed daily as a series of chefs and provisioners competed for prizes. Three corridors extended outward from the Table of Lucullus. The one to the left was home to the *Arts Ménagers*, where electric appliances, kitchen utensils, and everything else needed for a visitor's *batterie de cuisine* were on display. The middle aisle, the *Allée d'Honneur*, featured foreign products like Dutch beers, British teas and cheeses, Italian vermouths and Chiantis, Brazilian and African coffees, and samples of them all to taste. The right-hand aisle, *Vins et Alimentations*, displayed the wines and foods of France—oysters fresh from the beds in Arcachon, chickens roasting on spits, snails sizzling, cheeses and pâtés served on crusty rolls, and the beautiful "table wines" of France.

"The town was jumping, quasi-hysterical, injected with a mysterious supercharge of medieval pomp and Madison-Avenue-via-Paris commercialism," Mary Frances wrote. "I had gone to several banquets where ornate symbols were pinned and bestowed, with dignitaries several levels above me in the ferocious protocol of eating and drinking."[23] On her last day in Dijon she excused herself from dinner with Georges and Henriette Connes and headed for the venerable Crespin to savor a meal alone and snatch a taste of the past—a glass of dry white vermouth followed by a dozen *Portugaises Vertes Extra* oysters, a half-bottle of red Meursault, a dozen snails, and a ripe cheese from the Cistercian Abbey nearby, the same drinks and dishes she had savored there more than twenty years ago. "I sat back as I had done so often and so well in Crespin. Coffee was black and brutal."[24] The next day she returned to Aix.

Before her two visits to the Foire, Mary Frances had looked for accommodations for herself with one of the many upper-class Aixois landladies who rented rooms to long-term visitors. She was lonely in the impersonal surroundings of the hotel and tired of escaping to movies in the evening to avoid her small room. Separated from her daughters, she also wished to be able to enjoy at least two of her daily meals in the company of people who would be familiar. After a few futile attempts, she found accommodations with a Mme Lanes at 17 rue Cardinale, a few blocks north of the cours Mirabeau and a few doors away from the place des Quartre-Dauphins, with its seventeenth-century fountain sporting the eponymous dolphins.

The German, Italian, and American occupations had left their stamp on Mme Lanes in the form of a lingering defeatism, and the only way that she could maintain her household in the manner appropriate to her social status was by discreetly sharing her home and table with paying guests. She did this with great thrift and personal effort in a household of difficult women, including her unstable adult daughter and servants whose employment seemed to be chronically short-lived. Her boarders always came with appropriate recommendations, and she personally screened them. Mary Frances passed muster, but because the room she was to occupy was not yet vacant, Mme Lanes made the unusual concession of inviting her to lunch and dine at 17 rue Cardinale until it was. Sometime in late November, Mary Frances moved into the small, ill-heated maid's room on the top floor of the town house that Mme de Sévigné's daughter had once inhabited.

Filtered through Mary Frances's American eyes, the shabby gentility and supreme effort on Mme Lanes's part to set a table of many courses, many changes of china, and appropriate fish and fruit cutlery was both admirable and maddening. She longed for the day when her landlady would "accept her as another woman and not as one more outlander who paid for her food and lodging,"[25] but she found in Mme Lanes the same condescending attitude toward Americans that she had also discovered in former students and acquaintances of

Georges Connes who invited her into their homes. On one occasion she was openly insulted by a woman who had an ax to grind from her past college days in Dijon. "Tell me, dear lady . . . explain to all of us," she taunted, "how one can dare to call herself a writer on gastronomy in the United States, where from everything we hear, gastronomy does not yet exist? . . . Now that you have eaten this little French luncheon, so simple but so typical of our national *cuisine*, tell us just how you managed to invent such profitable fiction about one of our sciences, when even Brillat-Savarin could not! We await your dictum!"[26] In self-defense Mary Frances began to adopt a vocabulary— "They did not see me," "I became invisible"—that reflected her growing ability to be alone in places where she had once been with others; in short, she was learning to be a ghost.

During the fall of 1954, *The Art of Eating: The Collected Gastronomical Works of M.F.K. Fisher* appeared, and it was a success. The book featured "decorations" by the artist Leo Manso, an appreciative introduction by Clifton Fadiman, and a cover photograph by Man Ray, putting to rest the fears Mary Frances had articulated to Powell some months before: "I feel quite plainly repelled by the whole thing, and I wish I had never agreed to it . . . warming up a cold corpse, as far as I'm concerned, for the woman who wrote those books has been dead for years."[27] Reviewing the book in the *New York Herald Tribune*, J. T. Winterich pointed out that anyone who had not heard of M.F.K. Fisher would be introduced to "one of the haute cuisine gastronomes of all time."[28] Longtime admirer J. H. Jackson of the *San Francisco Chronicle* said, "In today's welter of cutie-pie cookery chatter, the conversations of M.F.K. Fisher on *The Art of Eating* are like a refreshing breeze flowing from the twin sources of sense and sensibility. She writes, in short, as one adult to another—practically, often profoundly, and always beautifully. If eating means more to you than a steak drowned in bottled sauces, then she's what you've been looking for."[29]

In *The Spectator*, Alan Brien called *The Art of Eating* a cookery book on the verge of being a novel, and he described Al and Chexbres as the problematic heroes, who seemed to travel with the author-heroine through a variety of landscapes and "bottlescapes." "They eat and love and talk their way into oblivion until she is finally left alone to cook her lonely exquisite meals which neither time nor tragedy can

force her to neglect . . . M.F.K. Fisher's egoism is childlike and total,"
he wrote. "Everywhere she goes waiters, chefs, peasants, innkeepers,
little boys who sing outside cafes, chauffeurs, bus drivers, ship's captains, everybody who is in the local-color business fall half in love
with her and Al (or Chexbres) and lay their art at her knowledgeable,
and appreciative feet."[30]

In his introduction, Clifton Fadiman dubbed M.F.K. Fisher a
"philosopher of food," who cut a wide swath through America's native
puritanism and related food to the larger human experience:

> Her subject is hunger. But only ostensibly so. Food is her para-
> mount but not her obsessive concern. It is the release-catch
> that sets her mind working. It is the mirror in which she may
> reflect the show of existence. For despite her denials, there is
> much in these five volumes about wars and love, much about
> death and joy and sorrow and indeed many of the major
> concerns of men and women. For all her awesome learning
> and authority, Mrs. Fisher writes not as a specialist, but as a
> whole human being, spiky with prejudices, charming, short-
> tempered, well traveled and cosmopolitan, yet with her full
> share of intolerances. She is a person, not a gourmet masked as
> a writer. Her passion comes from inside her, and it is a passion,
> not an enthusiasm or a hobby.[31]

That M.F.K. Fisher should be ranked with Brillat-Savarin, Fadiman
said, was her entitlement.

It is not known whether the publication of *The Art of Eating* or
Mary Frances's translation of Brillat-Savarin or her friendship with
Connes (who had once been mayor of Dijon) was responsible for the
Chevalière du Tastevin award given to her at a special dinner at the
Clos Vougeot in Dijon that fall. "A lot of whoop-ti-do cannily staged
for commercial reasons called P.R., I believe? It is an enjoyable show,
if much too long. The night I was there, there were a lot of women
guests, mostly German and Italian . . . By the time I was summoned
for the ceremony . . . it is very silly, and I was the only female and
thought I might be conspicuous but nobody was even listening . . . it
would not have mattered if I had been two-headed and bright green. I

thought the whole thing vulgar."[32] In a sense she had come full circle. She was now a minor local celebrity in the city where twenty-five years before, as an unknown, she had discovered the fine wines of Burgundy and tasted dishes like *tripes à la mode de Caen véritable*, *écrevisses à la nage*, and pâté de foie gras. Now she had moved on to another city where she was beginning to sketch the outlines of another inner map, drawing upon new experiences in places that would allow her to convey the need to be in a satisfying place, a need that would join the other insistent hungers for "food, security, and love."[33]

By the time the leaves on the plane trees flanking the cours Mirabeau turned color and began to fall, Mary Frances and her daughters had settled into a routine. At six o'clock Mary Frances met them at their school, and then they stopped at the Glacier to talk over the events of the day and enjoy a *goûter*, a snack somewhat comparable to English tea. After her own Cinzano and soda, Mary Frances would take them to Mme Wytenhove's apartment for their evening meal and return to Mme Lanes's for her own. And once a week, she escorted them to ballet lessons. In a letter to Donald, she was glowing in her reports about their academic progress. They were, understandably, not up to their normal grade levels, but in the trimester exams, Anna had an average of 85 and Kennedy 78, and both were speaking easily and even volubly. "Kennedy's accent is better than Anna's," she wrote. "While Anna has a slight Anglo-American intonation, being older . . . they still mix French and English. Quite often they go from one to the other without knowing it, but it doesn't worry me at all, natural stage . . . and I can slip into French when they are talking, and they go right on."[34]

Inclined to reward herself and her daughters on almost any pretext, Mary Frances often whisked them off to Marseilles for a day or weekend, and frequently took them on long walks followed by lunch at a local inn, or a picnic when the weather permitted. Gradually, she acquainted them with the towns and restaurants that were beginning to define her own private map of Provence. For Anna and Kennedy, it was an unforgettable experience. Their pattern was to go to the Madeleine on Thursdays, when couscous was served. On weekends they also went to matinees to see their favorite actor, Fernandel, in the film of the moment, and they spent occasional overnights at the

Hôtel Roi René, where they could take luxurious baths and enjoy room service. In a letter to Covici, Mary Frances described spending three days climbing up every thirteenth-century tower and exploring every dungeon in the Avignon region with her "Constant Companions."[35]

In mid-December, Anna and Kennedy left Mme Wytenhove's apartment and joined their mother at Mme Lanes's establishment, where they observed the rituals of her table with the same diligence that they applied to the difficult flow of adult conversation in their second language. Living in Aix soon became as familiar as living in Whittier or St. Helena. In Aix, however, there was excitement and even mystery, a veritable parade of vengeful gypsies, crippled newspaper vendors, and solicitous waiters that sent their imaginations soaring. They even befriended a mongrel Disneyesque dog and followed his exploits, amorous as well as gustatory—including his unmasking of a band of local crooks.[36]

Anna and Kennedy celebrated their first Christmas in France with Mary Frances at the Hôtel Beauvau in Marseilles, where they were joined by Anne and Sean Kelly, who flew across the Mediterranean from his air base in Casablanca. During the five days that Sean was with them, they stayed in both Aix and Marseilles, and Mary Frances kept a journal of their meals, from proper Gibson *apéros*—aperitifs— at the Roi René to the various restaurants in Marseilles where she played the role of "Gastronomic Tyrant," by selecting the dishes to be served in advance. "I hate a restaurant table cluttered with a dozen different dishes, all looking and smelling their own ways," she wrote. "So when I can I order in advance automatically, and this time I could."[37] Whether they were eating a bouillabaisse in a first-class restaurant or poached eggs in jelly in a fourth, they dined well, and Mary Frances concluded, "As Tyrant I can only blush lightly to confess that we ate some more *petites fritures mange-tout*[38] . . . They were perfect, everything they should be."[39]

From her first experience of Marseilles as a young bride in 1929, the city had not lost its hold on Mary Frances's imagination. That Christmas she introduced her daughters to the quai des Belges, the Rive Neuve, La Criée, and Notre-Dame de la Garde. They placed lighted candles in front of the life-sized *santons* in the Nativity scene in the vast cathedral, and with their aunt and cousin they dined at Surcouf, where Mary Frances watched her girls appreciate "the difference between a superb *bourride* and merely an excellent one."[40] The account of how they transformed the hat rack in their room into a Christmas tree, how the children explored the nearby shops on the Canebière and bought trinkets and sweets to decorate the tree, and how they breakfasted on caviar, hard rolls, cups of *café au lait*, champagne, and a magnificent *bûche de Noël* appeared in "The Mahogany Tree" in *Woman's Day* and later in a slightly different form in *A Considerable Town*.[41] It captured the excitement Mary Frances always felt in the ancient city, along with its dark and seedy underbelly.

After the holidays, with Anna and Kennedy back at school, Mary Frances decided to explore in greater depth one of the best pastry shops in Aix. It belonged to a petite, formidable woman who ruled over a kingdom of almond paste, chestnuts soaked in sweet liqueurs, and chocolates in all of their various forms. What intrigued Mary Frances the most about the shop was the rhythm of cakes, fruits, and bonbons that flowed through the large display window as one month followed another—candied fruits on such and such a date, sugared almonds for the baptismal season, confections for June weddings, strawberry-shaped marzipan for one date, snails and shrimp for another. She made an appointment with the proprietress and tried to explain to her that to a person visiting Aix the pageantry of the pastry shop windows was a mystery that she longed to solve, beyond the broad and obvious explanation of the seasons and the ingredients that they brought. But with each interview, the proprietress turned the subject to *calissons*, the specialty of Aix, and invited Mary Frances into the kitchen to observe their production. Although much later Mary Frances passed along the recipe for the little pointed ovals of almond paste to her readers, she never wrote the article that she wanted to write about the symbolism of the edible artifacts in the pastry shop window. Nor did she write a book about the *bonnes femmes* who cooked their marvelous meals during the Lenten competition held annually in Aix. It was the city itself that gripped her imagination, and she found herself exploring the narrow cobbled streets and passageways, the ancient churches, and the hidden fountains in the various courtyards.

In mid-January, preparations for the Carnaval d'Aix dominated the city. Floats were assembled, the numbers of gypsies and carnies swelled, and colored lights were strung along the cours. The revelry lasted for twelve days in February and featured two grand parades and a number of impromptu ones made up of visiting musicians and rag-tag revelers. There were costume balls for children and adults, and showers of confetti as throngs of people mingled, jostled each other, and moved in a frightening mob down the main streets of Aix. On the fourth day, as they watched the grand float of His Majesty Carnaval LVIII drive by, the surge of confetti throwers was so great that Mary Frances, who was not wearing a mask, was pelted in the face with a mixture of paper and tobacco and temporarily blinded. To compound the problem, Kennedy had become separated from her mother and sister and sought shelter with their favorite waiter at the Glacier. To someone who could not abide scenes of any kind, this display of mass confusion was more than Mary Frances could stand. After four days of what she described as "the scheduled cruelty of Carnaval," she escaped with her daughters to the island of Porquerolles until Lent began a week later.

After Easter vacation, Mary Frances began to think about Anna and Kennedy's transition back into the school system in the States. With her furniture and books in storage in St. Helena, she was free to enroll them wherever she thought best, and she entertained the idea of renting a visiting professor's place in Berkeley or even leasing an apartment in San Francisco, where Anna could enroll in the San Francisco School of Ballet and both girls could attend public school. But she still had to solve the problem of their keeping up a "well-bred" French, and she feared that even enrolling them in a parochial school with French nuns would prove to be inadequate.

So, in an impulsive moment, Mary Frances approached Mme Wytenhove about the possibility of "adopting" her sixteen-year-old daughter, Monique, for a year. Both of her girls were fond of Monique, and Anna, especially, admired her sense of style. Mary Frances thought that she could not only help Anna and Kennedy with their French but would also act as a bridge between them and herself as they approached their teen years. Although hesitant, Mme Wytenhove saw the advantages that a year in California would offer her daughter, and she agreed to the plan. But to Mary Frances's amazement, her sisters were shocked at the idea. Norah cautioned her that Monique's status would not be clear, and that Mary Frances's responsibilities in terms of the girl's health, safety, and education would be greater than she anticipated. Anne voiced concern about admitting an "outsider" into the family circle. Brushing aside their objections, Mary Frances started the necessary legal paperwork at the American consulate in Marseilles.

That spring, Leo and Barbara Marschutz, an artist couple Mary Frances had befriended in Aix, made her an offer she could not resist. They wanted to paint in Italy for a few weeks, and asked her to stay in their country *mas* at Châteaunoir, about twenty minutes from the center of Aix, and care for their chickens, kittens, and dog Whisky while they were away. Mary Frances took her daughters out of school, and they played in the hills with Whisky, gathered eggs every day, and grew rosy in the sunshine. Living in the country was a dramatic switch from the routine at 17 rue Cardinale and the long days at Ste.-Catherine, and Mary Frances, against the advice of Mère Tassy at the girls' school and the disapproval of Mme Lanes, decided to extend their country idyll by moving from Châteaunoir to Le Tholonet, a few miles farther from town, when the Marschutzes returned to their *mas* at the end of April.

Neglected after the war, the Château du Tholonet was in a state of disrepair, with only one aged woman residing in the main residence, although there was a farmer's family in one of the wings, a shepherd and his wife in one of the stone barns, and a gardener and his wife in the gate cottage. Mary Frances and the girls moved into the newly painted dormitory of the old stable house at the beginning of May. Although there was a local one-room schoolhouse where a tired school-marm taught four grades, Mary Frances was loath to enroll Anna and Kennedy. They would, she was told, acquire the local Provençal accent, but more to the point, she also felt that a few months of freedom were in order after the rigorous discipline of the past months. Just as her own mother had done, Mary Frances exempted her daughters from ordinary scholastic requirements.

While living in full view of Mont Ste.-Victoire and walking along the Route du Tholonet, Anna and Kennedy felt the unseen presence of Cézanne and were even convinced that traces of oil paint that they found in the cracks of tree trunks were remnants of the paints he'd wiped from his palette knife long ago. "They were his intimates in a strange way,"[42] Mary Frances wrote of her daughters. In her mind, such knowledge, and the adventures the girls had roaming the hills with the shepherd and his flock and playing with the village children more than compensated for the lack of formal lessons.

Living on the grounds of the old château was liberating for Mary Frances as well. No longer was she dependent upon Mme Lanes's kitchen for meals for herself and the children. And while they still frequented the Glacier and the Deux Garçons whenever marketing or errands took them into Aix, Mary Frances now had her first country kitchen in Provence. Her efforts to obtain foodstuffs in Aix and from the local market in Le Tholonet and to prepare the kinds of meals she wanted for herself and the children became a preoccupation that would inspire some of her most compelling prose. Breakfasts might be of canned grapefruit juice, large bowls of *café au lait* with brown sugar, slices of Dijon gingerbread with sweet butter and Alpine honey; noontime meals of new potatoes boiled in a broth of carrots, onions, and sausages (set aside for the evening meal), sweet butter, mild cheese, and a bowl of green olives and little radishes; and suppers of broth with thin slices of the reserved sausage, carrots, onions, chopped parsley, and celery tops served with slices of grilled toast, and a bowl of mixed peaches, pears, and pineapple. Descriptions of such meals tempt the reader of "Two Kitchens in Provence" to revisit vicariously the nine-by-nine whitewashed kitchen with its meager *batterie de cuisine*.

Without a refrigerator, Mary Frances learned firsthand that "the fish would spoil by tomorrow, the chops would be practically incandescent in thirty-six hours, and the tomatoes would rot in twelve. It was a kind of race between my gluttony for the fine freshness and my knowledge of its fleeting nature."[43] And when she had misjudged the amount of food needed from one marketing expedition to the other and there was only a dried onion and shriveled lemon left in the wicker tray on the old pine table that dominated the kitchen, Mary Frances and the girls walked into the village and dined on grilled *poulet* or a trout *meunière* at the Restaurant Thome.

In June, while Norah traveled in Germany with a friend, her sons vacationed with Mary Frances and her girls in the south of France. Anticipating their arrival, Anna and Kennedy had scouted the territory and made many more plans than could be accomplished during their two-week stay. Past the château and the mill, there was a pool called the End of the World, and when the weather grew warmer they swam there. Although they did not understand the language, John and David joined their cousins in following the old shepherd and his flock, wading in the stream, and even taking tea with some of the elderly ladies who had befriended Mary Frances in Aix. To further amuse them, the Marschutzes' dog, Whisky, usually ran down the hill from his home in Châteaunoir to romp with the youngsters at Le Tholonet.

While the four children played, Mary Frances revised the story about the death of their fellow passenger on the *Diemerdyk* and sent it to Volkening. She also worked on a book about the mongrel dog in town that she and the children had befriended. Although there had been some interesting material about Juliette Récamier in the Bibliothèque in Aix, Mary Frances told Covici that she had jettisoned the project because it involved so much reading and digging and research. As remiss as she considered herself for not pursuing the biography of the "old girl," she assured him that she continued to make lengthy notes for the "old-age project."

Living at the Château du Tholonet reminded her vividly of her former life at Le Paquis, and when she looked over the fields of wildflowers, she thought about the view she had shared with Dillwyn in Vevey. "There are at least ten different kinds in the posy the children picked yesterday for me . . . all those pink and purple vetches and dark blue lupines . . . And white daisies and clover," she wrote to Norah. "It gives me a strange feeling to have my *children* bring in what I last saw there with all of us."[44] Shortly after Norah joined them during the third week in June, Mary Frances began the task of packing their belongings in preparation for leaving Aix. In contrast to the idyllic days at Le Tholonet, the return trip aboard the *Vesuvio* was, as Mary Frances wrote to Donald, "a surprisingly unbelievable experience . . . we were about 52 days on a real hellship . . . I am writing about it, but nobody would ever print what I'll write, for it involves everything from Tito to 'white slavery' to pederasty."[45]

Because of the political unrest between Italy and Yugoslavia, so many refugees were fleeing Trieste that Tito had petitioned France not to let cargo freighters dock for passengers. Mary Frances, Norah, their children, and Monique therefore had to travel to Genoa—"7 of us to feed and lodge . . . a real catastrophe"[46]—where they waited a week to board the *Vesuvio*, a freighter that usually did not carry passengers. Once aboard, the complications of traveling on a ship with unknown ports of call multiplied, as did their days at sea. The trip, which took them from Genoa to Barcelona, Central America, and through the Panama Canal to their first American port, Los Angeles, and their destination, San Francisco, became the subject of many of Mary Frances's letters to friends left behind in Aix, and she wrote a story, "Announcement from Israfel,"[47] about its sinister aspects. The captain treated the cargo with more care than he did the twelve passengers. The lower decks were packed with miserable refugees escaping from Yugoslavia to Venezuela, the food was almost inedible except for the pasta, and the water undrinkable without a bit of brandy. The crew was mostly composed of criminals doing time, the saving grace being an innocent hand named Claudio, who as the youngest member of the crew was "owned" and protected by the strongest member. Mary Frances called him Israfel after the Koran angel whose heartstrings were a lute, and his presence seemed to ensure that they would all reach port.

The children amused themselves by playing chess, Scrabble, and other games that they devised. They also took photographs and wrote a journal of their voyage, which they presented to their aunt Anne for Christmas that year. Norah and Mary Frances rationed their reading to last until the end of the trip. Because the crew was so depraved, they also spent a considerable amount of time knitting within sight of the youngsters. But there were also unexpected delightful moments on the voyage. For Anna's saint's day on July 26, the cook made a *pièce montée* out of paper, dyed turnips, carrots, and radishes. And during the voyage Norah and her boys became acquainted with Monique, who told them stories in French and sang French songs with them. Months after the voyage, the children still referred to their experiences on "the dear old *Vesuvio*," and even Mary Frances admitted that she did not regret it at all.

When they docked in San Francisco, Norah and her sons returned to Berkeley, and Mary Frances picked up the yellow Ford station wagon that she had ordered while abroad. Then she drove to the apartment that her sister Anne had selected for her, at 1740 Franklin Street, down in the Van Ness Gulch before the climb to Pacific Heights. With a little bit of planning, the living arrangements were worked out. Monique and Mary Frances each had their own bedrooms, while Anna and Kennedy shared a room. They had brought eighteen trunks and suitcases from Aix, and Anne had previously arranged for the books and goods stored in Napa to be delivered. Not aware of the parking rules on Franklin Street, Mary Frances awoke the next morning to find that her new car had been towed. "Then an earthquake apparently jarred the gas oven, which later blew up in my face: 2nd degree, and nevermore any eyebrows or lashes, but it's fun to put on new ones, and there's no permanent damage thank god," she told Donald. "The skin-boys assure me that in a few more days (It's been four weeks now, one hell and three just purgatorish . . .) I'll be as lovely as ever."[48] These were the first of many adjustments to city living that they all had to make, including the need for Mary Frances to chaperone the girls everywhere, from the corner grocery to ballet and music lessons.

Anna and Kennedy attended the nearest grammar school, which was, as Mary Frances described it, "a real mish mosh racially."[49] Anna immediately fell in love with a tall fat Chinese boy, and Kennedy's three best friends were "Mexican, Chinese, and South Carolina Negro."[50] Anna auditioned for the San Francisco Ballet School and was accepted, and Kennedy began taking recorder lessons. Monique enrolled in Lowell High School, where she was placed in the senior year. Having already mastered conversational English, she adjusted more easily to her classes than to American high school social life, which included the brutality of football games and the horrid Jell-O salads in the school cafeteria.

San Francisco had long been a kind of refuge for the Kennedy family and Mary Frances in particular, but after living there for two months, she realized that she hadn't seen a single exhibit, movie, or play and had gone to only two restaurants—once to pick up a Siamese kitten from a waiter she knew and the other time to toast an old beau who had married. She played the role of chaperone, cook, and house-keeper from dawn to dusk. The girls were increasingly bored because they could not have bicycles or run and shout. Mary Frances soon began to think seriously about leaving the city.

Adding to Mary Frances's uneasiness was the fact that bringing Monique into their daily lives seemed only to compound the increasingly difficult relationship between her elder daughter and herself. She had never been very demonstrative with her daughters, but with Monique so far from her own mother and often somewhat lonesome, Mary Frances went out of her way to treat the French girl affectionately and to make her feel part of the family. Anna did not respond kindly to these displays. On New Year's Eve, a few minutes after honking horns, firecrackers, and gunshots ushered in 1956, Monique gave Mary Frances a bouquet of chrysanthemums she had hidden in her washbowl. "I kissed her cool cheek, so young, and felt moved by her youth and her distance from Aix and the family and sorry that I had felt cross and bored with her arrogant youth, earlier in the night. But as I tried to kiss Anna, lying tense and obviously awake on her made-up couch, she faked sleep. She is punishing me for some sin, perhaps that of bearing her," Mary Frances noted in her journal. "I was older by several centuries, temporarily at least. I was drowned by the noise of the bells of St. Saveur in Aix. I was wracked by guilt for unknown things I had done to make Anna remove herself from me with hatred, revolt, anger, disgust. I was a-tremble with fear of what I might even now be doing to Mary [Kennedy], still outwardly a loving creature. I was sick with doubts. And as I heard the cold hard raindrops and the foolish autos honking, I was excited by my own determination to continue my muddled course, to go on being me."[51]

By the time that Mary Frances and the girls returned to their apartment from a visit with Norah and her sons on New Year's Day, Mary Frances had made up her mind to move back to St. Helena as soon as she could find a suitable house. She told Georges Connes, "For me it's adventurous to decide I'm wrong about anything, the way I know I was about coming to SF. The transition from the little French town and the farm, to SF, was too hard on my girls. I know it now, but I never dreamed of it while I was doing it. So all right. I'm changing as fast as I can, to a peaceful little familiar wine-valley they know, where we'll have cat-dog-birds-garden. That takes some courage, don't you think?"[52] She planned to rent for a while and then probably purchase a house that would suit both her present needs and later, when her daughters went off to school, be a welcoming place for them to return. San Francisco would again become the refuge, a wonderful town for parties and fun, and St. Helena would be home.

In early February, Mary Frances, Anna, Kennedy, and Monique moved into Rancho Otranto at the end of Sulphur Springs Road. More isolated than the Red Cottage, the house was surrounded by vineyards and oak groves. Mary Frances told Connes that the old place was full of mystery and romance, as was the adjacent empty carriage house flanked by a little stream. Evelyn and Nelson Garden, who owned the property and even more land that extended into the foothills of the Mayacamas, were their only close neighbors. Getting back into the rhythm of up-valley life, the girls returned to the public school in St. Helena and the friends they had known a year and a half earlier. Monique, who seemed remarkably adept at adjusting to new experiences, attended the local high school, where Mary Frances's friends Tony Ten Broeck and Marietta Voorhees were teachers.

On the surface things seemed to go smoothly at Rancho Otranto, but the easy relationship that had existed between Anna and Kennedy at the Ranch in Whittier, in the Red Cottage, and especially at Le Tholonet was growing more difficult. Convinced that her mother favored Kennedy, Anna began to treat her younger sister with disdain, punishing her with verbal insults. Anna also recoiled from Monique, whom she had once thought "the most beautiful-kind-wonderful-exciting-person" who had ever breathed, alternating between fear that she might lose face with the older girl and indifference to her growing disapproval. It was Mary Frances, however, who seemed to bear the brunt of her daughter's wrath and scorn, and when she refused to be drawn into a quarrel that Anna was obviously "itching for," it only infuriated Anna more.

In an unsent letter to Norah, Mary Frances wrote at length about the developing problem:

I know of many things about me that torture Anna: the occasional expression of respect for something I have written, or a very rare picture of a TV show[53] or or or. Those things are hell for her, and she braces herself bitterly for the remark from a protective friend of mine, now and then, that I have worked for the picture or the story or or or. I am over-conscious of the fact that she is building up a jealous conviction that I have always kept her from being famous or beautiful or this-and-that because I wanted all the attention and acclaim and renown and so on for myself . . . that I have deliberately thwarted and stunted her. She is already telling me this: I have been on TV and she has not. Why? Because I have never given her a chance.[54]

This reaction itself was telling, typical of the way Mary Frances referred problems back to herself, and often her idealized self, instead of concentrating on the person with the problem. She seemed to be repeating a dynamic that she had entered into with her sister Anne, whom Mary Frances had implied was jealous of her own greater fame, years, and number of husbands.

Anne seemed to think her niece's behavior was typical of adolescence and reminded Mary Frances that her own behavior toward Edith had been problematic. She suggested that a boarding school might be the answer, as it had been for Edith. But inwardly Mary Frances blamed herself for the situation, and questioned if she should have shared more of her daughters' lives with Donald and not tried to raise them alone.

For his part, Donald had not shown much inclination to include them in his and Eleanor's lives. Kennedy, especially, was profoundly upset that she hadn't received a birthday card from him or even an acknowledgment of the letters she wrote to him. And Mary Frances had run out of answers to her questions about how busy he must be to have forgotten her birthday. She made it a point never to criticize Donald to the children, and never had any but positive things to say about Eleanor whenever the girls were present, but when Covici and his wife visited San Francisco early in 1956, Mary Frances decided to speak to him about Donald's negligence. Upon his return to New York, Covici made it a point to contact Donald and give him a first-hand account of his daughters, of how accomplished they were, and how their year in France had transformed them into winsome young ladies. He warned Donald that they would be out of his life completely if he didn't win back their confidence. Eleanor, especially, decided to do something about bringing his daughters into Donald's life.

Meanwhile, between driving the girls to Scouts, piano lessons, swimming, and school, Mary Frances completed the revision of *The Boss Dog* that spring. Although meant as a gift to her children, it was not exactly a children's book. The tale about the doggiest dog in Aix did, however, attempt to re-create something of the magic that a mother and her two daughters discovered in a Provençal city they grew to know and love. The story also captured something of the innocence of childhood, although the telling was deeply flawed by the mother's prim, artificial-sounding observations and the children's stilted vocabulary. Mary Frances repeatedly said that she spoke to Anna as to an adult and often resorted to sarcasm with her children, which may explain why the dialogue between the fictional mother and her daughters is so unconvincing. More to the point, Mary Frances romanticized and idealized her relationship with her daughters, and never allowed herself to explore in her writing for publication the darker side of the mother-daughter relationship that she reflected upon in her letters and, especially, her journals. Perhaps it cut too close to the bone.

She told Powell that the book seemed to be of interest to a handful of publishers, although they hinted that she might have to rewrite two of its seven stories. She even entertained the idea of appending several recipes for dishes that she and her daughters ate in the various restaurants mentioned in the book. But the manuscript was rejected, and she did not make much of its failure to attract a publisher. Although she resubmitted it in the 1960s, *The Boss Dog* was not published until 1990, when it appeared in a limited hardcover edition, followed by a paperback. Working on *The Boss Dog* triggered memories of the past year in Aix and Le Tholonet, and Mary Frances found herself "in a sort of pain about it, filled with half-understood yearnings, misgivings, regrets, and above all hunger. I am there. But I must not be."[55] She knew that she would write about Aix someday, if only to clarify her own tangled feelings about rediscovering the French language amid an old world of fountains and mysterious passageways, where even scruffy dogs knew the secrets of survival. But she was also aware that there she had been known as the *"Californienne,"* the out-sider, the pretend gastronome.

At the end of August, Mary Frances's tenuous connection with Aix was severed when Monique returned to France. After a little spree at the Clift Hotel in San Francisco, Mary Frances accompanied her to the airport while Anne stayed with Anna and Kennedy at the hotel. It was a particularly sad occasion for Kennedy, as the French girl's kind-ness toward her had compensated for Anna's increasing hostility.

"This will not be the letter I have in my head, the one I have been writing to you ever since I watched you go toward the plane at the San Francisco airport," Mary Frances wrote shortly after Monique's departure. "I, like you, was too full of words to talk. I was filled with affection and loyalty and admiration for you, my young friend who had come so far and dared so much to be with us. Let us go on now, I said, and see what the next step will be, in our relationship."[56] Mary Frances sent a few more letters that fall, telling Monique how much she was missed by students and teachers at the high school. Kennedy and Anna also wrote, but their friendship with the French girl was of a certain time and place. It did not endure. Writing about Monique many years later, Mary Frances said, "I know, though, that we all learned a great deal about how to cope with our inner worlds, thanks to the presence of a fourth person in our small and possibly rather in-grown actuality . . . And it seems impossible that deliberately as well as in our hearts, neither Monique nor the three of us have ever met again. I've never asked my girls if they wanted to see her, so truly loved during an important part of their lives."[57]

ELEVEN

One Verse of a Song

(1956–1960)

Oh Aphrodite, give what only you can give,
Be my ally, my co-conspirator![1]

—Sappho

Their many relocations in the space of the past three years had created a sense of *vagabondage* in her daughters' lives that Mary Frances
hoped to dispel when she purchased a house in St. Helena early in
the summer of 1956. And she immediately involved herself in making
the changes in it that years of neglect had necessitated. Each of the
girls chose a bedroom on the main floor, where they shared the large,
old-fashioned bathroom. There was also a comfortable living room
with a fireplace and bookcases, a spacious kitchen dominated by a
large round table, and a side room christened the Glory Hole, where
Mary Frances stored Dillwyn's paintings, important papers, and
books. Her own bedroom was a small room in the attic. But soon the
basement, with its high windows and sloped concrete foundation
walls, which were bolstered with a half-wall of stone, became the
most lived-in space. The ledge between the concrete and stone provided an ideal bookshelf, and the large wine storage space was named
the Pub. In time she also furnished a private bedroom and recreation
area in the coolness of this favored space.

After some time passed, Mary Frances had the basement windows

enlarged with panes of light amber glass. With the help of some local
Boy Scouts, she dug out the earthen floor and had a concrete floor
laid, which she covered with thick hemp mats. A year later, she added
a bathroom so that the downstairs bedroom could be used as a guest
room. Whenever temperatures soared in the valley, the basement was
a cool retreat for parties, meetings, and day-to-day living. Another favorite entertaining and play area was the patio in the back garden,
where a large fig tree shaded the tables and chairs, and flowers added
dashes of color to the privacy fence.

The room Mary Frances loved best, however, was the enclosed
back porch, which led directly into the kitchen: "The many windows
and the seams in the flimsy walls jammed and leaked now and then,
but we forgave everything for the bright welcome that seemed to
spread out from it the minute anyone came up the narrow steep back
stairs and inside. Its long row of windows looked out onto a giant fig
tree. The walls were a light clear yellow. The curtains were a soft red
plaid, and the linings of all the open supply shelves were the same
red. There were two good old rocking chairs and racks for fruits and
vegetables. The place was *reassuring*."[2]

Mary Frances now lived on a well-trafficked street and was caught
up in the day-to-day life of St. Helena. Juggling her roles as single parent, writer, Brownie Scout mother, PTA advocate, and Chamber of
Commerce member posed a challenge, as did her role as eldest sister.
Anne often visited, and either Mary Frances drove to Berkeley to see
Norah and her nephews or they came to St. Helena. Many of her
friendships also extended to the adult children of her friends. She became a mentor to her goddaughter Sylvia, Gloria Stuart's daughter,
when Sylvia decided to write cookbooks, and she and her husband
and their children were frequent visitors to St. Helena.

During those early days of Mary Frances's residence in St. Helena,
the wine industry in the Napa Valley was developing in ways beyond
the imaginations of the Italian, German, and French immigrants who
planted the first vineyards there. The valley's history of commercial
wine making had begun in the mid-nineteenth century, but it was all
but halted by Prohibition, and only gradually advanced in production
until the 1940s, when a few strategic decisions moved the wine industry forward. At the beginning of the decade a white-Russian émi-

gré, André Tchelistcheff, came to Napa at the request of Georges de Latour at Beaulieu and almost single-handedly changed wine making in the valley. Not only did he discover three distinct natural microclimates from north of San Francisco Bay to north of Calistoga, but he also saw that varietal grapevines unsuited to both the soil and growing conditions had been and were still being planted in these areas. He believed that the cool and moist climate of Carneros was similar to Burgundy, with its rich tradition of pinot noir. The middle of the valley, enriched by centuries of volcanic dust and warmer temperatures, was not unlike Bordeaux, with its great cabernet sauvignons and sauvignon blancs, and the northern portion of the valley, from St. Helena to Calistoga, was similar to the Rhône Valley with its distinctive red and white wines. Tchelistcheff advised the owners of Beaulieu to uproot and replant, and his systematic program of replanting was almost immediately followed by other wineries. He pushed to introduce additional changes in wine production by enlisting the help of scientists from the University of California.

In 1943, Cesare Mondavi purchased the Charles Krug Winery for his sons Robert and Peter to run as a family business. They, in turn, hired Paco Gould to promote their wines. Six years later, Paco initiated the concept of a "tasting room" for the public and "Sunday on the lawn tastings" by invitation only. He also enlisted the help of his friend Jim Beard, with whom he had formed the Napa Valley Vintage Festival Association three years earlier, and the services of wood engraver Mallette Dean to design a logo for his wine newsletter, called *Bottles and Bins*. At a time when there were only twenty wineries in the valley and only about five (Krug, Inglenook, Louis Martini, Beringer, and Beaulieu) making quality wine, these early efforts to enlist the support of the public for fine wines—and whet their palates—were daring.

By the time that Mary Frances purchased her home in town, other important events had signaled the beginning of a momentum that would double the number of wineries in the valley by the mid-seventies. Jim Beard, Paco, Mary Frances, and other wine aficionados initiated another series of wine tastings. The first, which was held at a local car dealership whose walls they decorated with wine posters, was a huge success, and the tastings soon moved to Spottswoode

Winery, where they became lavish garden parties. Planning for these and other events usually involved an evening of casual conversation and imbibing at one of the local Italian family-style restaurants in town or at a dinner served around Mary Frances's kitchen table, where the idea of establishing a wine library as a repository for winery records, wine labels and paraphernalia, and books about wine became an increasingly important topic of conversation.

To that end Mary Frances hosted a special dinner to ensnare Pinky Bynum, who had recently retired as director of the Huntington Library, to coordinate the venture. With enough red wine and roast beef (a dish Mary Frances executed to perfection) to turn the tips of Pinky's ears pink, the fledgling group was sure that he would agree to coordinate the wine library. But before they had unfolded their dinner napkins, one of the eager guests said, "Well, Pinky, the only reason we asked you here was that we want to get you roped into helping us start a wine library."[3] He froze and politely declined, but plans for the library continued.

Life in St. Helena during this time of gradual but determined change remained comfortable and far more simple than the social stratification that would develop in the Napa Valley in the late 1970s and 1980s. In an article comparing Napa and Sonoma that Mary Frances wrote for *Food and Wine* in 1979, she expressed her deep respect for the people she associated with when she first moved upvalley—for the butcher who hated his job but performed it with elegance and the plumber who "delicately flushed out my clogged sewage pipes." She also wrote about retired or active teachers, vintners, and other hardworking people who had a great capacity for drinking, eating, and conversing. "These people," she wrote, "lend themselves to Good Works, and build libraries and fight against bootleg subdividing and dubious contracts for dams and so on. They even serve on school boards, and even run for office. But underneath all this natural concern with what happens to their lands and their children, there is the stratum of plain conviviality that makes an occasional evening essential."[4] Mary Frances's home became a comfortable gathering place for family, friends, and neighbors, for wine enthusiasts and car-pooling parents alike. Childless couples like Paco and Romie Gould and the André Tchelistcheffs mingled easily with

Jim and Yolande Beard and Tony and Elsine Ten Broeck. "They meet, anywhere from three to twenty of them, and eat good simple food, and open a surprising number of their pet bottles, and talk a lot,"[5] Mary Frances wrote.

Participating in these many different activities, however, left little time for writing, and in a letter to her old friend Larry Bachmann, Mary Frances said, "I am at an impasse which I rigidly and fairly successfully (!) ignore most of the time . . . I refuse to continue being the Fisher of 20 and more years ago, which is what the editors want. And they do not like what I write as *this* Fisher. I can easily compromise and make enough money to take care of us. But I feel a great impatience and am risking the refusal of a lot of fat magazine stuff, for a few more months, to do a book [the Récamier biography] long overdue to Viking. Then we'll see. It's a professional problem, but also a moral one for me."[6] For years Bachmann, and Donald and Covici too, had been suggesting that she concentrate on novels, and Norah had hoped that *The Art of Eating* would finally signal the end of her sister's gastronomical writing. But Volkening's inability to sell the story Mary Frances had written about the elderly woman's death in Antwerp and the publishers' rejection of *The Boss Dog* manuscript the previous summer had been disappointments, and Mary Frances seemed unwilling or unable to recapture her earlier enthusiasm for the Récamier story, probably because she no longer identified herself with the beautiful nineteenth-century salonist as she had in 1945. She was no longer a "sexual cum intellectual refugee."

After her brief infatuation with Michel Le Gouis in 1950, Mary Frances had been in "the deep-freeze sexually." But since the beginning of 1957, she had been caught up in a conspirational scenario of public and private meetings with someone she described as her new "love" to her friend Powell: "Dearest Ghuce, I must tell you, the only person in this world to know besides my lover, that I am in love. I have loved peaceably and fairly quietly for about four years, and I know now that I went to Aix to contemplate my strength to remain peaceable and quiet (and unsuspected!). I found it. But now I find that it is not necessary. I am loved. Completely. God, Ghuce, only you can know the state of astonishment I'm in!"[7]

Marietta Voorhees was the drama teacher at the local high school.

A sturdy, striking woman with a commanding voice, she knew how to upstage anyone else in a room. A graduate of the University of California at Berkeley and a resident of St. Helena since 1930, Marietta lived with her widowed mother, Miss Eleanor, and had a collection of old and rare books in a library on the lower level of their home. Almost fourteen years older than Mary Frances, she was the second of two children from a troubled marriage, and, despite rumor and conjecture about ambiguous genitalia at birth,[8] she was raised as a girl and became a handsome woman, a strict and respected teacher, and the director of an amateur acting group called the St. Helena Players. Her passion for fine printing and literature as well as her keen interest in Jungian psychology were widely known in town, and a coterie of past and present students worshiped her from afar.

Mary Frances and Marietta had in common a great appreciation of books, delight in wordplay and humor, and an arrogance that could either attract at will or keep outsiders at bay. Articulate, witty, and expert at attacking each other's defenses, they played to each other's strengths and weaknesses. Always ambivalent about academe herself—she veered between admiring the mastery of a given subject and believing that creativity was more important than knowledge—Mary Frances was in awe of Marietta's intellectual accomplishments. And in Marietta, as in Dillwyn, Larry Powell, and Donald Friede, she found a conversationalist and a correspondent as well as a lover. For her part, Marietta basked in the feeling that she was loved by an author and woman she admired. At this particular time in their lives, they found great happiness with each other.

Given Mary Frances's three marriages and occasional affairs, there was little in her past to suggest that a same-sex relationship was a possibility. At The Bishop's School, although she called her idol, Eda Lord, "the most dazzling exciting human being I had ever met," and she was caught in one of the "same mushy, ignominious, and disgusting 'crushes' that so bored me in others," she also recognized that "it was the only kind of love I had witnessed, except between parents and children and siblings."[9] When she was under Dr. Frumkes' care in 1953, Mary Frances told him that she had had "a very good experience with a woman,[10] for the first time in my life, about six months ago. I have often been wooed by my own sex, but never felt any desire or need for their sexual love . . . This was the culmination or perhaps I should say 'one of the results' of some twenty years of trust and loyalty, and there is nothing to regret: it was fine. It will never be possible or necessary again, but as far as I know, I would never protest in any way if it were . . . that is, if it came about rightly."[11] It was only after Marietta admitted that she was attracted to her in 1957 that Mary Frances entered into a sustained relationship with another woman.

Mary Frances's secret liaison with Marietta revealed, among other things, her emotional state at this time. In letters and journal fragments she often portrayed herself as isolated and needy, a captive observer of her two daughters, and more than once she questioned, "Must I listen to nothing but their experimental prattle, their giggling talk of boys and teachers and girls, all love, love, love. Must I pretend a warm and even understanding interest in what Sally wore to folk dancing and how to slur from B to D on the flute? Part of the time I am interested . . . and then I'm saying, who is this stranger . . . and I yawn because I am lonely."[12] Mary Frances was forty-nine years old. Her lithe, trim body had betrayed her; she had added inches to her waist and a roundness to the once-angular lines of her chin. She was on the cusp of menopause, poised between a newfound freedom from the burden of caring for men and her responsibilities to her fourteen- and eleven-year-old daughters.

At sixty-two, Marietta was approaching the end of her teaching career and the loss of the adulation she had always enjoyed from students and the town's drama enthusiasts. She was also devoted to her aging mother, Miss Eleanor, whom Mary Frances made it a point to invite to lunch or dinner, in order to see Marietta as often as possible. Mary Frances also helped with a Junior Players club of about twenty or more participants, including Anna and Kennedy, offering her garage as a makeshift theater with a permanent stage. Marietta directed, and Mary Frances assisted with these productions in various ways, either helping with the scripts and publicity or making costumes and preparing snacks for tired thespians. There were other subterfuges. Because Mary Frances would not allow a television set in her home, she and the girls visited Marietta and Miss E. every Wednesday evening so that Anna and Kennedy could watch *The Perry Mason Show* with Miss E. Meanwhile, Mary Frances and Marietta drank aperitifs and conversed in the library. But more frequently, they were just two of many, dining around a table at a local trattoria or attending a cocktail party at the Beards' or Ten Broecks'. In April, Mary Frances mentioned to Larry, "I've been with him [Marietta] for 5 nights and days now, during the last two months—the gods are with us, eh?"[13]

Mary Frances began to write again, and told Powell, "I in turn ready myself to do a rather fat series of articles for a magazine . . . decided to break my non-contract pattern long enough to earn a little folding-money for a possible year in Italy with the children. I've done a few radio and TV and magazine things lately. The Récamier book is dead again. I've not yet adjusted my domestic and professional demands to my own secret schedule, but am not worried about being able to do so before much longer. I am well and alive, and in a stunned way I am happier than I have ever been in my life."[14] She had already completed "How to Catch a Sea Monster" for House Beautiful, and had approached Holiday about an article on dining in restaurants with children, drawing on some of the material in The Boss Dog.

In the March 1958 issue of Harper's Bazaar, the last paragraph of "The Editor's Guest Book" announced a series of articles on alcoholic drinks as a sort of "Baedeker of the reigning spirits." The first of the series, "Aperitifs: The Civilizing Influence," appeared without a by-line, but in content and style it was plainly the work of M.F.K. Fisher. She delightfully romped through the tantalizing possibilities of vermouth, cassis, Dubonnet, sherry, and many other drinks that contained the requisite 15 to 20 percent of alcohol, and told about the cafés she had frequented where she enjoyed leisurely sampling them all. Why the article appeared anonymously and why Mary Frances did not complete the series is not known. But "Aperitifs" was followed in June 1958 by Barnaby Conrad's "Rum and Summer Drinks" and in October 1958 by Sylvia Wright's "The Pale Spirits." The projected articles on whiskies and brandies and eaux-de-vie were never published, but the article on aperitifs begged a sequel, if not book, on the subject. "Being in love again has loosened my tight dry muscles," she told Hal Durrell, a fan with whom she had impetuously begun a correspondence. "I am writing easily, although there is always some resentment in me when I agree to do things for money."[15]

Despite the opportunity the Junior Players had given Anna to display her talents, and the other creative opportunities that life in St. Helena offered, the rift between her and her mother degenerated into open verbal insults, which hastened Mary Frances's decision to send her daughter to Anna Head, a boarding school in Berkeley. The school had an excellent academic reputation and a drama department of some note, and it was close to Norah and her sons. For moral support and some financial assistance, Mary Frances sought Donald's help. He was amenable, seeing an opportunity to reestablish his relationship with both girls, and also offered to pay most of the expenses involved in allowing Anna to spend some of the summer in Beverly Hills with Mary Frances's friend Jane Evans, whose daughter Barrie was going to drama school. While Anna was in Los Angeles, Kennedy visited her cousins in Berkeley, and Mary Frances wrote glowingly to Donald about her accomplishments. Kennedy was studying piano theory from a very demanding teacher and would begin lessons with a fine teacher in St. Helena in the fall. Kennedy was also taking advanced swimming lessons. "She is going to make an excellent swimmer, perhaps even show-stuff," Mary Frances reported. "I am delighted to have her do something better than Anna, who is inclined to dim her."[16]

Meeting Anna at the San Francisco airport in August, Mary Frances told Donald that she was "flabbergasted" to see her older daughter two inches taller in her first pair of high heels, lipstick, and a much shorter, very chic hairstyle. They had lunch together at Johnney Kan's and then went to Berkeley to purchase uniforms for Anna Head. Mary Frances also informed Donald that Anna was "shaping into a really knock-out creature, although still frighteningly young inwardly."[17] In her customary style, she downplayed Anna's problems that summer, which she had learned about from Jane Evans, who had reluctantly written to her about Anna's moods and difficulties in observing the "rules" of the house.

In September 1957 Anna went away to Berkeley, and Kennedy attended classes in St. Helena. But, Mary Frances wrote to Hal Durrell, she still drove to 4-H meetings, packed lunches, arranged visits to the orthodontist, and chauffeured Kennedy to school on wet days. "My need to write is cracking the whip and hurting me, right now. There is nothing to do about it. I am also a fairly clear-cut mother-domestic type."[18] Although she knew little or nothing about this gentleman, she encouraged his attempts to woo her with letters, and she answered his often intimate questions about her sex life and her emotional stability point by point. She also plied him with questions about bootlegged whiskey and other native American spirits because she was gathering material for the "drinking" book.

The need to seduce, even at a distance and through the mail, and her maneuverings to hide her relationship with Marietta from her St. Helena friends, however, often masked Mary Frances's bouts with depression and her deep feelings of restlessness about the lack of direction in her work. These and other unresolved issues were addressed only in her journal. "Temporarily I admit defeat. It is bitter to do so," she wrote in February. "But I seem unable to get to work. I feel dull and morose. Other writers have felt so and have gone on writing, doggedly and perhaps well. I have things to write about. But I have nothing to write toward, none to write to. That is my curse. It is an emotional one, and since I recognize it as such I should be able to cope with it. But for the moment I am not able to . . . I need to be directed for a time."[19] She was too proud to ask Marietta for help, and she had already assumed the role of established, confident writer with Powell. So the easiest way to cope was to seek distraction. It was a tactic she adopted for dealing with the more difficult problem of Anna as well.

In June, Anna returned from boarding school and Berkeley a very unhappy and confused adolescent. To Mary Frances's dismay, her daughter had taken almost an instant dislike to her teachers at Anna Head. She had also gravitated toward a group of girls who deeply resented the fact that their parents had sent them away to boarding school, and, in many cases, also to psychiatric counselors, because their conduct at home and at school was deplorable. After nine months in that environment, Anna's relations with her mother were more strained than they had been the summer before. She flatly refused her mother's advice to seek help from a professional counselor, a suggestion that only reinforced her conviction that her mother was the enemy. At a loss for what to do, Mary Frances decided to send both Anna and Kennedy to summer school at Parnell in Whittier. The Beards opted to send their daughter Susan with them.

Before leaving St. Helena for Whittier, however, Anna and Kennedy spent a week in San Francisco with Donald and Eleanor. It was their first vacation with their father in more than nine years, and they loved every minute of it, from getting picked up in a white limousine to checkout time at the Fairmont Hotel on Nob Hill. They went to the finest restaurants in town, toured Chinatown and the Embarcadero, saw a few plays, and went shopping with Eleanor. It was a week of fun and extravagance, and they entertained Donald with their fluency in French and ability to speak knowledgeably about couscous as well as Classic Comics. They also grew closer to Eleanor. That her father and stepmother were obviously successful in the publishing world, could afford to travel, and had acquired a weekend and summer place on Long Island was not lost on Anna.

When Donald and Eleanor took the girls home, they stayed with Mary Frances for a few days. The visit provided an opportunity for Donald to assess his former wife's financial situation. On the plus side, she owned the house and a car with a clear title, carried more-than-adequate insurance, and had enriched her bank account with the recent sale of Bareacres. But she had been living on capital from her father's estate for the past five years, which in another five years would be depleted. At the moment her professional earnings were almost nothing, because, she told Donald, she felt that she had to live life to the hilt for and with the girls, and could pick up her professional life four or five years later when they went off to professional school or college.

After summer school at Parnell, Anna expressed a wish to return there in the fall. Mary Frances was pleased with her choice, and there was a scramble to assemble trunks and boxes and send her off to Los Angeles, where friends would meet her and drive her to Whittier. Unhappy with the public school in St. Helena, Mary Frances took steps to find a suitable school for Kennedy. She decided on Anna Head for its challenging academics, but not wishing to repeat the problems that Anna had experienced as a boarder, decided to enroll Kennedy as a day student in the eighth grade and rent the lower apartment in Norah's home on Panoramic Way. "Kennedy takes entrance exams on September 3, and if all goes well will start school Sept. 15," Mary Frances told Donald. "I'll pick her up at 1 on Fridays and we'll come right up here, and stay until about 5:30 on Monday mornings. I will make a special effort to set up our weekend plans on the weekend before, to have people here for dinner or to go to see them, for we have made really good friends here and I do not want the relationships to go dead."[20] As for her relationship with Marietta, Mary Frances had already established her priorities, and Marietta knew that "the children came first."

When Kennedy failed to pass the entrance examination for Anna Head on September 3, Mary Frances was dismayed to learn that her younger daughter had just been sliding through the past two years at the local school in St. Helena, getting above-average grades not by cheating but by bluffing. Her math scores were on the fifth-grade level, and her grammar and spelling scores were very poor in spite of the A's she had received. The school's counselor recommended a program of tutoring for at least three months before she could qualify for admission to Anna Head. After a hurried search, Mary Frances hired a tutor and Kennedy joined her cousin John in the eighth grade at Willard Junior High in Berkeley.

Without a phone to distract her, and relegating most of her socializing to weekends in St. Helena, Mary Frances decided to work once again on her edition of Peter Cartwright's autobiography. "I don't know who cares but me," she wrote to Donald. "But *I care*. I think he was one of the ingenuous accidental giants of our whole American culture."[21] There is evidence that Volkening sent the 274-page manuscript, titled *Raise the Heavenly Shout: The Autobiography of Peter Cartwright*, to Viking, to American Heritage, to World Publishing, to Little, Brown, and to Putnam, with no success.

Perhaps it was working with the Cartwright material again that triggered the idea for Mary Frances's next project, or maybe it was the fact that she had more time to read her favorite Nero Wolfe and Maigret detective stories in Berkeley than she had in St. Helena—whatever the reason, she told Volkening that she was considering a book with the working title *Some of the Men in My Life*. The men included Peter Cartwright, Nero Wolfe, Maigret, Sherlock Holmes, and Brillat-Savarin, and she wanted to write about each and to explore why she had for so long had crushes on them. She told Donald, "There is a small something of both awe and sisterliness in all such relationships as the ones I must have with my real loves. It has since the first been necessary for me to feel shy and basically inexperienced, pupil not teacher, with the men in my life, whether of the mind or the body." And, she continued, the book would really be "a kind of literary love-story, a True Confessions of the middle-class American library-stacks." She concluded her letter with the observation, "Am fascinated by my statement, 'I play along with, now and then.' Who? Whom? What?"[22] Although she would allude often to her love affair with Brillat-Savarin, her romance with Simenon's hero, and her flirtation with Nero Wolfe, she did not develop the project to book length, but did write an article titled "A Few of the Men" in 1965, which appeared posthumously in *Last House*.

The year 1958 had been a difficult one for Mary Frances, with "the pill boys punching away" as they experimented with therapy for the increasingly painful arthritic problems in her hands and back and with an overwhelming feeling that all was not well in her girls' lives. She seemed unable to communicate with them with the same forthrightness she adopted with others. Like her own mother, she refused to broach the subjects of money or sex with them. The woman who had exposed her daughters to foreign languages and culture retreated into silence when faced with the practicalities of everyday life. Groceries were ordered by phone, bills mysteriously paid, schoolwork rewarded by extravagant forays into San Francisco or weekends in Sonoma. Anna set the table beautifully, but showed little interest in cooking. Kennedy did have her "baking station" in the enclosed porch, and she had mastered the art of cake and cookie making, but her first exposure to anything resembling actual meal preparation came when Eleanor Friede taught her how to make a vinaigrette. Part of Mary Frances still lived in Edith's world, where there were others to take care of day-to-day concerns. Another part of her believed that girls and women should be taken care of, a belief she often expressed as a solution to Anna's problems, although she herself not only projected the image of an independent woman but had been one, under duress, for long periods—a circumstance she perhaps wanted to spare her daughters.

In matters of intimacy she was equally reticent. She instructed her girls to read the instructions on a Tampax box, for example, when a mother-daughter conversation would have been appropriate and helpful. Kennedy remembered sitting at the kitchen table and talking to her mother about school, friends, and the events of the day, but could not recall discussions of more private matters or displays of affection between them. And years later, she realized that the innuendo, sarcasm, and even biting wordplay she had heard during Marietta's visits to their home had shaped her beliefs that people who loved each other treated one another that way.

Professionally, 1958 had been disappointing as well, and Mary Frances had drifted from one project to another without completing or publishing any of them. But the current living arrangement—divided between St. Helena and Berkeley—seemed to offer more time for writing than had been available the previous year. On a personal level, Mary Frances was still very much in love, and her relationship with Marietta did not seem to be adversely affected by her spending the week down in Berkeley. In fact, Mary Frances and Marietta had jointly purchased a house on Rail Road Avenue next to the St. Helena train station that had a diner on the first floor and some rented rooms on the second floor. Given the location, it is doubtful that they intended to live there, but their long-term plan might have been to turn the diner into a restaurant or a bookstore.[23]

On January 7, 1959, Mary Frances sent New Year's greetings to Powell, and commented on his recent observation that he found it necessary to "hoard his strengths at times." "Yes, we do wear out—pay a heavy price for knowing what we manage to know," she wrote. "But I would rather be me now, weary, blasé, arthritic, than the young unwitting almost unconscious me of Dijon or or or . . . The so-called holidays are over—many fine high moments and of course a few low ones—and now the girls are back at their schools and I am back at the typewriter (electric by now—much easier for me—). I am writing a kind of autobiographical biography of Dijon (!)."[24] Why her earlier life in Dijon suddenly became the subject for a book is not clear. Perhaps it was the pull of a simpler time, and the contrast with the changed city she had recently revisited. Although *Long Ago in France* would not be published until almost the end of her life, she initiated the project and wrote some chapters during this time in Berkeley, then apparently set them aside when she decided to prepare for another year abroad.

The possibilities for that adventure seemed endless, but the need to expand her daughters' educational opportunities was uppermost in Mary Frances's mind. The lure of returning to Vevey prompted her to write to Arnold Gingrich about the possibility of renting Le Paquis, and to inquire about admission to the École Pre Alpina in Chexbres for Anna and Kennedy. Unfortunately, Gingrich had turned the property over to his sons, who had already sold it, and she learned that the school was fully enrolled until 1961. Mary Frances then entertained the idea of putting the girls in a boarding school in northern Italy so they could learn Italian. When she spoke to Romie Gould about the plan, Romie invited Mary Frances and her daughters to join her and Paco at her family's villa in Cavigliano, Switzerland, in September, and she even offered to make the necessary arrangements to place the girls in the same boarding school she had attended in Lugano. It sounded like a perfect solution, and eventually Norah also decided to join her sister and give her three boys the experience of studying abroad for a year.

Mary Frances and the girls flew to New York to see Donald and Eleanor for Easter vacation. Anna and Kennedy stayed with the Friedes while Mary Frances "bowed out" and reserved a room at a hotel nearby. She kept her own schedule, met with Volkening and Covici, and dined with Eleanor, Donald, and the girls as often as possible. By the time they were ready to return to the West Coast, Mary Frances had convinced the Friedes that another year in Europe would be the best possible thing that they could give their daughters in "this shrinking, if not crumbling world."[25]

Although Mary Frances had repeatedly said that she wanted to take her girls to Italy or France for another year of schooling abroad "only if my love can be somewhere in the picture,"[26] Marietta was still employed as a teacher, and she was also reluctant to leave her mother for a substantial period of time. So Mary Frances departed from St. Helena with the promise that Marietta would visit during the summer of 1960. Meanwhile, Marietta assumed much of the responsibility for the house on Oak Avenue, which Mary Frances put at the disposal of family and friends.

On August 15, 1959, Mary Frances, Anna, Kennedy, Norah, and her sons John, David, and Matthew boarded a Norwegian ship, the

Taranger, and sailed from the Port of Oakland. "High-tailing it for Hamburg with a cargo of fresh lemons," Mary Frances reported to Eleanor and Donald. "This is the smallest and without *any* qualification the best ship I have ever sailed on."[27] She and her sister with their five children made up half of the passenger list, and they spent their days reading, swimming, splicing ropes with the crew, and playing bridge, canasta, chess, bingo, Scrabble, and Monopoly with everyone from the captain to the pantry boy. They landed in Hamburg on September 4, and traveled together to Cologne, where Norah and her sons took a series of steamers up the Rhine into Switzerland. Mary Frances, Anna, and Kennedy traveled by rail, visiting Ascona on Lake Maggiore en route to Cavigliano.

The Ticino, the Riviera of Swiss cantons, enjoyed balmy weather from March until November and offered its visitors ancient historic towns like Ascona, Locarno, and Lugano as well as rich Mediterranean vegetation, scenic mountains, and spectacular lakes. Carved out of the Duchy of Milan in the sixteenth century, the area was a rich blend of Italian culture, architecture, and cuisine combined with Swiss order and efficiency. Long attractive to artists, writers, and sportsmen, the valleys on the warm, sunny side of the Alps boasted stretches of open countryside and small villages easily accessible a few miles beyond the major cities. Although Italian was the official language of the canton, both French and German were also spoken. Mary Frances, along with her sister, daughters, and nephews, was introduced to the area by Romie and Paco, who were in residence at Casa San Michele, a historic stone building that Romie had inherited from her father and used as a pied-à-terre whenever she and her husband traveled in the Ticino.

The Friedes and Barrs stayed at an inn in Cavigliano and enjoyed "long slow walks, picnics in mountain meadows, waterfalls below our windows, good simple food." They learned how to hop on the electric trams that ran past the inn, and found pastry shops, post offices, and telephones in the three small villages along the route. On longer excursions into Ascona, Locarno, and Lugano, they rented *pedali*, the little paddleboats that dotted the lakes. "I swear you can hear Mary [Kennedy] giggle from here to the Matterhorn when she and John bump Anna and David's boat in the wake of a lake-steamer," Mary

Mary Frances Kennedy in Whittier, California, age six.

(This and all photographs not otherwise credited are reproduced by permission of Kennedy Friede Golden.)

Mary Frances's maternal grandparents, Bernard Holbrook (1836–1910) and Mary Frances Oliver Holbrook (1838–1920).

Mary Frances's paternal grandparents, Clarence Klaude Kennedy (1849–1933) and Luella Green Kennedy (1854–1933).

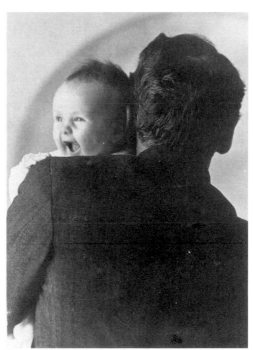

Mary Frances and her father,
Rex, early 1909.

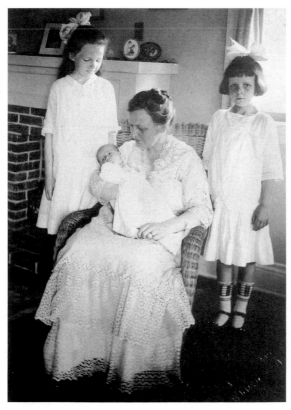

Mary Frances; Anne;
their mother, Edith; and
three-week-old Norah, 1917.

Mary Frances, Norah,
and Aunt Gwen, Laguna
Beach, California, 1919.

BELOW: Mary Frances
and Anne, ca. 1923.

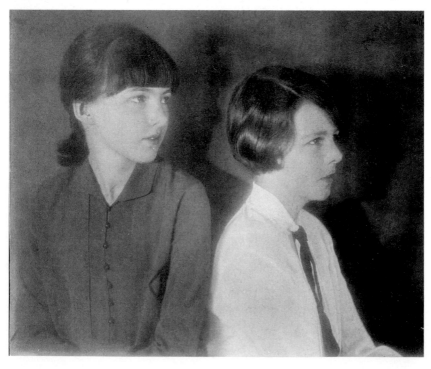

Sophomore class at The Bishop's School, La Jolla, California, 1924. Mary Frances is third from the left, last row.

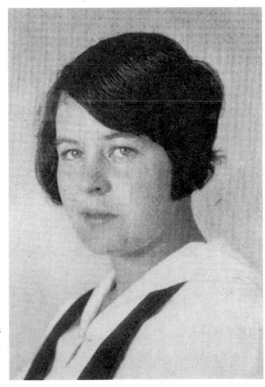

Eda Lord, a junior at The Bishop's School, 1924.

Rex, mid-1930s.

David, Edith, and Norah, ca. 1930.

Rex, Mary Frances, Norah, Edith (with her grandson, Sean Kelly), Anne, and David
at the Whittier Ranch, 1937.

Al Fisher and Mary Frances, Laguna Beach, 1932.

Mary Frances shopping in Vevey, Switzerland, 1936.

ABOVE: Dillwyn
Parrish at
Bareacres, in
Hemet, California,
1941.

Dillwyn at Le
Paquis in Vevey,
1937.

Publicity photograph of M.F.K. Fisher for *How to Cook a Wolf*, 1942. (Photograph by John Engstead)

One pose in a sequence of photographs for a *Look* magazine article (July 28, 1942). (Photograph by John Engstead)

Mary Frances and daughter Anna at Bareacres, 1944.

Kennedy and Anna at Bareacres, 1949.

Donald Friede and Mary Frances at Bareacres, 1945.

ABOVE: Anna, Kennedy, and Mary Frances in southern France, 1954.

David Barr, Anna, Mary Frances, Kennedy, and John Barr in Avignon, France, 1955.

ABOVE: Marietta Voorhees
and Kennedy in St. Helena,
California, ca. 1965.

Arnold Gingrich, in the
jacket photograph for *The
Joys of Trout*, 1973.

Dining/living room at Last House in Glen Ellen, California. (Photograph copyright © 1985 by Faith Echtermeyer)

BELOW: Mary Frances on the west veranda of Last House, ca. 1990. (Photograph by Richard Foorman)

May 25, 1983   *Jill Krementz*

Mary Frances and Charlie photographed by Jill Krementz in 1983.

Frances wrote to Donald. "I sit on the shore and slake my fears with a thimble-full of vermouth-gin."[28]

After eleven days of vacation, Norah and her sons left Cavigliano for Lausanne, where she rented an apartment in nearby Lutrey and enrolled her sons in the Lycée Jacard. Anna and Kennedy prepared for entrance into the Istituto Sant'Anna, reputed to be one of the strictest and finest schools in Lugano, and Mary Frances began to search for a *pensione de famiglia* where she could stay, take her meals, and be near her daughters. Just a short walk up the hill from the school on the Via Cantonale, she found one in an impressive old apartment house with a discreet "Room for Rent" sign in the window. She rang the bell and when Signora Donati opened the door, Mary Frances explained in her best French that her daughters were boarders at the convent school and she desired a room for herself with full pension. Almost immediately she settled into a spacious room with two windows overlooking the lake, and soon she began taking Italian lessons from Signora Donati's husband, a retired journalist who was not in good health.

Under the rigid regime of the Mother Superior, Anna and Kennedy were not allowed to share a room at the school because rooming with other students, who spoke either Italian or French, would facilitate proficiency in both foreign languages. During the first trimester they were officially "listeners" in all courses, with several additional hours a day devoted to private Italian lessons. For the first week, Mary Frances was allowed to visit them daily in the parlor for a short period of time, but after they were settled into their schedule, she could see them for only half an hour on Thursdays and from noon until five o'clock on Sundays. Once a month the girls were permitted to leave the school for a weekend, and on holidays they could be absent for longer periods of time. Kennedy found the school congenial in every way, and especially loved the chapel and the nuns. Anna hated it and grew sullen under the regime of early risings and bored with the girls who were her own age.

During October and November, Mary Frances took short trips away from Lugano to visit her sister in Lutrey, and in November she left for three days to meet Eda Lord and the British author Sybille Bedford in Schaffhausen. Although they had resumed their correspondence in 1952, Mary Frances had not seen Eda since their brief, sad meeting in Paris in 1937. When they met in the sunshine of the famous German-Swiss resort town, she immediately recognized a dramatic change in Eda; she was no longer the self-indulgent and unhappy woman of more than twenty years earlier. Eda had found a supportive companion in Sybille, and she was writing her first novel, *Childsplay*, based on some of her own childhood experiences, including losing her mother at a young age and being raised by her grandmother and then by the woman her father eventually married. Although she played Alice B. Toklas to Sybille's Gertrude Stein, Eda was happy, healthy, and engaged in her own work. Mary Frances enjoyed dining in the small cafés of the picturesque town with two women who were colorful, outspoken, and passionate about food and wine.

Mary Frances's meeting with the woman who had come into her life as a dazzling and talented teenager many years ago at The Bishop's School stirred many memories, and when she returned to Lugano, she wrote to Eda, saying that their recent meeting gave her "a new hold on life, to have seen for myself how firm your own is. I know that you are everything I recognized in you so long ago, tempered and refined and of course wearied by those processes."[29] Also enclosed in the letter was a five-page "Statement," a repetitive monologue entitled "I Love You, Eda," in which Mary Frances referred to her own fastidiousness, clumsiness, and confusion about how best to cope with the fact that "all my major actions have been shaped by my abiding love for you and consciousness of you."[30] Whether the expression of feeling was genuine or intended to flatter, it suggests that Mary Frances's teenage attachment to Eda resonated deeply because of her present relationship with Marietta. She closed her letter by saying that although it was quite possible that Eda had been a more important part of her life than she was of Eda's, to include Eda in her life once more meant very much to her.

Although Mary Frances mentioned that she was still working on the "drinks book," she seemed to divide her time in Lugano between travel and her daughters' schedule rather than her writing. There usually seemed to be a reason to shop for smocks or stockings in the limited time the girls were outside the convent walls, and they thought that the shops in Lugano were extremely stylish. In early fall there were bands and festivities associated with the Fête des Vendanges, and they watched the parade down on the quais and took a little boat to view it from the water. The Italian-Swiss lake country also offered boat excursions to small fishing villages like Morcote, where Mary Frances and her daughters climbed four hundred steps to see the thirteenth-century Chiesa di Madonna del Sasso, and stayed overnight in a small country inn. But their allowable time away from the convent was so short that they were limited in their travels, even though Mary Frances pushed the convent limits from time to time, as when she took Anna and Kennedy to see the controversial film *Hiroshima Mon Amour*, which they pronounced boring.

When Anna continued to rebel against the strict discipline of the boarding school, Mary Frances began to investigate the possibilities of *le ski* as well as ballet lessons for her older daughter and to consider switching the girls from boarders to day students the next trimester. In mid-November, Mary Frances located an apartment in nearby Paradiso, about five minutes from the girls' school by tram or fifteen minutes by foot. It was furnished, had wonderful heating and a modern kitchen, and would provide an opportunity for Mary Frances to prepare simple meals and to avoid the set times and polite conversation that ruled at Signora Donati's table, where the meals were plentiful but often pasta-laden. She rented it for the beginning of the year and planned to move in after the holidays.

Meanwhile, Mary Frances and Marietta wrote to each other frequently, and Elsine Ten Broeck and Yolande Beard kept her informed about what was happening in St. Helena. Mary Frances also sent letters to Anne, Sean, Volkening, and Powell, which filled them in on the details of learning Italian and exploring the Ticino and described the loneliness of the town when the weather turned cold and damp and the tourists departed. But her longest letters were often directed to Eleanor and Donald.

The expectation that a change of pace and place would be a tonic for Eleanor's chronic cough prompted Donald to plan an elaborate trip to Provence and the Côte d'Azur for the holidays. When they received his letter, Mary Frances and the girls excitedly coordinated "Operation Noël." They initially planned to meet in Nice, spend a few days at Porquerolles, and celebrate Christmas at their favorite Hôtel Beauvau, in Marseilles. Then they would drive to Aix and stay at the Roi René for a few days and return to Nice for New Year's. But when Anna enrolled in an intensive ski camp scheduled to begin on January 1 in Andermatt, they decided to celebrate New Year's Eve in Lugano instead.

For some reason, the Friedes' flight from New York was canceled at the last minute, forcing them to all meet in Marseilles on Christmas Eve. In their adjoining suites in the Hôtel Beauvau, Mary Frances and the girls repeated the marvelous feat of the coat-rack Christmas tree. Under it, wrapped specially for their father, was a miniature silver ice bucket with a bottle of champagne packed in cubes of crystal that the girls had discovered and purchased in an old tourists' shop on the Canebière that afternoon. (Mary Frances wrote about the silver and crystal *fantaisie* as well as other memories of Christmas celebrated in Marseilles in *A Considerable Town*.) A few days later, walking into the Roi René in Aix, Mary Frances and the girls were home again. Anna and Kennedy showed Donald their favorite meeting places, their former school, and the many cafés and restaurants where they had dined on *jambon, bourride,* and *crème Chantilly* less than five years earlier. They also drove to the Châteaunoir for a simple meal in the village inn before going on to Lugano.

On January 1, Anna departed for Andermatt. One day later, Donald left for meetings with publishers in London, and Eleanor, Kennedy, and Mary Frances spent the next three weeks taking short trips around Lake Lugano, going to the cinema frequently, and settling into their new accommodations in Paradiso. Although the apartment, located in a modern building overlooking Lake Lugano, was completely furnished, Mary Frances and Eleanor bought *boccalini,*[31] cups with handles that resembled small pitchers, which they used for drinking everything from wine to clear soups. They also took the train to Andermatt to pick up Anna, who had had to curtail her ski activities when she cut her leg while training.

While they were together, Mary Frances and Eleanor discovered that they had more in common than marriage to Donald Friede, and Mary Frances could see that Eleanor's concern and feelings for her daughters were genuine. They, in turn, were enamored of her and nicknamed her "Squeeker" because she was such a heavy smoker and woke each morning with a horrible cough and squeaky voice. When the girls went off to school, Mary Frances and Eleanor slipped into an easy pattern of work, conversation, and walks around the town. Whatever wariness there had been between them was dispelled. They had become friends, largely because Eleanor truly admired Mary Frances as a writer, and Mary Frances wanted Eleanor in her daughters' lives.

During February and March, Mary Frances was increasingly plagued by the chilly damp winds that blew off the lake and invaded her sinuses. None of the local Swiss doctors whom she visited seemed able to help her. "I continued to cough like a sick cow, and to sweat and shiver at perfectly spaced intervals," she wrote in *Map of Another Town*, and she longed to "lie in a meadow in the penetrating Provençal sun, and drink teas brewed from herbs picked that morning by my children."[32] She was convinced that if she could only visit Dr. Vidal, an Aixois physician in whom she had great confidence, she would be cured of this mysterious ailment.

She had first met Dr. Vidal in 1954 at Mme Lanes's boardinghouse, when he was summoned to treat one of the boarders. His remedy for a condition feared to be "Malta fever" (brucellosis, an infection usually caused by unpasteurized milk) or worse was simply rest, a bland diet, and aspirin for restlessness. A few months later, when Kennedy was bedridden and alarmingly lethargic, Mary Frances had brought in Dr. Vidal, who immediately recognized that her daughter's diet of rich pastries, eggs, milk, and ripe cheeses had contributed to a slowing of her liver functions. Again, his treatment consisted of a simple diet, almost no medication, rest, lemon juice and pure water, and avoiding the offending rich foods. Now, Mary Frances believed, he was the only one who could help her.

Besides, she decided, didn't Anna and Kennedy deserve a reward for more than seven months of intense study, with classes from eight to six and not a word of English? Never mind that they were only a month from completing their second trimester at Sant' Anna. Toward the end of February, Mary Frances wrote to Powell, "I want to take them here and there—maybe even to Le Turel . . . surely to Dijon, Beaune, Vézelay—maybe Paris—they were too young the last time—

and the next time they'll be on their own."[33] Anna had studied in at least seven different schools since leaving Whittier in 1953, and Kennedy six, but Mary Frances seemed oblivious to how this constant moving from place to place would affect them. She saw only the benefits of learning another language, meeting new and interesting people, and seeing as much as possible of the Old World. Although Kennedy would have preferred to remain at Sant'Anna in Lugano, where she had made many friends and truly loved the rituals and routine, she did not want to be separated from her mother and her sister, and she bowed to her mother's wish to go to Aix.

In mid-March Mary Frances rented an apartment in a large farmhouse in L'Harmas along the Route du Tholonet, about three miles from Aix. Norah and her sons rented a country house a short distance away. They arrived in Aix at the beginning of April. Spring in Provence was a visual treat of wildflowers and tender grasses in the countryside, and strawberries and fresh peas at the open markets. But Mary Frances's visit to her friend Dr. Vidal proved to be a disappointment. He still possessed the deep, calm eyes that had inspired her confidence, the fine voice, the sureness of movement. But he, like the doctors in Lugano, gave her pills to take. "I felt disillusioned but loyal . . . he had joined the pharmaceutical cabala [sic] . . . I let the hot sun and the meadow smells soothe me, and I put the pills down the toilet drain."[34] While Mary Frances slowly recovered by sleeping on the terrace in the sunshine and drinking herbal teas that Kennedy and Anna made for her, the two girls took over the household duties, frequently preparing liver for their supper because it was the only dish they knew how to cook.

While they were at L'Harmas, Anna and Kennedy resumed a program of lessons and tutoring, and Mary Frances bought them each a Velosolex bike with a small motor to facilitate their trips to and from Aix. They barely made it up the hill from the main road to the farmhouse, but enjoyed zipping around the infrequently traveled roads. As spring turned to summer, Mary Frances gradually regained her strength and energy, and began to prepare meals again. Living in the old farmhouse involved a deliberate pattern of shopping, sorting, storing, however precariously, and serving forth the bounty of the ancient earth. She wrote about her thrice-weekly trips into Aix to buy food and flowers at the Big Market in "Two Kitchens in Provence":

I would start out with three or four empty baskets, and a coin purse full of the small change essential to such hectic purchasing . . . I would add two kilos of soft sweet Valencia oranges from Spain, and a half kilo of lemons; two kilos of beans as long as hairpins and not much thicker; two kilos of country tomatoes smaller and more pungent than the big handsome ones from up near Avignon, a smoked sausage, some cheese . . . a kilo of fresh spaghetti from the fat woman by the fountain, and a clumsy bunch of pale-pink carnations . . . Sometimes I would want him [the cabdriver] to go faster, for I could almost feel the food in the baskets swelling with juice, growing soft, splitting open in an explosive rush toward ripeness and disintegration. The fruits and vegetables of Provence are dying as they grow . . .[35]

Warmer weather also meant houseguests. Eda Lord came to L'Harmas during Whitsun, and on one occasion she, Mary Frances, Anna, and Kennedy took the short bus trip to Marseilles for a special meal together at Surcouf, where they sat in the open window and dined on cold consommé, lamb grilled with fennel, and wild strawberries and watched the first communicants fluttering down the steps of Notre-Dame de la Garde. A few weeks later, when the Aixois teachers went on strike, Norah and her sons joined Mary Frances and her daughters, and they went to the small fishing village of Cassis south of Marseilles for two days. The entire village had been turned into a set for the filming of the movie *Fanny*. Leslie Caron, Charles Boyer, and Maurice Chevalier strolled on the pier, and at least half of the villagers were employed as extras and paid to play boules, fish, and drink pastis in the manner of 1924. "I doubt that either of us had ever felt much more contented, serene, reassured. Quite aside from being well and with our children and filled with various kinds of love, we were in Cassis, exactly as we should be at that moment in history and time."[36]

As July approached, preparations for the annual International Music Festival[37] were evident throughout the city. Rehearsals had already begun, and Anna got a job as an interpreter in the ticket office for a few hours before each performance began. On the first of July, the crush of tourists and the arrival of friends added to the excitement already in the air. L'Harmas became a gathering place, always stocked with wine, cheese, and bread. Jessamyn West came from Whittier; the Caronis, an Italian-Swiss couple, arrived from Lugano; and later in the month, Mary Frances met Marietta Voorhees at the train station in Marseilles and they taxied to L'Harmas. Anna and Kennedy had planned countryside picnics at nearby Bibemus, the Roman quarries that Cézanne painted, as well as sightseeing trips to Le Tholonet and Vauvenargues, recently discovered by Picasso. Mary Frances had purchased tickets for many of the festival performances.

But from the beginning of their visit together, Marietta found herself in an unfamiliar world in which Mary Frances and her girls moved with ease, and instead of the glorious reunion that had been envisioned, her stay at L'Harmas was filled with tension. She was newly retired and somewhat despondent about her future, and she felt keenly what she described as the loss of dignity and status that "real" work brings. Still bound to her aging mother, she also envied the freedom that permitted Mary Frances to leave St. Helena behind. Understandably, her anxieties dampened the spirits of those around her, and there were more than a few uncomfortable moments when Mary Frances made it clear that she was less than happy with the "state" her friend was in. Marietta replied that idyllic villages, beauty, peace, and leisure were not what she needed, and she made plans to spend more time in "literary" England before her return to California. Fragments of letters that she wrote to Mary Frances immediately after the visit expressed her unhappiness with the long-anticipated reunion. Marietta's time in L'Harmas had left her emotionally depleted; in her mind, the visit marked a change in her relationship with Mary Frances.

What Marietta had failed to understand from the beginning was the distinction Mary Frances had always made between "loving" and "being in love." In the elegant city of Aix-en-Provence, Marietta's real or imagined inadequacies, her "too little, too late" response to Mary Frances's love became all too evident. "I felt very sad that you ended your romance," Covici wrote in response to a very personal letter from Mary Frances in October 1960. "I am sure you decided what is best for you, but are we always sure what is the best?"[38] Although her deeply loyal, sometimes adversarial, relationship with Marietta would continue until Marietta's death in 1990, it ceased to be the all-encompassing love that Mary Frances had described to Powell in 1957.

A few days after Marietta's departure, Mary Frances's favorite cousin, Nan Newton, arrived with her husband and son, and there was another round of picnics and concert-going. Mary Frances and Norah hosted a big party at Le Tholonet for their cousin and friends, and they all returned to L'Harmas to watch the bonfires being lit on the top of Mont Ste.-Victoire in honor of St. John of Malta. Then Norah and her sons began a slow trip up to Rotterdam, the first leg of their trip back to California.

After the festival was over, Mary Frances reported to Eleanor that she had attended eighteen concerts and operas, a once-in-a-lifetime opportunity. Anna had finished her job as an interpreter on July 31, and she and Kennedy began a heavy schedule of tutoring in algebra, geometry, and French composition in preparation for their fall classes in Aix. During the month of August, Mary Frances was ill again with either an allergy or a virus, and the doctors advised her against staying at L'Harmas during the fall and winter months. "I am moving from this surprisingly lovely-beautiful-idyllic-heavenly farm, to some dour little rooms in town . . . it's impossible for me to be cook-maid-etc. etc. all alone, with furnace and fireplace, marketing, no car—the doctors say *no*, and part of me is really relieved. I dreaded some of it . . . And it will be much more *fun* for the girls to be in town (me, too!)"[39]

TWELVE

Illness and Healing

(1960–1963)

We need to trust something unknown, and to count on more than the actuality of a potion in the cup, a pill on the tongue.[1]   —M.F.K. Fisher

From the September day in 1960 when Mary Frances, Anna, and Kennedy moved into their aerie on the top floor of Aix's Hôtel de Provence, four flights above the narrow cobblestone street, they felt welcome. They had two rooms, the larger one with red tile on the floor and pink-and-yellow wallpaper, the small one a bit gloomy in color but filled with the sound of the fountain in the courtyard. Mary Frances and Kennedy shared the large room, which was furnished with an imposing marble mantel, two beds that served as couches during the day, and two large tables suitable for writing and schoolwork. Anna had just turned seventeen in August and had begun to date, and she wanted the small room for herself. The only other occupant on the floor was a long-retired law professor from the University of Dijon, who shared the toilet and separate bath with them.

The hotel was in the process of being sold, and there were few other guests. The breakfasts, served by the old night watchman, were ill-prepared. After the first few mornings of undrinkable coffee, Mary Frances decided that they would simply walk the short distance to the Deux Garçons for a quick *café au lait* before Anna went off to the lycée and Kennedy to the Bon Départ (equivalent to a junior high school). They usually took their midday meal in one of the restaurants on or near the cours Mirabeau, and after classes were over at six o'clock, Mary Frances and Kennedy would meet in a café nearby while Anna joined up with her friends. During the summer at L'Harmas, she had had a couple of serious relationships with students who were enrolled at the university, one of whom was black. "I knew that people I knew in Aix disapproved of this liaison, but I never discussed it with them," Mary Frances wrote. "As I remember I made it clear that if she ever married anyone who could not be a real citizen here [in the United States] I would come to see her wherever she lived with him where he WAS one."[2]

Free from housekeeping, marketing, and cooking, Mary Frances spent time crisscrossing the *vieille cité*, studying the subtle changes that had escaped her notice during the spring and summer at L'Harmas. She also continued to visit with Mme Lanes, still hoping that their relationship would slowly evolve into friendship, and she acquired new friends as she became a recognizable regular in the local cafés and shops. One such acquaintance was a young British student named Humphrey Stone, a recent Eton graduate who was trying to decide whether to attend Oxford or seek an apprenticeship in fine printing. Mary Frances and Stone shared a love of books and, despite the difference in age, became friends, maintaining a correspondence from that time on. She also visited occasionally with Georges Connes, Eda Lord, Sybille Bedford, and American friends traveling in the south of France.

To fill the solitary hours, Mary Frances began to write a new book. *A Cordiall Water: A Garland of Odd and Old Receipts to Cure the Ills of Man and Beast* incorporated scribbled notes she had accumulated over the years and found again in St. Helena when she unpacked boxes that had been stored away. Recent visits to Provence had also contributed to her knowledge about how "incantations and mystery, and ageless faith [became] the essentials of healing."[3] Her experience of "4 illnesses in 16 months"[4] with no sure diagnoses was undoubtedly a strong motivation for exploring this particular subject as well.

Mary Frances's interest in venturing beyond the limits of conventional medicine was long-standing. Probably beginning with

Grandmother Holbrook's visits to Kellogg's Sanatorium, she was curious about diets, and she had perused books on old-fashioned remedies and superstitions about diseases as a child. Later on, the inability of clinicians to find a cure for Dillwyn, and Donald's experiences with psychogenic pain, had added to her distrust of physicians, whom she labeled "pill boys." In selecting medical help for herself and her family she had always gravitated toward "alternative" doctors like Hal Bieler, who advocated natural childbirth and various nutritional regimes to promote good health. And she was impressed with her Aixois doctor, Dr. Vidal, although he proved a disappointment when he revealed himself to have become a "pill-man," in much the same way that the mortar-and-pestle pharmacies that had always been a mainstay in France had joined the rush to stock pharmaceuticals. She continued to consult Vidal, but she rejected most of his prescriptions, except for tranquilizers, which she occasionally used to "dull the razor's edge." And when she fell prey to a *crise de rhumatisme* in late fall, she agreed to take injections to relieve arthritic hip and leg pain, which was probably aggravated by climbing four flights of stairs several times a day. "Even the doctor himself [had] to bow to an occasional injection . . . I knew him to be brave . . . What I could not understand was how, and even why, he made me feel brave too."[5] She continued to be selective in her choice of physicians and medical advice, although in addition, contrary to all advice, she self-medicated with alcohol to control both internal and external pain.

However contradictory and inconsistent her approach to treatment remained, *A Cordiall Water* itself proved salubrious. Writing in English when she was thinking, speaking, and reading French allowed her to use her native tongue more effectively, she believed, and in the preface she cites Joseph Conrad and Vladimir Nabokov as two other authors who achieved a certain purity in their prose while thinking in two languages. While she believed that they were greater writers than she could ever be, she also felt that *A Cordiall Water* had a "pleasant honesty of style . . . For a few hours, while I was writing about horny cats and aching bones and nosebleeds, and all that clutter of life, I was stripped of banality, and I wrote simply in my native tongue, because I was temporarily detached from it and thus more aware."[6] She completed the book by December, and Volkening sold it to Little, Brown, in Boston, because Covici had retired from Viking.

That year Donald and Eleanor invited Mary Frances and the girls to celebrate the holidays with them in Paris. Mary Frances kept a "gastronomical log" of the trip, from their arrival on December 17 to their departure for Aix thirteen days later. Donald had reserved a flower-filled salon/bedroom at the Hôtel Meurice on the rue de Rivoli for them. When he and Eleanor arrived on December 19, the pace of dining and sightseeing accelerated, with de rigueur Dom Perignon aperitifs in the Friedes' suite, and lunches and dinners at Chez Joseph, the Ritz, and Prunier. "We went to the second-floor restaurant in the Tour Eiffel—none of us wanted to go that high, but the first floor was closed (as was the third), so Kennedy and Eleanor could not go on up as they'd planned, while Anna, Donald and I cowered at the bottom," Mary Frances wrote. "Ah well. It was a delightful meal, partly because the people were so much more alive and less homogeneously overstuffed: lovers and children and their parents of every class and color. We spent a long fine lunch time."[7]

On December 23 they went to a Russian place for music, and indulged in caviar, blini, borscht, and excellent vodka. Anna and Mary Frances went to Sainte Chapelle and then they all met Art Buchwald for lunch at Prunier. Mary Frances admitted that he was funny, but "I do not like him much."[8] That evening they dined at Taillevent, where Mary Frances ordered "*boudin* to DF's disgust—I think I ordered it a little to shock him—the peasant's traditional Christmas dish served in the Palace. Then, for the first time in my life I ate a truffle baked in pastry. Ah, it was delicious! And a salad of endive, and coffee. We drank a 1945 Bordeaux, whose name I forget, and then a '43 Haut Brion, very fine, in magnums (of course!). It was probably the best (most classically correct) restaurant for me since Foyot's, and not even DF's state of cosmic misery could spoil it completely."[9]

Many years later, Mary Frances's tendency to exaggerate got the better of these events. Her retelling of the dinner at Taillevent in a 1987 piece for the *San Francisco Examiner* put Donald and even Eleanor in a bad light. "The worst Christmas I ever spent was in Paris about 35 years ago," she wrote. She related how one of her "two very wealthy and unhappy dear friends" announced to a solicitous waiter that he was at death's door and ordered a specially prepared milk toast because it was the only thing he could eat. The other friend asked for nothing except black coffee, while Mary Frances ordered and savored a beautiful vintage Chambertin. She concluded the short piece with the caveat, "As I think of it now, it was not really bad at all. Of course, it was the pits gastronomically, but . . . it was Christmastime, and we were all together in a town we loved almost as much as we did each other."[10] In another piece, written years later, she reconfigured the lunch at the Eiffel Tower restaurant into a romantic tryst with a former husband.

On December 26, they left Paris in a chauffeur-driven Cadillac and traveled leisurely to Aix, stopping in Avallon, Vézelay, and Dijon. Shortly thereafter, Donald left for business in London, while Eleanor stayed on with them in Aix for a couple of weeks. By this time she and Mary Frances were close friends, and Mary Frances pointed out that in photographs they could easily be taken for sisters. Anna admired her stepmother's sophistication, her Bonnie Cashin designer clothes, and her Mr. Kenneth–styled hair. But it was Kennedy who bonded in a special way with Eleanor, recognizing that she cared for Donald and made his life both stimulating and easier.

Mary Frances and the girls crammed as much as they could into their remaining months abroad. This time Anna and Kennedy took in the chaos of Carnaval alone, while their mother avoided the noisy, crowded streets. Mary Frances continued to take them on weekend excursions, to Geneva for skiing or to Beaune to look at Flemish art. The highlight was a trip to Le Truel in the Aveyron, the home village of Georges Connes, where he and his father, Pepe, almost a hundred years old, visited the ancestral Les Penarderies each May. It was located in an area known as the Gorges du Tarn, a panorama of wild beauty, gaunt tablelands, gorges, howling winds, and flocks of sheep (Roquefort-sur-Soulzon, home of the famous cheese, was just twenty kilometers north).

"Les Penarderies is built like a stone doll's house," Mary Frances later wrote in "The Oldest Man," ". . . with four exactly similar rooms, two up and two down, and a stair in the middle, narrowing up to an airy attic and down to the cellars. There is a grass terrace in front, which falls off almost violently to the Tarn, a thousand feet below."[11] The isolated ancestral home offered minimal but adequate comfort. Mary Frances and the girls slept under mounds of blankets in the cool mountain air that rushed through the open windows. After the first evening, when Connes and his father laboriously prepared the meal, Mary Frances volunteered to cook, and over the next two days they gradually finished the chicken, cheeses, fruits, and bread they had brought along. On Pentecost Monday, they watched a procession of pilgrims, who looked like ants in the distance, climb the steep incline to the chapel of Notre-Dame du Désert.

Among the many French friends Mary Frances had made during her visits over the years, Connes proved to be one of the most enduring. His keen mind, Old World reserve and charm, and love of language were, no doubt, attractive to her, but Mary Frances also admired his political and military service and his commitment to the roles of father and grandfather as well as devoted son. His idiosyncrasies also amused her. A strong propensity to ignore any other moving vehicle on the roadway, his self-imposed rationing of tobacco, his slight awe of his father-in-law, who was a leading professor at the Sorbonne—all made him more approachable than his wife, who was the head of the English department at the lycée, and had been cool to her husband's students at the beginning of their acquaintance, though that barrier had long since been eroded.

Other French people remained strangers but became a crucial part of Mary Frances's daily life. The couple in the small flat across the narrow street, whose comings and goings, dining and drinking, and even lovemaking she observed whenever she looked out her window—and whose absence she eventually reported to the police—captured her imagination. So did the stream of people, mostly women and children, who walked beneath her window singing the "Marseillaise" during the Algerian insurrection, and the elderly men along the cours waiting impatiently for the newspapers to arrive from Paris with the latest news about the turmoil. These people and scenes would eventually find a home in *Map of Another Town*, published in 1964.

"If I stay here even a week longer we are lost," Mary Frances wrote to her "Aunt Grace," a dear friend of Edith's. "The Festival starts, and this year there will be *Dido and Aeneas* again, and *The Magic Flute* and *Così Fan Tutti* and and and . . . and the finest Cézanne exhibit ever assembled."[12] After a final weekend spree in Marseilles at the Beauvau, riding the five-cent ferry and gaping at the jugglers and tumblers on the quays, Anna, Kennedy, and Mary Frances left for Paris, then flew to Glasgow on June 30. Taking a last European fling before their return to California, they visited family friends in Scotland, then spent a week in London taking in performances of the Royal Ballet and shows in the West End, which had Anna in ecstasies, especially when they had a chance to go backstage. They spent a few days in Stockholm, visiting aristocratic Swedish friends who took them on a tour of various country estates. From there they traveled to Copenhagen, where they saw the Little Mermaid and drank beer in the Tivoli. The next day they flew home over the North Pole. Waiting for them in San Francisco was the Renault Floride convertible that Mary Frances had ordered while in France. "But swank as all hell as it is, it STILL costs less than an overblown Ford tub . . . I have asked for a dark green with black leather and top, but may have to settle for white with black . . . somewhat bebe-starlette for a staid dowager, but I really couldn't care less."[13]

Although Mary Frances's relationship with Marietta had diminished in intensity, she and her mother resumed their places as regular guests at 1467 Oak Avenue, and Mary Frances continued to support the efforts of the St. Helena Players. Most of her attention, however, focused on the Napa Valley Wine Library, for which Paco and Romie Gould and Jim Beard had raised seven hundred dollars in her absence. Incorporating donations of books from the university library at Davis, they inaugurated a Special Collection housed within the existing St. Helena Public Library and appointed seven trustees, including Mary Frances, to generate further interest in and draw up plans for the future Napa Valley Wine Library Association. Mary Frances became one of its most valued promoters, and she made the acquaintance of many rare-book buyers and sellers both in this country and abroad in her efforts to expand the collection.

A party for Anna's eighteenth birthday on August 15 was the highlight of the summer of 1961. Norah and her sons, Nan and Chuck Newton, June Eddy, St. Helena friends, and even Elsa Purdy from Riverside came to the celebration, which was also a farewell. At the end of August, Anna departed for New York, where Donald and Eleanor had made elaborate plans for her to take classes at the Neighborhood Playhouse School of Theatre and reside at the Studio Club. Donald insisted on paying for her education and even arranged a checking account that she could draw on for day-to-day expenses. But the restlessness, mood swings, rebellion, and impulsiveness that Mary Frances had tried to view as the last throes of adolescence did not significantly abate with Anna's coming of age. Moreover, thanks to her own denial about the gravity of Anna's problems, which she continued to believe a Prince Charming—preferably a wealthy one—could cure, Mary Frances failed to give the Friedes adequate warning.

From this time on, Eleanor and Mary Frances conducted an extensive correspondence. Initially the letters were pleasant accounts of shopping sprees for new clothes for Anna, delightful dinners at the Friedes' town house, and Anna's growing circle of friends and acquaintances. Donald repeatedly taught her how to balance a checkbook and manage her allowance, and Eleanor introduced her to many of their own friends. But increasingly the subtext of Eleanor's letters turned to concern about Anna's ability to function in the edgy world of aspiring New York actresses and actors. "No Anna never did anything about sending them [Pat and Doro Covici] tickets for the *Comédie* or thanking them for Christmas," Eleanor wrote, "but I was able to tell Doro that Anna had thought of it and wanted to. With not much said, I know that Doro is no longer hurt about this but in sympathy with whatever it is that makes Anna act as she does. Or does not. We all know she knows better."[14]

Meanwhile, Mary Frances decided to have Kennedy complete her high school education at the local high school rather than resume classes at a school in Berkeley. The decision proved to be a mistake in every way. Kennedy was aware that her life differed dramatically from that of her peers. She constantly asked why they could not live like other people, who had TVs and parties at home, and mothers who did not retreat to the Valley Hotel from nine in the morning until school was over in the afternoon, a practice that Mary Frances adopted in order to write without interruptions from phone calls or neighbors and that got Kennedy teased at school. Characteristically, Mary Frances ignored her daughter's humiliation and instead took delight in the rumor that she was carrying on a clandestine affair.

After her experience with Anna, Mary Frances believed that she was well prepared for Kennedy's adolescent behavior, but she had underestimated her younger daughter's reaction to being back in a community from which she now felt estranged. Kennedy developed a crush on an obese classmate named Michael O'Hagan, who had an after-school job working for the local undertaker, where one of his duties was to keep the hearses running smoothly. To Mary Frances's chagrin, Kennedy and Michael frequently drove up and down Main Street in one of the somber vehicles. Kennedy loved visiting Michael's home, where his large Catholic family gathered around the TV, had fun, and seemed "normal." The more Mary Frances objected to the romance, naturally, the more Kennedy was determined to pursue it, even though she sensed that Michael was destined to join the Christian Brothers. When Mary Frances caught him stealing money from her purse, she asked him not to visit the house again, and Kennedy found other ways to rebel.

During the fall of 1961, *A Cordiall Water* was published without much fanfare. The *San Francisco Chronicle* noted that the small volume led "into many corners of the world where she [M.F.K. Fisher] has found curious things."[15] Fanny Butcher gave it a brief nod in the *Chicago Tribune*,[16] and Elizabeth Janeway sampled some of the more unusual remedies for hangovers, colds, overeating, and fever in a more substantial review in *The New York Times*. Intrigued by folkways and folklore herself, Janeway felt that the book had great appeal for "those of us whose memories go back before the era of wonder drugs . . . to find fascinating echoes of remedies prescribed by grandmothers, aunts, and determined nannies."[17] Other reviewers echoed her comments about the book's distinctive prose and praised the evolution of M.F.K. Fisher's writing style. But *A Cordiall Water* had the same natural rhythms of speech that had always been a hallmark of her prose, and the same specificity of detail, evocation of mood, and deceptive simplicity that had long been her stock-in-trade.

Mary Frances had written about surviving the exigencies of wartime shortages in *How to Cook a Wolf* and had offered a handbook for getting by when faced with such challenges as dining alone and cooking in a studio apartment in *An Alphabet for Gourmets*. Both books contained recipes for soothing, comforting, and healing foods. In the latter she wrote, "I have used this bland prescription [Milk Toast] more than once upon myself, recognizing a flicker across my cheekbones, a humming near my elbows and my knees, that meant fatigue had crept too close to the fortress walls. I have found partaking of a warm full bowl of it, in an early bed after a long bath, a very wise medicine—and me but weary, not ill, weak, old, not very young."[18] A *Cordiall Water*, however, took the theme further.

Beginning with childhood memories of a book called *Nostrums and Quackeries* that Rex had kept in the revolving bookcase in his office at the *Whittier News*, Mary Frances focused on healing recipes and cures for everything from warts to hangovers, including a yogurtlike recipe supplied by a devout teetotaling Methodist who devised it for her father before He Heard the Call. She imparted an old-fashioned remedy for sore throats that her grandmother had used, described a little scapular of asafetida her second-grade Mexican friend Grace wore to ward off illness, and shared a recipe for wild jackrabbit dung tea, a brew to break a fever. She also recounted superstitions about the healing power of toads, freshly killed pigeons, herbs, plants, and grasses, about the mating cycles of farm animals, cats, and dogs, and miraculous cures effected by waters or compounds that she had learned while living in Mexico, Switzerland, California, and France. Using a parade of odd characters drawn from Brillat-Savarin, her neighbors at Le Tholonet, and relatives and friends nearer to home, she recounted experiences, real or imagined, that gave testimony to the efficacy of such folk remedies as a nightly saltwater enema, a mountain bitters *digestif*, wartwort, and the fat of marmots. The book included a very important component of nineteenth-century cookbooks; namely, the care of domestic animals. Using Blackberry, her favorite cat from the Hemet years, as a case study, Mary Frances wrote about feline self-healing and a cat's natural instinct for self-preservation, propagation, and purging. She also considered the legend and lore of aphrodisiacs and the dangers and cures of obesity, observing, "The severer a diet may be, the less effect it will have."[19] Some of the book's most affecting parts dealt with the theme of convalescence, and when it came to the passage from sickness to health, the critics were correct in saying that she wrote with more detail and immediacy than she had achieved in any of her earlier work.

While *A Cordiall Water* was being published, Mary Frances was writing against the clock to complete *The Story of Wine in California*, the project she'd undertaken a decade before at the behest of the San

Francisco Wine and Food Society and that the University of California Press was to publish. The initial plan for the book entailed photographs of California's vineyards and the winemaking process, to be taken by the Los Angeles–based photographer Max Yavno and accompanied by M.F.K. Fisher's text. When they began the book, however, Max Yavno's assignment was not coordinated with Mary Frances's plans for the text; then the funding proved to be insufficient, and the project stalled. While living in Berkeley in 1958, Mary Frances had completed most of the research, but then again put it aside. When she returned from Europe, she found that the photographs had been selected and the project was still viable. The task was not particularly to her liking, however. Writing to Powell, who had visited her in St. Helena in early November, Mary Frances said, "I'm on the last stretch of the wine book. It is easy to forget it, but I am determined to be shed of it by Thanksgiving."[20] Problems with the book continued, though. "I have been paid for the wine book, but now the Wine Institute wants me to do a lot of revision to turn the damned thing into a blatant ADVERTISEMENT," she told Eleanor. "I absolutely refuse. I always have and I always will. To hell with stuff like money. So tomorrow morning the president of the Institute and the director of the University Press are bringing me the galleys, and I have the check AND the contract all ready to tear into little tiny dramatic PIECES unless I win my point."[21] Mary Frances prevailed.

The family gathered in St. Helena at Christmas, and Mary Frances's newly acquired dog, Yee, greeted them. There were *santons* on the mantel, songs sung around the piano whenever Norah or Mary Frances played, champagne cooling, and friends and neighbors dropping by all the way to Twelfth Night. But after the excitement of the holidays was over and Anna had returned to New York, and Norah and her family to Berkeley, the battles between Mary Frances and Kennedy over rules of the house, dating, and companions resumed. The impasse became so intractable that Mary Frances took to writing letters to Kennedy instead of talking to her:

> I am typing this note to you, since recent experience makes me feel that it will be easier for you to read it than to listen to me. It is not an order in any way. It is a statement.

If by 3 o'clock on Sunday, tomorrow, January 14, you have not put your room and bath-shelves in order, I must do it myself. If I must do it, which I know you do not wish, I shall eliminate whatever I think is useless, like half-empty bottles without tops, old pieces of Kleenex, and so on. You will have to replace these things (including dirty laundry) at your own expense, and I shall stop all credit at Vasconi's, Lottie's, Buchanan's, and Goodman's, except with my written permission which you can carry with you for essentials. While you go through this increasingly disagreeable task of cleaning your bedroom, sewing equipment, closet, bathroom shelf or shelves, and back-porch cooking-table, I shall be more than glad to help you in any way I can.

I shall also continue to attend to doing the dishes, emptying the garbage and rubbish, stoking the fire on Sunday, and generally trying to keep the house pleasant and all four of us animals [including dog and cat] fed and warm. Any help you can give me in this is, as you well know, appreciated. But my statement still stands, about finishing your clean-up job before three o'clock tomorrow.

All my love . . .[22]

This infraction was slight compared to the offense that necessitated another letter less than two months later. Kennedy hurt her back at a school game and then lied to her mother about her condition and refused to see the family doctor. She proceeded to forge her mother's signature on two notes asking to be excused from physical education classes. "Perhaps I shall never know why you did this foolish and unnecessary thing, so clumsily . . . My confidence in you, and therefore in myself, has been cruelly jolted by this business, but my love for you is unshaken."[23]

In a letter to Eleanor and Donald, Mary Frances elaborated on Kennedy's lackadaisical scholastic performance: "she ambles along in a half-desperate inertia . . . doesn't read anything but comic books and an occasional copy of *Seventeen*, gets barely passing marks, is thoroughly disagreeable most of the time . . . Thank God (again!) I have been prepared for this weird phase by having Anna plunge into it first

. . . each time it is still something of a shock, however. There is nothing to do but live through it, and try to remember that it is surely as unpleasant on both sides of the fence!"[24] For her part, Kennedy felt as though she were "an outcast," a teenager who simply didn't live like all the other teenagers in town, and in retrospect she considered this the most difficult time in her young life.[25]

Since the end of January, Mary Frances had been trying to come to grips with the Aix material, and mentioned in a letter to Eleanor that she was "in a kind of moral chill about working on the Aix book, and am using you as a hot toddy or shot of adrenaline or something"[26] to ease the way into the work of revising the notes and "pastiches" she had written over the past two years. But instead of writing, she allowed herself to become preoccupied with short trips and friends' events. She encouraged visits from writers she admired, such as Robert Steele (whose pseudonym was Lately Thomas), who drove up from San Francisco with his family and his editor, Robert Lescher. In April she visited her sister Anne, who had retreated to Genoa, Nevada, with Bill Erskine, a tree surgeon and outdoorsman who had left his wife to marry her in 1960 after their affair in Sausalito. Together they owned a general store, which Anne helped to tend.[27] "It made me feel better than I ever thought I could about my sister Anne," she told Donald. "Now she seems to have attained a kind of serenity which I never dreamed possible. It is almost unbelievable to me that after fifty such destructive years this could happen to ANYONE."[28] During the visit Mary Frances found herself drawn to the austere mountainous landscape, which made the Napa Valley "seem almost painfully cluttered and *pretty*."[29] She also stayed with Norah in Berkeley that spring, and while visiting with her Berkeley goddaughter, Sylvia Thompson, Mary Frances agreed to write an introduction to Sylvia's first cookbook, *Economy Gastronomy*. When she returned home, she helped plan a "wingding" of a party to celebrate Miss Eleanor's ninetieth birthday. Kennedy pitched in by baking more than 250 brandy snaps, which Mary Frances described as "by far the best [cookie] at the party."[30]

Mary Frances's heavily annotated daily calendar for 1962 ended with the words "on May 27 I fell ill . . . Very bad summer. Hard on children. Well behind us all, I hope."[31] The symptom of the mysterious disease that her local doctor was unable to diagnose was severe pain beginning in the extremities and then spreading throughout the body. After weeks at the Seventh Day Adventist Sanitarium, the only hospital near St. Helena, she was transferred to the University of California Medical Hospital in San Francisco. Ten years later, she described her hospitalization as part of an indictment of the dehumanizing state of contemporary medicine: "I was *felled* by a mysterious illness (bouts of intense chest pain, increasing routine pain, inability to move or turn over or sit up because of the chest condition) . . . At UCMed I was First Prize Curiosity . . . new, rare, etc. At first I was put in the Tropical Diseases wing! Then I was shifted to a new Intensive Care wing for observation . . . once I opened my eyes and SEVENTEEN doctors and interns were standing in the room, watching me. I was hooked almost constantly to an EKG machine to monitor attacks . . . After about ten weeks, I began to cope with a combination of drugs to control pain."[32] Her doctors ultimately diagnosed that she was suffering from an inflammation of the collagen system, in which her body produced antibodies to its own substances. Norah made arrangements with two endocrinologists in Berkeley for immunosuppressive and steroid treatments. Meanwhile Kennedy lived with Marietta for a time and then went to Berkeley. In September, Norah enrolled her in the Convent of the Sacred Heart boarding school in Menlo Park and found a cottage for Mary Frances in Berkeley so she could be near her doctors.

Sometime during that summer, *The Story of Wine in California* appeared, with a foreword by Maynard Amerine, a professor of enology at the University of California at Davis, but Mary Frances was not able to acknowledge it in any way until much later in the fall. In answer to Powell's congratulatory note, she wrote:

About the wine book—I consider it a good hack job, but I am not excited about it. I think the only reason it was published, after some 11 years of shilly shallying, was that I finally said now-or-never. Ah well and ho hum. I was well paid. I think it is a slick job. (I dislike those heavy vulgar meaningless "gift" books, and am sorry my name is on one.) Oh—a needle to your blood pressure: a local review (Anon) says that *Maynard Amer-*

ine suggested that I write the text, *last year*. Murder. Well I was
very ill. I was in 2 big hospitals. Caught in the giant test tubes,
since the end of May. Very destructive to the family life, to my
finances, to *me*. Once I thought why can't I be flown to Hal
[Bieler]? But I was too ill. And he was in the last handwring-
ings of Elizabeth's [his wife] end. Now I am at least ambula-
tory.[33]

Implicit in Mary Frances's description of *The Story of Wine in California* were the limitations as well as the appeal of the book. Those
seeking a technical treatise on wine and wine making would not find
that level of detail within the text. Nor was the book a guide to California wineries, their proprietors, grape varieties, or types of wine. Instead, Mary Frances drew on her literary background, research skills,
and personal experience in the vineyards of Vevey to write knowledgeably about the romance of the vine, which Max Yavno had captured in
his photographs. Her text told the history of the grapevine in California
from 1769, the era of Junipero Serra, through the succeeding eras of
Chapman, Vignes, Haraszthy, Krug, and other major figures to the
years of increasing technical skill and corporate ownership. When
asked if Mary Frances had consulted his expertise, Maynard Amerine
simply shrugged and said that Mary Frances was her own authority
and "a damned good looking woman," a not too subtle way of convey-
ing that if the book was far from scholarly fare, it was nevertheless an
eminently readable introduction "to one of California's oldest and most
beguiling industries."[34] Mary Frances herself, however, rarely referred
to the book, and she omitted any reference to it in *Dubious Honors*.

During the fall of 1962, Mary Frances gradually recovered
strength while living with her dog in the tiny bungalow on a street
that featured a strange mix of blaring hi-fi music, zooming traffic, and
retired professors with hearing aids. Nearby were the "sadistic" clinics
where she had become a frequent visitor. The sudden death of her
cousin and friend Nancy Kennedy Newton on October 9 from pan-
creatic cancer was yet another cause of pain. She wrote to her uncle
Ted, "First I must tell you what perhaps you may have heard already,
that Nancy Jane died last night. She is the first of my generation to
leave. She was a very important part of my life, one of the best parts,

and I am thankful for that." Since college, Nan had been an intimate, "perhaps closer to me than either of us knew," Mary Frances wrote. "There are some relationships which send out myriad gangli, into the furthermost tissues of another's soul. When the person dies, these die too . . . And they must be dug out."[35]

Aside from occasional weekends with Kennedy, Norah was pretty much her only visitor. Mary Frances wrote: "I am usually rather voluble when she is here . . . reaction to the mute hours and days. I hope that before long I can start to vocalize (silently!!) on paper. I have a lot to say, of no importance except to myself, but it would be good to get it out of the way . . . Now all I feel is a kind of impotent and frustrating RAGE."[36] Some of the rage seemed to be the result of the Cuban missile crisis. "Suddenly I am touched with a chill that does not come from the foggy night," she wrote upon hearing of it. "My bones are cold. I turn on the floor heater, and shrug at its ease, thinking how little I care that in case of war there might not be that key to turn, that gas to burn . . . I am wrenched by the thought of my children and this cold news."[37] The crisis had an uncharacteristically pronounced effect upon her—she claimed to feel it almost as keenly as the death of Dillwyn—but she disdained the political posturing that ensued: "Great stuff. Big stick." Undoubtedly her rage was compounded by the chronic pain she'd been in and the helplessness she felt at her ongoing weakness. She was not even strong enough to answer the letters that had accumulated during the past five months, and when she did try, she wondered if she should:

> It is strange to pick up again the threads that have been stretched out to me. To what could they ever lead? I think of the woman in the tower, in Princess and the Goblin . . . that George MacDonald series which I loved. She sat critically in a tower room which one reached by following a thread, as I remember. Then there was the test of plunging one's hands into a kind of crucible of flaming roses. It did take courage. As a child I suffered and wondered if and why. But now as an oldering woman I wonder if I have the right to let people follow the thread. What do I have to offer them? Certainly no crucible of flaming roses.[38]

Her doctors repeatedly told her that her malaise was the result of having been ill for so many months, but more recently she had also recognized the old nighttime symptoms of sweating, heart thumping, and clammy skin that had invaded her nights in Hemet and Whittier and made every trip to Dr. Frumkes a challenge. Physically weakened, she was again slipping into depression.

Although she was in need of money, she had not finished the Aix book or accepted any magazine work. And she was unhappy about the turn Anna's life had taken in New York. In Eleanor's letters there were veiled references—"Anna has gone off a bit"—and mentions of non-attendance at classes, clothes and cash stolen, Village beatniks talking her out of her allowance, sessions with a doctor to determine whether she should see a psychiatrist, and Anna's decision to rent her own apartment instead of living at the Studio Club. There were more serious problems too, which Eleanor kept from Mary Frances. Meanwhile, the relationship between Kennedy and Mary Frances remained strained on the occasional weekend or evening they spent together. Hoping that a change of scene would be a tonic, Mary Frances took Kennedy to New York with her to spend the holidays with Eleanor, Donald, and Anna.

After returning to Berkeley, however, Mary Frances began to sleep constantly, napping in the afternoons and remaining in bed late into the mornings. She neglected correspondence, didn't even attempt to work, and evaded inquiries from Volkening. Eating, drinking, and even thinking became a bore. Norah urged her to write, but to no avail. Reflecting back on her condition, Mary Frances acknowledged that there were only two things that she managed to do with regularity. She faithfully walked Yee twice a day, and she did not let her person become untidy. After a few weeks, she pulled herself together enough to contact her endocrinologist, who prescribed antidepressants and recommended a complete change of scene. (Dr. Frumkes was retired by this time, and she never sought the help of another psychiatrist.)

In mid-January 1963, Mary Frances accepted her sister Anne's invitation to come to Nevada again. Anne arranged for her to stay in a guest cottage on the nearby Kimmerling ranch. The little square house had a pleasant living room with a large window that looked out onto pastureland and beyond to Genoa Mountain, which was sparsely covered with scrub pine. Mary Frances saw her sister and brother-in-law daily, and often rode along with her sister, who had a VW truck and "looked great at the wheel," when she drove into Carson City to the north or Minden to the south. There Mary Frances shopped for delicacies like sweetbreads to prepare for the evening meal, which was the most social part of the day in the tiny, isolated village where the wintry weather alternated between crystal-bright blue skies and snow-threatening clouds.

Mary Frances liked what she saw of the bars and family-style restaurants and the hard-drinking, hardworking, self-assured men and plain-looking women who frequented them, and she began to write about the town, Nevada's oldest settlement along the Emigrant Trail. It was not long before she settled into a pattern of reading, snoozing, and writing during the day, and walking to her sister and brother-in-law's store or nearby home for drinks and occasionally dinner. During the first days of March she noted in her journal, "I had written that in this country there seems to be no compromise . . . Anne said something like this, talking of people she works with and knows closely: 'Here there is no middle ground. You are drunk or you are sober. You are cold or hot, mean or kind and rich or poor.' And more. I asked why people get drunk and she and Bill said it was because of this lack of middle ground, this compromise. They get stoned, as Bill would say, when they are released even for a short time from the devouring need to farm, to get more land, to exist."[39]

The rugged beauty of the land, the blend of forgetfulness and kindness she came to accept in Mrs. Kimmerling, the pleasant drinks and simple dinners of stews and casseroles she shared with her sister and brother-in-law were therapeutic, and Mary Frances began to make real progress on the Aix book. On March 9, however, a dinner at the Erskines' was interrupted by a phone call summoning Bill, who was also a local volunteer fireman, to a fire on the Kimmerling ranch. Panicked that it could be in her cottage, Mary Frances immediately thought of her manuscripts. It was the main house, however, that lost much of its roof before the fire was extinguished a few hours later. Mary Frances immediately offered the Kimmerlings the cottage, which they initially declined, reassuring her that they could stay where they were while repairs were being made on the house. A week later, however, they were advised to move out, and they asked Mary Frances to vacate the cottage. To her relief, Helen Marshall, a friend of Anne's and a local woman of some sophistication, invited Mary Frances to stay in a vacant suite of rooms on the second floor of her house. Soon Mary Frances was settled again and working on the Aix book, intending to send a piece about her two kitchens in Provence to Volkening when it was finished. By April 3, she noted that she had almost completed what she wanted to do with the Aix material. "There is much that will never be written, of course, and much that I have written which I choose not to put into it . . . repetitive sometimes, too personal, uninteresting except to a few people like the children and Norah. I have no idea what kind of publishable book this may be, but all I care about is that I have written it."[40]

Meanwhile, Kennedy arrived for Easter vacation. After a festive dinner of grilled lamb and champagne at the Erskines' and several days of sightseeing, Mary Frances packed up her clothes, books, and the typescript of the Aix book. "Much has happened to me up here and I feel stronger and firmer for it all," she noted in her journal. "I shall sort it out gradually, and meanwhile my one hope (prayer really) is that when I get back to St. Helena I can stay this way, calm and uncluttered."[41] In her letters, she had described her residence in Genoa as "getting a divorce" from herself in order to come into focus again, so that she could come to grips with the question, "What next?"

Mary Frances had chosen to return to St. Helena for a short time to get adjusted to living alone in the house on Oak Avenue before returning to Berkeley for the remaining ten weeks of her lease. The important things, she felt, were to maintain the momentum she had achieved in Genoa, mend fences both of the garden variety and those involving her good, if demanding, friends, and rejoin the St. Helena community. After her experiences in Genoa, she even began to consider getting a woman lodger for one of the first-floor bedrooms and bath as well as developing a plan to serve a handful of regular diners a meal five nights a week. "I would not eat with my guests, nor would I encourage them to linger past 7:30ish," Mary Frances wrote to a bookseller friend, "in other words, it would not be at all your idea of chatting with 'literate creative people' while whipping up a cioppino!

This would be a pleasant congenial change from the ghastly coffee-shoppes in St. Helena. It would not be Dining With Miss Fisher at all . . ."[42]

When Kennedy's semester was over, Mary Frances joined her daughter in Berkeley, and Kennedy enrolled in a business course for six weeks before flying to Eleanor and Donald's beach house in Bridgehampton to celebrate Anna's birthday in mid-August. Feeling much stronger in body and spirit, Mary Frances began to move some of their belongings back to St. Helena on weekends, vacating the cottage entirely once Kennedy had gone. "I suppose that I am glad that I spent this strange year here," she commented. "I am not sure. But I do know that I did spend it, and that it is gone . . . and that I had better contemplate the next one."[43]

During her absence, the Napa Valley Wine Library Association had been legally incorporated, and bylaws were drawn up in 1963. Mary Frances was elected one of the trustees in charge of acquisitions. With André Tchelistcheff, Maynard Amerine, Louis Martini, Joe Heitz, and other Napa luminaries behind the organization, it flourished. Volunteers collected materials stored away in attics and forgotten vineyard office files that would probably have been lost had the association never existed. In addition to maintaining and enlarging the collection, the group sponsored tastings and, by the mid-1960s, wine appreciation courses. Mary Frances performed many services, from donating party food and preparing potluck dishes to lecturing in wine classes.

In her letters to the Friedes, Mary Frances reported on Kennedy's senior-year activities at Sacred Heart, and she also shared her professional concerns with Eleanor, mentioning that Rachel MacKenzie, an editor at *The New Yorker*, had asked to see more of her writing and that she had found a congenial editor in Mary Rackliffe, who was now working on the Aix book at Little, Brown. At the beginning of November, M.F.K. Fisher's name appeared on the cover of *Publishers Weekly*, and a two-page Little, Brown advertisement inside the magazine announced the forthcoming publication of *Map of Another Town*. Writing to Volkening, Mary Frances told him that she should have been pleased to have her name as visible as it was, but she felt quite resentful about the way her book was described in the ad. "It sounds like one of those quasi-whimsical diaries written by Fulbright mothers on how to get along on Daddy's puny dollars in a Volkswagen through Yurrup, with all the kiddies getting lost in the Catacombs and throwing up from the top of the Tour Eiffel."[44] Furthermore, she was dismayed by the Barbara Westman drawings that Little, Brown had commissioned to accompany the text instead of the Crespi drawings that she had submitted.

Still, her self-absorption seemed to be ebbing. The radio programs that she had always listened to were becoming more and more important in her solitary existence, and the news continued to carry an immediacy that had escaped her earlier in her life. Four people dead in the bombing of a black church, a nine-year-old black boy gunned down by two white men on a motorcycle, a sixteen-year-old black boy shot by a policeman who meant to fire over his head—such events triggered a visceral reaction in her that she could not shake, and she felt that "this thing has reached a point within me where I must soon do more than stand here." Yet "all around me are people I can no longer talk with, because of what they are finding out about themselves and what they do not want me to see."[45] She was referring to negative reactions to the recent Fair Housing Act and other examples of racial barriers and prejudice that now seemed to put her at odds with acquaintances and even long-standing friends. It seemed to her that conversations stopped or abruptly changed subject when she walked into a room or a market. Her abhorrence of quarrels and scenes, she reasoned, had previously prevented her from voicing her feelings and opinions, but now she remembered with shame past incidents when she had lacked the courage of her convictions.

The first involved a black couple who had worked at the Ranch for several years and suffered from discrimination when a local doctor refused to treat them. They left Whittier for a time, but were re-employed by her mother while Mary Frances was away at boarding school. When she returned home for a holiday, tired from the trip and still in her dark blue serge uniform, she was startled to be embraced at the kitchen door by the housekeeper she thought had left, and she inadvertently pulled away from the woman's floured hands. "The next morning," Mary Frances wrote, "my mother told me that Bea had come to her and said that I had changed, that I had pulled away from her, that the girls had changed me at school, so that I did not like 'her people' anymore."[46] Mary Frances tried to explain the mix-up to her mother, and invited Bea to her wedding a few years later, but never talked to the housekeeper about the misunderstanding. Now she regretted her retreat into silence.

The other incident had occurred years later, after she returned from Vevey to inform her parents of her intention to divorce Al Fisher. Invited to a minister's home with her parents, she listened as another guest retold the story of someone in her hometown who was charged with running down and killing two Jews. The woman merely concluded, "That is two less." The minister made no objection and even participated in an extended conversation about the difference between the names "Rosenberg (kike) and Rosenberger (all right)." Again Mary Frances had remained a silent ashamed observer. "What could I have done past the immediate shock and hurt of revolt on my part? I do not know now, and it is too late to find out about THEM. But is it not too late to do more . . . more, that is, than make myself pretty clear here, at least about my reticence, and with my children? I am not sure. I feel that a person like me, fairly skilled with the use of words, might be useful . . . *with* words . . ."[47]

At Christmas, Mary Frances organized yet another family celebration, which she referred to as her Genoa Christmas Caper. Sean, now married and the father of two sons, had recently returned to Washington from South Africa and brought his family to the reunion. Norah and her sons came from Berkeley, and Kennedy and Mary Frances arrived from St. Helena. Anna chose to remain in New York. "In this private report to you," Mary Frances wrote to June Eddy, "I shall be as blunt-malicious-bitchy as I want to."[48] And she described in detail how all of the guests took over the three floors of Helen Marshall's ranch house and the Kellys bedded down at the Kimmerling ranch. She and Norah provided a breakfast and lunch buffet each day, and Anne and Bill prepared a lavish Christmas buffet, which "enraged John, David, Matt, and even tolerant Mary [Kennedy]," when Anne provided them with a segregated Teen Age Bar, "where they had all of the fun and jollity of making their own hamburgers and pouring their own cokes (Both of which they shun like the plague for reasons of weight, skin, snobbism, and parental disapproval) without 'bothering' the grown-ups. Let's face it: she detests kids."[49] Mary Frances also noted that Anne looked unwell, but that her husband Bill was attentive and extremely helpful.

"This Christmas I was the oldest of the whole tribe, the matriarch. I had brought them all together. I felt basically responsible for the well being, the general tone, and yet philosophical about the forces of the unknown in everyone. Twice, and I think it is quite commendable that it was only that often, I felt so over-full of this, of all the neuroses and needs and tangles, and perhaps of the physical appetites, that I simply vanished into my end of the house, and I lay flat and turned off Dote, Dote the would-be Buffer-Patsy-Great-White-Mother-Bitch of all time."[50]

Soon, she hinted, she would do something meaningful with her life. "Come the New Year, I think I will take a nose-dive out of all this,"[51] she told her assembled family, and then said she was planning a sabbatical from being the number one "Good Citizen" of St. Helena and all the hostessing, costume making, speechifying, and boostering that entailed. She felt that there was some use for her experience as a "daughter-mother-writer-wife-human" someplace. The place was Piney Woods.

THIRTEEN

The Most Alone

(1964–1966)

I must choose another path from the mother-image.[1]   —M.F.K. Fisher

The Piney Woods School was founded in 1909 in rural Rankin County, Mississippi, as a boarding school for black teenagers. From the upper windows of the school, a view of miles of swampland stretched to the Gulf of Mexico about a hundred miles away. Where the land was cleared, corn and sugarcane fields dotted the landscape along with orchards of pecan and fruit trees, but basically the soil was poor and badly farmed. The school had its own post office and a general store managed by alumni. It was a part of the rural South that Mary Frances had never experienced.

Piney Woods was supported by Southern paternalists and Northern idealists who endorsed the school's adoption of the Tuskegee Institute model of vocational education, accommodationist rhetoric, and religious rigor in the tradition of Booker T. Washington. Under the leadership of the school's founder and president, Dr. Laurence Jones, the alumni worked tirelessly to support the school, and the endowment reached over a million dollars in the 1960s. At least half of the faculty were retired teachers from the North and Midwest who volunteered their services. The black resident teachers lived in separate buildings with their families and did not see much of the white faculty except in classes or at meals.

Mary Frances's first contact with Piney Woods went back to the early 1920s, when their gospel choir performed at The Bishop's School. Thereafter Edith received the Piney Woods bulletin and regularly sent donations of money and books, a practice that Mary Frances continued. In her letters to family and friends in the early months of 1964, Mary Frances wrote of her preliminary discussions with Dr. Jones about her plans to volunteer her services at the school and her reasons for doing so. First, her children seemed to be more settled. Anna, no longer intent on becoming an actress, was training to be a receptionist-translator for TWA. Kennedy had chosen to embark on a premed course of study at Russell Sage College in upstate New York. With both daughters out of the nest, living alone in the house on Oak Avenue seemed increasingly difficult, and Mary Frances was candid about admitting that she "had almost finished the active mother-role and that I am destined to go to waste unless I make some strong move."[2]

She had already told friends that she wanted to do something different with her life and had decided to teach, but except for the writing workshop in Utah in 1954 and various public speaking engagements during her career, she had no teaching experience. She also lacked sufficient academic credits to qualify for certification in public schools. But private schools like Piney Woods offered more leeway in the matter of credentials, and as the weeks passed, she entertained the idea of teaching English literature, basic composition, and home economics, and tutoring students in French, Spanish, and Italian at the school. She also mentioned that she might consult with the administration about keeping a record of her experiences, and possibly taking an advance from a publisher for it; if encouragement was not forthcoming, she intended to keep a private one. She even considered writing an article elaborating on her reasons for going. In a letter to Volkening, she said: "I'll be working with students in advanced high school and junior college who are preparing for the ministry, the law, teaching, and medicine. I'll also be working with students who have come from the most God-forsaken rural areas in the state. The main thing is that they will be there because they

WILL it, and not because it is the easiest coziest most indicated way
to social and economic success."[3]

That spring, Mary Frances shared her plans with her daughters,
sisters, and other relatives as well as her regular correspondents—
Aunt Grace, Gloria, June, and Larry Powell. She explained that she
was no martyr to the cause of racial equality, and "as for accepting and
being accepted, I honestly think that would soon take care of itself,
easily and thoroughly . . . there would be suspicion of my motives at
first, as is very understandable . . . so many white people want to
'help' but, are conditioned too far back to be anything but self-
conscious about it, and I seem to be born without a racial conscience
or whatever it is."[4] She was not being altruistic at all, she said repeatedly. She was doing this for herself because after so many comfortable
years in St. Helena and so many years of raising her daughters to be
citizens of the world, she now had her back to the wall and needed
Piney Woods as much as or more than the school needed her.

The responses were many and varied. Her sister Anne warned of
the austerity of the lifestyle with the observation, "How will you handle the absence of the morning vermouth/white wine . . . and the
evening block-buster . . . in that purified atmosphere?"[5] And she expressed her deeper concern that the whole scheme was a "misuse" of
Mary Frances's talents on those who would never be sophisticated or
cosmopolitan enough to make use of them. However, since the initial
commitment would be only for a year, the experience might be bene-
ficial as a distraction.

Anna was a great deal more enthusiastic. She regretted the fact
that she could not find the right words "to say something really deep
about a decision that I find world shaking and fantastic . . . It is impossible to say how much I admire you."[6] Other family members and
friends were equally supportive, although they did raise questions
about her health. But Mary Frances grew increasingly confident that
her medical problems would not be an obstacle. Whenever a twinge
in the shoulder or an unexpected pain in her chest triggered a flash of
apprehension, she initiated a regime of aspirin followed by painkillers,
without involving her local physician, Dr. Neil, or sending distress signals to Dr. Bieler. Her past illnesses, particularly the collagen defi-
ciency in 1962, had taught her to be constantly alert to physical

symptoms. She was also ever mindful of the problems attendant on aging. "I do not like to head for it with such meaningless speed as seems to be the case here in St. Helena. It is like shooting helplessly down a swift silent river. I want to catch onto a few overhanging branches, not to save myself but simply to feel them in my hands."[7] To calm her family's fears and likely some of her own, she scheduled a complete physical examination with Dr. Neil, who told her that she might as well be carried out of a place where she wanted to be rather than someplace else. She had already decided to get her feet wet at Piney Woods during the summer, when the faculty numbered only five teachers instead of thirty, and the classes were, for the most part, noncredit, before taking on a full teaching schedule in the fall semester.

Meanwhile, she admitted that professionally she was on "a shifting plateau." *The New Yorker* had published a heavily "bowdlerized" excerpt from the forthcoming *Map of Another Town* called "Second Time Around" in January 1964. Mary Frances told Aunt Grace that she resented the magazine's practice of "going through very demanding and often foolish or even presumptuous finaglings, once the story was accepted . . . last minute revisions, last *Last* minute consultations with lawyers about things like Libel and Invasion of Privacy, last last LAST minute style-changes demanded by Shawn Himself,[8] who had apparently not looked at the stuff until it was on the presses. I found all this boring."[9] Although she thought that Rachel MacKenzie was one of the most skilled, intelligent, and pleasant editors she had ever worked with in the rapidly proliferating world of magazines, Mary Frances announced that the story "The Oldest Man," now in the magazine's possession, would be her last. She knew that *The New Yorker* was the best of its kind—at that time it not only reigned in its literary reputation but regularly ranked first or second in the number of its advertising pages among consumer magazines. And she knew that being in the company of authors like Clifton Fadiman, A. J. Liebling, and Janet Flanner lent her a certain cachet. More to the point, *The New Yorker* paid well for articles and stories. But Mary Frances was not one to tolerate requests for revisions lightly (she had offered to return checks and/or withdraw material when changes were suggested or, worse, made without her consent). With *Map of Another Town* scheduled to be published in April, she vowed to forget magazine work and concentrate on writing the occasional book for a press that wanted to publish her because "I am me and not a projection of himself."[10]

She had charted new territory for herself in *Map of Another Town* by departing from the gastronomical memoir-cum-recipe format. This book is built not around meals but places—the cours Mirabeau, the Deux Garçons, La Rotonde, and other sites associated with the history and spirit of the town the Romans had founded more than two thousand years before, now re-created by M.F.K. Fisher's "own shadows, [and] inventions."[11] She subtitled the book *A Memoir of Provence*, and on one level *Map of Another Town* does recount how the author and her daughters familiarized themselves with the city where they lived and studied in 1954 and then again in 1960. On a deeper level, she develops the themes of permanence and change against the landscape of stone cathedrals, ducal palaces, and narrow streets, and in the pattern of feasts and fetes. The city that had for centuries lured the ailing to its healing waters becomes a symbol of her own search for both physical and spiritual health. When she writes about the Hôtel de Provence's being purchased by an outsider, a favorite waiter from the Glacier falling on hard times, and Mme Lanes growing comfortable in her role as landlady, she is telling the story of how things change but in some mysterious way stay the same.

Reviewers were quick to praise *Map of Another Town* as a stunningly written guidebook complete with notes on the history of the city and its principal sights, restaurants, local specialties, markets, and festivals. Dorrie Pagones wrote in the *Saturday Review*, "Although such is far from being Mrs. Fisher's intention, her memoir could also serve as a guide on how and how not to behave when living abroad . . . In the longest and best chapter in the book, '17 Rue Cardinale,' Mrs. Fisher details with sympathy, bafflement, rage, and love the formidable strength, the equally formidable extravagance, the maddening and inscrutable *Frenchness* of assorted French landladies . . . This account of two years she spent in Aix-en-Provence is given in a casually honest style that makes irresistibly attractive reading."[12] A short review in *The New Yorker* noted, "This is a book to be bought and read and never lent."[13] *Map of Another Town* was the first in a series of "place" books that M.F.K. Fisher wrote, and it was also in the vanguard of those "travel" books that capture the spirit of a city, town, or village and are deeply rooted in the sensory world.

On June 22, however, Mary Frances's thoughts were on Piney Woods. After designating Marietta caretaker of her house, she boarded the California Zephyr in San Francisco with her luggage and typewriter. In Chicago she transferred to a train bound for Jackson, about twenty miles from Piney Woods. Upon arriving at the school, Mary Frances wired Marietta: "After only a few hours, everything that I had wondered and thought about being here seemed almost too dim to remember, for at once I knew it to be right . . . *right*, I mean . . . in ways that I could never have imagined. I know this will reassure you and please you."[14]

Meanwhile, radio broadcasts and news coverage focused on the disappearance of two white civil rights workers from New York, Andrew Goodman and Michael Schwerner, and their black activist host, James Chaney, who were the first casualties of a project to send waves of politically mobilized college students into Mississippi, the most visible example of the intransigent Jim Crow South. "It was as if a righteous war had been declared and we were all ready to march off," wrote David Goines, a Berkeley activist. "Before 1964, the Student Non-violent Coordinating Committee [SNCC] had been putting out the message that the murder of Black civil rights workers was a common event in Mississippi, but that the rest of the nation didn't care. The main purpose of Freedom Summer was to create a presence in Mississippi so that the rest of the nation could no longer ignore what was going on there."[15] The discovery of the civil rights workers' charred station wagon in rural Neshoba County signaled an onslaught of acts of violence and bigotry that continued through the summer and fall of 1964. On August 4, the FBI would discover the bodies of Goodman, Schwerner, and Chaney buried in an earth-fill dam near Philadelphia, Mississippi. "Martyrdom," wrote Goines, "was the theme of the summer."[16]

Mary Frances, however, soon discovered that the administration, faculty, and students of Piney Woods School marched to the beat of a different drummer. During study hour there was no sound except the scratching of pencils on paper. The books in the impressive new library were well cared for—no mustaches drawn on pictures of Queen Elizabeth and other notables as at St. Helena High School. Motivational slogans were posted everywhere. She found the students "slowly and surely fighting their way toward being educated decent citizens, almost always from homes where their parents are not allowed to aspire toward education, even decency, and certainly not citizenship."[17] Although the radio brought news of flare-ups in other places, students and faculty alike attended chapel and worked quietly toward a better future. The "campus positively shone with optimism." As the headline of the local paper during that summer of unrest put it, "The Pupils [were] Too Busy for Trouble."

"I can't tell you how thankful I am that I came early," Mary Frances told Norah. "Really, I wonder if I could have managed without danger of depression or over-fatigue, if I had plunged into regular work with a big faculty ignorant as I was . . . This way I have not had to cope with a lot of other teachers."[18] She eased into teaching with a noncredit course on fables from Aesop to Thurber and also tutored a handful of students. She lived in the comparatively luxurious, air-conditioned mobile home of a faculty member who was away on vacation. She also ate most of her meals in the dining hall, which she considered disastrous because of the emphasis on starchy foods, spent the long day from five o'clock in the morning when the bell rang for rising until nine in the evening in an alternating schedule of teaching and various tutoring activities, and sweltered in humidity that often rose higher than the summer temperatures. Her letters to Marietta requested clothing she had neglected to pack, a book bag and various school supplies, books of riddles and tongue twisters for three newly arrived Mexican students whom she tutored, and a bottle of Angostura bitters to temper the harsh taste of the drinking water. Marietta sent the items, as well as posters for the bare walls of Mary Frances's permanent quarters and boxes of magazines and books.

Mary Frances enthusiastically wrote to Norah and her nephews, "For the first time in many years what creative energy I have is being directed toward other things than my professional and emotional self."[19] She embraced the role of "schoolmarm," and searched for lively texts for students to read or declaim, a necessary part of their preparation for chapel recitation. Eager to find out as much as she could about her students, she assigned compositions, only to discover that she had to spend an inordinate amount of time correcting them. Inventing assignments and lesson plans to fill up two hour-and-three-quarter periods per day kept her hopping.

Although a Sunday spree to nearby Mendenhall with one of her fellow teachers, including a meal at the locally famous buffet at a hotel there, was not exactly Mary Frances's idea of either a social or gastronomical event, she recognized the goodwill of the elderly ladies who volunteered their services at the school and occasionally dined with them. Her favorite by far was the incredibly frail, tiny old head librarian who presided over a collection of about 28,000 volumes. Before coming to Piney Woods nine years earlier, she had been a rare-book librarian at the University of Chicago, and Mary Frances found her to be "as gentle and remote as an old turtle." One or two others, who were almost as eccentric, were also of interest to her.

Mary Frances also dined from time to time with Dr. Jones, whom she described as still vigorous and accustomed to being venerated at more than eighty years of age. He spent most of his time fund-raising off campus. In his absence, the dean, Dr. Chandler, administered the academic programs at the school. It wasn't long before Mary Frances chafed under her directives for detailed lesson plans. Summarily dismissing Dr. Chandler's two scholarly books as studies of the "Syntax in Lord Byron's Earlier Works or something like that," Mary Frances described her to Marietta as "a white-haired delicate-faced woman who walks like a fat-bottomed duck but sits like a duchess . . . On foot she is a dauntless but somewhat ridiculous little figure . . . and I bet she covers every inch of this campus at least twice a day. I think she is probably tyrannical. She is obviously 'dedicated,' and has the detachment of an abbess. I plan NOT to tangle with her, no matter how."[20]

As the summer progressed, Mary Frances's popularity with the students became as obvious to the dean as her freewheeling methods. What Mary Frances described in a letter to her sister Norah as her deliberate intent "to woo" them, "make myself acceptable . . . break down fear, and suspicion and hatred,"[21] was succeeding. Mary Frances spoke about encouraging her students to work very hard, especially at using language and expressing themselves clearly and well.

Many of them, however, had little or no educational foundation to build on, and the going was slow. Nevertheless, her noncredit class grew from fourteen to twenty-nine members, with no dropouts except one for illness, and Dr. Chandler was so impressed that she changed the status of the course, assigning two precollege credits for it.

During the break between the summer and fall sessions, Mary Frances decided to go to the Friedes' beach house in Bridgehampton to help celebrate Anna's twenty-first birthday and to see Kennedy, who was apprenticing as a stage technician at a local theater for the summer and seriously thinking of changing her major to theater. Mary Frances was "itching" to visit with both of her daughters. While in New York she also planned to set some of her business affairs in order with Volkening, including her contract with *The New Yorker*.

Leaving the school, however, was not easy, and she described the two-hour wait for the plane in the Jackson airport as panicky in every way: "I was surrounded by men and women and their frightened children speaking Mississippi dialects, several Civil Rights workers were flying out, the plane was stiff with heavily armed police, and I grew more convinced that I could never come back."[22] Once aboard, Mary Frances had a "worth waiting for" double martini, and Donald met her at the airport with a chilled bottle of Dom Perignon, which they drank en route to Long Island for Anna's party. The visit passed quickly in the well-appointed beach house, where sea grass and sand stretched to the Atlantic and the views from every window were constantly changing seascapes. While Donald kept to his pattern of long weekends in Bridgehampton and midweek business at Doubleday in the city, Eleanor played hostess. She and Mary Frances sometimes prepared a lunch of newly harvested fingerling potatoes, caviar, and champagne to share with their neighbor Truman Capote and his houseguests. Anna, recently returned from a hitchhiking trek to Berkeley, showed up with several boyfriends, who came and went. Mary Frances attended *My Fair Lady* at the John Drew Theatre, where Kennedy was working during that particular performance. "It went slick as glass," Mary Frances wrote to Aunt Grace.

But under the seeming affability of the comings and goings at the beach house, tension steadily grew. Anna, increasingly unstable emotionally, had been dismissed from her TWA job and also seemed phys-

ically run-down, with an infected ear and a heavy cough. Mary
Frances suspected that she was pregnant as well. Eleanor and Donald
had kept Anna's serious problems from Mary Frances, but when
Anna's behavior began to monopolize the Friedes' time and energy,
Eleanor refused to assume further responsibility for Anna's actions.
Angry at Mary Frances's initial lack of candor with Donald and herself, Eleanor unleashed what Mary Frances described as her "suddenly open (instead of gracefully hidden) hatred"[23] toward Mary
Frances. In a letter to Sean Kelly, she admitted, "I became my most
objectionable self, dictatorial tyrannical nasty Dote, after some 12
days of day and night drama, and simply shipped her [Anna] to Norah!!!!! It was a question of her life or Eleanor Friede's . . . and after 3
full years of being responsible for Anneli [Anna], Eleanor had priorities. Since I could not quite request the Friedes to leave NY, the only
alternative was to remove poor bewildered exhausted Anna. Which I
did. Complete with Pekingese. Rest and food will soon set Anna up
again, and then I hope-pray-trust she will try to get work on the West
Coast. (This, and I say it completely without malice, will be easier for
her now that I am not there . . .) The main thing was to remove her
from the Friede orbit . . . I hope for a long time . . . Right now I am
very unpopular, especially with Eleanor."[24]

Mary Frances hoped that Norah, a trained counselor, would be
able to give Anna love, support, and direction, and that the companionship of Norah's sons, especially Matthew, whose company Anna
enjoyed, would also be good for her. But by transferring Anna from
the Friedes' to Norah, Mary Frances was once again asking someone
else to take on responsibility for the problematic daughter with whom
she could not cope. Moreover, by sending her daughter to Berkeley,
she was placing her in the heart of a subculture that was exploding
with drugs and sex and rebellion of every stripe. Hippies, park people,
flower children, ragged musicians, and addicts soon joined students
on the sidewalks and streets of the college community in the "New
Solidarity" united against the war in Vietnam, the Johnson administration in Washington, the university's board of regents, and any other
form of established authority.

To complicate things further, while she was in Bridgehampton,
Mary Frances received word that her sister Anne's health problems, as

yet not accurately diagnosed, were worsening. And she also learned that her trusted friend and editor, Pat Covici, was gravely ill. Within a few days, Donald pulled strings for plane tickets while Mary Frances scoured Greenwich Village for Anna's dog, keys, clothing, and other possessions that her "friends" had removed from her apartment. Although she did not urge her daughter to see a doctor to confirm her suspicions about her pregnancy, Mary Frances was beginning to realize that her earlier descriptions of a lovely, *gamin*-like, vulnerable girl who was unable to cope with the demands of the workaday world, "taking the PILL and knowing other bewildered people singing 'We Will Overcome' in Village coffee shops and smoking tea,"[25] were understated. Anna was not simply a victim of the *zeitgeist* sweeping the country, she was also beginning to reveal disturbing signs of a physical and psychological illness that even her mother could no longer deny.

In the middle of the domestic crisis in Bridgehampton, Mary Frances and Volkening negotiated a "dream-agreement" with *The New Yorker* for four or five stories or articles a year on some aspect of culinary history, introducing, as Mr. Shawn envisioned it, a series of cookbook reviews. Even though she said that the prospect scared her silly, she put aside any reservations she had previously expressed about the tyranny of Shawn and returned to Piney Woods to begin the fall semester.

When classes began, Mary Frances worked more closely under Dr. Chandler's direction, tutoring, preparing students for chapel recitation, teaching American literature to eleventh graders, and supervising the school newspaper, the *Pine Torch*. Soon, however, the daily routine, which left virtually no time for her own writing, began to pall, and the inadequacies of a volunteer faculty, a librarian who objected to books being taken off the shelves of the library, "especially by a NEGRO," and the overbearing personality of Dr. Chandler put Mary Frances's goodwill to the trial. Her letters were filled with requests for household items to make her apartment and shared bathroom more comfortable, and old cookbooks for *The New Yorker* articles she wanted to write. And, alarmed by the reticence of Norah's son John, who had been especially vague about Anna when he arrived from Antioch College for his own three-month stint at Piney Woods, Mary Frances begged Norah for word about her daughter's pregnancy, which had now been confirmed by a doctor. When Norah replied that Anna seemed calm and interested in taking some classes at the university and had found a small apartment and wanted to move some household items from her mother's house in St. Helena into it, Mary Frances was momentarily encouraged.

Toward the end of September, she and Eleanor resumed a cautious correspondence. "One of the most painful things in my life, which has had some pain in it, was to leave you on September 2 with a feeling of hurt and confusion,"[26] Mary Frances wrote. Inwardly, she felt that their relationship would never be the same again. To further compound her dismay, her nephew's presence on campus posed subtle problems as he "did his clumsy best to upset the strange place"[27] with the typical impatience of a self-styled liberal. Partly responsible for his being there, Mary Frances felt obliged to keep him "in line," while she wrote good reports about his activities to Norah.

Hoping to celebrate a calming Thanksgiving with Norah's family and visit Anna in her new apartment, Mary Frances flew to Berkeley. The holiday could not have been more difficult. Returning to Piney Woods after the long weekend, Mary Frances wrote to June (calling her daughter Anne and Anneli):

It interests me that twice in some three months I have been, through Anne, the center of real scenes, all saying that I have shirked my responsibilities long enough. (Sobs, shakes, recriminations, much beating of breasts . . . I just sit there blinking like a fish . . .) First Eleanor really blew her top, with a mad scene and then three days of stony silence . . . reason: I had fobbed off on her and DF a problem, and she could not and would not stand being kicked in the teeth again by Little Anne. So . . . I got Anne out of New York, in an atmosphere of bleeding hatred. Second time around, this past five days in sunny California has been one bitter bloody hateful scene, from both Anneli and Norah, but especially Norah, of resentment at my simply walking out on the fact that Anne is a homeless pregnant waif . . . what is her feckless mother doing in Mississippi? . . . is she not more important than a handful of Negroes? . . . does Norah not have her own life to lead? The thing is that

Eleanor was right, and Norah is right. I had firmly decided that I would stay only until May 24. Now I have been told, to put it mildly, that my place is in Berkeley, and the sooner the better. Norah has a very strong streak of the martyr, well known to me, and she will resent very much my "taking over" all her genuinely generous-thoughtful-helpful actions for Anneli's welfare, but when she last spoke to me, ICILY, at the SF airport, she seemed genuinely relieved, too, that I would be there to do the cleaning, marketing, and general mopping up. I shall have to quit here.[28]

When Mary Frances returned to Piney Woods, she asked to be relieved of her teaching duties in December so that she could return to California and live with Anna. But this move only exacerbated the situation, as both Anna and Norah replied, in essence, that she should not come.

Recounting the whole sorry affair to Connes, Mary Frances wrote, "It was a vital blow to me. I went right on teaching, and doing a great deal of soul-searching . . . I can tell you. I reviewed every act of my life, and dredged up uncountable ones from my self-conscious, and it was very painful. I asked myself why this thing, and then the abrupt and violent rejection from Eleanor, had come so close together. I acknowledged much that had been very wrong in me, in the long past as well as the immediate one. I saw that the endless physical strain of living at Piney Woods had perhaps sharpened my sensibilities and made me speak too pointedly."[29] For someone who had assiduously avoided arguments and confrontations, Mary Frances found herself in an unenviable position.

Having alienated Anna, Norah, and Eleanor, and troubled Kennedy, who could not understand the various rifts that had developed, Mary Frances sought refuge in her writing. She managed to send a "try-cake" to William Shawn before the end of the fall semester. The piece was unfinished, but she wanted to know whether her plan to discuss current gastronomical publications in relation to their prototypes from past centuries was what he had in mind. She also told him that she would be very interested in writing several more pieces on such topics as gastronomy for household pets, starting with the Empress of China's sleeve-dogs and her amazing diet for them; the feeding of infants and invalids; the diet of athletes from the early Greek runners to the astronauts; regional cookery; and books on wine and drink in general. Meanwhile, "The Oldest Man" appeared in the December 5 issue of the magazine.

With her house in St. Helena committed to various friends until May and because of the situation in Berkeley, Mary Frances decided that she would join Anne in Genoa in January. She also invited Kennedy and her nephew John to spend Christmas with her in Chicago. She planned to visit Aunt Grace and enjoy the holiday ambience of the city, with its array of performing arts, special exhibits, and hotels with excellent room service. Snapshots taken by John at the Drake Hotel picture a svelte Mary Frances sitting on a very ornate chairlike commode in the luxurious bathroom. She had lost more than twenty pounds during the past six months, and the photo shows her holding a glass of champagne and smiling broadly. After their week of theater- and museumgoing, walks in the snow, and good food and wine, Kennedy returned to Russell Sage College and John to Antioch. Mary Frances flew to Reno, where she was met by Anne and Bill.

Staying in a small cottage next door to her sister's home, Mary Frances "slept and ate and continued in a really non-Bhuddistic [sic] way to contemplate [her] navel and ponder on the strange change in [her] relationships with the few people close to [her]."[30] The more than ninety-year-old house with its sagging front and back porches became another refuge. Mary Frances focused her energy on the small attentions she could provide for her sister, whose digestive problems were exacerbated by self-medication. Anne, who had for some time distanced herself from Norah and who had always disliked Donald, was not surprised at Mary Frances's predicament, and welcomed her company.

She felt duty-bound to take care of her daughter, but Anna made it clear that she didn't want her help. Looking back on the snowbound nights and days of January and February 1965, Mary Frances wrote, "I began to come to life again, and got some writing done. Fortunately I sold some things I had written long ago, to keep the pot boiling. I thought a great deal about Piney Woods—the iron hand of Dr. Chandler, the librarian who didn't want books taken out of the library, the conformity. People want me to write controversial stuff about it, but I am still too close, and I do not want to hurt the old man who founded the school. He is a rascal, but he is also something of a real saint, in my eyes. I am making many notes, of course, and may some day be able to tell what I think is the truth about the basically noble but infamous place . . ."[31] She also began to entertain the idea that perhaps she could do more for the school and for racial equality by working for the students away from Piney Woods, although she still planned to return for the summer term. She answered letters that her former students sent her, and began to think of ways to get some of them out of Mississippi.

Meanwhile, Anna's mood swings brought angry recriminations against her mother as well as blithe reports of student sit-ins at Berkeley, the siege of Sproul Hall, and the mass arrest of students on December 3, 1964. She and her cousin Matthew were regulars at the local meeting places and movie houses, and she described Matthew's efforts at filming her dancing. These newsy items were often mingled with gracious little thank-you notes acknowledging the gifts Mary Frances had bought for her at Thanksgiving. By this time, Anna had identified the baby's father as a French student at Harvard with whom she had hitchhiked from the East Coast to Berkeley and back. He was aware of her pregnancy, but remained in Cambridge.

In contrast to Anna's pattern of acceptance and rejection, Norah's disapproving attitude toward her older sister remained constant. She insisted that if Mary Frances had to ask what people wanted from her there was no use telling her. "In one of Norah's letters," Mary Frances wrote to Marietta, "she said that one of the most unforgivable things about me was that I was 'so filled with self pity' that I was inhuman toward the needs of anyone else in the world. This has given me much cause for thought. My honest conclusion is that I am perhaps the most un-self-pitying person I have ever known. I have never in my conscious life said when something evil happened, 'Why did this happen to *me*?' I have, reversely, often felt very humble that so much that was *good* has come my way. I do not feel any self-pity *at all*, but only a kind of cold curiosity, when I say that I have been irremediably changed by this rejection in my life."[32]

Mary Frances received yet another rejection when in answer to her query about the starting date of the summer session at Piney Woods, Dr. Chandler informed her that there would be no classes for her to teach. Her sudden withdrawal from the school had given the administration enough of a reason not to invite her back, but her aggressive courting of the students also merited disapproval. Although Mary Frances rationalized the decision as stemming from Dr. Chandler's and other administrators' unhappiness that the students were beginning to trust her too much, and believed that Dr. Jones knew nothing of the decision, the disappointment was keen. It did not, however, dissuade her from pursuing other means to help the students at the school.

During days spent napping at unusual times and taking "drinkies" with Anne before lunch and dinner, and nights filled with confused dreams, Mary Frances began to draw parallels between the months she had spent in Mississippi and her illness of two summers before. "And the three months I have spent here, sleeping more and more and slipping into a confused half-life, at least mentally, are like the period in Berkeley when I was recovering (There with the help? of all kinds of experiments with drugs and so on, here with alcohol, and a gradual re-awakening to food-as-a-pleasure) . . . since I got the astonishing news that I am not wanted back at Piney Woods . . . This may force me so violently to readjust my plans, my thoughts, my hopes, that it will be like a physical transplant . . . I will be jolted into a new inner climate."[33] In a letter to Powell, written the same day, she expressed the realization that for the first time in her life she was "without any *raison d'être* except myself, and I am simply incapable of being an integrated human being all alone. I must have something or somebody to exist for."[34]

Time passed quickly in Carson Valley, and the snow line receded farther up Mount Genoa. Mary Frances had spent many evenings with Anne and Bill, and the old tension and envy that had marked her relationship with her sister seemed, if not a thing of the past, only fleetingly evident during their time together. Although she tried to concentrate on the *New Yorker* articles, writing was difficult given her concerns about Anna's nearing due date and the mixed messages coming out of Berkeley. With only Norah's word that she would call when Anna's baby was born, Mary Frances distracted herself with Jelly Roll Morton, Bessie Smith, and Fats Waller records and by decorating her cottage with sprigs of forsythia to force them into early bloom. She also looked forward to Kennedy's spending part of her spring vacation with her in Genoa.

On March 20, 1965, Jean-Christofe Chanderli was born at Herrick Memorial Hospital in Berkeley at 9:32 in the morning. The birth certificate listed a Michel Chanderli as father; he was French, twenty-four years old, and a student of geological studies at Harvard. He was not present at the birth of his son, and he showed little inclination to assume the responsibilities of a parent. As promised, Norah called with the news that mother and child were fine in every way. Mary Frances never wrote about the experience of becoming a grandmother, nor of her feelings about being separated from her daughter at this time. But a phone call from Norah two days after the birth of Jean-Christofe rebuking Mary Frances for not even sending Anna a bouquet via Western Union provoked Mary Frances to tears. She was too overwhelmed by her sister's harshness to respond, and she was equally taken aback by the birth announcement that Anna sent a few days later, with a picture of the baby and a handwritten loving note congratulating her mother on the birth of her first grandchild. In her letters, Mary Frances never referred to the fact that she was "exiled" from her grandchild for the first weeks of his life, but she described Anna as serene and beautiful and very happy with her handsome son. Kennedy left Genoa on March 24 and flew to Berkeley to see her sister and the baby before returning to college.

Coincidentally, on the day of Jean-Christofe's birth, The New Yorker published a story by M.F.K. Fisher called "The Lost, Strayed, Stolen." The ghost story with a surprise ending was set in England, and probably was one of the pieces that Mary Frances wrote in 1961 after her short visit there on her return to the States from Aix. She had also completed "Men in My Life" for Holiday, another reworking of earlier material once destined for the planned book on Sherlock Holmes, Maigret, Nero Wolfe, Brillat-Savarin, and Sam Ward. But the article on cookbooks that she had promised to write for The New Yorker was not forthcoming.

In the cocoonlike ambience of her little cottage, Mary Frances sometimes sabotaged her writing by drinking before lunch at her sister's invitation and then finding herself just over the edge of clear thought. "I am here to work, to pull myself out of a pit of non-existence I subjected myself to in Mississippi," she wrote in her journal. "This is deliberately destructive or at least dangerously careless of me, and in some ways it would be better if I let myself break a leg, instead of masochistically risk breaking my present lucrative arrangement with the magazine. I am defying reality."[35]

But she was not thrilled with the current crop of cookbooks. While she was still at Piney Woods, editors at *The New Yorker* had forwarded several review books to her and she had complained to Donald, "I am even more revolted by most of them than I planned to be. And I am shocked to reflect on their cost. Most of them, even if they were any good, which they are not, are simply impossible to pick up, if one by some idiotic coincidence ever planned to look for a recipe. Now and then there is a beauty, like the Larousse, which has just as much right as the Bible to be too big and too heavy. The rest are pretentious prestige-symbols."[36] She suggested that Donald use his innate good taste and publish a book to bring out the real connection between the kitchen and the parlor. Illustrate recipes with Man Ray's photographs or appropriate reproductions from the Museum of Modern Art, she advised, or use artworks like Brancusi's *Bird in Flight* and add recipes for roasted quail and *poulet de Bresse truffé*. "If these idiots are going to pay $22.50 for useless poorly written prestige-cookeries which are an offense to everything but the publisher's budget, why not combine business with pleasure and do a GOOD book to catch the super-snobs with their Braques down?"[37] To Donald's amusement, the cookbook editor at Doubleday saw real possibilities in the idea, if M.F.K. Fisher would agree to write it.

Meanwhile, Mary Frances finally began to work on "The Full-Orbed Dinner," which would place various cookbooks written by women in England and America into some kind of meaningful context. She started with a few old cookbooks like Ann Blencoe's 1694 *Receipt Book*, Mrs. Beeton's *Book of Household Management*, and Mrs. Marion Harland's *Common Sense in the Household*, which seemed to have endured because they were curiosities. Then she went on to discuss Fannie Merritt Farmer's *Boston Cooking-School Cook Book* and

Mrs. Simon Kander's *Settlement Cook Book*, cookbooks considered standard equipment for brides during the early part of the twentieth century until the all-purpose *Joy of Cooking*, published in 1931, established itself as the most popular guide to cooking ever published in America.[38]

In addition to these "durables," Mary Frances considered the "wonderful and occasionally hair-raising ephemera" usually published for charitable purposes. These do-gooder manuals were the predecessors of the Junior League spiral-bound collections, with recipes usually signed Dee Dee, Winkie, and Dottie Sue, and their tried-and-trues usually ran the gamut from Snickerdoodles to Chafing-Dish-Wiggle. These manuals were fodder for Mary Frances's perspicacious wit, and she verbally romped through the compilations of the First Congregational Church of Great Falls, Montana, and the Tampa Junior League's *The Gasparilla Cookbook*, which included misleading indexes, genteel and/or blatant advertisements, and ingredients unprocurable, like grouper chowder and Cuban bread. "Curiosity spices them all, whether it be clinical or merely snoopy,"[39] she concluded.

She reserved her salient dismissal for the "Dustbin School" of female gastronomical collections, usually signed by a frustrated author who divulges the shortcuts of the social "in" crowd for either charity or prestige. "Needless to say," she wrote, "these tricks are far from world-shaking, but they do have the titillation of snob appeal about them, and they serve their purpose."[40] Beginning with Mrs. William Vaughn Moody's Prohibition-era cookbook, published in 1931, and ending with two recognized authorities on modern gastronomy, she had kind words for *My Favorite Maryland Recipes* by Mrs. J. Millard Tawes, a self-styled "Governor's Lady," but she relegated Poppy Cannon's *The Fast Gourmet Cook Book* to the dustbin. The regional appeal of terrapin, clams, beaten biscuits, and spoon bread saved the former; Green Rice, made with an eight-ounce jar of toddler-food spinach, margarine, and cooked rice, merited a grimace instead. The article was cutting-edge M.F.K. Fisher in the *Art of Eating* mode, and she admitted that it was "fun" to write.

By June 1965, only three of Mary Frances's stories and "The Full-Orbed Dinner" had been published in *The New Yorker*, however, and Rachel MacKenzie had rejected more than three stories. In a letter to

Eleanor, Mary Frances confessed to being completely at sea with the magazine. "She [Rachel MacKenzie] liked the things but they didn't get past the boys . . . too far out, too vague, perhaps a tiny-winy [sic] bit sentimental . . . these were the thumbs down on three."[41] The lure of fiction, however, continued to be stronger than "writing about cookbooks and food the way I used to," she added. Meanwhile, Volkening was exploring the possibilities of a cookbook with William Targ at Putnam.

In April, Mary Frances waged "a terrible protest against the way life goes on."[42] She daily witnessed the slow "disintegration" of Anne, recently diagnosed with cancer, and chafed under Norah's angry detachment and Anna's fluctuating moods. Also, the school's rejection still smarted. "I thought I did a good job at Piney Woods," she wrote.

> But they did not want me to come back. I felt that way about Anna too. I thought it was wise for me to help her go to NY when she was 18. But she did not want me to come back . . . back meaning near her . . . Kennedy in her own equally subtle way has said the same thing. So what does one do next? IF I wait, I am told that I have been cold and disdainful and "rejective." If I continue to be Mama I am told that I am stupid. IF I do not send a Western Union Posy for the birth of my first grandchild, an historical event which moved me more than I need chronicle, I have "abandoned" my older child, a being I continue to hold close to me. So where am I? How close do I prowl to the new Compounds? How near do I sniff to the walls that have been set up?[43]

Despite Anne's urging her to settle in a more permanent way in Genoa, Mary Frances returned to St. Helena on April 27 and again became involved with the Napa Valley Wine Library. She also established herself as a regular at the wine-and-cheese gatherings at the bookshop that Marietta had purchased earlier in the year to occupy her time as a retiree. However, she seemed reluctant to visit her sister and her daughter in Berkeley, or even to take more cautious steps to heal the breaches with them. In a move initiated by Norah, Anna and the baby as well as Norah and Matthew drove to St. Helena during the Memorial Day weekend. Anna was warm and impersonal; Norah gracious and withdrawn. "I recognized with an equally deliberate detachment," Mary Frances wrote, "that something is forever gone from our relationships."[44] But with Jean-Christofe there was a new beginning and a new love affair.

That weekend, Eleanor called, with news of Donald's death on May 30. The heart attack had occurred while they were at Bridgehampton, and it was swift. Kennedy was grief-stricken, Anna less so, and only slowly did Mary Frances realize that "in deep ways [she] was again a widow."[45] Her only consolation was the fact that Kennedy had grown close to Donald while she was at Russell Sage, and her recent acceptance at Carnegie Tech, where she intended to major in stagecraft, had made him very proud. When Kennedy went to Bridgehampton that summer for another stint with the John Drew Theatre, the already strong bond that she had developed with Eleanor became stronger in their shared memories of Donald, and Mary Frances could feel her younger daughter slipping even further away.

Meanwhile, Mary Frances remained in correspondence with a number of her former students at Piney Woods, and devised a plan to bring a few of the promising ones with an interest in the performing arts or other professional ambitions to the West Coast. She tapped friends in Los Angeles for both funds and contacts in the movie industry, and enlisted their help in sponsoring her "escapees." On June 8, 1965, Mary Frances wrote to Anne about the scheme in cloak-and-dagger terms: "I am biting my nails . . . think I told you that I am quite deeply involved in the underground railway from PWS and we are getting at least nine young people out this summer, mostly to Oregon and Washington . . . all rather cloak and dagger. My new foster daughter, Barbara Ware, arrives on the 10th. Wow." She continued to encourage letters from former students, promptly wrote back to them, arranged for their transport, and even leaned on old friends to arrange lessons and provide other opportunities for her runaway students. When Barbara arrived in St. Helena, she invited the twenty-year-old woman to live with her, and introduced her around town as "my daughter." In a letter to Connes, she explained, "I am rewarded every day by seeing her native intelligence respond to my constant guidance. It is a most interesting experience, in every way, and it is very good for me and I honestly believe it will be good for this girl. She is a graduate of Junior College, and is preparing now, with the help of a couple of my friends, to take the state exams for Vocational Nursing late this month . . . My being able to feel even faintly useful to some young human beings has helped my morale immeasurably."[46] She seemed unmindful that to her own daughters, the "adoption" seemed another inexplicable example of their mother's disregard for their feelings.

The summer passed quickly, with rushed trips to Reno to visit Anne, hospitalized after an operation to remove an abdominal tumor. At the same time, Mary Frances was preoccupied with procuring dental work, tutoring, and part-time employment for Barbara, who had scored disastrously on her nursing aptitude tests. Mary Frances "pulled strings" to get vocational guidance testing for her. Although she ranked high in personal relations, Barbara seemed to have abysmally few academic possibilities. And St. Helena offered almost no social activities that were suitable for a strictly raised young black Baptist. Mary Frances really hadn't thought through the implications of bringing Barbara into a situation where she felt isolated and inadequate. On the other hand, Barbara was fond of Anna and Jean-Christofe, and on their occasional visits to St. Helena she took care of the baby and kept the house running smoothly whenever Mary Frances flew to Reno to see her sister.

On August 3, Barbara accompanied Mary Frances to Nevada and spent a week in Genoa helping her pack some books and belongings that remained in the cottage. They also helped Bill get the house ready for Anne's homecoming. But Anne's debilitating pain returned, more treatment was necessary, and then she never made it home at all. She spent her last days heavily sedated and pinned to her hospital bed with tubes "sticking out of her like a Dali drawing." On August 23 she lapsed into a coma. The next morning, her doctors advised her husband to return home for some rest, and Anne died alone on August 24, 1965.

Mary Frances immediately wired Sean, who had visited his mother in July before taking up his Voice of America duties in Léopoldville, the Congo. She followed the cable with a letter of explanation:

Your mother really did not suffer, as would another person. She had been sickly for a long time, as you know . . . really since she was born. When she finally went to Reno, she told me she was more comfortable after that first operation than she had been for months (She had been living for a long time on Scotch and paregoric, as we all knew.) In Reno so many tricks were pulled on her that she was kept heavily sedated, largely to prevent her moving about with all those damned tubes stuck into her, and she lived mostly in a dream, with moments of great clarity, but as far as we can tell, no fear for herself.[47]

Mary Frances returned to Reno immediately and helped her brother-in-law make the necessary arrangements, promising to return to help him sort out Anne's things. She never wrote of her grief or of her tangled feelings toward her sister; she only consoled herself with the knowledge that she had been with Anne in the final and "surely the best season of her life—serene, happier than ever before in her troubled years, amusing, relaxed."[48] Inexplicably, however, until the end of her own life, Mary Frances increasingly wrote disparagingly about Anne in her letters to friends, acquaintances, and even strangers. Whether her exclusion from Anne's will was yet another rejection she could not forgive, as Sean has suggested, is unknown, but her antagonism was undisguised.

Meanwhile, Barbara had become increasingly unhappy in St. Helena and began to cast about for something to do in San Francisco. Feeling that she could no longer be responsible for her and with a deep sense of failure, in October Mary Frances insisted on accompanying her back to her home in Mississippi. On her return trip to California, she stopped in Genoa to assist her brother-in-law in carrying out Anne's last wishes. Never had the still, clear air of the small town been so inviting. Apples and leaves lay everywhere on the grass, and the purple Michaelmas daisies still bloomed. While she went through her sister's incredible number of gloves, dresses, and jewelry, Mary Frances thought again about working in the solitude of the white cottage next door to the Erskine home. But sensing a deepening dependence on the part of her brother-in-law, and perhaps even a romantic interest, she decided against it, although she toyed with the idea of

living in Nevada City for a time to get some serious work done or perhaps even escaping to another place.

When Mary Frances listed various "escape hatches" in a letter to
Eleanor, including Norah's offer of the use of the old house that she
and her friend Lida Schneider had purchased in Jenner, on the northern California coast, Eleanor advised:

> I think I do know what you mean about not being able to just
> concentrate on your writing . . . perhaps you have gotten into
> the mental habit of considering your writing something you do
> "on the side," or when it happens, and that the essential life is
> bringing up two little girls, or teaching youngsters how to artic-
> ulate. But you could, perhaps, start thinking in the other direc-
> tion—that the writing . . . is the essential, and what you must
> devise is some satisfying filler for the time, lots of it, when you
> can't be at the typewriter. A matter of reversing the balance . . .
> It is *wrong* to neglect *now* the very special talent you have, and
> anything less than putting IT in first place is neglect. Or eva-
> sion.[49]

She also suggested satisfying time fillers—the house in St. Helena,
activities at the Wine Library—and a tougher attitude toward well-
meaning drop-in neighbors.

The advice echoed similar words from Volkening, and Mary
Frances knew that with the contract he was negotiating with Bill Targ
at Putnam for a compilation of offbeat "dated dishes" and her existing
New Yorker commitments, she would have to concentrate more diligently. The trouble was, she told Eleanor, "I don't think there is any
importance AT ALL, in anything I write. I write pleasingly, and sometimes well. But so what? I have known a lot of writers, and have always been basically amused by their frantic insistence upon being
WRITERS. I don't think I have the right attitude. I mean this. I don't
know who could ever convince me that it would matter one toot-
in-Hell whether I wrote an article for *Holiday* or not. So, yes, I have
come to consider what I write 'on the side' . . . and suddenly there is
now more of that. And what is left?"[50]

As the holidays approached, Mary Frances decided to gather the family, including Eleanor and Bill Erskine, together in St. Helena. She knew better, but she stuffed the turkey with oyster dressing the evening before she roasted it on Christmas Day, and virtually everyone ended the festive day with cramps and nausea. It was a good story in the retelling, but an embarrassing way to end what had been a year of disasters. After family and friends had all departed for Berkeley, New York, and Genoa, on the third day of 1966, Mary Frances scribbled in her notebook: "End of Xmas vac. Bath, supper, check out house: fireplace, lights, radio—Upstairs—rain—Always on watch, listening for non-people." The fragment was titled "The Most Alone." It concluded with the words "This is best."[51]

FOURTEEN

Cara Maria Francesca

(1966–1967)

Sometimes I feel so amazed, and so excited, to think that we actually started something last May, that I cannot believe it. But I do believe it. I cannot imagine life now without that.[1]   —M.F.K. Fisher

In mid-January 1966 Mary Frances was asked to deliver a lecture series for the spring session at the University of California at Berkeley Extension Center. Titled "Menus of Mankind," the series promised to "trace the development of cookery and dining, as a social and aesthetic phenomena over six thousand years," and the lectures, which were to be presented on eight successive Mondays at the Walnut Creek campus in the early afternoon and in the evening at the Berkeley campus, were designed to explore the foods of Greece and Rome, Elizabethan England and the Renaissance, cookery and dining in the Romantic and Victorian eras, mid-twentieth-century "packaged" meals, and beyond. "At this point I dread the whole caper, but it will give me a chance to see Anna and even Norah, and I think it will be good for my morale whatever that may mean . . . The applications are surprising, and I'll have about 250 in classes . . . each one. No papers, thank god again."[2]

When the series began on February 21, 1966, Anna invited her mother to spend Monday nights with her and her son Chris. But after two stayovers, the deteriorating physical condition of the apartment and Anna's bruises confirmed Mary Frances's suspicion that her daughter was again moving into a "manic" phase and was involved in an abusive relationship from which she was either unable or unwilling to extricate herself. "I was disturbed to find, in one 12-hour day when I took care of JC [Jean-Christofe], while Anna was in Berkeley . . . that Chris was very withdrawn . . . he slept perhaps nine hours, and preferred to lie by himself in his play-pen, sucking his thumb or a bottle. This is not right for a strong child of one year. Anna's friends told Norah that Chris is left completely alone for long stretches. He is obviously withdrawing in self-protection. When he is with her he is very whining and noisy, and her remedy is to give him something to eat and put him down again, and close the door. Kennedy, your sister is a sick girl again."[3] From then on Mary Frances seldom saw Anna, but checked into a motel after the evening session and returned to St. Helena the following morning.

In letters to friends, she noted that the series was proving to be more arduous and time-consuming than she had initially anticipated. The lectures did, however, expand her earlier forays into culinary history and old cookbooks, and by so doing they also helped her gather her thoughts about assembling a collection of "dated dishes" for the book Bill Targ wanted her to write. Going through her recipe file "for the real monstrosities in it," she said, "I found that there were too many decent recipes to ignore. Most of them were family hand-me-downs, the Tried-and-Trues . . . things like Cousin Aggie's Spanish Buns and other relics from the plain days in American cooking, attributed to friends or cooks, or even close relatives."[4] But during the course of collecting recipes, she began to reject the idea of simply focusing on the "off beat," and she submitted a plan for three or four main sections with recipes from a "tight but fairly eclectic file of personal cooking." She wanted "to bow firmly and openly to a list of perhaps five easily procurable and completely standard texts . . . Rombauer's *Joy of Cooking*, *The Boston Cookbook*, *Larousse Gastronomique*, *Escoffier's Cook Book*, and perhaps that near-classic by Julia Child and her associates about French cooking 'made easy' . . . it is used increasingly by amateur cooks, who are my main readers, I suspect. This book [will be] about how I like to cook, most of the time, for people in my world."[5] She wanted her cookbook to be about meals, recipes, and cookbooks that were meaningful to *her*—"the sensual and voluptuous gastronomical favorites-of-a-lifetime, the nostalgic yearnings for flavors once met in early days."[6]

Due in no small measure to the efforts of Volkening, doors that she had not walked through before were opening. Demand for her thoughts about everything from Victorian household manuals to gourmet dining was increasing, in part because of her recent publications in *The New Yorker*, but also because of the sudden surge in America's food consciousness. The early 1960s had ushered in *une frénésie culinaire*; food was becoming one of America's favorite performing arts, thanks to the success of Julia Child's *French Chef* TV series, James Beard's widely read cookbooks, and Craig Claiborne's insightful restaurant reviews in *The New York Times*, which popularized fine dining at that bastion of French cooking, Le Pavilion, and other fine restaurants. At the White House, Jacqueline Kennedy employed a French chef and presided over formal dinners replete with French wines, and in Manhattan, devotees of French cooking rushed to Dione Lucas's Egg Basket to learn how to flip omelets. Cooking schools proliferated, and magazines rushed to publish recipes for coq au vin, boeuf bourguigon, and pommes de terre dauphinoise. Child, Beard, and Claiborne were the triumvirate of culinary luminaries whom editors sought out for articles, recipes, and interviews, and M.F.K. Fisher soon joined their ranks.

The acceleration of her professional activities left Mary Frances little time to dwell on her personal difficulties. On a whirlwind trip to New York arranged by Volkening in May 1966, Mary Frances squeezed in a day with Eleanor and Kennedy, who arrived exhausted from Carnegie Tech. On the other two days, she and Volkening negotiated a contract with the book division of Time-Life for the first book in a series to be called Foods of the World. Richard Williams had been named series editor, to be assisted by Irene Saint. A staff of at least thirty people would work on each book, which would feature the cuisine of a given country, handsomely showcased in color photographs, packaged together with a small spiral-bound book containing only the recipes. Money was no object—they wanted a stellar lineup. M.F.K. Fisher would do the volume on France, in tandem with consulting editor Michael Field, a former concert pianist turned cookbook author, cooking school instructor, and sometime East Hampton restaurateur.[7] Julia Child would be a consultant as well. "I agreed to the essentially fast tough professional operation because of the editor, Michael Field, whom I admire, and because I can go to France for a month or so FREE. The deadline is October 1," she wrote to Aunt Grace. "I got along famously with the various editors and research people who will work with me. Actually, for what I am to do, I need none of them, but have not told them so! They are very serious and dedicated and grim and so on. I hide my inner jaunty detachment. I get a fat sum, which seemed 'wrong' for me, for I have never dealt in such terms."[8] The prospect of more than a month in France on an expense account, especially during the major music festival in Aix, and the chance to revisit friends and renew acquaintances, eased whatever pangs she felt.

The letter to Aunt Grace detailed other projects that Mary Frances had recently completed, not only the lecture series but a review of Martin Gardner's *The Secret of Cooking for Dogs* and the publication of her story "The Changeover"[9] in the April 30 and May 14 issues of *The New Yorker*. Almost lost in the letter was Mary Frances's casual mention of a "kind of date" in San Francisco arranged for the forthcoming weekend with a man she had known for about twenty-seven years. "He and his wife bought Le Paquis from Timmie and me. He is the publisher of *Esquire* magazine," she wrote, and added, "Oh, his name is Arnold Gingrich. He wrote that he had to spend four days in the City on business, and would like to save one for me if I would show him 'the other side.' So I plan to go down in time to give him an exhausting tourist whirl, complete with one-hour Bay tour and so on. He will never be the same again. As I said, it sounded like fun, before I got into this new deal with Time-Life."[10]

Arnold Gingrich, man-about-town, amateur violinist, fly fisherman, author of several books, astute publisher, dapper dresser, and longtime admirer of M.F.K. Fisher, may or may not have been interested in more than an insider's tour of the City by the Bay. But after the twenty-four hours they spent together, including Sunday night at the venerable Clift Hotel, Mary Frances became his "Cara Maria Francesca" and Gingrich was her "Dear Bouncy Boy." Their meeting in San Francisco was the beginning of an affair that would continue, albeit at long distance, until Gingrich's death in 1976.

In many ways the liaison was inevitable. As an early contributor to *Coronet*, the mistress of Le Paquis, and a writer of note, Mary Frances was on Gingrich's Christmas card list, and, for some inexplicable reason, in 1952 he had sent Mary Frances an announcement of his third marriage to Jane Kendall. At the time, Mary Frances was living at the Ranch in Whittier, and she responded, "I did not know that you were divorced![11] You may tell your wife that I've long carried a quietly burning torch for you myself, and that it's a good thing for me that I was kept in the dark . . . I couldn't possibly have afforded a futile trip to NY."[12] Offhand as the remark may have been, undoubtedly it made an impression on Gingrich, because when Jane's health sharply declined and she became virtually bedridden in 1964, he had renewed his earlier correspondence with Mary Frances.

They continued that correspondence now, and more. Witty, charming, and cosmopolitan, Gingrich's letters provided both pleasure and distraction. He praised Mary Frances's current pieces in *The New Yorker*, and he also brought her up to date on his own literary activities, including the recently published *The Well-Tempered Angler*. In an elaborate exchange of letters planning their next tryst, she inquired about his work at *Esquire*, his writing activities, and the nature of Jane's illness—a new exercise, after a long hiatus, of "the direct approach," about which she had recently written a piece, not yet published. "It should not be said about me, even by myself, that I sit like a hungry spider waiting for a succulent *partner*. I like people who are different from me sexually, and am stimulated by them. They trust me. Most of all I think I like men, who think of themselves as men, inert and unquestioned *men*. But I also like people who are not settled in one sex or another. Here I am not quibbling, for my approach is still direct. I make a lot of people turn away, or at least off, from me, by being so open in my assertion that I like people, men or, women or, this or that or."[13]

With Gingrich in her life, she became again the significant other, and his almost daily letters and phone calls made her feel adored and needed, even as *New Yorker* deadlines and her trip to France approached and Gingrich's delivery date for *Toys of a Lifetime*[14] drew near. On June 18, four days before her departure for France, he wrote, "Damn it darling, I can't bring myself to say goodbye, godspeed, even good happy landing and all that. I keep hanging on your shirt tails like a wailing baby . . . And you've been so wonderful about writing me—far more than either expected or deserved—and how wonderfully you've written me, too, my god, I have your last three letters memorized better than I have my fiddle pieces. How I love and cherish you and your every least and last word."[15]

Mary Frances boarded her flight determined to keep "a not too sketchy list of meals for fun." In her unpublished "Paris Journal," she did, in fact, carefully note memorable meals, including the double martini and mixed nuts, followed by a turbot entree and "few bites of Gruyère" that she had enjoyed on her flight to Paris.[16] It was the first time she had visited the city without a family member, a lover, or a former husband as a companion. At the Hôtel Continental on the rue de Castiglione, she took a room on the top floor that in 1938 had been part of the maids' attic quarters she and Dillwyn had planned to rent as a winter retreat from Le Paquis. Now remodeled, the small mansard rooms had large windows, and a few even had small balconies that overlooked the rue de Rivoli and the gates to the royal gardens of the Tuileries. Slightly to the left, the gray buildings of the Louvre came into view. Mary Frances learned that down the corridor and in the room that she and Dillwyn had planned to use as a bedroom, Janet Flanner had been residing for almost twenty years. Having met the *New Yorker* columnist at her sister Hildegaard Flanner Monhoff's home in Calistoga only a few months earlier, Mary Frances quickly slipped a note under Flanner's door to reintroduce herself.

Mary Frances admired the endurance of Flanner, sixteen years her senior, who "was the darling of the management, the waiters, room service, and the bartenders, especially."[17] Soon they were savoring chilled melon, grilled dorade, and Sancerre at La Méditerranée, across from l'Odéon, or attending experimental theatrical performances and films. She found the doyenne of *The New Yorker* "effusive, amusing, kind, and cold," and was attracted to "her sureness of power."[18] That Flanner was one of the few people permitted to visit the ailing Alice B. Toklas, who resided in a nursing home in a suburb of Paris, only added to her mystique, as did her retreat to Orgeval, her lover Noel Murphy's country home, every weekend, and the bouquets of fresh flowers she brought back to the hotel on Sunday evenings.

Gingrich had encouraged his son John, who was living in the city, to invite Mary Frances to "somewhere in the milieu where you play, for a drink and a bite,"[19] and he also pressed his friend Charles Ritz to invite Mary Frances to the Ritz Hotel for a drink, because she "is my great friend, and certainly America's greatest gourmet-writer."[20] Contrary to many accounts that Mary Frances wrote about being Flanner's "errand girl," however, she spent most of her time in Paris with Michael and Frances Field, who had arrived in Paris earlier than she, and with the staff members of the Time-Life Paris bureau, who were in the process of selecting a "typical" Parisian family to photograph for the projected volume. On June 26, after a light repast of Bollinger Brut with Parma ham that she savored in the Grande Salle of the Gare de Lyon, Mary Frances boarded the Mistral, bound for Dijon, where she planned to stop over for dinner with Georges Connes and his wife before continuing on to Marseilles and Aix-en-Provence.

Once established at the Hôtel Roi René in Aix, she was amazed at the number of tradespeople who still recognized her and greeted her as she made her way along the cours Mirabeau into familiar restaurants and cafés. Sitting over a gin and vermouth at the Deux Garçons, she watched students returning from their baccalaureate exams at the lycée. And once again she wondered if perhaps she had left Aix too soon, before her girls had grown "clearer and stronger" and more prepared for adult life than they now seemed to be. In the days that followed, Mary Frances experienced again the familiar sights and sounds of the ancient city, dined with friends, and observed the influx of visitors and performers arriving for the annual music festival. She also wrote a note to Mme Lanes to arrange a visit.

However, Mary Frances's account of living in the eccentric woman's boardinghouse in *Map of Another Town*, in which she used Mme Lanes's real name,[21] had embarrassed and enraged Mme Lanes's in-laws in Paris, and they had warned her never to speak to the American author again and even urged her to consider legal action. So when Mary Frances attempted a visit, she was ordered from the stairwell by an irascible servant who told her never to return again. "Today, no matter how detached and polite I remained outwardly, I was really *furious*," Mary Frances wrote in her diary the day before her fifty-eighth birthday.

Her differences with Mary Frances seemingly resolved, Norah arrived in Aix with Matthew on July 4 for a four-day visit before going on to Venice and Greece. During the time they were together, Norah arranged a festive belated birthday dinner for Mary Frances at Surcouf's in Marseilles, and they spent a Sunday afternoon visiting with Leo and Barbara Marschutz in the garden at Le Tholonet, followed by a quiet supper in the local café. On July 8 Mary Frances parted from them and returned to Paris, where she accompanied the Time-Life staff to the boulevard Montparnasse to meet with the family that had been selected—Annie Boulat, her husband, and her two children. The staff planned to photograph the family in their apartment and in their rebuilt stone farm cottage about forty miles south of Paris. Mary Frances would introduce them in the text as a typical young French family and explain how they exemplified traditional French ways of entertaining, picnicking, gardening, and shopping.

Meanwhile, the Fields, their teenage son, and a friend of his had already settled into Julia Child's second home, La Pitchoune, built on the estate of Child's coauthor, Simone Beck[22]—Simca—in Plascassier, near Grasse. Mary Frances arrived on July 11, and the next few weeks were a whirl of dining and socializing, interspersed with work on the book. She was grateful for the chance to visit Eda Lord and Sybille Bedford, who lived for part of the year at La Roquette-sur-Siagne, a short distance from Plascassier, and spent many of her evenings in the company of the Fields, although Michael's approach to researching authentic French cuisine—which seemed to consist of dining in one-, two-, and three-star establishments—struck Mary Frances as somewhat superficial. She wondered why the Fields kept the refrigerator so understocked, except for iced vodka and dried salamis, and why the highly touted culinary instructor avoided cooking in the kitchen that Julia Child had outfitted with professional equipment. Before their time at La Pitchoune was over, even Beck was questioning the choice of Michael Field for the project. In *Food and Friends* she wrote, "When he dropped in looking for hints, I was glad to give them. But I was flabbergasted when one day he asked, 'Could you show me how to make a brown roux?' "[23] That, Beck concluded, was like a science teacher asking about the composition of water.

Still, despite her growing boredom with Field, Mary Frances wrote in her journal, "Increasingly I feel this wild trip came at exactly the right time in my life, to intensify everything good, wipe out some recent bitter times, strengthen me for What Is Next . . ."[24] She had grown quite fond of Beck, and in a sense had even become acquainted with Child after three weeks of drinking coffee in her kitchen, sleeping in the shutter-darkened guest room, and sitting on the patio that looked out over the meadows stretching toward Grasse. The experience did not quite prepare her, however, for the first firm handshake with the Cantabrigian in tennis shoes who towered over most of the other people meeting the flight from Paris at Boston's Logan International Airport on August 3, 1966. As Child recalled a decade later, "I so well remember meeting you at the airport, and we were expecting a diminutive creature, but you were a nice big girl."[25]

Each woman brought considerable gravitas to this first meeting. By 1966 Child's career was skyrocketing. Volume 2 of *Mastering the Art of French Cooking* was under contract, and her name, TV series, and one-of-a-kind voice, in person and on the page, lent considerable authority to whatever she said and wrote. Mary Frances had a solid literary reputation based on ten books, her translation of Brillat-Savarin, and an impressive résumé of stories and articles, but her books had a much smaller audience. She was, as she liked to portray herself, "the Emily Dickinson of Oak Avenue." But both personally and professionally Mary Frances sensed that she was on the brink of great change. "For the first time in my so-called adult life I seem to be on largely uncharted courses,"[26] she confided to Child later that day, as they drank chilled wine in the shade of the garden behind the Childs' newly renovated home on Irving Street in Cambridge, where Mary Frances was a houseguest.

The next morning Julia's husband, Paul, introduced Mary Frances to Harvard Square, and as they strolled back to Irving Street, they watched the students tossing Frisbees across the lawn of the Divinity School. There was an immediate meeting of minds and spirits between them, thanks to shared literary and artistic interests and because of the pivotal role France, especially Paris, had played in their coming of age. Her relationship with Julia developed more slowly, but Julia told friends that Mary Frances was a woman of considerable life experience, and an intellectual. It took Julia a while to figure out Mary Frances's more subtle sense of humor.

Mary Frances and the Childs had lunch with Richard Williams, the Time-Life series editor, who was intent upon broadening Julia's role in the project. He also indicated that he and his staff were pleased with the photos and the progress that Field and Mary Frances had made in France, and he asked her to meet with the New York staff before she returned to California. First, though, Mary Frances "hitched a ride" to Maine with Julia and Paul, who were on their way to the Childs' family cabin in Bernard on Mount Desert Island. The trip proved to be a congenial way for Mary Frances to get to know the Childs better and also to see Kennedy, who was working at the Kennebunkport Playhouse that summer and falling in love with a young man who was the resident stage manager there.

In a "bread and butter" letter sent from the Hotel Dorset in New York a few days later, Mary Frances addressed Julia and Paul as her "Chers Nouveaux Amis" and thanked them for an end-of-summer interlude that she considered "a mysterious reward" after her earlier restaurant-hopping with the Fields. She also met with the editorial board of the Time-Life series and learned that they were proposing that the first draft of the introduction she had written in France be divided into a shorter general introduction and several chapter introductions. The shifting overall plan of the book was beginning to reflect the differing opinions of the increasing number of people involved in the project, and Mary Frances privately felt that it did not bode well.

While she was in New York, Mary Frances and Gingrich saw each other as often as possible and dined at the Richelieu and the Charles V. To their mutual delight, they discovered that their feelings for each other had been enhanced rather than diminished by their separation. Before she left, he gave her a ring, and after returning to St. Helena, Mary Frances wrote:

> Thank God you still find my [me] satisfactory-and-satisfying, after our Stolen Moments last week! I was scared about it, NATURALLY. I think wearing the top of the black and white linen dress inside out, for the first time in an endless series of appearances in it, was some indication. I was astounded to see what I had done, when I repaired myself after lunch in the TL "ladies." I love knowing a man who notices what I wear. It is

almost a lost sensation for me, after some 18 years of self-appointed immolation or whatever it might be called. One correction: my neck is not lovely. It is the worst thing about me at my present age. I think . . . with my waistline perhaps. Ah well and Ho hum. Please continue to like it.[27]

She confessed to being "startled" to know that Gingrich loved her. "Perhaps it is natural in women, who have seen and felt a great deal and have lived more than their share already, to be baffled and afraid when they are offered even more . . . ???"[28] She cautioned him against mistaking her for a "Dream Image" because he was enamored of her writing, as she felt that Donald Friede had done, to their mutual harm. But with a pampered, difficult wife rendered semi-invalid by a stroke, he rejoiced in the "miracle of timing" that had brought him and Mary Frances together after so many years of admiration from afar. He pressed her for assurances that there was nobody else.

"Carpe Diem has been my private touch-word for many years now, and I'd be glad to let you move in on it,"[29] she answered him, even as she acknowledged that she would never want Gingrich to leave his wife for her, especially "because of the tragic happening to that lovely creature . . . So, here we are, two grown-up people very aware of each other, but you are married . . . I don't think that you are either unfair or unrealistic to want me to be your girl, because apparently I have been for a very long time. And I am enriched to know that you want me."[30] During the rest of August and into September and October, they wrote to each other almost every day. "I haven't ever felt as overt as this—not since I was sixteen," he wrote to her. "It's good there are three thousand miles between us this minute or I would have you spread-eagle and gasping—I don't know what's got into me all of a sudden—maybe a full bottle of Fleurie that I drank all by myself at Midtown."[31]

The letters between New York and St. Helena contained the trivia of vineyard parties, bits and snatches of Napa gossip, and reports on books in progress, and they also explored the implications of their relationship. At times Mary Frances teased Gingrich with descriptions of what she was wearing—or not wearing. In other letters she wrote about her abhorrence of jealousy and her guardedness about physical contact:

About keeping or giving away my physical self, I'll keep it . . . I am by nature unable to be casual, sexually, and am what is somewhat carelessly referred to as a one-man woman. When I kissed you in the Buena Vista, that was IT for me, and the idea of much more than a handshake with anyone else is almost violently distasteful and even impossible. (I never kiss anyone on the mouth, except my lover . . . not even my children or parents . . .) This very basic and relentless characteristic of mine makes life rather dull at times, and has been deplored by several people for various reasons. But that's the way I am. So . . . Fortunately I have never been one for dalliance. Naturally I like to have it shown to me that I am attractive, in one way or another. But I have absolutely no need to prove that I am a woman by dangling the scalps . . . I have always held the insufferably smug opinion that if I want a man to love me, he will. I refuse to take a man from another woman, whereas most women feel that is the ultimate proof of their success.[32]

Her words about taking a man from another woman may have a false ring to them, but they also convey an ambivalence about casual sex, about her unabashed seduction of Dillwyn Parrish, and about her passionate, if brief, affairs.

When Gingrich hinted at another trip to San Francisco, Mary Frances said how difficult it was to be in love and not actually live with her beloved, "scared of trying to get along on a taste of it now and then, a snatched few hours, a tidbit here, a nibble there,"[33] reminiscent of her earlier relationship with Larry Powell. But she told Gingrich that she did want him to see her home in St. Helena, and more to the point, see her *in* her home, as one more step in understanding her. She suggested that he bring along a third person to keep them "vertical," a definite tease.

In early September, while she was writing almost daily to Gingrich and under pressure to complete the Time-Life manuscript, Anna's problems again interrupted Mary Frances's routine in St. Helena. Over the past year her daughter had veered between being a self-styled manager and booking agent for a number of rock groups and wandering along the California coast with a gypsylike band of hippies determined to live off the land. She was also in and out of various communal apartments until Norah offered her and Chris a place to live. Since spring, she had not only rejected any advice or contact with her mother, but had also denounced Norah when her aunt requested that she conform to a few minimal rules of the house. By mid-August Anna's situation had worsened to such a degree that the juvenile authorities threatened to put her son in foster care if she refused treatment. With Norah's help, Anna was admitted into Herrick Hospital, put under the care of a team of psychiatrists, and ultimately released into her mother's care on September 4.

They both moved into Norah's apartment, and Mary Frances also took a room at the Berkeley Inn in order to work on the Time-Life book during the day and be with her daughter as much as possible in the evening. When writing to Gingrich, Mary Frances described her daughter as physically weakened and underweight, confused, and frightened. "One tragic thing about Anna is that for almost exactly five years she has . . . ruined every single chance she has been given to be independent of the patterns and people she so hates . . . social rules, family patterns, all that . . . I have often read, and agreed through empathy, that psychic disturbance can be the worst thing to happen in a family. Now I know. One feels very helpless."[34] Gingrich continued to write to her in Berkeley—Mary Frances hastened to assure him that Norah would not even give a second thought to the flurry of mail she received at her sister's home—and during this complicated and trying time, their correspondence sustained her.

Following a rigid schedule of writing at the Berkeley Inn during the day and being with Anna, Chris, Norah, and Matthew in Norah's home the rest of the time, Mary Frances completed the Time-Life manuscript and sent it to Williams in early October. Using maps, culinary guides, and her own experience, she had verbally toured the eleven French provinces that for centuries had signified great food, celebrating everything from the fish, apples, and lamb of Normandy and Brittany to the *garbures*, foie gras, truffles, Cognacs, Armagnacs, and wines of the Bordeaux region. In the introductions to each province, she describes the sequence of dishes that might compose a family meal and identifies the specialties of each region. Michael Field and the consultants and staff supplied recipes, both simple and sophisticated, for hors d'oeuvres, bread, soups, fish, poultry, meat, vegetables, salads, cheese, and desserts.

An unexpected sequence of memos, letters, and editorial corrections followed Mary Frances's submission of her text. The food historian Waverley Root, whom Time-Life had hired to review the first draft, concentrated his comments on small but important details; Child's comments were far more substantive. In a letter to Mary Frances she went out of her way to note, "I have read and written as though you were not O*U*R F*R*I*E*N*D*, which seems the sensible thing to do."[35] Her main objection was that while she thought Mary Frances's text was "poetic" and "evocative," she also had "an overall feeling that the French are over-romanticized and the Americans underestimated, as though France was seen with loving pre-war eyes, and America viewed from the super highways with every once in a while a meal with the TV-dinner set."[36]

Mary Frances had described Annie Boulat in both her Parisian and country kitchens, explaining the hows and whys of her marketing at the outdoor stalls on the rue Mouffetard or picking fresh radishes at her neighbor's farm in the country. As Mary Frances portrayed her, she was a prototypical French housewife who could handle a *mousse au chocolat* and a *potée* with equal skill. Child objected to the portrait, which didn't conform to her long-held conviction that the French bourgeoisie considered domestic cooking a menial task. She added that American families knew their way around the kitchen far better than most French families did, and American kitchens were much easier to work in. Child admired Mary Frances's stories and anecdotes, but she took a dim view of any comment that "degraded the red-blooded American way of life." She preferred to avoid "digs" about folkways, gelatin salads, squeezy-fresh bread, and inferior grandmothers, and advocated instead a tone of urging on. At issue were each woman's impressions of France, which were formed under different circumstances, at different times, and in different places.

Volkening had a copy of Mary Frances's manuscript in hand before receiving the four-page commentary from the Time-Life people and the twelve pages of editorial suggestions from Julia Child. He phoned Mary Frances to prepare her for them and suggested that she cope with some of the comments in order to be able to accept the initial advance. But after Mary Frances received and read the many requests for revisions, she called Volkening on October 31. She had decided, she said, to return all the material to Time-Life on condition that they not use her name in any way. Relaying her agent's reaction to Gingrich, Mary Frances wrote, "[Volkening] congratulated me and said that he was very proud and happy."[37] She also added that he thought that announcing her decision to "Mr. Luce's Creatures" would throw them into hysteria.

In a detailed letter to Williams, Mary Frances said that she would expect no further remuneration, and that the editorial staff could salvage the 38,000 words she had supplied to them, "depersonalized," of course, in order to arrive at a suitable text. She also wrote to Child the same day, thanking her for her help and encouragement, and hoping that she had not let her down. She felt that the whole endeavor had been a mistake on her part and that she was not really the right one for the job. But she added that she had been immeasurably enriched: "I have met you both, and Michael and Frances Field, and the fascinating family of the fascinating Simca."[38] She concluded by saying that she was very much in debt to the Luce empire.

"I myself slept more serenely last night than for a long time," Mary Frances wrote to Gingrich. "This has been foreign to my nature from the start . . . and as for giving up the first payment, it matters not at all to me. I can easily get into productive work again for the NYer, which I have completely stopped for the past 5 months, and go about the Putnam job with a clear mind. Well . . . end of little story. I have met some fascinating new people, and have had a chance to have two breakfasts and two lunches with you . . . and of course have seen old friends in France . . . I hope you don't think I'm a rash foolish person about the T-L decision. Committee editing is simply not for writers like me, and I feel also that Dick Williams, who has been devious with me, has his back against some wall he has kept hidden until now."[39]

After another exchange of letters and several phone calls, on November 5 Mary Frances reached a compromise with Williams, who had sold the idea of "name" writers to the powers-that-were at Time-Life and wanted M.F.K. Fisher's name on the first volume in the series. She spent the next two days going over every directive from him, Julia Child, Irene Saint, Waverley Root, and researcher Helen Isaacs, and writing ten pages of comments in response, saying for the most part, "Omit///cut out . . . agree///do as you wish."[40] After a considerable amount of rewriting, Williams traveled to St. Helena, where Mary Frances was again in residence, and showed her the revised manuscript for her approval. There was a bit of minor "blackmail"— Williams suggesting that her check might not arrive unless Mary Frances allowed the use of her name—and in the end she capitulated.

As it turned out, her decision would prove to be far more professionally advantageous than she realized at the time. After the subscription brochure on the series was published, Mary Frances wrote to Volkening:

> The most surprising people, *nice* people, even dear good friends, are saying and writing to me the damnedest stuff about the glossy publicity in the Time-Life throwaway. I feel as if they actually had no conception of what I have been trying to do since I was nine or so: be a good writer. They call me long distance and scream happily at me, "MF, you're *in*! You've *made* it!!!" . . . just because of a hammy toothy shot in the subscription gimmick . . . Actually it hurts me. You can add this to your file on the Sensitive Soul Syndrome. Or am I simply being peevish? Or snobbish, perhaps? I suppose if some obscure reviewer had linked my name, referring to one of my books pre-doomed to complete nonentity, with someone like Colette or V. Woolf or or or, I'd feel happy as a fat cricket.[41]

The experience did nothing to make her reconsider her tendency to regard herself as her own best critic, or to believe that when she submitted a manuscript, it was an "honest" piece of work that required little or no editing. She canceled copyediting changes that appeared in the page proofs of the Time-Life book, and at about the same time also encountered difficulties with her editor at Putnam. When she had signed on "to write a nice quiet book about my recipe file," Bill Targ had requested that she send each chapter when she completed it. Although she sent one or two pieces to placate him, she refused to send any more material until the manuscript was completely finished, because, she said, "I don't work that way."

Moreover, she continually made grudging remarks about *The New*

Yorker's proclivity for commas. Sentence structure, punctuation, and a sophisticated vocabulary she considered to be her stock-in-trade, and she had little respect for editors who "tinkered" with her prose style, and even less respect if they questioned her judgment. Volkening frequently resolved these author-editor entanglements. As a literary agent and as a friend, he had served Mary Frances well, and at this point in her career he served her more than well. As she faced Anna's medical, housing, and personal debts, the need to sell articles and collect royalties became more pressing. Writing had become more than Mary Frances's refuge; once again, it was a financial necessity.

Julia Child's comments on her manuscript notwithstanding, the eighteen months between the contretemps with Time-Life and the publication of *The Cooking of Provincial France,* in January 1968, brought a deepening of the relationship between Mary Frances and the Childs. Since their initial meeting, invitations to visit again and even to meet each other's friends were extended, often in an indirect way. Child was eager to introduce Mary Frances to James Beard, and she wrote, "[He] will be in San Francisco around the middle of September [1966], and I do hope you meet. We are extremely fond of him, and he was unbelievably generous and kind to Simca, Paul and me when we first arrived in New York with our great-unknown selves and cookbook. I think he has done much to set the tone of friendliness among cooking types, which is so different from that sniping and back-biting that goes on in France."[42]

In an effort to include Mary Frances in the current food "establishment," Child went a step further. "Judith Jones of Knopf will possibly get in touch with you," Julia wrote. "She is our editor, and we love to work with her. She said she 'wanted to feel you out' I believe. No harm in that!"[43] As a young editor at Knopf, Jones had initiated a correspondence with Mary Frances some time before Julia's comments, and she followed Mary Frances's reviews and stories in *The New Yorker*. "Reading your recent essay ['The Anatomy of a Recipe'], in *The New Yorker* . . . particularly your look at the Aresty book,"[44] she wrote, "set me to brooding again on how much we need a delightful, informal sort of social history of food that would romp through the ages, picking up all sorts of telling bits about the whys and wherefores of eating habits . . . my own thoughts keep revolving around you."[45] In response, Mary Frances mentioned the "Menus of Mankind" lecture series she had given at the University of California and the planned "Gastronomy Recalled" series in *The New Yorker*. She indicated that under her contract the magazine had the right of first refusal to her articles, but said that she hoped perhaps Knopf would be interested in publishing her books—if and when.

More introductions would be arranged on both sides of the Atlantic. Learning that the Childs would be in Plascassier early in 1967, Mary Frances urged Eda and Sybille to contact them at La Pitchoune. As connoisseurs of fine wine and food, they knew both the London and Provençal culinary scene. Eda was a good friend of the painter and food writer Richard Olney, who had left the States in the early 1960s and taken up residence at Solliès-Toucas, in the hill country north of Toulon. And it would not be long before Simca, James Beard, Elizabeth David, and eventually the wine merchant Kermit Lynch and the innovative restaurateur Alice Waters were also drawn into these concentric orbits around Provence: Mary Frances also wrote to Julia about her wish to write the text for a book of Paul's photographs of France, which had "rocked" her because she felt that he had captured the view behind all of her experiences in that country: "I am limited and would have to do an approach to your work through myself . . . people . . . the senses. I don't know if this would be right, perhaps too simple."[46] For so many reasons, both personally and professionally, Provence continued to beckon her. As Anna's situation in Berkeley deteriorated and Mary Frances also found herself coping with Kennedy's serious involvement with James Wright, a callow Midwesterner whom neither she nor Eleanor considered to be a suitable mate, it beckoned harder.

Three weeks before Christmas 1966, Mary Frances invited Anna and Jean-Christofe to St. Helena. Kennedy remained in New York, where Wright gave her a ring, and Mary Frances had their engagement announced in the society pages of *The St. Helena Star*. On December 25 Mary Frances prepared the festive dinner for her elder daughter, grandson, Norah and her sons, and Bill Erskine. The holiday marked the last time Mary Frances saw her brother-in-law. After returning to Genoa on January 5, 1967, he hanged himself in the back of his general store, where some friends discovered his body a few days later. More than five years earlier, in a backlash of scandal, he had left his family and the San Francisco Bay Area to be with Anne. After her death, he realized that he could neither return to his former life nor adjust to living alone in Genoa. On more than one occasion he had turned to Mary Frances for comfort and more, but she had made it clear to him that she could not and would not be her sister's surrogate. Now she had the pain of yet another suicide in the family to contend with.

In February, Mary Frances returned from a monthlong trip to southern California, where she visited with June, assisted Dr. Bieler with a new book that he was writing, and got back on his diet regime again. She offered to rent a place in Berkeley in order to lend Anna and Norah a helping hand, but they declined. Mary Frances reacted by immediately gaining back some of the weight that she had lost; she also suffered about a week of jitters, stressful nights, and panic. At the end of February she wrote in her journal:

> Here is another night when I want to write about my Third Re
> jection. But I cannot. I have sat over a glass, two glasses, of gin
> and vermouth, and then I have eaten a rather good supper of a
> peeled cucumber and a small head of endive with some slightly
> dreadful dressing which would not be on Hal's agenda, and
> now I am creative but tiddly . . . There is a lot of guilt in this. I
> went to Hal's with difficulty: I was supposed to go for a month
> in November, but could not leave Berkeley, or so I felt then and
> still believe. Then I arranged for January. I felt conscious of
> some resentment from Norah . . . she would say coldly that it
> was "nice" that I could flit about at will, and so on, the impli
> cation being that she was chained to her job, her children, and
> the presence of Anna and Chris. If she read this, she would
> deny it. I still was conscious of it. I finally did go to Hal's,
> rather doggedly. I am glad I did, even though I am because of
> many conflicts negating much he did for me.[47]

Whether her frayed nerves and physical state were a delayed reaction to Anna's demands on her spirit, or to her resuming her old eating and drinking habits, or to the fact that in Norah's eyes her trip to southern California represented yet another neglect of her responsibilities, Mary Frances could not answer. But having been rejected by her daughter for a third time and by her sister for a second, Mary Frances reluctantly acknowledged that Anna and Norah "are better together than I am with either of them, because of our natures. I admit this with regret but fully."[48] She remained in St. Helena.

In mid-March, Mary Frances began what she called "a series of short hops" to Berkeley, San Francisco, New York, and Hemet. Writing about her "very cluttered-sounding safari" to Gingrich, she described beginning it with a shopping trip in Berkeley, during which time she returned a wild pink dress that she wouldn't be caught "dating Hitler in." In New York, Mary Frances met with Targ at Putnam, had lunch with Volkening, and visited the offices of *The New Yorker* with a hastily devised scheme to procure office space there for herself. Enlisting the help of Kennedy and Eleanor, she even looked at ads for studio apartments within walking distance of the magazine. Although her plan for an extended residence in New York seemed primarily a career move, she seemed willing to explore a less distanced relationship with Gingrich, and while in the city she met him as often as possible. Kennedy had no knowledge of the affair; Eleanor, no doubt, suspected it. On Easter Eve, Eleanor hosted a dinner party in Mary Frances's honor, inviting Michael and Frances Field and James Beard, from whom she recently had taken a series of cooking classes. At the gathering, which was the first time Mary Frances actually met the flamboyant culinary showman, Beard was quoted as saying, "Now all we need is to have Julia and Paul here . . . The Big Four." "He was being polite about me," Mary Frances wrote to Child, "for I am not in any way in your class, except now and then with a snippet of Deathless Prose."[49]

Eleanor had also arranged an opportunity for Mary Frances to meet Kennedy's fiancé on Easter Day, but the fact that it was Eleanor and not Kennedy who suggested the meeting only contributed to Mary Frances's opinion that James Wright was unsuitable for her daughter. Her attitude didn't change when she met him. He wore a beard, had been engaged at least three times, had, as she put it, "a silver-cord" attachment to a widowed mother in Illinois, and, because he had taken a fellowship in the drama department at the University of Wisconsin, Kennedy would be forced to leave Carnegie Tech. But Mary Frances could see that her daughter was in love with him, and she bowed to the inevitable. She had more difficulty accepting Eleanor's growing enthusiasm over the arrangements for the wedding, which Kennedy wanted to take place at the Bridgehampton beach house. Feeling more than ever cut out of her daughters' lives, Mary Frances wrote, "What should I do next? Should I simply *resign*, as one would from a club (or, by suicide, from the human race)? Should I continue to maintain this too-large and expensive house with the fallacious and even vampirish premise that it is HOME, where the girls' things are stored? Should I say to my children, 'I am going to live for a few years in Provence. Get in touch with me when you feel like it'?"[50]

On March 28 she went to Hemet to see her former neighbor Fredrika Van Benschoten. During Mary Frances and Dillwyn's years in Hemet, the aristocratic lady lived in a comfortable white house on Crest Drive near the base of the dirt road that led to Bareacres. Through letters and visits Mary Frances had remained in contact with her and followed her into the vagaries of old age, as she did Aunt Grace and Uncle Ted. Now that Fredrika was moving into a nursing home, Mary Frances offered to help her close her home and make the transition. "The days in Hemet have not yet come into focus," she wrote to Kennedy, "but they were fantastic . . . one more long chapter in my magnum-but-unwritten-opus on old age."[51] From Fredrika's orange grove, Bareacres looked as beautiful as ever. The trees that she had planted with Dillwyn and Rex had flourished. The main house and the workroom-garage they had built were the same. The only change was a straight road up the hill where only a curved dirt road had existed. The town of Hemet, on the contrary, was undergoing a vast expansion into a retirement trailer park, and the apricot groves that Mary Frances and Dillwyn had looked down on from Bareacres had long ago been cleared to make room for bungalows. Yet, she confided to Gingrich, the days of the visit with Fredrika were dreamlike.

Mary Frances returned to St. Helena via Berkeley, where, she said, "I got the word that it was not wise, right now" to think about relocating to New York. Norah thought that although Anna was showing definite improvement, she was not ready to be on her own. In truth, Mary Frances thought that Norah simply could not accept the idea of her sister leaving the peripheral scene, although she plainly did not think it wise for her to be part of the main one. Nevertheless, "I killed everything pronto, and re-adjusted myself," she wrote Gingrich. "I am very good at that, by now."[52]

To further add to Mary Frances's chagrin, Gingrich sent her a copy of a small Chicago magazine called *The Literary Times*, which had published five of his letters to Murrah Gattis, a professional admirer and contributor to *Esquire*. The "Selected Letters" contained Gingrich's advice on how to improve certain articles, encouragement about continuing writing, and a reference to devouring popcorn with his wife during their frequent visits to drive-in theaters. After reading them, Mary Frances wrote, "Of course the thing that has really hurt me is that I now see that you write almost exactly to 'Dear Murrah' as you have been writing to me, and even at the same time. That is the crux of it."[53] The letters, however, were different in substance and tone from the almost daily "bus" letters that Gingrich wrote to Mary Frances on his ride from Ridgewood, New Jersey, to New York City, and Mary Frances's disproportionate reaction seemed to be attributable to her frustration with the Berkeley situation. "Well . . . the whole thing was a body-blow to me, and I tried very hard to cool off, and then wrote at least five letters telling you *why*, and then I fell back on the when-in-doubt-don't technique. I don't mind the risk of irritating or even insulting you, but I honestly *cannot stand* the thought of hurting you . . . you the man . . . you my Ginger. So if I have done so, I must pay for it by a new loneliness . . . I feel that the apparent compiler of the 'Selected Letters' is a ruthless arriviste, and that you have been had."[54]

Surprised and hurt, Gingrich tried to set the record straight, and Mary Frances again raised the question of whether she was simply another "toy," the pretty M.F.K. Fisher of two-plus decades ago, in Gingrich's collection. Mary Frances's criticism undoubtedly echoed the capricious insults his wife often lobbed at him, and when his continuing letters to Mary Frances seemed despondent, she telegrammed and offered to continue their "ritten romance." In June, Gingrich made every effort to arrange a meeting when Mary Frances came east for Kennedy's wedding. "I've long felt that when one thing goes wrong, the chances are pretty good that everything will go wrong, and if what

I had with you is gone, maybe I deserve to have it go, as part of the consequence of my failure. Look let's have lunch."[55] Arriving in New York a few days before the wedding, Mary Frances and Kennedy met Gingrich for lunch at one of his favorite restaurants. He was smitten all over again, and she decided that she was not prepared to end a relationship that added so rich a dimension to her emotional life. As she often signed her letters, she was his "Girl fren from the West."

Mary Frances spent some time shopping and going to the movies with Kennedy before they went to the Friede beach house in Bridgehampton the day before the June 10 ceremony. The groom's younger brother and mother were present, as were Eleanor's brother, sister-in-law, and mother, along with a few of Donald and Eleanor's friends. Even Dorothy Covici, who had lost Pat three years earlier, arrived with cookies and chopped chicken liver. But Anna and Norah were not present, nor any of Kennedy's other relatives. Mary Frances gave her daughter away while the groom's brother and Eleanor were best man and matron of honor. Dressed in a white eyelet shirtwaist dress, Kennedy carried a bouquet of lilies-of-the-valley that had been gathered in the flower garden. Waves from the Atlantic accompanied the wedding music, and champagne toasts on the sandy deck celebrated the occasion. "The wedding was, as such rites go, perhaps the most beautiful in the world," Mary Frances wrote to Aunt Grace, "and I got back to St. Helena in time to do the wine lecture at 7 the next day . . . photo finish . . . too much excitement for my aging emotions! But everything is fine by now, and I am about to start work on the book [*With Bold Knife and Fork*] again, and another thing for the *NYer* to put in its icebox."[56]

During the summer of 1967 two different scenarios played out. After an unseasonably cool spring, the summer in St. Helena was moderate, and visits of relatives and friends, including Sean and his family, Georges Connes and his wife, and Judith and Evan Jones, were distracting and pleasant. Mary Frances's engagement calendar listed "shrimp tarts" served to Marietta and her mother, "easy stuff because of her double clickers,"[57] and Cornish hens roasted using Julia's instructions for chicken, which didn't crisp them enough. Simultaneously her private journal was a sad record of Anna's appearances in St. Helena high on drugs, and discouraging sessions about her condition with health authorities and psychiatrists in Berkeley. Mary Frances sensed that her daughter was beginning a new downward spiral. By mid-June Anna stopped seeing her doctor and began moving from apartment to apartment, to whatever scene in Berkeley seemed momentarily attractive. In mid-August Chris, now two and a half, was picked up by the authorities "rambling and filthy across a six-lane highway . . . He is in Juvenile Hall, and is in fine shape," Mary Frances wrote. "I think that I must try flatly for legal custody, but am waiting until I know more from Anna's doctors."[58] Recognizing that she was in serious trouble, Anna checked herself into the psychiatric ward of Herrick Hospital during the latter part of August. Mary Frances's meetings with lawyers, psychiatrists, authorities, and doctors began again. "Anna is off on another tear, willy-nilly," she wrote to Aunt Grace. "I can only sit by and wait for the crash, apparently . . . As for Chris, he is a strong handsome child, and making normal progress now after the deprivations of Anna's last flight. He is very attractive, and more than of average intelligence, I think. I find him sadly tempestuous and undisciplined, and here I speak as a doting grandmother, I know. I fear for trouble ahead."[59]

As was her habit during periods of stress, Mary Frances tried to work things out in her journal. "I have been waiting for about three days now to write a kind of report on myself, which goes on in my head and changes complexion with the hours and the weather, both within and without. I think the next page is indicative of my general feeling of displacement, readjustment, whatever it is . . . I know that I am not in focus."[60] Although her authorship of *The Cooking of Provincial France* had propelled her to new heights in the culinary establishment, she was too distracted to recognize its impact. And although her relationship with Gingrich had resumed, she was too unnerved to enjoy being in love, and too weary to care.

FIFTEEN

Reading Between the Recipes

(1968–1970)

Should I try to bring up to date my grandmother's receipt for Boiled Dressing or Addie's Sister's Pickles? And if so, why? Yes, this is a strange confrontation, partly with my own past, and the recipes will prove it, no matter how grudgingly or triumphantly.[1]   —M.F.K. Fisher

"I thought that the Mission Accomplished feeling, and a good night's sleep, would be all I needed," wrote Mary Frances after she closed Anna's small flat in Berkeley and moved her daughter and grandson to St. Helena in mid-January 1968. What actually followed were fourteen days of battling a bronchial infection with an unremitting cough and fever that necessitated doctor's visits and penicillin injections. Conscious only of the "two lost children upstairs," Mary Frances convalesced in her basement bedroom and literally willed herself back to health so she could provide the clothing, shelter, and good food that her daughter and grandson needed "to repair some of the destruction of the past months and years."[2] For the greater part of 1968, Anna and Chris stayed with Mary Frances at 1467 Oak Avenue, and Mary Frances balanced the care of her daughter and grandson with the demands of her writing career.

As scheduled, the first cookbook in the Foods of the World series was published in January 1968, and Time-Life planned an elegant party at the Four Seasons the following month. Julia Child was enthusiastic about the book and told Mary Frances, "On the whole I think things are pretty good. I am most anxious to see it, aren't you? I am sure it will be most swish and handsome."³ On the day of the party, Craig Claiborne's review of *The Cooking of Provincial France* appeared in the daily *New York Times*. Incisive and authoritative, Claiborne's comments left only M.F.K. Fisher's contribution unscathed: "Mrs. Fisher knows whereof she speaks, and she knows how to say it, whether nostalgically about a 'Munsterplate' with onion and caraway seeds on a Sunday afternoon in Alsace, the soupe aux poissons of Provence, or the clafoutis or fruit tarts of Bordeaux. She has authority, experience, memory and a pen to admire and envy."⁴

Claiborne went on to rap Child's knuckles for not correcting the failure of the "former concert pianist" Michael Field to make a serious distinction between the recipes identified with the provinces and those developed under the aegis of haute cuisine. "What naiveté makes anyone include fillets of sole bonne femme in a volume on provincial French cooking . . . [or] coquilles Saint-Jacques à la Parisienne with its sauce Parisienne?" Claiborne wrote. "One suspects that these recipes were in somebody's files and were—in their opinion—too good to resist including." Claiborne's review dismissed the book, which, he believed, "could have been a grail-like monument to good taste."⁵ Despite his review, the success of the Time-Life cookbooks was guaranteed by more than 500,000 subscribers to the eighteen-book series. And even Mary Frances thought that the first book was "a pleasant surprise." She wrote to Child, "I decided to let the whole slick series come along."⁶

Yet controversy continued to plague the volume. At the Four Seasons party, the food famous were overheard sniping that the image on the jacket was a meringue, not a soufflé. There was deeper embarrassment at Time-Life when the French edition appeared. The publisher had hired Robert Courtine, Frances's "most-feared gastronomic critic"—a man who occasionally used the pen name Le Grincheux (the surly one)—to write an introduction and footnotes to the French edition. John Hess, Paris correspondent for the *Times*, was one of the first to translate Courtine's additions, and in his article "Time-Life Cookbook: It's Self-Roasting," he adroitly quoted them: "Rebuking the authors, Mr. Courtine advises that *cotriade*, a fish soup, 'is in fact not at all spiced' . . . Where the authors say a quiche Lorraine should be followed by a cold bird, Mr. Courtine retorts, 'Why the devil should it?' and he advises against judging the quality of a restaurant based on the terrine maison,[7] saying, 'the real gourmet will shun it like the plague.' "[8] In New York, Time-Life editors admitted that "they had not had Courtine's footnotes translated until after the French edition was ready for publication, and suggested that the Paris office had been derelict in letting them slip through. Then everyone concerned set about putting the best possible face on the affair."[9] When Hess called Mary Frances for a comment, she archly replied: "I feel that Mr. Courtine has a right to his opinions. I don't think the book is important in France. If I were French, I wouldn't give it the time of day. Even if I were American—and I wrote the introduction, after all—I wouldn't."[10]

In an article in *New York* magazine titled "Critics in the World of the Rising Soufflé (Or Is It the Rising Meringue?)," Nora Ephron skewered the current culinary "world of self-generating hysteria," using the controversy over *The Cooking of Provincial France* to ask whether the food milieu was possibly even more ingrown than the theater world and the music world. Apparently it was. "The food world is smaller. Much more self-involved," she wrote, "and people in the theater and in music are part of a culture that has been popularly accepted for centuries; people in the food world are riding the crest of a trend that began less than 20 years ago."[11]

Dropping names and dishing with abandon, Ephron discussed at length the two factions of the Food Establishment. On the one side were the home economists, writers, and magazine editors who, industry-oriented and mindful of the needs of the average housewife, lined up on the side of shortcuts, kitchen gadgets, and convenience foods. The other group consisted of purists who championed the merits of haute cuisine and worked tirelessly to develop taste. "The Big Four of the Food Establishment—James Beard, Julia Child, Michael Field, and Craig Claiborne—are all purists," Ephron wrote. "They are virtual celebrities. Their names conjure up a sense of style and taste; their appearances at a benefit can mean thousands of dollars for hospitals, charities, and politicians."[12]

Child sent a copy of Ephron's article to Mary Frances with the comment that she and James Beard found it hilarious: "I don't think we would if we didn't come off mostly unscathed," she wrote, "although the remark about my Bavarian Cream hurts."[13] For her part, Mary Frances thought that the article was "delicious," especially because she knew so many of the individuals involved. As an afterthought she added, "I have not met Craig Claiborne, but for years he has sent me books and I have exchanged little notes with him and he has invited me to Long Island and so on."[14] A few years earlier, the publisher Stein and Day had approached Mary Frances about writing a biography of Claiborne, and she had declined, not because she did not regard him highly but because she considered writing a biography about a living subject simply too difficult. Still, all of this gossip about the Food Establishment offered a diversion to Mary Frances, who chose to live in a little town in the Napa Valley and did not publish a cookbook every year or endorse the newest can opener or create recipes for the Northwest Pear Association. Julia Child was not as far removed from the internecine quarrels of the food world, although living in Cambridge and Plascassier insulated her to a degree from New York City's Balducci–Bloomingdale's–Coach House circuit.

Many of the letters that Child sent Mary Frances at this time detailed her attempts to refine instructions in order to get a recipe just the way she wanted it. For her part, Mary Frances bluntly criticized the growing practice of lifting recipes from published cookbooks and fobbing them off as original the way so many second-rate cookbooks did. She was convinced that "rarely like a great planet, comes a BOOK: Mrs. Beeton's, Mrs. Rombauer's, Montagne's [sic], yours. Willy-nilly, they are enough."[15] Her basic belief was that there was no such thing as an original recipe, and that even the greatest dishes were adaptations. She never questioned her improvisations on standard Americana recipes like Captain Jensen's Delight, a fish casserole. "I can say that probably not a single recipe I ever used has sprung virgin from my brain," she wrote in the essay "A Recipe for Happy Hens."[16]

Under the terms of her agreement with Putnam, *The New Yorker* planned to publish ten chapters from *With Bold Knife and Fork* before the actual release of the cookbook in October 1969. Beginning on September 7, 1968, Mary Frances's essays on hunger and enjoyment, recipes, secret ingredients, pickling, innards, rice, and casseroles appeared in the magazine under the umbrella title "Gastronomy Recalled." "I think the title Mr. Shawn likes for what he plans to run is rather pompous . . . or something," Mary Frances wrote to Henry Volkening. "It rings very faint bells of everything from *Remembrance of Things Past* to *Brideshead Revisited*."[17] She also had problems with Targ's suggested titles for the book until he finally agreed to her choice of *With Bold Knife and Fork*, a phrase from Boswell's *London Journal*. Arnold Gingrich had proposed it, and she thought it captured the flavor of the book.

Nostalgic and witty, the shortened and edited chapters that were published in *The New Yorker* evoked memories of nursery dishes and childhood treats, of special feasts and comfort food. "There is not a recipe in the book that would ever get past the door of a really classical kitchen . . . and people like Craig Claiborne, Jim Beard, Mike Field, and even my loyal and dear friend Julia Child are going to be really embarrassed by my whole approach to 'family cooking,' "[18] she confided to Volkening. Later on she wrote to Child, "I at once wondered what on earth you'd think, for it ["Gastronomy Recalled"] is not gastronomical at all, but instead very limited, like something a Jewish Arab would write if she had been brought up in Tunis . . . or an English girl in Addis Ababa perhaps. Well, I feel relieved, and much more, that you like the stuff. I hope it will continue to amuse you now and then. Some of it will of course be shudderful."[19] After the first few articles appeared in *The New Yorker*, Mary Frances's fan mail escalated. "I suppose the nostalgia in the pieces did the trick," she wrote to Volkening. Her words about mashed potatoes and gingerbread evoked memories of childhood experiences in her readers. They wanted to communicate with her, to confide in her because she had confided in them.

Despite the success of *The New Yorker* series, however, the world seemed too much with her, and in 1968 "the weather without" as well as "the weather within" was frequently disturbing. Mary Frances insisted that she would not have a TV in the house, but she regularly listened to the all-night radio talk shows and followed the news. With the escalation of the Vietnam War following the Tet offensive, student unrest escalated as well. The assassinations of Martin Luther King, Jr., and Robert Kennedy also contributed to what Mary Frances called "the national ordeal of shame." She followed the national conventions to nominate the presidential candidates with avid interest. She told Aunt Grace that she felt "a real distaste and occasionally a kind of anger, about the state we seem to be in, politically and otherwise. So much is going on that I *hate*. And I am really very unsure about HHH [Hubert Horatio Humphrey] . . . I simply don't put my trust in him. But where else to turn, right now? (There is still a lot of talk about a write-in for McCarthy . . . it might be wisest.)"[20]

Then came the Democratic convention in August, when young people were clubbed and tear-gassed in the streets of Chicago, mirroring the chaotic spectacle of the student riots in France a few months earlier. In a letter to Connes, she wrote that she felt "abashed, perhaps even ashamed, about a lot of things that have been happening in my country lately," but she continued, "You had *les jours de mai*, and even of June."[21] She also told him about her nephew John Barr's soul-searching regarding military service and his conflicting thoughts about fleeing to Canada or Switzerland to avoid the draft. As for herself, she said in one of her last letters to Dr. Frumkes, who was in very ill health, "I don't want to become an expatriot [*sic*], although lately I feel very uneasy about the basic dignity of being an American . . . I think often of you, and always with heartfelt gratitude for what you taught me about 'the art of survival.' "[22]

As far as the "weather within" was concerned, her romance at a distance with Arnold Gingrich had become slightly less ardent, although Mary Frances continued to assure him that he made her feel wanted and needed and loved in a way that no one else did. Responding to a question about the current man in her life, Mary Frances told Aunt Grace, "He is married! (To a hopeless and completely helpless paralytic and former alcoholic . . .) He has been yearning for me since about 1939, and is determined to marry me as soon as poor Janie dies, which I doubt she will do for many years, for she is cared for like a rare orchid. He is rich and witty and attractive and all that, and I wouldn't mind going on a world-tour or safari or something with him. But marriage? I am simply too sot . . ."[23] Mary Frances had already decided that Gingrich had no realistic intention of establishing her as his mistress in New York. He would always welcome her company at breakfast, lunch, or dinner whenever she visited the city, but he was scrupulous about sending and receiving letters only at the office and not phoning from the home he shared with Janie.

Mary Frances's friendship with Marietta also became more complicated and troublesome, in part because of Marietta's niece, for whom Marietta had recently assumed the role of surrogate mother. Marietta wanted the two most important people in her life to enjoy each other, but the niece was jealous of Marietta's emotional ties to Mary Frances, and Mary Frances resented being drawn into what she considered to be a foolish situation. When Marietta accused her of being intolerant, there were angry verbal exchanges, followed by hurtful letters, although Mary Frances continued to supply aid and comfort to Marietta and her aging mother in their long-standing routine of lunches, suppers, and "fivers."

The vagaries of the "weather within" also encompassed Mary Frances's arm's-length relationship with both of her daughters. Since Kennedy and Jim had married and moved to Madison, Mary Frances had been convinced that her daughter would fall under the spell of her Midwestern mother-in-law, "a good pie baker,"[24] and Jim, whom Mary Frances described as someone who would eat nothing but "meat, potatoes, and desserts,"[25] and who forced his food preferences on Kennedy. It didn't help that when the couple had paid their first visit to St. Helena the previous year, Mary Frances had grandly met them at the San Francisco airport in a chartered plane to fly them up to Napa and proceeded to criticize meat processors, knowing that her son-in-law's deceased father had been one. Jim had stormed out of the house on Oak Avenue, and the tension between him and Mary Frances continued. Meanwhile, just as Mary Frances feared, Kennedy grew closer to her mother-in-law, who accepted her for what she was and didn't burden her with expectations as Kennedy felt her own mother had always done.[26]

Ongoing concern about Anna's condition, which was finally diagnosed as manic depression, also plagued Mary Frances. The commitment of time and money alone was burdensome. Mary Frances drove Anna to doctors' appointments in Napa and helped pay for her dental work. Although Anna occasionally substituted for the teachers at the preschool, where she was remarkably effective with the children, she often abused her mother's credit in shops around town. And life with a three-year-old could be trying. "Chris is on my nerves, now and then . . . he is a wonderful sensitive strong intelligent little boy, eager to be friends . . . he loves *people*," she told Aunt Grace. "His mother has a strong guilt-feeling about the badly checkered past she gave him, and now feels that she must make up to him by almost complete permissiveness . . . Chris is cruel and bullying with her, and he will scream and whine and spit. NEVER WITH ME."[27]

Meanwhile, Mary Frances's relationships with Julia and Paul Child, Michael Field, and James Beard on the culinary front, and with Rachel MacKenzie at *The New Yorker*, were deepening. Closer to home, her name appeared on every important winery's guest list, and she did not want for invitations to tastings, concerts, and dinners with friends. She lectured on the pairing of wine and food at Jim Beard's wine classes whenever she was asked to do so.

Writing about Edith's Avocado Cocktail and Canadian Potted Cheese and Grandmother's Boiled Dressing in her *New Yorker* essays brought back memories of the smells and tastes she had experienced in the dark kitchen on Painter Street and in the much larger and brighter kitchen at the Ranch. Referring back to Aunt Gwen's delicious "camp" cooking during their extended vacations at the Kennedy beach house in Laguna also brought her childhood idol into sharper focus. "I have decided to try to write about her, after so many years of putting it off," she told Aunt Grace. "It is too complicated to handle, by now . . . as more or less of an adult I understand so much (too much) that was mercifully Greek to me when I was younger. I see now, for instance, that there was a complicated relationship between Edith and Aunt Gwen because of Rex. And so on. Some of what I now see does not make my mother look the way I want her to look, even to myself. I am trying to avoid all of this. But if I do, am I writing a true picture? I wish I had done it twenty or thirty years ago! Perhaps I'd better stick to the hot stove, on paper anyway . . ."[28] Nevertheless, in the late summer of 1968 the early sketches and notes for a memoir began to take shape—as did another important relationship.

One August day in Glen Ellen, just over the Mayacama Range from Napa, a houseguest at the Bouverie Ranch teased her host, the cosmopolitan boulevardier and conservationist David Pleydell-

Bouverie, into making the acquaintance of M.F.K. Fisher. Led to believe that it was a disgrace not to know "the only great writer who lived within a hundred miles of me," Bouverie told an interviewer, "I got her [M.F.K. Fisher's] address, and I wrote to her, and she said that she wouldn't come to lunch, but that she would ask *me* to lunch if I'd like to come."[29] With *Life* magazine columnist Shana Alexander as companion, Bouverie drove to St. Helena a week later and met Mary Frances. Under the fig tree in the garden, she served her guests a cold crab bisque with chunks of ice-cold fresh cucumber in it, croissants, and, for dessert, a hot peach garnished with hot fresh strawberries. "That was our lunch," she noted in her daily calendar. "It was the first meal we had together, with some good Napa mountain wine."[30]

By the end of August, Mary Frances had visited the Bouverie Ranch, and what she saw interested her. The grandson of William Bouverie, the fifth Earl of Radnor, David Bouverie had grown up in huge cold historic houses in England and escaped to America in the early 1930s, when he was twenty-one. Attracted to the temperate climate of northern California, he acquired about five hundred acres that had been destined for development in the Valley of the Moon in Sonoma County. Since then the Bouverie Ranch had become a subject of perennial interest in architectural, home and garden, and society magazines. Bouverie had designed and built eight country-style buildings, including a barn, a bell tower, a recreation building, a hexagonal guesthouse, caretakers' houses, and the main house, where he lived. Passionate about overscaling, he artfully arranged big pictures and big pieces of furniture in quite small rooms, hung a nineteenth-century French chandelier from a wisteria-draped trellis over the terrace, and banked his swimming pool with white roses. In this setting Bouverie entertained "a mixed lot," including artists, writers, actresses, self-made millionaire farmers, and British aristocracy—"the Queen of England or the Chinese laundry man," as one of his household servants said. The ranch was designed for indoor and outdoor dining, poetry readings and chamber music, hot air balloon parties, and picnics within a circle of sequoias in the lower part of the canyon.

At a much earlier time the Pomo Indians had held secret rituals in the caves under the cascading waterfall on the property. But through the years, various owners had cut down groves of oak and madrone, plundered the trout streams, and even sold some of the volcanic rock to build Jack London's Wolf House on the west side of the valley. Under Bouverie's ownership the pastureland bloomed with more than two hundred kinds of wildflowers before prize cattle settled in for the summer, the streams yielded steelhead trout that swam inland to spawn there from the ocean some fifty miles to the west, and deer, mountain lions, rattlesnakes, and birds once again thrived.

Thanking her host for his hospitality, Mary Frances wrote, "It was good in every way to see your beautiful place, and to eat and drink so pleasurably, and to listen to your deft use of your own wordings about things, but probably the real charge came from seeing, even fleetingly, some of the paintings." She was referring to canvases by Mathias Withoos and John Singer Sargent, including *The Ships at Whitby* and the portrait of Edward Vickers. Mary Frances closed her thank-you note with the words, "I would like to tell you sometime about the true reason I came to lunch today."[31]

By the end of September 1968, Anna and her son had grown stronger in body and spirit, and Anna began talking about moving into an apartment or small cottage nearby. She actually found a two-room cottage in one of the vineyards in St. Helena, but her stay there proved to be short-lived. There were few people in the valley with whom Anna wanted to associate, and the Berkeley scene continued to draw her; soon she had entered another manic phase, which, thanks to her renewed strength under her mother's care, came on slowly and lasted longer.

Depressed by her inability to keep her daughter stable, and separated from Kennedy, who was expecting her first child in Madison, Mary Frances dreaded the coming holiday season and decided to celebrate Christmas away from St. Helena. Impulsively, she invited Norah and Matthew to take the Zephyr to Denver with her and stay at the Brown Palace. After being stalled in a snowstorm for several hours en route, they arrived late on Christmas Day and foraged for something to eat. Four days later, Mary Frances received word that her second grandson, Sybren Alexis, had been born on December 29, 1968.

Once back in St. Helena, Mary Frances turned down a number of articles for *House Beautiful* and *Family Circle*, and Time-Life's offer to engage her for the volume on the American Southwest. She did, however, accede to a request from her friend Sam Davis to write an introduction to Funk and Wagnall's *Cook's & Diner's Dictionary: A Lexicon of Food, Wine, and Culinary Terms*, which he had compiled. The project had a special appeal to her, since dictionaries had lured her since childhood, but the book was not a commercial success. Still, it was her sixth introduction. With her increased visibility in both literary and culinary circles, an introduction by M.F.K. Fisher had become a sought-after prize.

For the moment, however, writing about her childhood in Whittier claimed most of her attention. In February she wrote to Connes, "I am working on a 'memoir' of my childhood in a small California town in which I belonged to a minority group of Anglicans (35?) among 4000 Quakers . . . I try to remain completely honest and unadorned, in my approach to the subject. It will never be published . . . my view of the hypocritical smug self-satisfied Quakers is prejudiced, especially now that our president is one . . . I knew his family, and Norah went through high school with him, and when I worked for my father for six years before his death, when Mr. Nixon was running for vice-president, I was much involved in local politics."[32] And in early summer she told her cousin Weare Holbrook, "I am gradually hewing out some remarks about being a minority-group child in a Quaker ghetto. It is tough to stick to my actual recall and not embroider. Good exercise. Probably unpublishable. Interesting aspect of religious and racial prejudices . . . also ethnic, with Grandmother so adamantly North-of-Ireland-Iowan in that land of Thees and Thous and daily snubs."[33] Memories from the past—some pleasant, like the aroma of strawberry jam in the kitchen, and some troublesome, like Edith's disdain for their Kennedy grandparents during those early years—came back into her consciousness. With grown children and grandchildren of her own, she sought to come to terms with Edith's shortcomings and Grandmother Holbrook's dominating spirit. For the first time she was not writing for someone she loved or writing for hire, but for herself, and returning to a world that was in every way more congenial to her spirit than the contemporary world around her.

In spring Gingrich visited Mary Frances, and, instead of keeping up the pretense of checking into the Buena Vista Motel, he stayed at

1437 Oak Avenue. Mary Frances pampered him with lovely little meals, they visited a few wineries, she even modeled some new clothes that she had purchased for him, but their lovemaking was disappointing. When he left, she wrote one of her famous "not sent" letters. "I asked you if you had ever tried to curb your childhood habit of gobbling so that you could get more pleasure from the act of eating itself, and you said, 'No . . . why should I . . . I like it this way.' Well . . . I think that it would be artificial, and an induced thing, for you to slow down on your sexual satisfaction. And that lets me out, for I am a woman who must live alone most of the time, and whose sensual and sexual and voluptuous pleasures need to be attained at another speed after she has been brought out of the frigidaire where current culture and she herself have placed her . . ." The crux of the matter was that mentally she and Gingrich were compatible, but physically "we are not good; you come on fast, pretty much the same way you eat, greedy boy munch, munch, and here I am a woman who has had to turn herself way-off-and-far-low sexually, expected to be ready for the quick lay and then the exhausted blissful sleep of an overtired man."[34] It was the first time she had written so candidly about their sexual relationship, and within the context of what she described— "you pounce-gobble-finish, and I nibble voluptuously"—she spelled out her ideas about the pleasures of the bed as well as the table and the ambience that should accompany both. Referring to his inability to satisfy her adequately, Gingrich apologized profusely in his next letter: "If we can still say 'joke laff' without constraint and I'm sure we can, then whatever damage was done is only momentary and remediable and everything is still great with us and will only be greater."[35]

During the summer of 1969 the annual flow of visitors to St. Helena continued, and in a letter to the Childs, who were staying in Plascassier, she wrote, "I am dormant, temporarily . . . or lying fallow, or something like that. A lot of people come through the Valley, and this is the best restaurant and pub north of San Francisco, and instead of sitting cross-legged and chanting Om Ram Om Ram or like that, I cook while I meditate. I make a lot of cold things based on Provençal cooking."[36] An English friend from Aix, Humphrey Stone, and his wife, Solveig—whom she increasingly referred to as her "English children"—visited, as did Georges Connes's wife, son, and daughter-in-law. At the end of July, Gingrich paid another short visit, bearing gifts.

At the same time, Mary Frances was being drawn into David Bouverie's social circle. She attended a luncheon at the Bouverie Ranch for Her Royal Highness the queen of Jordan, and she wrote about informal gatherings there of San Francisco's patrons of the arts, whom Bouverie, as chairman of the Arts Council, was tapping for donations. The idea of being a part of that world appealed to her; "I collect people," she told Gingrich, instead of violins and fly-fishing equipment, as he did. She believed that people were easier to acquire and easier to discard. And, no doubt thinking about the convenient arrangement that Julia and Paul enjoyed in Plascassier, where they had built a home on Simone Beck's property, she began to lay the groundwork for a similar arrangement on the Bouverie Ranch.

Meanwhile, Mary Frances learned that Kennedy and her family planned to move to Oakland, where Jim had secured a position in the drama department at Mills College. "He continues to be very hostile to anyone connected with her [Kennedy's] life before they married, which of course makes me the prime villain in the piece," Mary Frances confided to Connes. "I am sorry about this, but think Time will soften his viewpoint."[37] The move enabled Kennedy to see Anna from time to time, but she was involved with a one-year-old and the sisters did not share many interests as adults. And neither had much time for visits with their mother. As she had done so often in the past, Mary Frances began to seek out a refuge, believing that "it was pointless for me to sit alone in St. Helena waiting for her [Anna] and Kennedy to toss me an occasional kind word."[38]

For a time she thought about going to Japan and staying with Shizuo Tsuji, the expert on Japanese cuisine who had sought her out in April, met her in San Francisco, and extended an invitation to her to visit Osaka. But after reading books on Japanese cooking, practicing with chopsticks, buying a set of Japanese language records, and drinking floods of tea, she abandoned the idea as too impractical. Meanwhile, Eleanor, currently employed as a senior editor at Macmillan, was overseeing both an autobiography and a picture book about Paris that Maurice Chevalier was writing; when she suggested that Mary Frances might be interested in translating Chevalier's books and offered her winterized beach house in Bridgehampton to work in, Mary Frances accepted gladly. She saw in the Chevalier project another opportunity to cull material for her "old-age" book, as well as a possible trip to France in spring. She wrote to Dr. Bieler, "this time I acted in pure self-interest and self-protection. My sister Norah is stonily disapproving of my leaving St. Helena, but everyone else seems to think it a fine idea!"[39]

On October 7, 1969, in a letter addressed to members of the family and her closest friends, she wrote, "I have decided upon something which I know promises me times of regret and loneliness, but after long thought I feel that it is wise. I shan't be home this Christmas, to welcome you to the real warmth and love that is always yours when you want to accept it. For more than fifty years I have been 'the oldest in the family,' and because of my nature, have enjoyed almost every aspect of planning some sort of celebration at the end of the year. By now I think that I should hand over that role to younger people, if there are any who want to play it."[40] It was a dramatic gesture, but the truth was that neither of her daughters would have joined a holiday celebration if she had planned one, although she had learned all too well how to play the role of matriarch with others. She confided to Gingrich that she felt shaky emotionally. "I think I must get the hell out of here or I'll turn into a doomed slavey to my own image of hospitality . . . For people keep coming. It is my own fault, I need to feed my ego by being generous, a good provider, etc."[41] And a few months later in another letter to Dr. Bieler, she mentioned that she was "in a real bloc there [St. Helena] about working. All I did was cook and care for a constant stream of people, and mop up their tears, and wait for more. I could not finish a single thing. And not only do I earn a living with what I write, but it is the only thing that fulfills my creative nature, now that I have finished child-bearing and, apparently, sexual life. I was turning into a vegetable."[42]

Meanwhile, *With Bold Knife and Fork* had been published in late September 1969. It featured more than 140 recipes, indicated as doable or impossible, delectable or avoidable according to Mary Frances's opinion—and all of them only secondarily included for their own sake. "This book is about how I like to cook, most of the time, for people in my world, and it gives some of the reasons,"[43] Mary Frances wrote in an abbreviated six-line preface to the book. But uppermost in her purpose was an exploration of the forces that made her instinctively reject her grandmother's stringent food preferences and accept the indulgence of one of Rex's broiled steak dinners or a slice of ripe French cheese. She mined recipes to re-create meaningful experiences from the past. Through Grandmother Holbrook's Boiled Dressing, Mary Frances introduced readers to the woman she considered largely responsible, through reverse example, for her eventual "hedonistic" enjoyment of the pleasures of the table. Her mother's "dark, heady broth," which traditionally cured a bout of flu, remained a lasting tribute to her mother's love, as did her Lady Baltimore birthday cakes and divinity fudge. Sevruga caviar eaten with Rex and Edith Kennedy at the Café de la Paix stood for the perfect shared moment. "We ate three portions apiece, tacitly knowing it would never happen again that anything would be quite so mysteriously perfect in both time and space."[44] And Mme Bonamour (Rigoulot)'s cheese soufflé, savored in Dijon, seemed at the moment and for all time thereafter the perfect dish. She also paid tribute to Julia Child as the "culinary arbiter of at least this much of our century," and included an account of Child's five months of work to achieve an infallible recipe for French bread.

Mary Frances had written a much longer introduction to the book, but apparently decided not to submit it. It is noteworthy, however, for the additional light it sheds on her motives for writing the book. "Should I try to decipher and put into language recipes written to me from Bern ('Bischofsbrot' measured in grams and deciliters) and Ireland ('Slim Cake' measured in breakfast cups and fruit spoons)? Should I try to bring up to date my grandmother's receipt for Boiled Dressing or Addie's Sister's Pickles? And if so, why? Yes, this a strange confrontation, partly with my own past, and the recipes will prove it, no matter how grudgingly or triumphantly."[45] The same sense of wistfulness for a happier time and place that infused the stories and sketches about Whittier that she had begun sending to Volkening also pervaded the recipe collection and the unpublished introduction, strengthening the tone of déjà vu or what one of Fisher's critics labeled the "nouveau pastoralism"[46] of her later work. About Edith she wrote, "The more I remember about her, the more I like her. And I always did like her . . ."[47] Being a mother of two adult daughters and a grandmother herself had brought her closer to the woman she described as "voluptuous and amusing, which in family lingo often means lazy and manic-depressive."[48] The observation highlighted the probable hereditary link among Edith's mood swings, Rex's bouts with depression, her own alternation between frantic journeying and hostessing (which some of her family and friends suggested was manic) and depression, David's tortured vision, and Anna's recent diagnosis.

The reviews validated Mary Frances's reputation as a persuasive writer as well as a practical "provider of feasts." "The recipes are guaranteed to produce excellent fare; but the meat of this book, if one pardons the obvious pun, is the delightful manner in which Mrs. Fisher presents her comment on the whole business of making good food fit to eat,"[49] wrote Friede Gruenrock in *Booksellers*. Yvonne Horton in *The Christian Science Monitor* compared Fisher's enjoyment of food to that of Charles Dickens in *Pickwick Papers*. In *The New York Times Book Review*, Nika Hazelton praised her as an "erudite, original, fluent, and complicated" writer who "stands alone," but she believed that even Fisher aficionados might find that "her editors allowed her to give in too much to archness and mannerisms."[50]

Packing her Whittier manuscripts, a still-unfinished article on frozen foods for *Esquire*, and the Chevalier material, Mary Frances arrived in New York in early December. She stayed with Eleanor at 45 West Twelfth Street and spent the next five days having "three breakfasts, five lunches, and four dinners"[51] with Gingrich, Volkening, Targ, Judith Jones, Shana Alexander, and other New York contacts. She and Eleanor then drove to Bridgehampton, stopping first in Southampton to rent a typewriter. Although part of the beach house was shut off from use, Mary Frances had an adequately heated bedroom, bath, living room, kitchen, and study to occupy, and Eleanor's Vauxhall for trips to the village and to Sag Harbor, about eight miles away. In a letter to Anna she wrote, "I am finally *in* here, after a wild five days in NY and then two nice ones here with Eleanor. She left about 5 last night, and since then I have been watching and listening to a nice storm, with waves as far as the horizon, all blowing sideways in the strong east wind, and handfuls of sleet rattling against the windows now and then. I love it."[52]

On December 16, she returned to New York and then went to

Washington, D.C., to visit her nephew Sean Kelly and his wife and two sons, who had recently returned from fourteen years in Nigeria. Two days later she returned to New York, where Gingrich was supposed to meet her at Penn Station. But he had misread the schedule, and they searched for each other for more than an hour. Revisiting the incident, he wrote, "When I think of the recriminations, and reenactments, and re-recordings, and blows by blows, that I would have been subjected to by practically any other female on earth—you become a greater miracle for me each day."[53] They went to a little Italian "joynt" for an extended lunch that Mary Frances pronounced pleasant in every way. "Maybe we should just meet surreptitiously in off beat dives in Hong Kong, Paris, places like that . . . how about Cody . . . or Guadalajara?"[54]

Although Mary Frances had anticipated her first Christmas Eve away from her family, there was a certain poignancy in the way she described her holiday with Eleanor in Bridgehampton. In a letter to Norah she wrote, "I miss being near the few people I love, and I miss having an animal friend."[55] On Christmas Day she prepared chicken breasts with mushrooms for their dinner. Snow began to fall, and they relaxed in front of the fireplace with vintage champagne. Eleanor returned to the city the next day. By the first of the year the weather had turned more forbidding, and after enduring an unabating nor'easter (the subject of the story "The Wind-Chill Factor") and being warned about power and communication failures by the local fire department, Mary Frances realized that she had to vacate the beach house and obtained living quarters in a family-owned tourist house in Sag Harbor. The house was located on the main street of the town, and she could walk to the post office down near the harbor, shop on the way back, and return home in less than twenty minutes. Jottings in a fragmented journal record barometric pressures, wind speeds, and waves that she saw first from the large living room window in Bridgehampton and then from the icy streets in Sag Harbor. "Things go well here," she wrote to Marietta. "I have periods of mild depression. I feel that I am too self-centered (Shades of my sister Norah's summing up!). I really do not mind being alone. But I do get bored being alone with myself, since I feel basically inadequate."[56]

Letters to Gingrich, Norah, and Eleanor detailed the amount of work that she was able to accomplish despite the fact that she could not type later than ten o'clock in the evening because of the "paper thin walls." She completed the article on frozen foods and dinners for *Esquire*, which she thought quite "funny," and which Gingrich praised: "I *love* what you did with the TV dinners. I didn't think it could be done. But you raised their importance from the level of trivia to important philosophic significance. Beautiful piece, even by your standards."[57] She then told Gingrich, "I have done all the Chevalier stuff available, of course in my inimitable style. It is not very exciting . . . he is turning it out simply to see his name in print again—I'm afraid . . . there is no fire, no passion."[58] According to Eleanor, Chevalier rejected Mary Frances's translation as an embroidered rewrite and a misrepresentation of what he had written. Caught in the middle, Eleanor diplomatically resolved the situation by gradually downgrading Mary Frances's involvement in the Chevalier project to writing an introduction to the book.[59]

During the three months that Mary Frances lived in Sag Harbor, the Whittier reminiscences occupied most of her time. Eleanor came out for weekends whenever the weather permitted, and Mary Frances returned to the beach house with her to entertain guests or socialize with the stalwart artists and writers who braved the winter storms of the Hamptons. At these gatherings Mary Frances met the writers Jean Stafford and Narcisse Chamberlain, the artists Frances Miller and Paul Cadmus, and the culinary writer and instructor Bert Greene, who along with his companion owned an upscale cookware shop on Long Island. Gingrich also called once or twice a week, and continued to send his daily letters.

At a time when she was imposing a sense of order on her own childhood, which she admitted was "pure hell" to do in any kind of objective way, Mary Frances was also trying to put her adult life into some kind of perspective. The sudden and unexpected death of Al Fisher on January 3, 1970, which she only learned about in late February, prompted her to write to his surviving sister, Elizabeth. "In the past few months I have found him much in my mind," she wrote, "and have been considering, and even phrasing a letter to him, to thank him for all the good things he gave me . . . and perhaps to ask him if he would like us to meet again. I know that I dealt him a grievous blow when I had to leave him, but I thought that perhaps a reiteration of my unfaltering affection and admiration might please him a little. I was too late."[60] Since their separation in 1938, Al had gone on to have a successful career of almost thirty years as an English professor at Smith College, had married and divorced two more times, and had fathered a son and two daughters. "It is an odd feeling," Mary Frances wrote to Connes, "that by now the three men I have been married to have died. They were all unusual beings, and enriched my life immeasurably, both for good and evil of course."[61]

No longer anticipating going to Paris to work with Maurice Chevalier, she postponed a trip to France until the fall, when she and Norah could visit the island of Porquerolles, the "Escape Hatch" so designated by herself and her daughters when they had resided in Aix years earlier. "It is impossible that you have never been there," she had written to Norah. "I myself have a strong 'feeling' that I should return . . . In October-November it is wonderful."[62] The island, the largest of the group called the Hyères, boasted one village with a few fishermen's cottages, a hotel, training facilities for the French navy, a historic lighthouse, and beautiful beaches bordered by pine and eucalyptus woods. Depending on the embarkation point—Toulon, Giens, or Hyères—and the weather, the boat trip from the mainland could be thirty minutes or more than an hour and a half. Mary Frances also tempted Norah with the observation that after Porquerolles there would be Aix and Marseilles to revisit.

By the beginning of March, Volkening had negotiated a reprint of *The Art of Eating* with Macmillan and had sold Mary Frances's "The Wind-Chill Factor" to *The New Yorker*. A few weeks later she wrote to Gingrich that she had only a few more hours of work on the Whittier book. "It is rather like feeling the place where a tooth has been pulled,"[63] she said, and added that after concentrating on one project for so long, she found herself overstimulated mentally, dreaming in chapters and often in columns of small print. By the end of the month, however, she told her family and friends that she would be very happy to shed the layers of warm clothes, return to her home in St. Helena, and put her garden in order. Stopping in New York, Mary Frances again saw Volkening and Judith Jones, who expressed an interest in Mary Frances's reminiscences about Whittier, and she had lunch at the Four Seasons, Le Mistral, and the Brasserie with Gingrich. Referring frequently to his visit to St. Helena the previous spring, Gingrich pursued the question of what had "turned Mary Frances off."[64] She made light of it.

When Mary Frances arrived back in St. Helena on April 3, she had already tentatively decided to ask David Bouverie to consider the possibility of her living on his ranch. Her house was too large and expensive to keep up, and she was tired of either renting it or putting it into the hands of friends. She also continued to believe that her involvement in the various activities of the town and wineries, and her role as hostess for family and friends, hampered her professionally. But before she took steps to set her plan in motion, she first wanted to stage a fitting celebration in honor of the centennial of the house at 1467 Oak Avenue. As a first step, she engaged the artist Judith Clancy to design an invitation with a sketch of "The Grand Old Lady" on it. Then she gradually drew up lists of approximately 150 people whom she planned to entertain in a series of three "Champagne and nibbles" parties in August.

In early July, Gingrich visited St. Helena again, and he went away thankful for all the attention and exquisitely prepared foods and wine lavished on him. While flying back to New York, he wrote in his "Boeing" letter, "You could see, I hope, how happy I was to be in the Bamboo Shack again, and understood without our talking about it why I didn't go near the stairs to the eyrie [MF's third-floor bedroom] again. It will be a long time, if ever, before this criminal has any urge to return to the scene of his crime . . . For all the pleasures of sight and sound and touch and taste that you gave me for the best parts of three days, I thank you."[65] During the summer Mary Frances also entertained Humphrey and Solveig Stone, who were staying near Stanford University, where he was consulting on fine printing. Sean Kelly and his family arrived from Washington, D.C., and the Steeles visited from San Francisco. "It was a wildly interesting summer," she wrote. "Enjoyed every minute of it. I'll never do it again."[66] She had already quietly contacted a real estate agent about selling "The Old Grand Lady."

"I would *love* you to live on the ranch," was Bouverie's response to Mary Frances on July 5, 1970. "In some trepidation I called my gentle local lawyer . . . and to my delight he said yes it *could* be done in the way you suggest, with a legal document full of mutually protective clauses."[67] Bouverie wanted to add another house to his already significant compound, but did not have the ready funds to do so. So they agreed that Mary Frances would sell her house and use the money to build a small two-room cottage on the ranch.

On July 16, Mary Frances told Gingrich, "I must talk with you, and soon, about what I am planning to do with the next months and years of my life. I like to think it will matter to you."[68] During the next few weeks she gradually disclosed her plan to sell the house and take a long trip to France with Norah. On August 7, after sending her description of the forthcoming "Autumn Safari" to him, she wrote:

> These are my plans for the rest of it: build a slightly palatial two-room shack . . . that's *shack* on the Bouverie Ranch, and move over there before June 1, 1971. I have sold this house, to the McIntyres who understand its real karma, good friends of mine who will help it more than I ever could or did. I am actually lending David B money to build a small house he has had on his master plan for many years. On my death, or if he predeceases me, all I have invested will be repaid at the rate of $5,000 annually to my heirs. He is designing the shack to my really eccentric specifications, and it will be "interesting." I've told Kennedy about it, and June, and Norah, and they are very happy. I've not yet been able to talk with Anna, but I doubt that she will really get it . . . It is really quite traumatic, for all of us in our different ways . . . And that is one reason these wild Centennial Bashes are such a good idea, although NOBODY knows.[69]

It was only after the very lively and successful open-house parties on August 12, 14, and 17 that she told some of her closest St. Helena friends that her new home would be on Bouverie's ranch in the Valley of the Moon.

Mary Frances's reasons for leaving the Napa Valley were complex, but the most compelling one was that her daughters were living their own lives in other places. Kennedy's visits were infrequent, and Anna had entered into a serious relationship with Stephen Metz, a caring young man she had met in Berkeley. Mary Frances had a recurring worry of being found dead on the kitchen floor with a warm glass of champagne and a half-eaten pear on the counter. Mortality was ever on her mind. Recent word that her aunt Grace Holmes was gravely ill in Chicago seemed one more bow to the inevitable scenario of aging. But more disturbing was her friend June's series of cerebral hemorrhages during the summer, when she was enjoying her new home in Laguna Beach and her much younger lover. "June's disaster has given me much to think about,"[70] she wrote to Gingrich—and, no doubt, a renewed sense of *carpe diem*. David Bouverie's personality and lifestyle were enormously appealing to her; she found his guests well traveled and interesting, and the assortment of employees on the ranch an endless source of material. Although the ranch was less than an hour's drive on the steep mountain road that wove over the Mayacamas from the Napa Valley to the Sonoma Valley, the psychological distance from St. Helena to Glen Ellen seemed immeasurable. Mary Frances was more than ready to go.

In addition to voicing his "jealous as hell" objection to the move, Gingrich added a word of caution: "When I think of the three bashes, running into the scores of dozens of items and up into the probably hundreds of people—well, I shudder to think of your instant availability as hostess of *an* even *larger* establishment than the one you are quitting after eighteen years. There can so easily be this or that little do for only eighteen or eighty-eight, two or three times a week, which you will undertake without batting one of your shadowed lashes—as now. There will be instant MFKFPF [Mary Frances Kennedy Fisher Parrish Friede], on tap, *jour et nuit*. Well, it's either a hell of a drawback or an attraction—*ça dépend*."[71]

By way of answer, Mary Frances told Gingrich that her motives were just the opposite; she wanted to break the pattern of "dear old lady with the big house and the hot stove." Just as it had been a distancing move to spend the holidays and three months on Long Island the previous winter, her future in a small house, with perhaps room for only one guest, would be an opportunity to be alone and working. "I am moving from a three-storey Victorian house with nine beds and two couches (!!!) to a one-bedroom cottage purely and solely to break the continuing pattern of open-house . . . also described as the best bar-restaurant-hotel in Northern California."[72] She ended her letter by saying that she had at least two more books that she wanted to write.

Mary Frances was not unmindful of the protection that a staff of employees and servants living on the ranch provided; neither was she impervious to David Bouverie's charm, rugged good looks, intelligence, and cosmopolitan flair. Although not sexual, the relationship between them was intimate, their letters teasing, loving, gossipy, and, during the time that her *palazzino* was being built, filled with Mary Frances's preferences. She wanted a Pompeian "live-in" bathroom with shower, oversized tub, tile countertops, and red walls for paintings and artwork. She also envisioned a private study-bedroom connected by a large book-lined foyer to a busy room incorporating a kitchen, dining space, "hearth scene," and "living room." "I am horrified at the thought of having to decide about My Last Kitchen Sink and all that," she wrote to Bouverie, "but it will be fun with DP-B [Bouverie]."[73]

During the fall, construction began, and Anna and Stephen Metz, who had been married in the late summer, moved to Portland, where Stephen planned to continue his graduate education. Among the photos and mementos Mary Frances saved from the summer was a 1970 guest register with the inscription "A house of strengths and grace, knowing and storing more joys than sorrows." It had been signed by almost two hundred friends and neighbors. On the inside cover there was also a small poem in her handwriting: "Voici la maison où Dote demeure—on y chante, on y vit, et parfois on y pleure."[74] Although she knew that she would return to the celebrated house on Oak Avenue, it was no longer hers. The thought of escaping to the places she loved in France became irresistible.

SIXTEEN

Alive Again

(1970–1973)

Everything, inside and out of one's self, is more intense in Provence than anyplace else I know or know about. Salt is almost dangerously saltier. Foods that grow from the earth taste stronger, or subtler, or stranger. If a person feels unwell, he is usually more miserable there than he would be in Sussex or Mendocino County, and if he is exhilarated and happy, it is immeasurably better than it could be anyplace else.[1]   —M.F.K. Fisher

M ary Frances and Norah began their journey to France on October 8, 1970, with a flight to Vancouver, where they boarded a train and for three days "bucketed" to Montreal. From there they flew to New York City, joined Eleanor for a farewell lunch, and sailed "Second" on the SS *France* to Le Havre. After a few days in Paris, visiting with Janet Flanner and revisiting the quai Voltaire, Brasserie Lipp, and Sylvia Beach's bookshop, they went on to Dijon, where Mary Frances wanted to savor again the experiences that she and Norah had shared there so long ago. The city, moreover, was a good jumping-off point for the canal-side village of Corbigny, where they boarded the *Palinurus* for a leisurely barge trip south on lap two of what Mary Frances called their "watery spree." The trip along the canals was pleasant, and Mary Frances sent her impressions of it to Gingrich. Her descriptions were so evocative that he encouraged her to publish them.

From the beginning of November, Mary Frances and Norah lived across the road from the house occupied by Eda Lord and Sybille Bedford in La Roquette-la-Siagne. Four years earlier Mary Frances had stayed nearby in Plascassier, where she had made the acquaintance of several people, including a chauffeur named Raymond Gatti, who frequently was hired to drive people around in his Mercedes, and, of course, Julia Child's collaborator Simone Beck. Thanks to Michael Field, she also knew many of the restaurants in the area.

In the wake of Child's fame, and with Beck's cooking school as a draw, Plascassier had become a gathering place for the American culinary establishment, while farther west, in the hills above Toulon, Richard Olney attracted a different but no less impressive group of chefs, writers, and wine connoisseurs to his home and to the vineyards south of Marseilles. During the last two months of 1970, all these culinary mavens, including journalist Bert Greene, flocked to the south of France. In fact, Greene had told a select few in New York that he was going to the Côte d'Azur *with* M.F.K. Fisher. So when he and his companion arrived in Mouans-Sartoux, he quickly invited Mary Frances and Norah to dine and to visit various places with him.

Eda also told Olney that her high school friend M.F.K. Fisher would be staying in La Roquette, and she broadly hinted that she, Sybille, and Mary Frances would be delighted to dine at his home in Solliès-Toucas. Having already been told by his agent that M.F.K. Fisher wanted to write about him, Olney extended an invitation. After aperitifs in the garden, he served his guests a meal of artichokes *poivrade*, a roulade of sole filets with a *mousseline* of sea urchins in aspic, *daube à la provençale*, a *macaronade*, a rocket salad, cheese, and a raspberry sorbet. Each course was enhanced by a vintage wine from his famous cellar, and he published the menu shortly after the event in the French food-and-wine magazine *Cuisine et Vins de France*.[2]

Years later, Mary Frances described the approach to Olney's house as one of "climbs" without a flashlight and "impassable roads except to herds of sheep."[3] She also told Beard that although it was a superb dinner, the wines and words were endless. In 1990, when Olney read her letter in Evan Jones's biography of James Beard, *Epicurean Delight*, he disavowed almost everything she had written about the visit. "No one climbed the hillside," Olney countered in his memoir *Reflexions*. "They were driven up in broad daylight. There were no herds of sheep and, except when comfortably settled in a chauffeured car, M.F. glimpsed no heights or depths. Nor did Eda and I 'prance up and down in the abandoned quarry'—we passed the evening at table in front of the fireplace. When Raymond [Gatti] returned at midnight, everyone was amply lighted, on ground level, from the house to the car. A very unlikely story."[4] The version that Mary Frances related to Beard, no doubt exaggerated, had been meant for his eyes alone. She never intended it to reach Olney.

The dinner at Solliès-Toucas, however, was only a prelude to another meeting between Mary Frances and Olney at La Roquette later in November, when he was a houseguest at Eda and Sybille's home for a few days. The first evening he was there, Mary Frances prepared cold shrimp tails set in their congealed cooking butter in paper cases, Eda produced an admirable *navarin*, and Sybille made a macédoine of fresh fruits in kirsch. After dinner, Mary Frances asked to speak privately to Olney; according to his account, she confided that she felt that Sybille was very bad for Eda and sought his help in "separating them." Olney responded by saying, "I told her that I was not into breaking up friends' love relationships." He added, "She was not pleased."[5] If, in fact, Mary Frances thought that Eda's relationship with Sybille was destructive, she did not communicate it to anyone else. And, more likely than not, Olney was engaging in a bit of tit-for-tat.

Mary Frances did not know that when Eda and Olney had discussed her books, neither of them considered them to be of much merit. Olney labeled them full of "silly pretentious writing," probably because he disapproved of Mary Frances's lack of formal culinary training. Eda's dismissal was influenced by Elizabeth David, whom both she and Sybille knew well. The revered British food writer made no secret of her disdain for M.F.K. Fisher's forays into culinary writing, and she had even confided to Olney, "Of course I am not supposed to say this (muffled laughter) but I do find her [M.F.K. Fisher's] writing to be TOoo detestable."[6] There was and continued to be a subtle rivalry between the two women, spurred on by many comparisons in both the British and American press,[7] and Olney openly sided with David. Mary Frances seemed oblivious to any criticism of either herself or her writing, and she never criticized David's work.

James Beard was also staying at La Pitchoune that fall, testing recipes in Child's kitchen for his new book, *American Cookery*, and receiving outpatient care for obesity at the Clinique Médicale et Diététique in Grasse, where he soon grew restive under the constraints of a salt-free, low-calorie diet. When Norah left La Roquette to return to the States in early December, he welcomed the companionship of Mary Frances to distract him from his health problems. With Raymond Gatti at the wheel, they drove through the foothills of the Alps, visited the Maeght Museum near St.-Paul-de-Vence, and stopped at the faience museum in Mostiers-Ste.-Marie. After Julia and Paul Child arrived at La Pitchoune, they frequently invited Mary Frances, Eda, and Sybille for dinner. By mid-December, Paul Child's twin brother and his family arrived in Plascassier, as did Judith and Evan Jones. Beard departed for St.-Rémy, and Mary Frances, determined to repeat the scenario of spending the holidays alone, left La Roquette for Arles. In her thank-you note to Child, she wrote, "It will be odd to play the role, by now familiar and quite comfortable of course, of a ghost in Arles. I'll drift among the pre-Christian carvings, and hope to find a Midnight Mass where there will be the pipes and drums and a lamb bleating."[8]

In the middle of a season when families celebrated the holidays at home and tourists were few, Mary Frances discovered that the Hôtel Nord-Pinus had very few warm rooms during one of the worst cold spells that had gripped Provence in years, and that the bar and restaurant were closed for the season. She visited the Saturday market with its stalls of bric-a-brac, fruits, vegetables, and poultry, as well as the Christmas Market, the international salon of *santons*, St.-Trophime, and the underground Roman galleries, and ate mediocre meals in whatever brasseries and restaurants were open. In the mornings before these forays into the cold and gusty winds that roared through the city, she lingered over breakfast in her room and wrote about her solitary holiday. Although she initially intended only to share her impressions of the holiday with Norah, she later published "Looking Alone at a Place" in *As They Were*.

From Arles she took the train to Avignon, where it was even colder, and then she boarded one of the last trains bound for Marseilles. Staying at her favorite Hôtel Beauvau, she looked out on the rough waters of the Vieux Port, now virtually closed to fishing boats, and welcomed the Joneses, who were en route from Plascassier to New

York. After their departure, Mary Frances wrote to the Childs, "Judith left a nasty pile of work [revisions of *Among Friends*] for me (I'm *not* one of my own small loyal band of Fisher Fans!), and we had some fun as well, in spite of cruel cold—and the most delicate ravioli pasta I ever ate, at the Jambon de Parme—a very good *loupe au fenouil*, but poached, at La Cintra—we planned one more splurge at the New York, but didn't make it . . . Today there are 22 fishing boats at the Quai with their catch, instead of the 2 or 3 of the stormy days."[9] The spell of frigid weather had broken, and Mary Frances decided to fly to California before a return of inclement weather made traveling difficult again.

After five days in transit because of flight delays, technical difficulties, and bad winter storms in the British Isles, Mary Frances landed in San Francisco. When she returned to St. Helena the next day, she found with considerable dismay that the McIntyres had virtually taken possession of the house on Oak Avenue, breaking their rental agreement, which stipulated that she could occupy the house until her new home was completed. They had removed paintings from the walls and stacked them haphazardly in closets. Her papers and files were piled indiscriminately in the small first-floor office and in the basement, and perhaps most annoying of all, hundreds of books that had been left on shelves in the living room in a certain order to complete her work on *Among Friends* had been packed into unmarked cartons and moved into the basement. After futile attempts to revise her manuscript and salvage the situation, she wrote to the McIntyres, saying that she was professionally adrift and horrified over the breach of their agreement with her. She then spent the months of February and March sleeping in the basement of the St. Helena house during the week and staying at the Bouverie compound over the weekend. "This whole period," she wrote to Gingrich, "is rather like a serious but not fatal illness . . . or like getting a divorce from somebody you've loved dearly but can no longer live with."[10]

When Bouverie's friends Genie and Ranieri di San Faustino, who lived in San Francisco and rented the Hexagon House as a weekend retreat, were not in residence, Mary Frances worked there, sometimes sharing space with *San Francisco Chronicle* columnist Charlie McCabe. At other times she used the guesthouse. She complained to

Gingrich, "Split living is not for me . . . I'm really displaced, no matter how welcome I am here at the Ranch, and it is an uneasy feeling. It almost got me down for a couple of weeks, but now I have simply put myself 'in transit' until I'm really *gone* from St. H. That will be easier than I feared, because the McIntyres have so completely changed the whole ambience of what was once our dear old Bamboo Shack. I don't want you to see it again, nor anyone who loves it. I myself have said goodbye to it. But unfortunately I must still be there, four or five days a week . . . all my papers are there, and I am continuously moving car-loads of books and stuff."[11]

One of the advantages of staying part-time at the ranch was seeing the evolution of her house week by week, and she became so involved with the progress of the interior that she arranged picnics for Norah, Kennedy and her family, and friends from St. Helena to show off the newly tiled floors and soaring beamed ceilings. When the time for occupying the house drew near, her English "children," Humphrey and Solveig Stone, who were still living in Palo Alto, helped her pack and move books from St. Helena to Glen Ellen. By April 1, Mary Frances was in residence in her new home. To celebrate the event, Humphrey Stone mounted a stylized grapevine mural of aluminum paint on gun metal over the doorway to mark the entrance into Mary Frances's newly christened Last House.

Situated on a knoll overlooking a meadow, the house was a considerable distance from the main road that stretched from Sonoma to Santa Rosa. Protected by fencing and a sign that read "Trespassers Will Be Violated," its location discouraged casual visitors. Mary Frances also had the added security of the Bouverie staff, any of whom she could easily reach by phone. For added protection, she had a panic button with her own signal to press if she needed assistance. The custom-built *palazzino* showcased Dillwyn's paintings and the various posters from France that she had collected over the years. On the shelves that lined the walls in the foyer and the two main rooms, she arranged her vast library of more than five thousand volumes according to subject, from cookbooks to witchcraft. Antique furniture and treasures from her former homes, including her grandfather's revolving bookcase, her mother's teacups, her glass-doored spice cabinet, and a decoupage globe that Gloria Stuart had made for her, added a patina of age to the striking newness of the home. She slept and wrote in one room, prepared meals and entertained in the other. A spacious bathroom with art-filled walls and dressing room lights separated the two rooms.

Although it had been difficult to work during the transition from St. Helena to Glen Ellen, Mary Frances had revised sections of the Whittier book, scheduled to be published by Knopf that fall, and had written an introduction. Under the collective title "The Enclave," four chapters had already appeared in *The New Yorker* during the last four months of 1970, and two more were scheduled for January and May of 1971. Other publications kept the Fisher banner flying too. At Macmillan, Eleanor republished *The Art of Eating* in early February 1971, with jacket blurbs by Michael Field, Shana Alexander, and Arnold Gingrich. Following the introduction that Clifton Fadiman had written for the 1954 edition was a two-page appreciation by James Beard, in which he recalled reading *How to Cook a Wolf* while he was in the army in World War II, and then searching for more of M.F.K. Fisher's books. He put the greatest emphasis, however, on the impact of her words and how they touched the reader's own emotions, sending them away "with a desire to love better and live more fully."[12]

In early May, Michael Field, who had been teaching, writing, and demonstrating recipes at a feverish pitch, died suddenly of a brain hemorrhage. And James Beard, who had been hospitalized in New York after returning from the south of France, had, against all advice, resumed his hectic travel and teaching schedule. Mary Frances disapproved of the frantic pace of these culinary trendsetters, and she asked Julia, "*Quelle vie! on se demande pourquoi?*"[13] But she herself was also playing a more significant role in the increasingly trendy food world, and her articles lent cachet to culinary and nonculinary magazines alike. Commissioned by *Playboy* to do an article on New Orleans, she agreed to spend a week in the Crescent City. Citing the problems of a woman of a certain age dining alone, Mary Frances requested an escort as a condition for accepting the assignment, guaranteeing that she would not end up behind the aspidistra or, even worse, next to the powder room in restaurants and bars. The magazine agreed to send along a young staff writer named Douglas Bauer.

He proved to be an ideal companion, happy to begin the day with a dozen oysters on the half shell and to try out a couple of restaurants at lunchtime. He was also perfectly agreeable to an afternoon nap before they resumed their round of coffeehouses, restaurants, and jazz bars later in the day. "Trying to write about New Orleans is trouble," she wrote to Gingrich. "People think you have to sound like Tennessee Williams or the Underground Gourmet or maybe Mark Twain."[14] She told him about a nearly disastrous meal at Antoine's and a perfectly satisfying one at Galatoire's. The first draft of the article exhibited her finely tuned sense of place and her ability to catch the essence of a town: "Behind its soft drawl there is the machine-gun rattle of what may be the smartest Public Relations Bureau in modern times. Behind the languorous smell of magnolias and rum and the salty sexy whiff of cool oysters on the half shell there is the reek, no matter how discreetly siphoned off by the omnipresent air-conditioning, of diesel engines, oil, sweat, tidal sewage, electric furious Big Business . . . commercial success everywhere, around all the edges of the hundred blocks of building Bienville drew in the sand in 1718."[15] Unfortunately, the article was never published because Mary Frances did not agree to the changes the editors proposed, and she withdrew it.

After she returned to Glen Ellen, Mary Frances invited Gingrich to visit Last House in early June. Now that their relationship had reached a comfortable plateau, and their frequent letters chronicled everything from what they were wearing to the books they were writing, he was curious to see the *palazzino* that had replaced the "Bamboo Shack," and to meet the owner of the compound. The first weekend in June, Mary Frances took the bus to the San Francisco airport, where Gingrich awaited her with his rented car. After sampling fresh crab and dry white wine at Fisherman's Wharf, they leisurely drove northeast toward Sonoma, where Mary Frances showed Gingrich the town's plaza and historic buildings, and they stopped for a dry Gibson. A half hour later they turned into the main drive and Gingrich saw Last House. Gingrich approved of it all—Bouverie, the location, the amenities. He could now imagine her, he wrote, tending plants on her patio, preparing meals in the light of the large window looking out over the madronas, and writing with the ranch bell tower in view.

During the summer of 1971, Mary Frances entertained many other visitors and guests at Last House, gradually assuming the role of Bouverie's hostess as well as "writer-in-residence." She usually greeted the San Faustinos as well as the "Squire" with a welcoming drink when they arrived from San Francisco or places farther away. At other times, because Bouverie's guests were curious about the new house that he had designed, Mary Frances would invite them to "peek" and have a glass of wine with her before they gathered at the Main House to swim in his pool and dine.

Despite her frequent avowals that she and "Squire Bouverie were as amiably sexless as two bulbs in a flower-bed, two potatoes in a bin,"[16] when Gingrich expressed discomfort with her new role Mary Frances assured him,

> Don't worry about my having been "turned . . . into Madame Butterfly!" It is true that I've been on hand for a lot of local capers, largely by choice, but I don't regret it at all. It helped enormously to ease me from one pattern of life into another . . . I am no longer sitting in a too-big house waiting to have somebody come and stay there with me: children, friends, all that. I am no longer the woman whose children have grown up and whose husbands have died, dusting the corners now and then and trying to write. I have put all that behind me, and am as free as I ever will be from the demands, enjoyable and otherwise, of family life. For them I have deliberately substituted a simpler personal life, more independence in eating-working-sleeping-dressing-etc. I often find it a puzzlement, but I've made my choice, and this is the way I'll live until I'm no longer able to. The past *été mouvemente* has been very good for my spirits: I have proved that I can handle social situations I'd almost forgotten about . . . and that I need a great deal of solitude. I'll get that now, judiciously spiced with little forays into the world.[17]

She went to San Francisco from time to time to see art exhibits or attend concerts, usually followed by dinner with Norah or friends. She also visited Kennedy and her family in Oakland, and she continued to be active in the affairs of the Napa Valley Wine Library. Old friends like Marietta, the Ten Broecks, the Beards, and Paco and Romie Gould drew her back into the social life of St. Helena, where she often spent more time than she thought wise taking part in the wine classes organized by Jim Beard and the almost nonstop wine-related activities of the Goulds.

In the early 1970s, Julia Child was also participating in the California wine and food scene with greater frequency, and she brought her assistant, Rosemary Manell, and sister, Dorothy Cousins, into Mary Frances's orbit. By the same token, when the Childs visited Last House for the first time in December 1971, they met Bouverie, his cousin, the titled Isobel Radnor, and the San Faustinos. The Childs stayed in the Guest House, and every effort was made to keep JWs (Julia Watchers) away. Mary Frances prepared a *menudo* in their honor, accompanied by Sonoma wines and local sourdough bread. The next day they were guests of Robert Mondavi.

Mary Frances and the Childs kept up a steady correspondence dominated, unsurprisingly, by food and travel. Mary Frances was an improviser, creating menus of three soups and two apples, and dinners of clam chowder and marinated fruits. Child, on the other hand, proposed to take a lot of the "la-dee-da" out of French cooking and substitute the logic of French technique. She was known to test and retest recipes, conquering the variables. Mary Frances was freewheeling in the kitchen, finding what she wanted in Escoffier, Rombauer, or *Mastering the Art of French Cooking* and adapting recipes with abandon. As cooks and as writers they also differed in complexity and style. Child's prose was straightforward and instructive. Mary Frances's was evocative, personal, and sensual.

For all her socializing, there were also days when Mary Frances pursued her role as RR (Resident Recluse) and tried to cope with unpacked boxes of papers and manuscripts temporarily stored in the carport attached to her house. Although she assured Gingrich that she was "turning up astonishing proofs that while I am in much more control of my skills now than I was years or decades ago," she also noted that she did not have "the old creative necessity, or urge, or goad, or whatever it is/was."[18] She decided to seek a publisher for *The Boss Dog* again and contemplated how much revision her early edition of Peter Cartwright would need. As for the unfinished manuscripts, private notes, and other papers she pored over, she was already considering what to do with them all. She had been approached by Elizabeth Wector, a former trustee of Radcliffe College, about a possible gift to the manuscript collection at the Schlesinger Library. When she learned that Julia Child had already made arrangements to deposit her papers there, she decided to do the same.

In the meantime, *Among Friends* was published in the fall of 1971, not only introducing M.F.K. Fisher's readers to new pleasures of culinary memory, but giving them a sense of the exclusionary social and religious milieu in which she had spent the first twelve years of her life. As a remembrance of time past her account was also focused and fueled by a decade of civil rights marches, feminist consciousness raising, student protests, and other events that had helped to heighten her interest in social and political issues. The "courteous but cabalistic withdrawal" of the Society of Friends that she had unhappily experienced during her childhood was, in her view, simply another version of racial intolerance.

Unlike her other books, which were a mix of memoir, culinary history, narrative, and recipes, *Among Friends* concentrated on presenting the anatomy of a small town and the community that dominated it during the years of Mary Frances's childhood. But rather than presenting a sustained narrative, like James Joyce's *Portrait of the Artist as a Young Man* and Colette's *My Mother's House*, Mary Frances's bildungsroman was a collection of tales and vignettes that her editor assembled into three sections—"The Family," "The Town," "And Beyond." In "The Family," Mary Frances focused attention on the people who provided the love and security that kept her insulated from the almost daily taunts and snubs of the young members of the Society of Friends. She wrote at length about Rex, the would-be adventurer with an inextinguishable gleam in his eye, and about Edith, the young editor's wife who shielded herself from social slights by escaping into British novels, weekends at Laguna Beach, and occasional getaways to Los Angeles and beyond before health problems caused her to retreat to her suite of rooms.

For the first time Mary Frances also wrote about her deep feelings for Aunt Gwen ("related by love alone") and Gwen's family, former missionaries who established themselves as members of a minority of about thirty Episcopalians in a Quaker community of five thousand. In the warmth and shelter of their ramshackle kitchen and in the company of Aunt Gwen during summers at Laguna Beach, Mary Frances and Anne were transported into a world of "stiff upper lips," *The Jungle Book*, savory battered onion rings, fried egg sandwiches, and steamed mussels. Mary Frances also included other members of her extended family, beginning with Grandmother Holbrook, whom she depicted as the censor of pleasure in all of its palpable forms, the family's financial mainstay, the pillar of the local Christian church, and the one responsible for the procession of missionary housekeepers and cooks through the household. Despite its doctrinal exclusivity, Mary Frances described "The Town" itself as a fascinating organism, dominated by Whittier College and the businesses that stretched along Philadelphia Avenue. In this setting, she brought to life her teacher Miss Newby, her best friend, Margie Thayer, oddballs like Charles Somerville (one of Rex's "Lame Ducks"), and a host of other characters.

In the third section, titled "And Beyond," Mary Frances explored the Kennedy family's refuges—Aunt Maggie's fruit ranch in Valyermo, Los Angeles for lunch at the Victor Hugo and an afternoon at the theater, and Laguna Beach, which had provided safe haven for the renegade Episcopalians, Southern Baptists, and "plain heretics" who fled Whittier on the weekends to picnic and enjoy their freedom. Also beyond Whittier were the worlds that opened to Mary Frances through books that lined the walls on either side of the living room fireplace. She wrote, "In Whittier, our 'sets' and 'series,' the Classics and the trash, the borrowed once-is-enough books from the library and even Margie Thayer . . . all those phony cures for cancer and falling hair in the book in Father's office . . . they helped make one a more sensate and occasionally coherent person, or so I like to assume."[19]

Despite Mary Frances's effort to look clearly at her childhood and its setting, her stories were, as always, embellished in the telling. Anne's playground love affair, an enticing suspicion planted about Rex's fondness for the cook "Anita Perdita," even the frequency of Edith's pregnancies were played up—perhaps consciously, to reflect the youth of the narrator, but their inclusion revealed an authorial voice that could not resist the lure of a good story. And, depicting herself as the heroine of nearly every tale, Mary Frances reinforced the dual image of herself as a freewheeler in small matters (like hiding the comics page in the fold of a book of Bible stories or skipping school to visit the circus), but always essentially the good child: her mother's dedicated helper, a dutiful granddaughter, her sister's guardian, and her father's oldest and brightest daughter.

Highly selective in both her inclusion and omission of character-revealing incidents regarding Rex and Edith, Mary Frances chose to credit Grandmother Holbrook for developing her gastronomic awareness, without whose puritanical counterexample "I probably would still be swimming in unread iambics instead of puzzling over the relationship between food and love, painting Zen-begotten abstracts instead of observing the glandular reactions to a pot of dark broth in my hungry guinea pigs, my loved victims. I would not be this *me* but some other, without my first years in Grandmother's gastric presence."[20] It was in Whittier that the "gastronomical she" was born, her powers of observation were sharpened, and a certain *je-m'en-fichisme* became a means to detach herself from what was going on around her. And there was evidence of the adult she would become: the aggrieved daughter, wife, mother, friend, the woman who abhorred a quarrel and who, when depressed, would seek the privacy of her room rather than show her weakness, the cook who knew the power of a stew as well as the writer who knew the power of pleasing on paper.

Despite her unreliability as a narrator, the story she told was so compelling that her memoir became the sourcebook for M.F.K. Fisher's early life. Readers and fans rely on its image of her as a child and cling to the picture of a swashbuckling Rex beset by intolerant Quakers and an Anglophilic Edith as a prairie princess unable to cope with the domestic scene. Grandmother Holbrook and Aunt Gwen are elevated as culinary and spiritual influences, while Anne is subjected to an extraordinary suggestion: "It seems clear to me that organically, chemically, biologically she should never have been coaxed through her first two years, when she was trying so hard and innocently to escape."[21] "This is an amazing observation to me," Anne's son, Sean Kelly, wrote. "Here we have an older sister, who has played around with the occult enough to know the implications of an expressed death wish, calmly suggesting that it might have been better if her younger sister had died in early childhood. Does it get much worse than that?"[22]

The publication of the book brought favorable responses from critics like Jean Stafford, who wrote in *Vogue*, "This memoir of M.F.K. Fisher is a needle in the arm filled with nectar and ichor, and distillations of irony and wondrous corn and sassy razzmatazz and tempered temper tantrums and tolerance."[23] Others were more qualified but still enthusiastic: "As autobiography, this is not an important book; but it is delightful reading, not only because of the subject matter, but also because of its style—witty and charming, decidedly well written."[24] The family response was a matter of greater suspense. Norah's acknowledgment after receiving the book led Mary Frances to respond gratefully, "Yes, it was pretty reckless of you to break the Embarrassed Family [H]Ush! Thank you though . . . what you think and do not think matters very much to me."[25] Dr. Bieler's positive reaction also pleased her. "Thank you for telling me you liked the book about my being a child. I wrote it without thinking of readers, and now that they are writing to me, I wish I had done it much better. The reactions are good: the people who were happy children recall their happiness as children, and the ones who led dreadfully sad lives as children seem to dwell on what might have been."[26] And Mary Frances told Judith Jones, "I continue to get astonishing reactions (all good) to the Whittier book . . . So far I have not heard from anyone who was affronted by it, but probably, as Quakers, they would not write anyway. A few people qualify their amusement and so on . . . the old thing of 'I don't always like what you say, but I like the way you say it . . .' And I get really interesting letters from people who once sat next to my father at a football dinner or went to the same beauty-parlor as my mother. I try to write to them all, and unfortunately they reply lengthily and eagerly . . ."[27]

Isobel MacLaren, a Kennedy friend, wrote to dispute the depiction of her family and to disclaim "the scene in which Gwen and I are unpacking my brother Fred's trunks after his death in the war, nothing of the sort took place."[28] Many of the Quakers in Whittier, moreover, were not pleased with their portrayal in *Among Friends*, and they took special issue with her statement "Some of them [Quakers] were sanctimonious bastards," neglecting to quote the rest of it: "Some were truly gentle and fine, almost worthy of my parents."[29] On local TV shows and in articles members of the community expressed their indignation, but in Mary Frances's view their protests were only a further indication of the dull clannishness of the town.

M.F.K. Fisher's *Among Friends* was not the only one of her books to cause a stir in the last months of 1971. Knopf also published a revised edition of her translation of Brillat-Savarin's *Physiology of Taste* in December, and the new edition attracted more attention than the original limited edition had in 1949. A *New York Times* review focused attention on *The Physiology of Taste* as a "book of 18th-century pleasures, composed by the only *philosophe* of food," and praised M.F.K. Fisher's translation as "far superior to the earlier one by Arthur Machen; Mrs. Fisher's English is unstilted and flowing. The notes, however, are the glory of the book . . . Mrs. Fisher does not explain Brillat-Savarin, she reacts to him . . . With notes like these, it is regrettable that the book has been designed so that they appear at the end of each section rather than at the bottom of the page. M.F.K. Fisher and Brillat-Savarin are too united in spirit to be so far separated in print."[30] Clifton Fadiman, in a lengthier appraisal, spelled out how the Parisian jurist used gastronomy as a key to unlock the cabinet of the whole man. "Mrs. Fisher (in one of her many 'glosses' that add a truffle flavor to the author's own plain prose) goes to the heart of the matter," Fadiman wrote. "The book is 'a well-balanced expression of one thinking man's attitude toward life.' That is it." And he added, "His twenty 'Aphorisms,' thirty 'Meditations,' and his twenty-seven 'Varieties' find their locus in the palate . . . And all this is dressed in a style that replicates his mildly eccentric, generally mellow, comically pedantic, tolerant personality. He is not really a good writer—with her lovely, informative glosses his translator quietly writes rings around him—but he is a *true* writer."[31]

With Macmillan's edition of *The Art of Eating*, her translation of *The Physiology of Taste*, and *Among Friends* all published in 1971, Mary Frances had a successful year, and she had also entered into a productive relationship with a publisher she had long wanted to be associated with and an editor she respected. Relocating to the Bouverie Ranch, she had broadened her circle of acquaintances and friends, and during the trip to the south of France she had established "a new plateau of mutual enjoyment" with Norah. Only her daughters, who seemed to be busy with their families and content with their choices, remained both emotionally and physically distant. Although they urged her to join them and their families in either Oakland or Portland for the holidays, Mary Frances reverted to self-imposed isolation, turning aside even Norah's invitation to come to Jenner for Christmas Day. In her private journal she wrote, "Why am I doing this? Why is this the third Christmas in a row that I've run away from? This year I am almost perversely alone again and suddenly astounded at the basic vanity I am displaying. I suspect I have withdrawn this way because I no longer find myself physically able to dominate, to be the driving force, the planner, the creator of a rendezvous of family and friends."[32]

A series of last-minute invitations interrupted her solitude, however. When Elsine and Tony Ten Broeck asked to stop by on the day before Christmas, she prepared an impromptu lunch for them, and she joined the ranch's housekeeper for a drink later that day. When she returned to Last House, she had a gin-vermouth, and instead of the caviar she wished for, she settled for a tin of mediocre lobster pâté and Melba toast. The next morning Marietta called and said that she and her mother would drop by and wish Mary Frances a Merry Christmas. Although she would have preferred to be alone, she received them graciously and prepared a simple lunch. She had had visitors and phone calls, packages, flowers, and mail. Reflecting on the day, she wrote, "I now realize that I have been mistaken and that I shan't do it again . . . Next year, and without seeming to be Head of the Clan too much, I might be able to do something to re-unite good people . . . instead of sitting here like a stuffed toad waiting to be visited and telephoned and pampered."[33]

Inexplicably, less than three weeks into 1972, Mary Frances started "to fall apart." Fearing another spell of the kind that had hospitalized her in 1964, Norah drove her to the hospital in St. Helena for a complete physical examination. Mary Frances described her ordeal: "I spent two days getting the works, and came home late Tuesday. I am in good shape: heart, spine, blood. Enlarged liver, which I have had since I was a small child. Signs of arthritis (my hands). So there was nothing more that could be done for me there, and the rest is up to me: eat more, drink less, and not overwork. I have to take an anti-depressant for a time."[34] A month later she wrote to Dr. Bieler and was more explicit about her continuing "shakes, chills, deep confusion, and depression." She also told him that her present state was probably the result of having broken with the physical side of being "mother-wife-daughter, etc., etc."[35] Living in a small house, secluded by choice, and responsible only to herself, Mary Frances was beginning to feel that she must take further steps to remake her life.

She also had reason to believe that she was physically "deteriorating fast," that she was aging precipitously. She was unsteady on her feet and had a noticeable tremor in both hands, which left her insecure about driving, seeing friends, even managing the three steps from one room to the other. Although her weight remained stable, between 158 and 162 pounds, she noticed a growing thickness around the middle of her body. It was, she told Dr. Bieler, "hard on my vanity." Instead of plunging into her work, she felt apathetic, even lazy. She concluded, "I'll be 64 in July. I would like to live for another decade or so, if I could do it gracefully. But for the past few weeks I have felt like a piece of clay in the rain, growing more shapeless and meaningless all the time. *It's boring.*"[36]

By the end of March she informed Dr. Neil that she had stopped taking the antidepressants he had prescribed, and she told Gingrich that she felt like she was "out of jail literally"[37] and ready to complete the introduction for Paco Gould's memoir and send off an article on death and dying called "Notes on a Necessary Pact" to *Prose.* That spring Mary Frances also hired Erika Hubblitz, Norah's tenant and a part-time editor at the University of California Press, to organize her papers for the Schlesinger Library. It was a strange feeling to be going over all those early scraps of paper, she told Gingrich, and she regretted that it seemed, at least to her, that she wrote the same way in 1942 that she did now: "I'd like to be *better,* for god's sake."[38]

During the late spring she made the acquaintance of two ex–New Yorkers who had opened a kitchenware shop in the center of Sonoma called The Sign of the Bear. Richard Foorman and Gene Quint were gourmet cooks, interested in wine, and knowledgeable about the theater and music. While still living in New York they had contacted

Eleanor about how best to meet Mary Frances, but she surprised them one day by simply dropping in to their shop to buy something. From their first dinner together, their friendship grew, and they frequently invited her to accompany them to wineries in Sonoma and musical productions in San Francisco.

David Bouverie was also in residence again, and the number of houseguests and special events escalated. The poet Maya Angelou and her friend Paul du Feu, who were living in Sonoma, were frequent guests at the ranch, and Angelou read at Bouverie's annual musical and literary soiree. Another frequent guest was the British author Jessica (Decca) Mitford, who lived in Berkeley with her husband. The summer also brought a number of Mary Frances's friends and relatives to Last House. Sean Kelly and his family stopped for a few days on their way to Bangkok, and Nan Newton's son Chas, now studying wine making at some of the major wineries in the Napa Valley, was often a dinner guest and occasionally a house sitter.

In midsummer, Anna and her son, Chris, arrived from Portland. Four months into a difficult pregnancy, she showed the familiar signs of slipping into another manic phase, as had happened in her previous pregnancy. After the brief and disturbing visit, Mary Frances wrote to Gingrich, "Norah has said that I am the most self-centered person she has ever known, and that may be so. But I honestly do not feel that my love for Anna and Chris is self-centered. I want, more than anything, for them to be strong and well, and, and. Parent-talk! At the same time, and after some thirty years of doing every thing I knew how to, to reach this goal, I find that my own self esteem and *amour propre* and whatever it may be called is in a precariously depleted state, and easily undermined. And after a bout with Anna I am left like a fish flapping on the beach at low tide . . . low morale, great despondency and spiritual insecurity . . . all that."[39] By August Anna was in a crisis unit in Portland, and her husband was in a dangerous state of emotional collapse. He sent Chris down to Jenner to be placed in Norah's care.

An added sorrow during this almost surreal summer was the death of Mary Frances's longtime friend June Eddy in Laguna Beach. She had been a friend for more than thirty years, had shared Mary Frances's passion for Jelly Roll Morton's hot jazz before bebop reigned, and had been a welcome distraction during the early 1950s, when Mary Frances and her daughters lived with Rex on the Ranch in Whittier. She evidently felt the same, because she left Mary Frances a bequest of several thousand dollars in her will.

In September, Mary Frances flew to New York at Volkening's urging, whereupon he informed her that he was resigning from Russell & Volkening after managing her publishing affairs for more than twenty-five years. He had already made arrangements for another agent, Tim Seldes, to represent her. After they had been introduced, Volkening and Mary Frances went to lunch at his favorite restaurant, where the waiters and management knew his ritual of at least six Old Grand-Dads during a business lunch. The two of them spoke of the loss of Volkening's wife to lung cancer, and of his own battle with the same disease. Afterward, he hailed a taxi for them both and held Mary Frances's hand until she left him on Twelfth Street in the Village. He blew a kiss out of the back window and waved goodbye. The next morning he went into the hospital and died shortly thereafter. Mary Frances concluded her unpublished tribute to him with the words, "I respected HV as a man and as a literary agent, ethically and otherwise. I loved him as a warm if very reticent human being."[40] "Henry V," as she often referred to him, had served her long and well, always urging her to work more, but remaining patient with her during her long periods of self-doubt and insecurity.

Without his gentle goading and encouraging words, Mary Frances seemed unable to focus on another book about Provence. But she began talking about returning to the south of France again if Norah would accompany her. For her part, Norah had decided to sell her house on Panoramic Way, and by the end of the summer she also had reached a decision to retire from her counseling work in the Berkeley school system and live in Jenner. In November she was ready to book passage on a transatlantic freighter, but Mary Frances began to draw back from the proposed trip. Her first concern was Anna's imminent delivery after a complicated pregnancy, and there were also nagging questions about Chris's well-being during his mother's latest breakdown. Furthermore, she told Norah, she was unable to think about writing again. "I have several reviews and articles outlined, and their material in order . . . but the thought of tackling them is repugnant to me. I blame this on the Radcliffe job flatly.[41] It has done something to my spirit, like snapping a light switch. I am turned off. I never want to write again. I have a lot to say, but why say it? It has been a shock to me, probably, to have to look at the printed product of a/my mind . . . The only justification for it was that I used my one small talent as best I could." And then she added, "I never lied." She abruptly concluded the letter with the observation that the change of scene might be a goad, and might make writing meaningful to her again in much the same way that "plowing a little matters to an old plowhorse."[42]

On December 3, 1972, Steve Metz called from Portland to say that Anna had given birth to a strong baby boy, whom she had named Matthew. After offering her congratulations to her son-in-law, Mary Frances hesitantly asked if she was still on her daughter's "black list." He told her that Anna did not want any contact with her, and Mary Frances bowed to her wishes, thankful that this time the estrangement was only with her daughter and not with Norah, as it had been when Anna's first child was born. The anger and resentment between Norah and herself at that time had slowly given way to understanding, and now they were comfortably companionable, carefully avoiding topics that neither really wanted to pursue. Their forthcoming trip to the south of France promised to be one more step in reestablishing a pattern of mutual trust.

Mary Frances and Norah flew to New York on January 19 and spent the night at Eleanor's town house. The next day they boarded the *Colombo*, a small liner bound for the Mediterranean, where they had arranged to disembark at Cannes and continue on to Salon-de-Provence. After a week crossing the Atlantic, however, their plans went hopelessly awry. Thanks to the capriciousness of the Italian line, they sailed directly to Naples, and they had no choice but to make their way to Cannes via Rome, where two of their six valises were detained and, unfortunately, burglarized. To further complicate matters, after only a few days they realized that staying in Salon, which had seemed to be a typical Provençal town where one could walk anywhere, was impossible without a car. The restaurant scene was bleak except for Boissin, and a decent pied-à-terre was not available. They abandoned the idea of staying in the country, boarded a bus for Marseilles, and found a studio apartment on the eighth floor of a plain concrete building at 41 avenue de la Corse.

The two-room flat had a little cupboard in the bathroom with a two-burner gas plate and three battered saucepans. It was the kind of challenge Mary Frances enjoyed. Within a few days she and Norah had acquired a salad bowl, some wineglasses, a sharp knife, and cloth for bedspreads for the studio bed in each room. Mary Frances slept and worked in the smaller room. Norah used the larger room, which also doubled as their dining room because it had three chairs and a kind of buffet for dishes. A balcony stretched across both rooms, providing a view over the Basilique St.-Victor and the Fort St.-Nicolas on the left. The quai du Port was directly across from them, and to the right they could follow the quai de Rive Neuve, which led to the Hôtel de Ville and the Canebière. The south of France had again become a welcoming place.

Marseilles offered a steady stream of activity: fishing and leisure boats entering and leaving the harbor, fishwives selling fresh seafood along the quai des Belges, tourists mingling with the locals in old cafés and restaurants lining the streets, church bells pealing, and 1974 Citroëns speeding through the narrow streets. The places they frequented were all within walking distance, and the neighborhood was dotted with shops selling excellent cheeses and breads and pleasant local wines. A few times a week they ate at one of their favorite restaurants, but for the most part they lived inexpensively and simply on what they could prepare themselves. Years later in *As They Were*, Mary Frances described "the least dignified of a lifetime of kitchens" in a preface to a piece that she had written in 1966, called "Two Kitchens in Provence": "We ate as close as possible to one of the windows, shut against the mistral, open to the warm sun. The foul little bath-kitchen produced miracles of good plain food from its two pans, and we bought some plates and bowls of Provençal pottery, and two sturdy wine glasses, so that everything tasted better. Salads were easy. So was good *café au lait*, and we soon learned where to find the most commendable croissants, the most pungent mountain honey. We could get local cheeses, and homemade pâtés sent to our shopkeepers by cousins in Normandy or Alsace. Now and then we bought a little roasted chicken from an elegant catering shop on the Rue de Rome. And the *vins rosés* were ever-flowing."[43]

Often disappointed with the produce available at the market, which was shipped in from Israel and Portugal, they would board the bus and in thirty minutes arrive in the center of Aix. At either the Big Market, held three times a week, or at the smaller Marché aux Herbes, they could purchase fresh green beans, tender zucchini blossoms, radishes, and seasonal fruits and carry them back like trophies to their apartment. But nothing in Aix could compare with the Flower Market in Marseilles. Mary Frances observed, "We go like hypnotized chickens, strolling up and down and humming uncontrollably and unconsciously. Right now the cheapest are huge heaps and piles of anemones, both long and short stemmed. Carnations, which are strictly 'Provence' to me . . . and lovely little prim posies of pinks and daisies . . . we also have three little pots of local herbs: rosemary, thyme, tarragon."[44]

Mary Frances took care of her correspondence in the morning, and because she wanted to write about the mysterious attraction Marseilles had always had for her, she began to gather old maps and information about the city. Meanwhile, Norah spent much of her time studying the legends, myths, and general "cult" of Mary Magdalene in Provence. The Abbaye de St.-Victor, which was close to their apartment, was a source of documents, as was the Bibliothèque Mejane in Aix. Short trips to St.-Maximin also yielded more information because it was commonly believed that *la Sainte Pénitente* was buried in the basilica there.[45]

Usually Norah returned to the apartment at noon, and they ate a simple lunch that Mary Frances had prepared—a soup, vegetables in a vinaigrette, or a tasty fish stew. An avid moviegoer, Norah often then went to see a film or the two of them would explore the out-of-the-way places of the city in the early spring afternoons. They also took advantage of performances at the Opera House and plays and reviews trying out for Paris, and entertained Humphrey and Solveig Stone, who had come from England to see them. They visited old friends like Leo and Barbara Marschutz in Aix, and before leaving Marseilles went on a final spree to the family home of Georges Connes in the Aveyron. On May Day, Mary Frances told Gingrich that everything was going too fast. "I swear the withdrawal pangs grow worse with age . . . it's very hard to leave, no matter how much I look forward to some things about being home again. I simply feel like more of a whole person, here . . . and I resent wasting time being only partly alive, no matter how enjoyable it may be."[46] Mary Frances and Norah left Marseilles on May 20 and went directly to Nice. Three days later they flew back to the States.

During what had been an extremely cold January in the Sonoma Valley, most of the eucalyptus trees on the north side of Last House were severely damaged, and all but a few of them fell to the chain saw. Their loss simply added to Mary Frances's feeling of *dépaysement*. But the June weather was beautiful and, as Mary Frances wrote in her journal, "constantly interesting to me."

SEVENTEEN

Other Places

(1973–1980)

Friends kept the hearth warm and the animals happy, and other friends let me stay in their own places when they were away. It was a vivid period of slow wandering, very rich like a carpet I had often trod before I realized that it was there.[1]   —M.F.K. Fisher

After Mary Frances returned from Marseilles her health slowly but discernibly declined. In July and August of 1973, she wrote at length to Dr. Bieler describing her "strange attacks," and Dr. Neil treated her for a cerebral-vascular condition that she described in her journal: "There is a kind of SNAP in the brain waves, and an immediate feeling of alarm and anguish, as if things were going too fast and the whole system might explode."[2] The attacks were accompanied by a rapid heartbeat, deep breathing, and prolonged chills with uncontrollable shivering. Gradually the tremors and light-headedness subsided, and fatigue followed. Mary Frances breezily shrugged off what she called her "Victorian vapors," but the symptoms persisted.

While not housebound, she found trips to Santa Rosa for dental care and to St. Helena for Wine Library meetings more tiring than usual. She opted to nap more and curl up on her bed with a favorite Simenon, and she nibbled on her zucchini "mishmash" or a few spoonfuls of comforting soup instead of eating full meals. In early 1974, a persistent pain in her shoulder necessitated a series of medical and chiropractic examinations. Mary Frances told Norah that the

X-rays showed she was "as horny with spurs and deposits as one of the pre-historic reconstructions in the Smithsonian." "It has interested me, these past months," she wrote, "to realize the difference between internal pain, in liver or heart or guts for instance, and the kind that invalid a person's extremities . . . arms-legs-hands-feet-shoulders-elbows-knees. The inner kind is mysterious. The second kind is plainly ugly and cruel, but in a deliberate way it is acceptable and real."[3] In addition to Valium and other drugs, Dr. Neil now had Mary Frances on a daily regime of aspirin tablets for arthritis.

Bothered by persistent pain and lethargy, Mary Frances told Norah that she had not only abandoned the Marseilles book, but had stopped being a writer—for good this time. "Of course I have often withdrawn for a time . . . what is glibly called Writer's Bloc. But now I think I am a real dropout. And the interesting thing is that as far as I can tell, except for occasional grabs from my subconscious during dreams, I am relieved. I simply do not want to *write*."[4] She added that her correspondence was sadly neglected and she really did not care. Puttering around Last House, keeping pots of herbs and flowers watered, and "playing hookey as cookey" was the only thing that held her interest. She prepared vegetables in savory vinaigrettes, and baked cookies that she served with jellied fresh fruits.

When Bouverie was at the ranch, an ever-changing sequence of his friends and acquaintances arrived and departed. When he was in New York or abroad, Mary Frances often lived in the midst of strangers who rented the Main House or were "guests." During those times she felt that the ambience at the ranch was impersonal and less secure, and occasionally in her letters to Norah, she even questioned her wisdom in choosing to live there. Nevertheless, her daily calendar suggested that she managed to maintain a vigorous schedule of "dinners in or out," as "one long parade of very nice but basically tiring people"[5] visited her at Last House.

In addition to her long-standing friends from St. Helena, she counted among her guests the various local authors whose company she enjoyed. Albert Kahn, a dedicated Communist who wrote a biography of Stalin's daughter, and his wife were dear friends, as were the San Franciscans Frances and Robert Steele. Photographers and artists also made their way to Last House.[6] On one of her visits, the artist Judith Clancy began to sketch Mary Frances, and gradually she assembled the line drawings into a portfolio. Mary Frances described the likenesses of herself as "catching the sinister cherub . . . quite interesting,"[7] but she was not pleased when an editor selected one of them to illustrate an article.[8] But older friends like Larry Powell had virtually disappeared from her life. "I never hear from LCP any more," she had written to Dr. Bieler in 1972. "It gave me a pang to have him move definitively to New Mexico . . . He was in St. Helena two weeks ago, with many people I know, but did not have time (or inclination?) to call me. Where are the snows of yesteryear?"[9] When Powell did finally visit to introduce his current, very much younger mistress, Mary Frances took umbrage at his "horniness." At seventy-one he wanted to marry a woman of thirty-five and divorce Fay, "cuckolded patiently for some fifty years," and who for that period of time had contributed to his "image of respectable marital bliss."[10] Gloria Stuart, who believed that Mary Frances had betrayed her years earlier when she persuaded her to burn the manuscript of a novel she had written, also absented herself.[11]

Increasingly, Mary Frances turned to much younger friends, like the Glen Ellen writers James Pendergast and his wife, Margaret, who brought new ideas into her life and regarded her with a certain awe. Her growing guest list also included a number of adult children of her friends and former friends. Gloria Stuart's daughter, Sylvia Thompson, and her family often made their way to Last House or extended hospitality to Mary Frances when she was in the Los Angeles area. Grown-up sons and daughters of the Steeles and the Conneses, her sister Norah's sons, and her cousin Nan Newton's son Chas were frequent visitors as well. Mary Frances told Gingrich, "I get vicarious enjoyment from young people, being deprived by fate and circumstance from seeing my own very often."[12]

Yet she was increasingly reminded of her inadequacies as a mother and grandmother, as when Chris chose to vacation in Jenner and spent only a day with her in Glen Ellen. Kennedy's infrequent visits were also a source of disappointment, as was the nagging suspicion that Kennedy's son, Alex, was closer to his paternal grandmother than he was to her. Anna's contact with her mother was erratic. During the spring of 1974, after sixteen months of what Mary Frances described as "touch me not" behavior on Anna's part, phone calls and letters began to arrive from Oregon. Then in June, Steve Metz visited Last House with Chris and eighteen-month-old Matthew to explain that he was filing for divorce, because there were significant issues between him and Anna and he had doubts about the paternity of the child Anna was now carrying. He also told Mary Frances that he would be suing for custody of the children. Although she loved seeing her grandsons, the meeting was uncomfortable because Mary Frances decided to stick by Anna. In December, she went to Portland to testify for her daughter at a custody hearing.

"Anna is always The Waif," Mary Frances wrote, "but she has great dignity when she is in her present mood (a sad resigned one). The new baby Sylvie [born on September 28] is lovely, a tiny child very much like Anna, very dainty, but really not as lovely as A was . . . dark eyes not quite as huge, dark hair not quite as fantastically thick and silky."[13] Although the presiding judge postponed the decision until March 1975, ultimately the court granted custody of Matthew to Steve. Chris and Sylvie were assigned to the care of Anna, who took them to Astoria, Oregon, where they lived on welfare. "Well, I send her a big tuck-box about every three weeks, and she has the stamps, and she also has state-county-gov't checks," Mary Frances told Norah, "but she also has, at last count, something like 9 animals, not counting fish etc, plus the two children and herself, to house and feed and clothe . . . in two rooms as last reported. *No go.*"[14]

Norah, in addition to enjoying closer relationships with her own children and grandchildren, and even Mary Frances's grandchild, also had the company of her longtime friend and colleague Lida Schneider, who was also recently retired and shared the house with Norah in Jenner. Since their graduate studies at the University of Chicago, they had been friends, with similar interests, and they traveled and volunteered in many community organizations together. Faced with Marietta's offer to share a home now that her mother was no longer with her, Mary Frances gently but firmly rejected it. It was too late, Mary Frances said. Intimate living made too many demands, and she had convinced herself that "this increasing *remoteness* is devoutly to be wished for."[15]

More to her liking was the role of hostess at Last House. "It amuses me to find myself turning into a very minor Eminence Grise here on the West Coast," she wrote to Gingrich in 1975. "Younger people like to come for lunch and make little notes! (They are hungry and thirsty, and someday will write better than they do now.)"[16] It was, in fact, not a new role. In the early 1960s an aspiring food journalist named Jerry DiVecchio had contacted Mary Frances. As a beginning writer for *Sunset*, she had hoped to persuade Mary Frances to give a "pep talk" at an editorial session. Although Mary Frances turned down the invitation, she did invite DiVecchio to visit her in St. Helena, where they went on one of Mary Frances's famous picnics. An enduring relationship ensued. "To be in her life was by invitation only," DiVecchio remembered.[17] During the 1960s and 1970s such invitations were rare, because Mary Frances spent long periods of time away from California, but as her culinary reputation grew and she became more identified with Sonoma, her correspondence with food writers, interviewers, and potential cookbook authors multiplied, and she ended most of her responses by giving her unlisted phone number and directions for driving up from San Francisco.

The region itself was vastly growing in prominence in the culinary landscape, and she had become an established highlight of the region. The cookware entrepreneur Chuck Williams was expanding his California-based business, sales of California wines and produce were skyrocketing, cooking schools proliferated in the region, and a handful of California chefs attracted enthusiastic audiences both on TV and in person. Whenever James Beard appeared at an event or taught cooking classes on the West Coast, he made an effort to visit Last House and occasionally brought his friend Marion Cunningham. Child did the same, and her assistant, Rosemary Manell, who lived in nearby Belvedere, became a frequent visitor, as did Mauny Kaseburg, a Seattle food writer who was an acquaintance of Child's. Food consultant and PR maven Maggie Waldren, from Sausalito, joined the ever-expanding group of Last House visitors. With good food and wine on the table, the established and the aspiring mingled, and Mary Frances became the fixed center of a widening culinary circle.

When Simone Beck taught a sequence of cooking classes in the Napa Valley in 1974, she invited Mary Frances to visit and shared the news that Julia Child could not bring herself to tell her friends,

namely, that Paul would soon undergo coronary bypass surgery. The
word reached Mary Frances at a time when serious health problems
and death were claiming many of the people Mary Frances had been
close to. Earlier that year she had learned of Georges Connes's passing in Dijon, and she told Gingrich that she felt absolutely lost without him in her life. In 1975 Aunt Grace died, leaving Mary Frances
bereft of a confidante, and in October Dr. Bieler passed on. "I have always been attracted to people older than I," she wrote, "so the falling
off is inevitable."[18]

Mary Frances said that these deaths reminded her that time was
passing and she must attend to more than "the heady prospect of lazy
naps and little walks and vague ponderings,"[19] although between 1974
and 1976 she did very little work on her Marseilles project. She did,
however, publish two articles—an "Ode to the Olive" for *Travel and
Leisure* and an essay for *Esquire*'s Americana sequence, devised to
usher in the Bicentennial year of 1976. In the company of Joan Did-
ion, Jean Stafford, Julia Child, James Villas, and other notable authors
who deconstructed quintessential American subjects like shopping
malls, Coca-Cola, corn, and fried chicken, Mary Frances wrote about
apple pie: "The fact that it came from England, with the Pilgrims up
North and the Cavaliers down South, long before we were a nation,
and that it was probably brought in recognizable form to England by
William the Conqueror in 1066 or so, cannot mar the fine polish of
how we feel about apple pie as a part of our comparatively youthful
heritage."[20]

Now Mary Frances encouraged fan mail to such a degree that all-
day marathon sessions with her typist became weekly occurrences,
and she supplemented the services of her longtime Napa typist by hiring Margie Foster, a young Glen Ellen neighbor, to help primarily with
correspondence. But Mary Frances continued to answer personal letters herself. Letters gave her license to exaggerate, to be witty—even
devastating—to reveal a range of emotions that conversation seldom
permitted. And although she frequently wrote the same thing to many
different correspondents, she adopted a distinct persona when writing
to each. She also used letters as a warm-up to get into an article or
story. She called it "a self-indulgence," but her compulsion to communicate waved that consideration aside. At a time when driving and

traveling were becoming increasingly difficult, letters were her main-stay.

To Norah she expressed her deep satisfaction that her younger sister was a vital part of her life again. "I may be in a state of general puzzlement," she wrote,

> but one question is clearly and forever answered for me by having lived with you for the past months [in Marseilles]. It was one of the richest experiences in my whole life, very warm and intense. It was even better than two years ago, perhaps because I'm older and know a little more (Wishful thinking . . . ?). I learned a great deal, mostly about your thoughtfulness and wisdom and forbearance, even when I "sat there pontificating," and of course there were creature comforts: Listel et al, black olives, enough empty shells to build a small jetty . . . Who else in this green world would have understood the complex pleasure of sleeping in those beds . . . and accepted the 4th-floor shudder so fatalistically in that elevator."[21]

Over lunch at Last House on March 4, 1976, she raised the prospect of sharing a similar experience again and the hope that it might goad her into completing her book. But the next day she had doubts about another trip. Writing in her journal, she questioned whether Norah really enjoyed her company or was motivated by a sense of duty because Mary Frances's declining health made traveling alone difficult for her. Mary Frances was also dissatisfied with herself. "There is an imperative (compulsive) need to start a thing and then drop it, ignore it, even forget it. I suspect that it started with my apparent interruptions in what would usually be a speedy finish of the Marseille book," she wrote. "By now I *want* not to end things. It is odd . . . It is a form of braggadocio, of cock-snoot: I know I can do what I have to do, but by god I don't have to do *this*."[22] The appeal of being in Provence, however, was stronger than her deep reservations, and she decided to forge ahead with an itinerary.

Three weeks before Norah and she departed for France, Arnold Gingrich's weekend telephone calls signaled a sharp decline in his health, evidenced in part by slurred words and complaints about sleeping problems. One of his last calls was especially touching, and Mary Frances wrote, "Arnold, for a split particle of time yesterday, you spoke directly to me and I knew that we are fine happy loving people together, no matter what the distances and vagaries. I shall always hear your voice, speaking straight to me, ME, instead of chitchatting about the weather and the buses and how many trout you caught that morning and how the lesson went with Deane [Gingrich's violin coach]. For a second in time, we spoke. Lucky us."[23] The next day Gingrich underwent exploratory lung surgery, and on April 15 Mary Frances left the States in limbo about his condition. "I am one of his many sub-rosa 'toys,'" she recorded in her journal, "and after some 35 years of involvements, professional and personal, am still un-official as a Concerned Citizen."[24] The frustration of having to de-pend on his staff at *Esquire* for information about him only sharpened her sense of being an outsider. Unlike on her previous trips, there were no flowers or letters to greet her when she arrived at the Roi René in Aix, and Mary Frances eventually learned from his secretary that Gingrich had started a debilitating sequence of chemotherapy treatments for lung cancer. Trying to distract him, Mary Frances wrote to him frequently, reporting in great detail on the various musi cal events she and Norah attended and the guests they entertained.

Although it had been only three years since Mary Frances and Norah had last visited the south of France, they found Aix dramati-cally changed. Restoration of public buildings, initiated by André Malraux in Paris, had quickly spread to other towns, and in Aix, with the help of Beaux-Arts grants and local pride, important buildings were encased in scaffolding, and sculptors, masons, and plasterers were removing the cracked stucco that hid the honey-colored stone beneath. Recently designated Le Centre, the core of the old town now boasted pedestrian zones. Boutiques and smart shops joined a new wave of restaurants and bars. The Deux Garçons remained a fa-miliar landmark on the cours, but the venerable café seemed al-most exclusively patronized by students dressed in Levis, sloppy gray pullovers, and clogs, with an occasional Italian "buck" in a skintight leather suit and orange crash helmet roaring up on a Moto Guzzi mo-torcycle.

Mary Frances and Norah decided to make Aix their home for the next few months and began searching for an apartment that was within their budget. Following a tip from the hotel's concierge, they found one on the rue Brueys, two short blocks from the cours, town hall, cathedral, and Rotonde. It featured one very large room on the first floor, with newly painted white walls, red tile floors, authentic black beams across the ceiling, a kitchen alcove, and a large dressing room. Mary Frances told Eleanor, "Norah works every day at the Bibliothèque Mejane, and this time 'round may actually get that book [on Mary Magdalene] into shape! I work here at the apartment, and while I feel that I'm creaking with rust, I'm at least *working* after 2+ dead years. We buzz all day with small delightful jobs: a long drink on the Cours, the wonderful open markets, an occasional concert or movie—walk a lot, eat lightly but very well, drink rosés and dark vermouth with an occasional gin for a spree—sleep well."[25] The only discordant note was the noise from motorcycles racing by outside from morning until late at night.

Beginning on May 30, the Humphrey Stones vacationed in Aix for ten days, followed by the Childs, who were en route to a series of cooking classes at the Gritti Palace in Venice. Mary Frances and Norah had arranged a long and leisurely lunch for them at an outdoor café, and while symptoms of aphasia were obvious in Paul's groping for words and frequent mood shifts, the meal brought back memories of happier times. So did Mary Frances's reunion with Eda, who came for a visit after a winter of cobalt treatments for cancer of the throat, looking wasted and very ill. When she departed for England, they both knew it would be their last visit.

Later in June, the Joneses, accompanied by Judith's mother and aunt, arrived and stayed at the Roi René for a week. By Judith's account, Mary Frances made the elderly women feel young and even flirtatious. Lingering over aperitifs on the crowded cours, Mary Frances entertained them with stories about Aix and the happy periods of her life spent there.[26] Nowhere was the hold that time past exerted over time present more evident than in Mary Frances's letters to her daughters. "There are so many things I see and hear that make me think of you," she wrote. "You are children I see, and *lycéennes*, and, and—I see you coming down the Cours, out of a movie, in the market—It's very nice, and I feel lucky."[27] Living in Aix turned back the clock to a brighter time when Mary Frances was needed as a mother and was compelled to write.

On July 9, 1976, Mary Frances received a cable informing her of Arnold Gingrich's death. Because she knew that he had dreaded a drawn-out dying, his quick death was a relief, but also one more loss to reconcile. When his associates asked her to write a testimonial, however, she told Kennedy, "No sir! I admired the man for 35+ years, with growing affection and enjoyment, and any 'anecdotes and comments' I might make would hardly be of general interest."[28] She chose to remain silent on the bond that had answered some deep need in both of their lives, and the empty space left by the cessation of his frequent gifts, almost daily letters, wit and publishing gossip, constant praise for her writing, and love.

At the end of July, Mary Frances and Norah flew from Marseilles to England to visit the Stones and their two daughters, Mary Frances's godchildren. "It seemed like a good piece of preventive therapy," she wrote in her journal. "And seeing the Stones, if an extra demand on our strength, will most probably be tonic too—the wee children, the renewed contact with Humphrey and Solveig, our mutual affections. How wily we are being, how self protective."[29] Seeking "to make a neat and tidy re-entry into Earth-orbit," they arrived in San Francisco on August 4, spent a night at the Clift Hotel, and returned to their respective homes the following day. "The re-entry was chancy," Mary Frances wrote. "But by now Norah and I know its risks and seem to have handled it quite well."[30]

During the months after their return, Mary Frances revised and sent a story about the constant noise in Aix to Rachel MacKenzie at *The New Yorker*, and she set the beginning of 1977 as a personal deadline for completing the Marseilles book. She had written various chapters over a period of time and worked on it in Aix without books or reference materials, so she had to review everything and decide what was lacking. The process proved to be time-consuming and tedious. When the Joneses visited in October, she felt that she had a better perspective on what remained to be written, but as always, she chafed at editorial suggestions, however well meant. Often when Jones pointed out repetitions of words or phrases to her, Mary Frances solved the problem by dropping the passage. "She simply disliked going over her own work,"[31] said Jones. By mid-November, Mary Frances told Jones, "I have a general plan: an introduction, 3 or 4 sections on the men and women and the Old Port, and then a conclusion. But if you read the stuff in pieces, it may take a more interesting form, as happened with that lovely job you did on shaping *Among Friends*. It is a real bore, right now, to get this stuff ready to read. It involves my long hand, then revising, then sending to Napa to be typed from the cassette I have made, then correcting, etc., etc. But if it pleases you, what does it matter?"[32]

As the holidays approached, Mary Frances told Norah that she hoped the completion of the Marseilles book would redeem her year "to whimper."

> Now and then I say it is nothing but self-pity, but that is not quite true. I feel very *angry* about the way people have to exit. It was cruel to make Eda submit to an obviously useless surgical interference so late in the game. After that biopsy, why not just keep her warm and as comfortable as possible? DAMN. As for Arnold, I do *not* think he should have had almost three months of kimotherapy [sic] for the terminal lung cancer that had progressed to his brain before it was even detected lower down. DAMN. As for Bob Steele, he chose to sweat it out, and while the last months of life were increasingly sad, he died as "naturally" as one can with Parkinson's . . . at least peacefully and among dear friends. Now about Ranieri [San Faustino]: The first tumor has shrunk a little, but a new "node" has developed. And so on. DAMN.[33]

Because of her husband's prognosis, Genie San Faustino planned to give up their lease on the Hexagon for the coming year. Their absence at the ranch would be one more loss.

After the New Year, *The New Yorker* renewed Mary Frances's annual "first reading" agreement, even though William Shawn had rejected her article on "noise pollution" in Aix, citing the need to make the magazine less nostalgic, and Tim Seldes suggested that she turn down the agreement. But she had been working on several short pieces that she felt only *The New Yorker* would publish, and after what she considered an interminable year of contrived Bicentennial cookbooks and food articles, she was "itching" to do some gastronomical reviews for the magazine. Moreover, she sensed that the momentum she had gained while completing the Marseilles book would carry over into other projects.

That January she gave up her "disciplining" journal, which was usually reserved for periods of depression, and she sent a piece on "beachers"—beach picnics—to Frances Ring, the current editor of *Westways*, the automobile club magazine. "I plan to write some more stuff for it, because I want to break away a little from the NYer set-pieces. They take good hard work, but I like to do looser stuff too. I have a few things planned in both patterns."[34] After establishing a good working relationship with Ring, who continually strove to upgrade the literary content of the magazine, Mary Frances proposed a series of articles on California cooks, chili, enchiladas, the Wappo Indians, "Slow Stuff," and Halloween.[35] Jones also urged her to start pulling together material for a possible third book on Provence in a trilogy begun with *Map of Another Town* and "the Marseille book."

In July, Mary Frances met with Jones in New York over some details relating to the Marseilles book, and she also talked to her about arranging a meeting with Robert Lescher. Years earlier Mary Frances had been introduced to him when he was Robert Steele's editor, and he and his fiancée, Susan, had crossed paths with her during the winter she spent on Long Island. Now that he was well established as a literary agent, Mary Frances thought that she would feel more comfortable with him than with Harriet Wasserman, who was handling most of her affairs at Russell & Volkening, and she decided to take the appropriate steps to end her long relationship with the agency that had served her so well. Mary Frances and Norah then spent a week at Eleanor's home in Bridgehampton, where the effect of the ocean and the company of the artists and writers she had met there over the years proved to be calming.

Knopf published *A Considerable Town* in the spring of 1978. "The book about Marseille is a series of explanations of what I've seen and sensed there," she wrote to Rachel MacKenzie. "I suppose it's rather like *Map of Another Town*, but of course I'm not the person who wrote that."[36] Different in focus and tone, *A Considerable Town* was the work of M.F.K. Fisher the *flâneuse*, or stroller, who went wherever caprice or curiosity led her. Recounting her experiences of Marseilles from her first visit as a young bride in 1929 to her extended residence in 1973, she gave herself over to a series of moments that had played out in the old city. The history, scenes, and sensual appeal of the place, as well as the quality she called *insolite* (mysterious, unknowable, indefinable) that she tried to convey to her readers, also drew something indefinable out of her as a writer. In no other context does M.F.K. Fisher paint a gastronomical still life with quite the same brush strokes, as evident in this description of a typical Marseilles restaurant: "Often, in a window opening onto the street, as a crown of the display inside, there will be a kind of *pièce montée*, a Dali or Carême sculpture of one stunningly graceful *loup*, posed for an endless second with a great pink shrimp in its mouth, as it leaps from a high wave of smaller red and blue and silver fishes over piles of oysters, mussels, urchins, clams." Scattered throughout *A Considerable Town* are also lush descriptions of the flower market, eerie speculations about a blood-spattered concrete sidewalk, images of short hefty Marseillais driving taxis along the Canebière, and glimpses of the shrill-voiced fishwives selling the daily catch on the quai des Belges.

Introducing the book with an item taken from an eighteenth-century map of Marseilles that identified the city as "a considerable town of Provence," Mary Frances imposes a personal vision on France's second city. She describes the port as the scene of a manhunt that delayed the sailing of the *Feltre*, the Italian freighter on which she, Al, and Norah were booked in 1932. She re-creates the restaurant where, as a guest of Dillwyn's mother, she embarrassed her hostess by ordering not one but two dozen Belon oysters for a first course. Doctors and interns come to life when she is rushed to a hospital for treatment after a bad fall from a curb. (Here she invents a context for her notes on the differences between American and French medical practitioners.) Throughout the book she concentrates on the changes wrought by time: the metamorphosis of La Criée when the legendary fish market moved from the quai des Belges to a cave of a building on the Rive Neuve, and the slow decline of the restaurant Mont Ventoux from elegance to closure.

In no other book, moreover, does M.F.K. Fisher's fascination with the supernatural come across more convincingly, although it is a theme of other occult tales like "A Possible Possession,"[37] "The Lost, Strayed, Stolen,"[38] and "Legend of Love."[39] Marseilles's reputation as the world's wickedest port, based upon a history of plagues, invasions, crimes, drug trafficking, and prostitution, created an indefinable karma that M.F.K. Fisher believed to exist "in pockets on this planet filled with what humans have left behind them, both good and evil, and . . . any such spiritual accumulation can stay there forever, past definition of such a stern word."[40] Within the range of her experience, Stonehenge was one such locale, radiating good or evil depending on "one's ability to accept non-Christian logic." But there were other places—the cathedral in Dijon, the deserted ancient town of Les Baux, and a small village she called Askhaven in England,[41] where the aura of evil spirits was so overwhelming that Mary Frances knew she had to leave the place at once.

Neither malevolent like Les Baux nor serene like Mission San Juan Capistrano,[42] Marseilles had a deeply religious spirit that countered its violent history. The city "is 'Christian' now, in the sense that this form of worship is the last manifestation of its ageless need for altars, altars behind altars, idols behind idols. It needs something to shout to and to dance around, to curse and to beseech, and because it is a natural gathering place on the globe for such human necessities, saints and sinners have collected there around the Vieux Port as irrevocably as water runs downhill."[43] The sight of the gold statue at the pinnacle of Notre-Dame de la Garde near the entrance to the Vieux Port was always her first glimpse of Marseilles, whether from bus or train. "And there she was! Across the crowded waters of the Vieux Port, high in the sky, golden in the sunlight, the colossal statue seemed to ride the basilica, the fortress, the Crag, the city itself, as if she were the figurehead of a ship forever safe from danger. I knew that at night she would be lighted, a symbol to tired travelers and ships at sea, and that the grave sound of her mighty bell would ring for them, for me."[44] Still, it was the fortune-tellers, cabalistic signs, tarot cards, and teeming life in the deep warrens that stretched from the quai du Port that excited Mary Frances's imagination and sent her strolling along streets and into squares where the guillotine once stood and layers of ancient bones were buried.

Marseilles also represented the beginning and the end of many of her journeys and was the scene of holidays with her children and short escapes from the routine of their studies, as well as the setting for meals with a husband, a former husband, and a husband to be. With her sister she had gone through the paces of day-to-day living there, improvising meals, entertaining friends, leisurely discovering a surly fishwife here and a majestic bouillabaisse there, visiting a midsummer garlic fair and a wintry *foire aux santons*. The pace of her strolling allowed her to take in every detail and "explain why the place haunts me and draws me, with its phoenix-like vitality, its implacably realistic beauty and brutality."[45] The equation of Marseilles and *insolite* helped her to understand the connection between the town and herself, and provided more than a hint about why she had returned there so often between 1929 and 1978.

Although M.F.K. Fisher's literary reputation does not rest on *A Considerable Town*, within the canon of her works the book is important. She wrote it at a time when she doubted her ability to write another book, and it proved to be her last book that was not, in the main, a collection or reconfiguration of works written and/or published earlier. When *A Considerable Town* appeared in the spring of 1978, admiring reviewers welcomed another "distinctly *un*-city book from dear M.F.K. Fisher—'dear' because Mrs. Fisher stands to so many of us, wherever we live, in the office of an endlessly entertaining and slightly mysterious aunt. She has written one such book before, about Aix-la-Chapelle [*sic*], but in *A Considerable Town* she develops the genre much further, and weaves a meditative, discursive, and sometimes enigmatic spell about that Chicago of European seaports, Marseille."[46] Other reviews, like Anatole Broyard's in the daily *New York Times*, were more qualifying in their praise, citing "a good tour," but a failure to look deeply into the soul of the city.[47] Increasingly critics judged her work against Auden's 1963 comment, more often than not quoted out of context: "I do not know of anyone in the United States today who writes better prose."[48] As Broyard was quick to note, not only was that statement a bit extravagant, "but that celebrated prose stylist several times uses 'hopefully' as a dangling adverbial modifier."[49] Taking a knock-her-off-the-pedestal tone, other critics drew attention to stylistic tics that a copy editor ought to have gently discouraged. And Rhoda Koenig questioned the tone of Fisher's vignettes, "more *New Yorker* than Marseillais—many of the stories— Christmas in a hotel room, an encounter with an angry taxi driver, a walk with some nervous visitors—end on a note that is mildly benign or mildly quizzical or mildly despairing—anyway, mild."[50] M.F.K. Fisher's devoted coterie of readers, however, welcomed the book.

Meanwhile, Mary Frances's influence continued to be felt in the expanding culinary community, and Carol Brock, founder and president of the New York chapter of Les Dames d'Escoffier, an organization now a few years old, wrote to Mary Frances about their wish to confer the title of Grande Dame on her, as they had previously bestowed it on Julia Child and Ella Brennan. "At first," Mary Frances told Eleanor, "I was rather sniffy about them . . . a bunch of food PR people, I thought. But now I know more about the group, and approve its aims to make qualified females welcome in large fine kitchens. So I agreed to be there . . . I've made it clear that I don't want my 'appearance' tied in at all with the publication of the Marseille book. I'm hoping Norah will feel like coming along . . . I'm really quite at a loss on planes and getting into taxis and so on. But I don't want her to feel like a Guide Dog."[51] Between the invitation and the actual event on April 29, 1978, plans changed from a "noon-thing on a cruising yacht" around Manhattan to a gala dinner at the New York Public Library. As requested, Mary Frances sent a suggested guest list that included Julia and Paul Child, Judith and Evan Jones, William Maxwell and Edith Oliver from *The New Yorker*, Robert and Susan Lescher, Eleanor Friede, and Bert Greene, who had also been involved in planning the event, which was now headlined "An Evening in Honor of M.F.K. Fisher." Mary Frances told Child, "I've got a new 'outfit' (About time!), all of which will stay invisible behind the dinner table. But I'll feel fine, inside. On to Marseille! Or Aix! Or or or . . ."[52]

Having decided to use the trip to New York City as a stepping-stone to another visit to Provence, Mary Frances and Norah flew to Marseilles on April 30 and then went on to Aix and Le Tholonet. With only one month abroad planned, they decided to make a base at Thome, the village inn, traveling to other places on the weekends to escape the influx of guests at the lengthy *fiançailles* (betrothals) and christening parties, "all very noisy and Breughelish," that took place on the château grounds. The arrangement proved to be congenial, and they spent a weekend apiece in Marseilles and Nice, and two weekends with the Childs at La Pitchoune.

With taping of the *Julia Child and Company* television series completed, the Childs were looking forward to a summer of relaxation. Mary Frances, Norah, and Genie di San Faustino, who had joined them for a week, found Julia and Paul in good spirits and La Pitchoune bathed in sunshine. The grasses that stretched across the meadow in front of the house were green and lush, and the roses that grew beyond the shaded terrace were in bloom. At noon they typically dined on the front terrace in the shade of the mulberry tree that Paul had planted in 1970. Child would prepare dishes like zucchini blossoms dipped in "Beard-Child Beer Batter," boned and stuffed chicken, mesclun salad, and cheese. Crisp white wine enhanced the meal, which often lasted far into the afternoon. During one of these visits Julia mentioned that *A Considerable Town* was not exactly her own impression of Marseilles, which dated back to her residence there in 1951. Mary Frances agreed that they were bound to have experienced the city in completely different ways. The visit remained, as Child said, "familial" and as it should be.

But other aspects of the trip were not so idyllic. While in Le Tholonet, Mary Frances developed a sore throat and a harsh cough, and her arthritis worsened, limiting her walking. When it was time to leave on June 5, she thanked Norah for tolerating her slow pace and bothersome coughing during the trip. From the Nice airport to Glen Ellen they were twenty-four hours in transit. Mary Frances described the Nice–Paris segment of the trip aboard an Air France carrier as the only civilized part of the "basically non-human and tedious experience . . . At 10:30 a.m. a handsome steward begged us to accept a glass or two of Moet Brut, with four really delicious little sandwiches. From then it was downhill all the way."[53] Although traveling was increasingly difficult, her words also reflected the fact that her opinions, always forthright, were becoming more critical as she approached her seventieth birthday.

Perhaps nowhere was her "bite" more apparent than in her appraisal of many of the young women entering the culinary field who visited Last House. "I seem to be in a period of knowing lively, attractive, ambitious (ruthless) women who write about gastronomy in general," she wrote to Child, "and most of them have been influenced by Julia Child . . . followed you around when last you were in San Francisco . . . stayed one week with Simca [enrolled in her cooking classes in Plascassier], etc."[54] Frequently they wrote about their first visit to Last House, describing their attempts to create the right impression with a gift of food, and, of course, the meal shared with "the gastronomical she." Mary Frances's demeanor to them was always hospitable, but her comments about them to others were frequently scathing. Rosemary Manell brought up an aspiring chef whom Mary Frances described as a "prototype of every over-bright striving Jewish girl who ever fought her way through universities in New York, Princeton, and finally on to Taiwan! She now explains with delicate somewhat Oriental gestures the past-present-future significance of every dish, bowl, spice, and whiff of every dish she presents."[55] Mary Frances labeled the cook and the "ToFy" dishes boring. "As far as I know," she wrote to Norah, "she never studied cooking, or even *cooked*. But by now she is establishing herself in 'food circles' as an authority on all Chinese cuisine . . . Like Americans who have lived a year in Germany or Italy, she rattles off long sentences and then smirks as she apologizes, and even in Basic English her talk, which never ceases, is liberally smattered with strange vocal howls which she says are Chinese expressions."[56]

Not all of her visitors, however, were so summarily dismissed. Possibly in one of her "testing" modes, Mary Frances extended an invitation to Marion Cunningham and Alice Waters, the young owner-chef of Berkeley's Chez Panisse, to join her for lunch at Last House on March 6, 1978. Searching for something to bring to a writer she greatly admired, Alice filled a basket with Araucana eggs, wild chanterelle mushrooms, a few handfuls of salad greens, and a few bottles of Domaine Tempier Bandol rosé wine. "Our hostess was disarmingly gracious," Alice recalled, "but when she said how flattered and pleased she was that I offered to cook, and asked with eager curiosity what lunch was to be and what I had brought in my basket, it became uncomfortably apparent that we had not perfectly understood one another on the telephone . . . Perhaps she had slyly planned to test the resourcefulness and sincerity of my cooking . . . Lunch was a success."[57]

When Alice proposed a small party at Chez Panisse to celebrate

Mary Frances's seventieth birthday, Mary Frances accepted but wrote
to Norah, "I'm glad you don't mind giving me more moral support at
another quiet little birthday party that threatens to be a bash. Thank
God for your support. I mean, I was indeed turned off yesterday when
I got Alice Waters' latest bulletin including a printed invitation. It
proved me wrong again, or at least 'naïve until death,' as Timmy said I
would be. But I think it is a genuine like for me that lets her invite a
few PR people to her quiet little bash . . . God knows what we'll eat
disguised as garlic."[58] The dinner, on the evening of July 25, 1978,
proved to be memorable. Using the titles of some of M.F.K. Fisher's
books, the meal consisted of a selection of oysters in remembrance of
Consider the Oyster, followed by four courses redolent of Marseilles.
A Considerable Town inspired snails sauced with Pernod, tomatoes,
and garlic; charcoal-grilled rockfish with wild herbs and anchovies;
spit-roasted pheasant; bitter lettuces with goat cheese croutons; and
three plum sorbets in orange-rind boats. The dinner concluded with a
Muscat de Beaumes-de-Venise suggested by *A Cordiall Water*. A few
years later, Mary Frances remembered the evening as a culinary highlight and the restaurant as "quite an experience . . . You must get
there, by hook or crook, when next you are near San Francisco," she
wrote to Eleanor. "It's a small restaurant run by my young friend Alice
in its tenth year by now, and very famous. Really, the food is the best
I have eaten in America . . . in a public place, I mean."[59]

Just as M.F.K. Fisher's name on an event drew crowds, a "blurb"
by her sold books, and the supplicants were many. Frequently she indulged the author but voiced her disdain for the book to others. "I 'accomplished' another letter to a writer," she wrote to Norah. "I find this
an increasing chore in deception and ambiguity . . . People send me
their books to 'criticize,' but God forbid that I do. Well, I did it again,
and although the book makes me gag quietly . . . I think I showed it to
you . . . a world-shaking new theory that since we must eat to live, we
should enjoy it . . . [The author] finds big cocktail parties very 'sensual' because of all the finger-food. She likes *dîners à deux*, where one
eats in the bedroom, ending with very smooth chocolate mousse in
two goblets but with one spoon."[60] Established authors also came
within her shooting range. She gingerly referred to Raymond Sokolov's
Saucier's Apprentice as "a mixture of commonsense and 19th Century

romanticism," its author "a blushing newcomer, an amateur fumbling his way toward the sauce pots . . . The Woody Allen of *la haute cuisine*."[61]

At the same time, she urged on those she admired to greater literary heights. James Beard ought to write another book in the narrative style that had distinguished his autobiographical *Delights and Prejudices*.[62] Child should "write something that is completely for *you* without any editorial demands except your own and Paul's. End of presumptuous and unsolicited opinion."[63] Yet she herself continued to write introductions to other people's books. They simply asked, and she obliged whenever possible, and there seemed to be no pattern to the various introductions that she began writing in 1952. Sometimes the subject—tea, California food and wine, a train station—was congenial. Sometimes the author—Angelo Pellegrini, Alice B. Toklas, Maurice Chevalier—was someone she respected or found fascinating. Often she honored a request because of friendship.

In the fall of 1978 Mary Frances's longtime friend Shizuo Tsuji asked her to introduce his *Japanese Cooking: A Simple Art*. To prepare for the assignment, she accepted his offer of a two-week trip to Japan to sample the cuisine of that country and observe its preparation. Tsuji was the James Beard / Jacques Pepin / Julia Child of Japanese cooking, with a series of cooking schools, publications, and disciples dedicated to Japanese *ryori* (national food) at its best. He had also studied French *haute cuisine* and offered postgraduate courses in both Chinese and French cuisine at the École Technique Hôtelière Tsuji, his school in Osaka. An admirer of Mary Frances's prose, he had met her about twenty-five years earlier after she wrote to him for information about sake for the Wine Library, and he in turn requested information about the Foire Gastronomique in Dijon. Whenever he was in San Francisco he invited her to dinner, and Mary Frances had entertained him and his associates in her home, but she never expected the one-step-below-the-imperial-family hospitality that he proposed to lavish upon her now.

She took Norah with her, and they arrived in Osaka on October 1. Mary Frances kept a journal of the markets they visited, the private classes with Tsuji and his chefs, the exquisite multicourse tasting dinners in Osaka, Kobe, Kyoto, and Tokyo, as well as the private luncheons at the school and in renowned noodle and tempura shops. With a new appreciation for the aesthetic, cultural, traditional, and religious aspects of Japanese food, Mary Frances concluded, "After two weeks in Japan I must admit with real astonishment that if I could eat as I did there under my friend's subtle guidance, I would gladly turn my back on Western food and live on Japanese *ryori* for the rest of my life."[64]

Mary Frances was thrilled by much of what she experienced—the visual excitement of unfamiliar vegetables, the seduction of a good dashi, the symbolism of "one thin slice of molded fish puree shaped like a maple leaf and delicately colored orange and scarlet, to celebrate autumn; a tiny hut made of carved ice, with a little fish inside made of chestnut paste and a chestnut made of fish paste; to remind a guest that he was born on a far-north island, an artfully stuffed lobster riding an angry sea of curled waves of white radish cut paper-thin."[65] But her experience of Japan was dimmed by her sense of the enormousness of the cultural gap between East and West. The language barrier was obvious; less so was what Mary Frances called "the latent paranoia" induced by the country's constant overcrowding. She deplored the almost militaristic discipline that kept order in the streets, the crowded transportation system, the teeming sidewalks. She objected to the omnipresent male dominance and to the nation's dedication to amassing great wealth, exemplified in the rare delicacies available only to the rich.

Although she was determined to "strike while the iron was hot" and write the introduction to Tsuji's book as soon as she returned home, it proved to be more difficult than she had anticipated. "It's really very hard to keep it straight-line gastronomy . . . I keep shooting off on 'asides and footnotes' . . . everything from chauvinism both national and male, plumbing, even toothpicks (They might qualify?)," she wrote to Jones. "I'm trying to write as a naïve (dumb dumb) awkward Westerner . . . it would be presumptuous to be anything else, after two weeks in Osaka!"[66] In an earlier letter, Mary Frances had made the same comments to the Childs, adding, "I went into a kind of doze when I got back from Japan, partly on purpose. I could not see how to write two consecutive words about the whole experience. Then on November 12 it all fell into fine clear focus, and I got a lot done and planned the whole job."[67]

Three days later Mary Frances experienced severe abdominal pain and was rushed to the emergency room at the Sonoma hospital for what she called a "surgical caper" to remove some scar tissue that had grown around an adhesion from an operation in 1941. The operation and recovery proved to be traumatic. Under the influence of painkillers and sleeping pills, she fantasized horrible plots against her. The television suspended in the corner of the room became a malignant eye recording her every move, and the nurses were demonic. It was only after she was moved from the recovery room to her own private room, where she spoke to Kennedy and Norah, that she realized she had processed the televised tragedy of Jonestown, Guyana (where the members of a California-based religious cult were forced to commit mass suicide), as one long hallucinatory attack on her sanity. "Suddenly I was lying like a drugged animal in a glass box in Sonoma, and there the two women were, drawn together by something much stronger than any other tricks of Time and Circumstance," Mary Frances wrote to Jones. "Now that I am well and strong again, they may never really meet again. But I know that Kennedy was given new strength and confidence while they were together."[68] Despite the postoperation nightmare, Mary Frances was serene in the thought that after many years of estrangement, her daughter and her sister had reconciled their differences because of her great need.

Returning to Last House, Mary Frances healed slowly, but her voice had been reduced to a whisper. The throat specialist prescribed cortisone to treat what he diagnosed as a paralyzed vocal chord, not uncommon in postoperative states. "For the first time since The Pickle [recent operation] I am having to be a little dogged about depression-apprehension-the blues. That is why I am telling you about it," she wrote to Norah. "I wonder how I could stand to speak for the rest of my days in this breathy croak . . . how I could ever dictate letters or material . . . what dear little children like Lukie and Oliver and Alex and Chris and Sylvie would think of me . . . how people I love to talk with could sustain even tolerable chitchat with me."[69] She had been forewarned to do as little talking as possible, and in a state of deep dismay she replayed the tapes that she had recorded when working on the Marseilles book to listen to the way she used to sound.

By December 20, 1978, Mary Frances's voice was still "squeaky" but sufficiently audible to give a brief address to the first twenty-nine graduates of the California Culinary Academy in San Francisco. She considered the academy, like the Napa Valley Wine Library, a cause worthy of promotion. In her remarks she noted, "A lot of you will go on as professionals, which I have never been . . . and I tremble for you. I worry about you, because of what you are getting into, in this age-old yet challenging business of nourishing people. You already know how the history of eating is really the history of mankind itself . . . wars, plagues, invasions and inventions. Human hunger, and its satisfaction, is the root of everything that has happened, before and after that apple in the Garden of Eden." She admired their dedication and hard work and hoped for their integrity in a world of fast food, convenience foods, substitutes, fillers, and stretchers. That eleven of the graduates were young women pleased her greatly. James Beard was visiting San Francisco at the time, and Mary Frances had invited him to join her at the graduation, adding even more excitement to what a San Francisco Chronicle columnist called "a landmark event for San Francisco gastronomy."[70]

The following spring Mary Frances was asked be a keynote speaker at the dedication of the new Napa Valley Public Library, where the Napa Valley Wine Library would have its own wing. Since the beginning of the organization in 1963, the collection of books and materials on wine making, grape growing, and the history of the wine trade had grown to more than a thousand volumes. Its annual wine tastings had become a showcase for Napa Valley wines, and its wine-tasting courses had been repeated some seventy times.

As the last day of the last month of the 1970s drew near, Mary Frances sent greetings to her friends. To Judith Jones she expressed her reluctance to assemble the pieces from the past for the "Places" book, and to Norah she recounted "a really fine dinner party" in a Sonoma restaurant on December 29 with the Childs, Alice Waters, Bob Finigan, Gene Quint, Richard Foorman, and Rosemary Manell. The next day when the bell in the tower on the Bouverie Ranch rang in the 1980s, her thoughts were of New Years past—with Dillwyn in Delaware, with Rex in Whittier, and alone in Bridgehampton, where she had toasted in the 1970s. During the next few months of 1980 she would write:

It is very simple: I am here because I choose to be . . . My eyes are undependable by now, so I do not drive. A young friend takes me marketing once a week. And my legs are not trustworthy, so I have given up walking that can be wonderful here on the Ranch . . . I move about fairly surely and safely in my *palazzino*, and water the plants on the two balconies. I devise little "inside picnics" and "nursery teas" for people who like to sit in the Big Room and drink some of the good wines that grow and flow in these northern valleys. I work hard and happily on good days, and on the comparatively creaky ones I pull my Japanese comforter over the old bones, on my big purple bedspread . . . and wait for the never-failing surcease.[71]

The decade of "other places" was over.

EIGHTEEN

Garments of Adieu

(1980–1992)

The lost self changes,
Turning toward the sea,
. . .
In robes of green, in garments of adieu.[1]
—Theodore Roethke

Although the 1940s had been M.F.K. Fisher's most productive period, the 1980s would be the apogee of her public recognition. At Knopf, Judith Jones encouraged and supported her efforts to complete a book on various places that had been especially meaningful to her, and she urged Mary Frances to finish her old-age project. In 1981 the newly founded Berkeley-based North Point Press began a vigorous program of reissuing M.F.K. Fisher's books in handsome paperback editions. A series of beautifully printed limited editions of *Spirits of the Valley*, *The Standing and the Waiting*, *Answer in the Affirmative*, *The Oldest Living Man*, and *The Boss Dog* was also published. And M.F.K. Fisher's introduction to Judith Clancy's drawings of the Gare de Lyon, *Not a Station But a Place*, was a loving tribute to the first-class restaurant buffet that had been a way station on many of Mary Frances's comings and goings.

Articles and interviews ran in magazines and newspapers ranging from *Ms.*, *Omni*, *Newsweek*, and *Bon Appetit* to *The New York Times*, *Los Angeles Times*, *San Francisco Chronicle*, and *The Boston Globe*, most of them repeating Auden's famous quote and including elaborate descriptions of Last House and whatever foods and wines the reporter had sampled there. The journalists also took away Mary Frances's tales, tall and otherwise, about writing jokes for Bob Hope in Hollywood, Rex's long-standing feud with William Randolph Hearst, and Al Fisher's near-neurosis when a Gypsy's warning that he would be either rich and famous or dead by the time he was thirty didn't come true. M.F.K. Fisher became the most quoted and quotable gastronomic grande dame in the ever-expanding American culinary landscape. Even her two calico cats, Zazie and Nipa, became iconic features of the scene.

Like them, she played an intriguing game of cat and mouse: inevitably amusing yet unpredictable, too, a woman who could purr contentedly one minute and rake with her claws the next. She had a habit of baiting those who entered her orbit, and then deciding whether she would invite them to remain there or not. For example, there was the young writer who visited Last House and later discovered a dead mouse in her totebag, and the woman who desperately wanted to write an "official" biography and was stopped dead in her tracks. Mary Frances was described as "the existential epicure," "an American Colette," "a national treasure," "the doyenne of food," "a culinary pornographer," and "the Sonoma Sibyl," and she increasingly used visitors as a vicarious means of escaping Last House and as a distraction from her writing.

The book on places, which Lescher and Jones thought she could easily pull together by using previously published and unpublished material, posed more difficulties than she thought it was worth. In September 1980 she abandoned it because going over her own material again proved to be so difficult, and because the treatment of a palsy-like condition, as yet undiagnosed, brought about periods of mental confusion. She described her reaction to the medications she was using: "Within 24 hours I had never known anything like it: I could not finish a letter, a thought, I could not decide a simple financial problem. I felt scrambled. I was an impotent, helpless mess."[2] In desperation she wrote to Jones that she could not complete the places book: "This back-out, tossing in the towel, reneging, was extremely painful, as you more than anyone but perhaps Norah will understand."[3]

That she seemed to be deteriorating physically at a rapid pace led her to question if she could continue to be a creative and self-sustaining person:

> It is a strange admission, but I think I can state honestly at this point in my life that I doubt that ever again I do any real work at my job, which has been to use words in order to tell other people about what may be important to them . . .
>
> But now I feel tired. I want to stop. But I don't know what will happen when I do, and that puzzles me and perhaps scares me a little.
>
> Later still . . . I am wondering how firm and all-encompassing this decision is. For instance, do I stop reading and replying to mail? Do I ditch all the admiring and even loyal admirers? And do I stop paying bills? . . . I feel tired and such tiredness is the enemy.
>
> I suppose that is why I want to stop being MFK Fisher. I never had any idea I *was* this small image until a few years ago, and now I feel humble about it, and startled.
>
> So do I have a printed statement made, to send to any and all correspondents except my purveyors of heat and light . . . ? "Mary Frances Fisher thanks you for your letter, and regrets she cannot reply, except with all good wishes."[4]

Despite what she wrote in her journal, however, Mary Frances's appointment calendar for the fall of 1980 noted visits with the Los Angles–based journalist Ruth Reichl, her old friend Ward Ritchie, James Beard, Marion Cunningham, and an initial interview with Marsha Moran, the young Glen Ellen woman she would soon hire as her secretary. And it was in the midst of this time that William Turnbull and Jack Shoemaker, North Point's publisher and editor in chief respectively, came to make their case for a series of reprints that they had previously explored with Robert Lescher. More than ten years later she wrote, "Dear Bill and Dearest Sir, which is the way I always think of you . . . I remember the first time you came here. I felt very shy and was surprised and appalled to hear myself refuse you the rights to publish a novel and instead urged you to bring out a book that had not sold at all well . . . So I suggested that you republish as a tri-cake *A Cordiall Water*, and as I remember, I felt very sheepish sending you off looking rather downcast and disappointed."[5] There was, however, an immediate synergy between North Point's mission and Mary Frances's personal and financial needs. She developed a strong friendship with Shoemaker and Turnbull, and a social relationship with their small, dedicated staff and other North Point authors, like Evan Connell, Michael McClure, and Anne Lamott, which was sparked by annual North Point staff picnics, often held on the Bouverie Ranch.

When *A Cordiall Water* came out in 1981, Clifton Fadiman hailed its publication. "The North Point Press, a brave little outfit in Berkeley, Calif., has just retrieved for us *A Cordiall Water*, first published in 1961. Of all her works, M.F.K. likes this best . . . She may be right."[6] Seeing her favorite book in print again was a psychological boost, and it, together with a visit from the Joneses in December of that year, seemed to have ended Mary Frances's block about resuming work on the places book.

In January 1981 she decided to hire Norah to assist her in reviewing cartons of previously written pieces, some published, some not, from which she selected twenty. Starting with a brief introduction to the neighbors and friends who populated her childhood memories of Whittier and contributed to her self-image as a "child of an inner ghetto" and ending with a description of Last House, she toured the "other places" that had become points of reference in her life: ice cream parlors in Los Angeles, Burgundy inns, kitchens in Provence, Laguna Beach, the Arles where she passed a solitary Christmas, the Gare de Lyon, and Eleanor's Bridgehampton beach house, among others. Food frequently framed the scenes. She remembered the sensual thrill of an "Easter Special" composed of several flavors of ice cream, sauces, and chopped nuts. She recalled the feeling of being "generous, warm, floaty" after breakfasting on French bread, sweet butter, Parma ham, and brut Champagne in the Gare de Lyon. She shared a wealth of simple experiences made complicated by circumstance. Taken together, the pieces formed a verbal kaleidoscope of secret palaces, private ghettos, lodestar kitchens, and enticing places that were intensely memorable to M.F.K. Fisher.

As They Were was a successful publication for Knopf, but also something of a critical conundrum. Raymond Sokolov's lengthy review in *The New York Times* paid tribute to the literary merit of Fisher's works over the past five decades, and he expressed hope that this new anthology would "take the gastronomic curse off Mrs. Fisher and convince a world quite ready to acclaim her as the doyenne of food writers that she deserves much higher status."[7] That someone highly regarded as a "food writer" and a brilliant stylist also continued to dazzle her audience with a much broader range of subjects was also noted in *The Christian Science Monitor* and the *San Francisco Chronicle*. In a *New Yorker* article called "Female Pilgrims," John Updike reviewed Louise Brooks's elegant little memoir *Lulu in Hollywood* and M.F.K. Fisher's *As They Were*. "Mrs. Fisher is, indeed, a poet of the appetites—what she calls, 'our three basic needs for protection, food, love.' Of the last, in her own life she tells us little in this collection . . . and sometimes expresses satisfaction in her withholding. This is autobiography as a highly articulate animal would write it, crammed with sensual event and devoid of social rationale."[8]

Some reviewers were harsher about Fisher's repetitions, eccentricities, and "cutout characters to support a ferociously narcissistic vision," as Carolyn See wrote in the *Los Angeles Times*. "Fisher, because she is so passionate, headstrong, self-centered yet accessible, 'open' and yet so closed, makes the same demands on us as a supremely irritating friend."[9] Mary Frances commented on the review, "It was the only bad review the book has had. A really sour frustrated exhibit by a sour frustrated woman, who plainly hated to be handed a Fisher book to review."[10] She also claimed that in response to a "thank you letter" to her reviewer she received a "tearful apology."

Three months later she told Norah that she had "skimmed" *As They Were*, because she had been getting touching and even unsettling reactions from fans. In the process, she realized how mistaken she had been to refuse to read her published work all these years. "Thanks mostly to you and your patience with my distaste for my own stuff, it is all right . . . I found some of the stuff in the book quite interesting."[11] Although she found the story about motorcycle noises in Aix boring at times, she also discovered her preoccupation with the effects of sound, which had also appeared in her account of the holiday in Arles, in the crash of the storm on Long Island, and in the "blasty mariachi band in Chapala."

A few months later, however, her feelings about the book had shifted again. She objected to the title—"It's no good." She had wanted *Other Places*.[12] And in an exaggerated account she told an old friend, the lexicographer Sam Davis:

> I can't feel any real interest in the book, I am sorry to admit. It is the only thing I have ever published that has ever made its small advance, and it does something to my ego to feel that it is a phony. The reasons are now quite clear to me for this basic distaste. I wrote it, or rather compiled it, at the request of Judith Jones, my editor, in order to have a book about other places than Aix and Marseille so that Knopf could publish it in hardback, even as a flop, and then incorporate it in a three-book paper volume for Vintage . . . I have never done such an assigned job, and I froze on it and could never have brought it to Judith without my sister Norah's kind and patient help. And then Knopf changed places, and published and touted it as an autobiographical summary, and sold it separately to Vintage, and is publishing the other two books in a single "travel" volume . . . It is humbuggery. I resent having this book thought of as autobiography.[13]

She steadfastly referred to the twenty pieces as "reports," not memoirs.

In 1982 North Point Press reprinted M.F.K. Fisher's *Not Now But Now* with an afterword that revisited her reasons for writing it. She wrote about Donald Friede and Pat Covici's encouragement and her own hesitation about undertaking the novel. She also disavowed any resemblance between herself and the heroine, Jennie. "I decided to make up the whole thing and tell it through a person as totally as possible unlike myself, both physically and morally. I knew I could tell dreams and spin yarns, although always I must depend on some of my own experience." She then said, "The female Jennie appears everywhere, often with heedless cruelty or deliberate destruction to her docile associates, and then slips away in her little snakeskin shoes . . . Of course I had to borrow from my own life, since I do not remember any other."[14] Speculation about "was she or wasn't she" the prototype of Jennie dominated the reviews, which far outnumbered those garnered by the 1947 edition. Her perceived-to-be reclusive life on the Bouverie Ranch only served to generate more curiosity about the *real* M.F.K. Fisher.

"By now I have manufactured protective tricks, for pure survival," she had told an interviewer years earlier. "I am still affronted, or at least taken aback, by some type of assault upon my so-called privacy. But I know that if a person permits the kind of book I have written to be published, he or she must consider it *open*. I am basically naïve, as [Dillwyn] Parrish said of me, but I am also very conscientious, and I don't like to promise more than I can give. That is why some of my fan letters need a lot of attention: I have become another person's substitute for something. It pains me but it is my fault."[15] One of the paradoxes of Mary Frances's public persona was that few of her friends were really intimates, but she easily managed to make everyone who knew her feel needed and special. Her behavior was often interpreted as manipulation or seduction (and she was particularly charming and feminine when a man was present), and she knew how to invite, cajole, flirt, and joke her way into the limelight. But whenever a person came too close, she simply retreated.

In 1980, Mary Frances's "Why We Need a Women's Party" appeared in *Newsweek*,[16] followed in 1981 by an interview with Ruth Reichl in *Ms.* magazine.[17] Both pieces generated considerable commentary for M.F.K. Fisher's advocacy of a third alternative to the country's two-party electoral system. "They [journalists] think that I am a 'pioneer women's libber' and therefore will be a good object for an interview for some off-beat journal they free-lance for. They do not yet realize that women have been independent since Eve bit that apple," Mary Frances wrote in her journal. "I am no prophet or forerunner or whatever these young worshippers-at-the-shrine want me to be. I was raised to believe and know that men and women share an equal responsibility, for earning sustenance and raising wanted children."[18] Abhorring the shrill voices of "feminists," Mary Frances basically thought the women's movement was contrived and not particularly worthy of her attention. However, she also acknowledged that since the days in Laguna Beach when she earned less than Al for cleaning beach houses, she had known that women were consistently underpaid and underestimated. She applauded the rise of women from the prep station to executive chef in the culinary profession, and firmly believed that when Mary Cassatt "let herself be a woman, she painted in a way no man has ever tried to copy."[19]

Enlisting Mary Frances's name in another current cause, Alice Waters and the winemaker Richard Graff invited Mary Frances to be on the board of directors of the newly founded American Institute of Wine and Food. But Mary Frances did not like Graff and refused to allow her name to be used in the promotion of the group. When she reluctantly wrote an article for the inaugural issue of the AIWF-sponsored *Journal of Gastronomy*, she took aim at those who "love to cook" but lack taste and wrote about a "Mama Mia" spaghetti dinner to which she had been invited on Long Island that would have raised the hackles of any gourmet. It was the revenge of a culinary-literary sensibility over "rot-gut red" and "imitation Parmesan cheese."[20] When the editor David Thomson wrote to Mary Frances and suggested changes that would perhaps make the piece better, Mary Frances replied, "I really want to help you but simply cannot rewrite or gear my mind to do much more than thank you."[21]

She had also become very prickly about interviews. After an unpleasant exchange of letters over the inclusion of what she considered "off-the-cuff" remarks in an article in *Women's Wear Daily* in September,[22] she vowed never to give an interview for an article unless she had the right to approve its content before publication. When Maya Angelou interviewed her for a major article in *People* in October 1982, she insisted on reviewing the page proofs.

"I'm trying now to condense some 45 years of doing research on Old Age into a short introduction to the collection of stories Knopf will bring out next spring," she wrote to Larry Powell. "I think I told you . . . took a quick look at all the cartons of clippings and articles and notes and so on I'd gathered for so long, and simply baled them up, for Radcliffe. I'm too old to write what I always thought would be my 'best' job, and really I am not qualified to tackle it: I'm not a scientist or a sociologist or an economist or or or. And the so-called serious stuff about Old Age is already over-handled by everybody from Simone de Beauvoir to Dr. J. C. Gluckemhimer. So Norah and I took a good look at some old stuff, and I'd been writing about age for years."[23] Ten of the stories had been published in *The New Yorker* over a period of eighteen years, and some of the earliest—"The Oldest Man," "The Weather Within," and "Moment of Wisdom"—show the wonderful eye for detail and the personal voice that distinguish M.F.K. Fisher's style. Other stories, like "The Kitchen Allegory," a tale of how a mother prepares favorite foods for a visit with her daughter and grandson but fails to connect with them on any level, do not end so much as fade into a feeling of unease. And the stories that border on the supernatural, like "The Lost, Strayed, Stolen," in which an American tourist encounters lost souls in rural England, and "Diplomatic, Retired," a tale of an aging Foreign Service officer who meets his inner self, seem artificial and contrived.

Neither the title, *Sister Age*, nor the introductory narrative explain Mary Frances's interest in aging, a subject she claimed had preoccupied her since her twelfth year. Was it the presence of Grandmother Holbrook and visits from aging relatives during her childhood, and her sense of their isolation? Or did the many natural and self-inflicted deaths she grieved as a young woman result in a deep feeling of loss that always remained with her? Or was dying, surely as basic to human experience as eating, an art that she felt deserved far more attention than it received in the sterile world of modern medicine? She did not say.

When *Sister Age* was published in the spring of 1983, the book jacket touted: "Not only the best book she has ever written, it is one of the best anybody has written on [the] subject."[24] And with the growing interest in gerontology from the mid-1970s on and the popularizing of the theme in everything from Broadway plays like Edward Albee's *All Over* to self-help books, Mary Frances's book found a market and a niche. But critics like Michiko Kakutani of *The New York Times* observed that while many of the characters in these stories are approaching old age, their loneliness stems not from age but "from the fact that they either have no one to love or are themselves afraid to care."[25] David Lehman, in *Newsweek*, focused his attention on Fisher's ability "to evoke, in pitch-perfect sentences, an emotion or sensation 'too mysterious to accept with equanimity' "; but he also wrote, "Not everything in *Sister Age* succeeds . . . Ghost stories like 'The Lost, Strayed, Stolen' and 'The Reunion' suffer from an excess of whimsy, and Fisher sometimes resorts to trick endings whose charm quickly wears off. At her best, she writes about 'loss and love and other forms of dying' with the same gusto that characterizes her omnibus volume *The Art of Eating*."[26] His was not the only review that linked *Sister Age* with M.F.K. Fisher's earlier work and earmarked as the "best pieces" those stories that read like memoirs.

Thanks in large measure to Lescher's efforts, from early summer and accelerating into the fall of 1983, many of M.F.K. Fisher's books were reprinted in Britain by Chatto and Windus and Pan Books. In an interview with British journalist Paula Weideger, Mary Frances responded to the unprecedented phenomenon. "To have 11 titles published in half a year is a little like a painter being given a large retrospective exhibition. It's very flattering, but it amplifies the sound of the death rattle as well as the sound of applause."[27] In March 1983, the noted British cookbook author Jane Grigson journeyed to Last House. But Elizabeth David, who visited the wine critic Gerald Asher in San Francisco every year during the 1980s, declined to meet Mary Frances. "What on earth would we two old women have to talk about?"[28] was her response to Asher's suggestion.

America's culinary community, however, could not get enough of M.F.K. Fisher. *Gourmet* featured a major profile of her by Elizabeth Hawes, with photos by Jill Krementz. Mary Frances and Norah were invited to appear in one of the party scene preludes to *Dinner at Julia's*, the stylish television series that was being filmed in Santa Barbara. Judith Jones accepted the Silver Spoon Award for Mary Frances in New York City. North Point reissued *Among Friends*, and Lescher arranged for Vintage to publish *Two Towns in Provence*, incorporating *Map of Another Town* and *A Considerable Town*.

Having been bothered for more than a year by failing eyesight, Mary Frances had a lens implant operation on July 13, 1983. Five weeks later she entered the hospital for a hip replacement. For almost two months Norah and Kennedy took turns being with her during hospital stays and convalescing periods at Last House. Mary Frances told Larry Powell that she enjoyed every minute of being with them. "I am a medical miracle," she said, "with not a single hitch in my amazingly fast recovery, and for that of course I blame the whole extraordinary success of both the implant and the hip replacement on Hal Bieler's diet of zucchini and 'calcium broth.' Suffice it to say that although I am currently bored silly by hours of physiotherapy, I am childishly thrilled to graduate from a clunky walker to a comparatively elegant chromium cane."[29] By mid-September she was able to navigate Last House on her own and even venture out with friends at the wheel. She had become in her own words "a bionic woman," worth at least $3,000 in pure titanium.

With improved vision and able to walk without severe pain, Mary Frances returned to work with gusto. By occasionally escaping to her sister's house in Jenner for short periods, she completed five pieces for magazines, and she wrote to a friend, "I seem to be depending more than usual on nostalgia in what I am doing for magazines. It is easy and people apparently like it. But I am really not pleased, because it is *too* easy. I want to work harder, on something more gritty and tough, and I plan to get into it shortly."[30] Just as the old-age book had been talismanic over the years, her "Secret Project" took shape in her imagination, and was often alluded to in interviews but not divulged.

By this time she had come to depend on her secretary, Marsha Moran, to assume daily responsibility for business mail and correspondence. After leaving her position at a bank in Sonoma early in the afternoon, Marsha would pick up mail and then would spend three or four hours with Mary Frances, paying bills and taking dictation. On Saturdays, Marsha's husband, Patrick, also a writer, typed from Mary Frances's dictation and together they worked on articles and the "Secret Project." Although at first she found it awkward not to type her own material, Mary Frances soon felt comfortable dictating even personal letters to Marsha. And as her messages grew shorter, she began using specially designed stick-figure postcards that came to signal a note from M.F.K. Fisher.

On November 18, 1983, at the annual *Los Angeles Times* Book Prize ceremony, she received the Robert Kirsch Award for lifetime achievement. With Norah as companion, she flew to Los Angeles the day before and checked into the New Otani near the *Times* building downtown. Although she begged off from the cocktail party for publishers the first evening, she attended the award ceremony and the dinner for fifty-five "chosen few" the next day. In a deliciously malicious letter to Bouverie, she described the "piss-elegance in true

Hiltonesque" ambience of the hotel, the sashimi bar that seated six people by appointment only, the way she and Norah "literally reveled in mocking everything and everybody," and a dessert that to her summed up the entire experience: "A tall 'sherbet glass' filled with layers of fruit sorbets and heavy mousses, topped with raspberry syrup and bits of walnut, and with a leaf of Belgium endive stuck in each."[31] But she enjoyed meeting Walker Percy, Thomas Keneally, and Seymour Hersh, whose books had been awarded prizes.

From 1950 to 1985, Mary Frances had written twenty-three prefatory pieces for other authors' books. She told Powell, "I seem to have gone through the classical period of any older writer's life doing prefaces and introductions for my friends, and right now I have four new books to look at because my name's on the cover along with the real writers! The only one I really care about is a foreword to the new edition of *The Alice B. Toklas Cookbook*."[32] Lescher sold the *Toklas* introduction to *Vanity Fair*. "I must have spent a good twelve hours on the telephone with two editors and a copy editor from *VF*, going over every single paragraph, word, and grammatical structure of that silly Toklas thing, which I had loved writing and which I now will barely recognize as very British rather than completely American prose," Mary Frances complained to Judith Jones. "I told Bob [Lescher] that from now on I must flatly refuse any possible connections with Conde Nast. I told him I was truly sorry if this would cause him any embarrassment, but *too bad*. I really do hate to be unpleasant with Bob, because he always comes through as a poor wounded butterfly type, completely the 'gentleman' and making me feel like a clumsy oaf, and I know that neither of us is that."[33]

At the end of 1983 Mary Frances had submitted various records to the accountant who prepared her income taxes and included an estimate of 299 meals served to people who visited her professionally. In the ensuing years, the number increased substantially, and the listings in her detailed appointment calendars reveal an ever-changing configuration of relatives, friends, and neighbors. Julia Child continued to visit when she conducted cooking classes at Robert Mondavi's winery in Napa, and Alice Waters and film historian Tom Luddy from the Pacific Film Archive brought up dinner and a movie projector to show old Marcel Pagnol films. On another occasion, Alice ordered roses for

Mary Frances from the famous rosarian Rayford Reddell, who, in turn, made her acquaintance by sending baskets of Sea Pearl roses to Last House. Old friends like Romie Gould from St. Helena introduced Mary Frances to young writers who were producing house organs for the rapidly proliferating Napa Valley wineries and hoped for an article from M.F.K. Fisher. Food journalists Antonia Allegra, Jeannette Ferrary, Sara Moulton, Ruth Reichl, Joan Nathan, and Mauny Kaseburg joined Jerry DiVecchio in seeking both professional and personal advice. In Mary Frances they found a good listener, a raconteur, and sometimes a challenging critic. Some young aspirants hung on her every word, running errands and attempting to ingratiate themselves, but for the most part, Mary Frances devised mechanisms that protected her from becoming bound to any outsider who desperately wanted to be the only insider. She was not always wise, but she was inherently shrewd, and she kept her front door revolving, especially when she felt she was being used.

In family matters, she held to a high standard of personal loyalty. Even if they had done something to annoy her, her relatives were always welcome at Last House. No matter if she disapproved of her nephew Sean's decision to divorce, he was a Kennedy, and she told his wife that, having raised his sons honorably and supported her, he should be free to marry the woman he had loved for years. And although she had disliked her cousin Ron Kennedy from the time of his adolescence, Mary Frances nevertheless entertained him and wrote encouraging letters to him as she had done to his father, Ted, her least favorite uncle. When Kennedy's marriage to James Wright failed, she supported her daughter's decision to put the needs of her son first rather than divorce the man who had betrayed her, and offered whatever help might be needed.

She could also be unthinkingly cruel. She told an interviewer at one of her guest appearances at the Herbst Theatre that both of her daughters were "sterile" and were academic "dropouts." Kennedy, who had completed her bachelor's degree and was contemplating working for a master's degree, was in the audience, and was devastated.[34] And Mary Frances made no secret of her younger daughter's weight problems, criticizing her eating habits and offering dieting advice. It was, of course, her penchant for an irresistible story at any cost, but Mary Frances's frequent references to "roasting her small plump daughter in the oven" were deeply hurtful to Kennedy. And more than one of Anna's doctors had already told Mary Frances that she was partially to blame for her older daughter's psychological problems.

After a ten-year separation, Mary Frances and Kennedy visited Anna and her children in Portland in 1984. Due to distances both geographical and emotional, Mary Frances's daughters had really grown apart as Anna embraced a rustic life that included raising goats and another failed marriage in 1977. Mary Frances wrote, "I am happy in every way that we met again. I know we all dreaded it for our own reasons and also shared ones, but it seemed to me that after the first tough few minutes there was little if any strain, emotionally."[35] And as critical as she occasionally was of Norah, whose silence she often interpreted as disapproval, Mary Frances had come to depend on her for support in dealing with health problems and assistance in her writing projects. Because she felt strongly that Norah should not disrupt the pattern of her life in Jenner, she staunchly refused Norah's offer to relocate near Last House. But Mary Frances did express her "wish and want and hope to die in [her] own home"[36] to her, as well as to Anna and Kennedy.

Mary Frances also stood by old St. Helena friends like the Ten Broecks, the Beards, and Marietta, whom she often openly disagreed with and thought adopted the role of "Little Old Tottering Lady" a bit too obviously. Although she completely disapproved of Yolande Beard's decision to place her husband in a convalescent home and never quite forgave her for it, when Jim died on December 26, 1983, Mary Frances rallied around his widow and offered to write something about him for the *Napa Valley Wine Library Report*. "The four Beards were the first people my little girls, Anne and Mary, and I met when we came to St. Helena in about 1950 [1953], and I still nourish myself on the immediate recognition that Jim and Yolande and I felt that fine summer day. It has never stopped, and like all such basic happenings it cannot be explained . . . which is why I'm so obviously mumbling and fuming in the present non-explanation . . . Perhaps the easiest thing, for now anyway, is to say that Jim Beard was one of the few truly courteous people I have ever met."[37]

Although Mary Frances frequently had fun at David Bouverie's expense, narrating at length his preoccupation with his appearance, morning weigh-ins, and other vanities, her annual appointment calendars also record special private dinners she cooked for him when he celebrated a solitary birthday or holiday. When he was present at the ranch, they telephoned each other daily, and he would drive her to the local market; on more than one occasion, armed with a shotgun, he responded to her message that a rattler was being held at bay by her cat. When interviewers and television cameras appeared, he also cautioned her about overexposure in the media. But by the mid-1980s Mary Frances was caught up in the apotheosis of M.F.K. Fisher.

North Point had brought out a paperback reprint of *Among Friends* in 1983 and a revised and pared-down edition of *Here Let Us Feast* in 1986. Later that year Shoemaker published the third reprint of her translation of *The Physiology of Taste* with a handsome cover designed by the Berkeley artist David Goines. During the last two years of the 1980s North Point also reprinted each of the five books that had been gathered together in 1954 under the title *The Art of Eating* in stunning editions with cover photographs by Man Ray, George Hurrell, and John Engstead. These elegant, widely distributed paperbacks played a key role in the M.F.K. Fisher revival. "Now stuff I wrote 35, 40 years ago is selling like peanuts," Mary Frances told a *New York Times* interviewer. "They're saying, 'She's good.' I *was* good then."[38] It was a bit of swagger, but it was also true that she had always liked the freshness—"naïveté"—of the early books.[39]

At an American Booksellers Association meeting held in San Francisco, John Harris, editor of Berkeley's Aris Books, and a group of friends including Mary Frances reportedly had a discussion about forgotten culinary masterpieces, and she casually mentioned a book called *Fine Preserving* (1967), by Catherine Plagemann. Intrigued, Harris tried in vain to find a copy of the book and finally asked Mary Frances if she had a copy he could look at for a possible reprint. She obliged, and Harris discovered not only a little gem of a book, written by a dedicated gardener and cook who did not want the delicious condiments she had known in her childhood to be lost forever, but also Mary Frances's extensive marginal notes. He immediately contacted Mary Frances, who took out a few "Tut-tuts" and added one of

Edith's recipes and a few more comments. By arrangement with the Plagemann family, Aris Books published *Fine Preserving: M.F.K. Fisher's Annotated Edition of Catherine Plagemann's Cookbook* in 1986, in an edition illustrated by Earl Thollander and designed by Patricia Curtan. The cachet of Mary Frances's name on the cover sold the book and brought it to the attention of Craig Claiborne, Marion Cunningham, Carol Field, and Joyce Goldstein, who, among others, hailed the book as a superb culinary resource. The John Harris connection also brought Aris Books authors Michele Anna Jordan and Peter Reinhart, and other Sonoma County cookbook authors, to Mary Frances's door, leading to more agreements to write introductions and supply jacket blurbs.

But not all of the visitors to Last House were in the culinary community. Henrietta Humphries, a financial consultant in San Francisco who escaped to the valley on weekends, met Mary Frances at a time when her life was in transition and enjoyed Mary Frances's sympathetic ear and quick wit. Henrietta, in turn, invited Mary Frances to art exhibits and other events in San Francisco. Poets and writers like Anne Lamott, Joel Redon, and Barbara Quick sought Mary Frances out, and she encouraged them to send their manuscripts to her. She often initiated relationships with writers who had reviewed her work, and gave advice to writers in search of topics. A casual acquaintance might even lead to an invitation to write her biography. In 1987 she revoked the stipulation that her papers at the Schlesinger Library remain sealed for twenty-five years after her death and gave access to a few writers who intended to write biographies, memoirs, or books involving her life and career. One of them was James Pendergast, who taped his conversations with her over a period of at least two years. Mary Frances also gave Berkeley author Barbara Quick several interviews and permission to read unpublished materials, and opened the door for Quick to conduct interviews with a number of friends. Lescher raised cautionary flags, reminding Mary Frances not to grant blanket permission until she had read the material intended for publication. He also was concerned about the number of people competing to make a documentary film about her. "I understand that you somehow feel an open-door policy is best . . . I do want to recommend that you make a choice."[40]

Last House became the stage for the last act in Mary Frances's life. Perhaps her penchant for role playing, which began at the stove in Whittier and took her from dutiful daughter, protective sister, and occasional cook to Hollywood mistress, wife, mother, writer, and grande dame, was the only way she could cope with situations that were increasingly beyond her control. Whatever the reason, living out what sometimes verged on a comedy of manners became a way of life, and a way of accepting the humiliations and dependencies of serious illness. When the house became too crowded or her voice gave out, Mary Frances retreated to her room. And when she felt the burden of entertaining yet one more stranger, she would summon the "Bear Boys," her nickname for Gene Quint and Richard Foorman, or other friends to help her with her guests. She did not seem to consider the possibility of slowing down, or becoming more selective about her company.

In 1986, three years after her hip replacement, she had two dislocations, the second of which left her sprawled in agony on the bathroom floor until her driver entered the house, found her, and summoned an ambulance. Urged by Norah and Kennedy, Mary Frances reluctantly hired Mary Jane Jones as a companion and proceeded to enclose the carport to create a room for her. Losing her cherished privacy was difficult, but in time Mary Frances got caught up in some of Mary Jane's preferences, often joining her in her room to watch television. When Mary Frances acquired a VCR, which she informed everyone was not a TV, they also enjoyed old films with a bowl of popcorn at the ready. She even adopted some of Mary Jane's cooking "tricks," like baking chicken thighs with a coating of mustard.

Mary Jane also enabled Mary Frances, now dependent on a wheelchair, to travel. When Mary Jane wanted to participate as a runner in the Bay-to-Breakers race in San Francisco, Mary Frances accompanied her. They stayed at the Stanford Court, courtesy of hotelier Jim Nassikas, who liked to entertain the culinary famous. On another occasion, rather than refuse an invitation to be the featured guest at the first annual John Greenleaf Whittier Bookfaire at the Whittier Museum on December 12, 1987, Mary Frances asked Mary Jane to go with her. On the short flight she felt the pull of Painter Street all over again. She went to see Kennedy Park and the magnificent trees still growing on the long-gone Ranch. "I knew I would come back some-time because I have some ghosts to lay to rest," she told a reporter for the local paper. "But I never thought I'd come back as the honored guest of a literary affair."[41] After a series of receptions and dinners with Bookfaire organizers, Mary Frances told a friend, "I was so impressed by the fine reactions of all of the people . . . I forgot my own petty thoughts, and was filled with admiration and a certain sense of humility . . . and I met a few people who remembered my father with great admiration."[42] The event went well, even though Mary Frances fell ill and had to stay at the new Whittier Hilton for a week before she was able to fly back to San Francisco.

On April 4, 1988, Mary Frances and Mary Jane flew to New York City for an AIDS and Meals on Wheels benefit at the Rainbow Room. She told Norah, "I spent three days making a film that will be shown, since I refused to go in person. Then it was told to me that if by chance I would go there, they'd raise double the sum easily. So off we go . . . we're going to stay at the Plaza in a suite, and I plan to see absolutely nobody, that is besides some 2,000 people in the Wainbow Woom, except Squeek and Bob Lescher and Bert Greene."[43] The event premiered a video of M.F.K. Fisher sponsored by the Walnut Board. It was the last trip she and Mary Jane took together.

As July 3 approached, elaborate plans to celebrate Mary Frances's eightieth birthday were well under way. Henrietta Humphries had written to friends near and far asking for letters, reminiscences, and good wishes for a Birthday Box to be presented to Mary Frances at a $100-a-plate dinner at an East Bay restaurant. Covering the event for the *Los Angeles Times*, Ruth Reichl wrote, "On this occasion Craig Claiborne calls her 'a national treasure' and wine-maker Robert Mondavi toasts her by saying 'you've raised the image of food and wine in this country.' "[44] In San Francisco on July 6, a tribute called "A Conversation at the Public Library" was followed by a dinner at a Cambodian restaurant organized by filmmaker Barbara Wornum. A few months later another gala at the Herbst Theatre was given in Mary Frances's honor. Herb Caen featured it in his *Chronicle* column:

With the Symphony and opera in full swing, Van Ness Avenue was as crowded at night as Market Street was during the day.

Stars, Modesto's and Harry's Bar were packed. Over at Herbst
Theatre, the literary and gastronomical world was honoring author and legend M.F.K. Fisher—Mary Frances to her friends—
on her 80th birthday, which has lasted about a year "and I'm
getting tired of it," she said. A beauty for every one of her years,
she is admired by her peers for some of the best prose ever
written by an American—clean, precise and totally her own. It
is ridiculous to characterize her as a food writer—her range
covers all emotions and sensations—but nobody has written
about food better than she. After KQED's Sedge Thompson
had interviewed her onstage, chef Alice Waters and food critic
Patricia Unterman unveiled a banquet backstage for Mary
Frances and her friends, as Don Asher played dreamy background piano. Corn cakes and Chinese caviar, cold oysters and
hot sausages, *fraises de bois* in tiny pastry shells—a fantastic
spread for an amazing woman, who took it all in with regal satisfaction. "What's the best thing about being 80?" Sedge asked
her. "Never having to be 80 again," smiled M.F.K., sipping on
her favorite, which she calls "One Two Three"—Campari, gin,
and dry vermouth.[45]

From the beginning of their relationship, Jack Shoemaker had long
hoped to bring out a never-before-published book by M.F.K. Fisher.
In 1983 he suggested a collection of kitchen pieces, but "Two
Kitchens in Provence" was already the centerpiece of *As They Were*,
which Knopf was publishing that year. At some point Mary Frances
had also sent him her unpublished edition of Peter Cartwright's autobiography, which he returned with the comment, "I wish I could feel
a bit more adventuresome today, but this book really stymies me—I
don't think your regular readers would respond to it and I wonder how
we could get it into the marketplace that welcomed *Mary Chesnut's
Civil War Diary*. You can see how confused I feel about it."[46] In 1987,
however, when Knopf passed on Mary Frances's collection of revisited
introductions, she offered it to Jack Shoemaker. On the eve of her
eightieth birthday, *Dubious Honors*, with a spiffy jacket photo by Jill
Krementz, was North Point's birthday present to her.

M.F.K. Fisher had been writing her autobiography for most of her professional life—the oblique narrative of her early life and first two marriages in *The Gastronomical Me*, her Hollywood years and third marriage in *An Alphabet for Gourmets*, her role as mother in *Two Towns in Provence* and *The Boss Dog*, her childhood revisited in *Among Friends*, and her life through recipes in *With Bold Knife and Fork*. Now, in *Dubious Honors*, Mary Frances revisited her life as a writer; in effect she became the self-appointed critic of M.F.K. Fisher. Probably influenced by two of her "introducers," Clifton Fadiman and W. H. Auden, who had both collected their prefatory pieces,[47] she gathered twenty of her forewords and afterwords to other people's books as well as the introductions and revised introductions to her own books. She wrote of her pleasure, and sometimes her reluctance, at the "dubious honor" of lending her name to other writers' works. Because the pieces were arranged chronologically, they also reflected her changing attitudes on a variety of subjects. An introduction to the second part of the book traced her development as a writer, acknowledging her debt to agents, editors, publishers, family, and friends, and offering background information about her works. Characteristically, she often wildly exaggerated the circumstances of their publication or offered irrelevant but interesting commentary. Although she parted company with Judith Jones at Knopf over the advisability of publishing this kind of book, her judgment prevailed. She never warmed to Jones's suggestion that she assemble an *M.F.K. Fisher Reader* to showcase her best pieces.

Mary Frances's determination to orchestrate the final chapter of her private life as well as her literary life prevailed as well. For reasons known only to her, she had asked Mary Jane to leave in June 1988. A series of more or less eccentric helpers took her place, including a young sculptor, a crystalogist, and a young woman who had a habit of dipping into Mary Frances's medications. Her secretary, Marsha Moran, tried to keep the situation in hand, and was relieved when Mary Frances's grandson Chris obtained employment in a restaurant in Santa Rosa and took up residence at Last House in the fall of 1988.

A Sonoma writer named Kathleen Hill, who had met Mary Frances at the Depot Hotel a few years earlier, also helped to keep the household running. Kathleen had not read any of Mary Frances's books, was not a "groupie," and indicated she "was only interested in [Mary Frances] as a person."[48] She said there had been a kind of "electricity" between them on their first meeting, a shared passion for life and zany sense of humor that had played out in a scheme to dress up as nuns for Halloween one year. After they had spent a few months conversing on a number of topics, Mary Frances had suggested that Kathleen tape their conversations. As Mary Frances's eyesight diminished, Kathleen also read her work in progress to her. Now Mary Frances needed another pair of eyes as well as a voice to make her whispers known.

Since Mary Frances's trip to Oregon in 1984 and Anna's visit to Last House in 1986, their relationship had substantially improved. "I'm so glad you have a good memory of being down here," she wrote to her daughter, "because I certainly do think of it just as you say! It was a strange wonderful dream. It was especially good for me, because I saw you and Kennedy together and most of the kids, and we sent up a kind of candle flame of being from the same cloth, not of the same cut but very alike . . . I'm fumbling here, but it was as if we were several pods from the same branch, perhaps seeds from one pod . . . anyway, it was fun from beginning to quick end."[49] Their continuing exchange of letters at this time provides a welcome glimpse of Mary Frances as a generous and encouraging mother and grandmother, sending lagniappes to her loved ones. The letters also show Anna as the free spirit she had become through her work in elementary education and by writing and staging little plays with junior acting groups in Portland. "Dearest Dote, a very quiet weekend. I awoke once during the night thinking of Aix and how lucky we were that you showed us how to taste, smell, touch, and savor from birth. That was my thought as I awoke, and I prayed a small 'Thank you' in your direction. And here it is in concrete form. Much Love, Anna."[50]

For some time, Mary Frances had dreamed of another extended stay in Provence, and during the fall of 1988 she made plans to lease Kermit Lynch's house near Bandol for three months and then perhaps Julia Child's La Pitchoune for three more months. She wanted to introduce Chris to the French countryside she loved, and both Kathleen Hill and Jay Perkins, founder of the Sausalito cooking school Cordon Rouge, volunteered to accompany her. She wrote jauntily to

Eleanor, "I'm taking off for France on October 14 to spend hopefully three months in one house and then three in another. I'll send you the address of the first one soon. This all seems pretty crazy, but why not? And I count on seeing you there. Why not again? And especially if Kennedy could come along!! It's something to work on."[51]

Ongoing hip problems, however, forced Mary Frances to cancel the trip, and she entered St. Mary's Hospital in San Francisco on December 7, 1988, for another operation. At first she permitted only Kennedy to visit her daily, then she asked Henrietta Humphries, who lived near the hospital, to bring her real Scottish oatmeal every morning for breakfast. Henrietta also recalled a 4 a.m. phone call from Mary Frances telling her that death was near and asking her to come to the hospital at once and bring a tape recorder. When Henrietta arrived, Mary Frances taped her "last wishes" and a rambling account of her hospital stay and resistance to physical therapy to rebuild muscle tissue around the hip joints. After two weeks, she returned to Last House.

Less than a month later, she was hospitalized again in Sonoma, and Norah and Kennedy hired a live-in nurse when she returned to Last House. But Mary Frances rebelled against doctor's orders, refusing to do the exercises therapists prescribed. Told to buy a particular kind of therapeutic shoe, she bought a pair of stylish leather flats with Kathleen Hill's help, doing her best to thwart efforts to fit her for a brace.[52] She resented the way saleswomen talked down to her, and she balked at nurses who went to extremes to keep her from falling out of bed or hitting her head on the car door. In exasperation, she enlisted the help of Kathleen to tape her thoughts on what she considered the demeaning rhetoric, the kind of "baby talk" that health providers used when conversing with patients.

By this time Mary Frances and Kathleen had also worked out a plan to tape their dialogues, with the intent of publishing them. They talked about the experiences they'd had with the shortcomings and often fierce pride of a succession of German, French, and Italian landladies, which Kathleen transcribed and edited into a piece they tentatively called "The Cuckoo and the Landlady." But when Norah read it to her, Mary Frances refused to have her name associated with it, although she allowed excerpts to appear in Long Ago in France. In a lengthy letter to Lescher, Mary Frances claimed she hadn't realized how serious Kathleen was about having the project published,[53] although she assured him that she considered Kathleen a "dear and good friend."[54]

"Although it made her feel good to have so many people adoring," Kathleen said, "she often got jittery when people were coming, which is part of the reason why I was so often there."[55] She claimed to have facilitated Mary Frances's last affair, with a certain former military officer who lived on the East Coast and began writing fan letters to Mary Frances in the mid-1980s. Naturally, Mary Frances encouraged him to visit. On more than one occasion when he came west, Kathleen entertained his wife in the living room while the general and Mary Frances communicated in her bedroom.[56] Kathleen also brought Thanksgiving and Christmas dinners to Mary Frances and coaxed her to eat. Ultimately, she provided welcome distraction as Mary Frances embarked on her "last great adventure—death."[57]

That it was proving to be an expensive adventure weighed heavily on Mary Frances, and she urged Lescher to sell previously published material to small presses for limited editions to help pay for the nursing care she needed. Meanwhile at Last House, Kathleen, Marsha, and Norah reviewed unpublished pieces. Henrietta Humphries remembered finding the typescript of *The Boss Dog*, which Yolla Bolly Press brought out in a limited edition in 1990 and North Point published in 1991. When the travel writer Jan Morris contacted Mary Frances about a book on Dijon for the "Destinations" series she was editing for Prentice-Hall, Norah helped her choose selections from *Serve It Forth*, *The Gastronomical Me*, and *With Bold Knife and Fork*, which Mary Frances wove into "an essay in recollection"[58] called *Long Ago in France*.

By the spring of 1989, Chris had left Last House to live in Santa Rosa. In a letter to Anna, Mary Frances wrote that she had hoped to take him to France or some other place in Europe where he would be exposed to a different way of life, but she did not think that he was interested in learning foreign languages or meeting strange people. "Anneli, you know that I am disappointed in what I have been able to do for Chrissy. I had hopes of helping him grow more established as an artist, for one thing. But at least he knows that I love him without question, and I hope he will count on me always. I think his last days here have been rather thin ones, emotionally at least, but that is only natural in a small ménage geared to the comforts and care of an old woman."[59] Another person conspicuously absent from Last House that spring was her friend Marietta. Poor health and doctor's advice had induced her to enter a nursing home in the Napa Valley. Out of loyalty, Mary Frances paid the rent on Marietta's bookshop and organized a group of friends to keep it open in case Marietta recovered and could return to it, but Marietta died at the age of ninety-four. Her relatives found Mary Frances's letters among her possessions and returned them. Mary Frances burned them immediately.

With her voice reduced to a whisper, and the work on Barbara Wornum's video frequently halted because of funding problems or her hospitalizations, Mary Frances agreed to make another video with Kathi Wheater, a graduate student enrolled in the film program at San Francisco State. She also agreed to Kathleen Hill's plan to contact Bill Moyers, whom Kathleen had known in the Peace Corps, about a possible television interview. And at the end of July 1989, David Lazar, a professor of English at Ohio University, came to Last House for a three-week visit to interview Mary Frances and gather information for an anthology of interviews tentatively called *Conversations with M.F.K. Fisher*. A "scrapbook" of photographs with a text of appropriate quotes from M.F.K. Fisher's books, for North Point Press, was also in the planning stages. In 1990, Mary Frances saw an exhibit at the Napa Valley Museum on James E. Beard, assembled by Jennifer Garden (granddaughter of Mary Frances's St. Helena friend Evelyn Garden), and was so impressed by it that she asked Garden to organize an M.F.K. Fisher exhibit.

Then, in January 1991, her work was recognized in a way that she could not have planned or anticipated. "Almost every gastronomer has some kind of literary predilection," she had written in 1949. M.F.K. Fisher's election to the American Academy and National Institute of Arts and Letters honored that predilection and secured her literary reputation. Announcing the honor, *The New York Times* noted: "M.F.K. Fisher is the first culinary writer to be elected to the Academy and Institute of Arts and Letters."[60] Two days later the editorial page carried the following: "Calling M.F.K., who has just been elected to the American Academy of Arts and Letters, a food writer is a lot like calling Mozart a tunesmith . . . Celebrant of 'pickled peaches like translucent glass' and 'soufflés that sighed voluptuously at the first prick,' Mrs. Fisher is like no other writer in the august group of which she is now a member. But, then, M.F.K. Fisher is like no other writer anywhere."[61]

During Mary Frances's last two years, visitors brought elaborate comestibles for lunch and dinner to Last House and marveled at the pace of activity they found there. "Fisher had taken several phone calls ('Not this week, dear. Monday'd be marvelous. Come and have lunch with me. I have to go to work at two') and received a visitor during our morning interview, a neighbor who stopped in to bring her a bouquet of large yellow mums,"[62] Katherine Usher Henderson wrote. Although she could hardly speak above a whisper, she answered phone calls herself. Interviewers and visitors reflexively lowered their voices, but she insisted they speak normally. She became enraged if she heard anyone whispering to Marsha or Nina Ingram, her nurse, or any other caregiver. And everyone bowed to her wishes to work privately with Marsha every afternoon. Her "Secret Project" and two more books, based in part on journals that were being read to her, were in progress.

Initially she thought that she had destroyed all of her early journals when moving from Hemet to Cheviot Hills with Donald Friede in 1947. But a number of them had surfaced while Norah was going through published and unpublished pieces for *As They Were* and *Sister Age*. "I picked up one, and read about a page, and was literally shocked to find that less than two weeks after I married my first husband or rather was married to him, I was wondering why on earth I had done it," Mary Frances wrote. "Until I read that page, I'd been thinking since at least October 1929 that I was a blissful, dewy eyed, ignorant and completely fulfilled young female! So who was that woman that wrote that page? So here's a whole new can of worms, maybe."[63] She had fragments from her precollege summer at Laguna Beach, extensive entries from Bern and Adelboden, and journals from her residences at Genoa, Nevada, vacations in Paris, and periods of illness in St. Helena.

Written with more candor than her published works, her private journals gave testimony to Mary Frances's many vulnerabilities. They also explored the "art of dreaming"—her efforts to learn more about the life of the unconscious and subconscious and how to direct it. During the 1940s she and Larry Powell had experimented with the idea of "willing a dream" and for a while had kept notes of their dreams. Throughout her life she frequently retold her dreams to other people in letters and conversations, and occasionally used them in her stories.[64] Her journals also recorded her bouts of depression through the years and the isolation she often felt: ". . . almost frantically depressed . . . nobody to tell of this—not sister, not friend—a private thing. A private anguish."[65] And her journals revealed her intentional use of alcohol: "slow gentle *deliberate* alcoholic destruction since lethal message in Berne of husband's [Dillwyn Parrish's] death, although he lived for three years more . . . gradual conditioned increase of consumption. 30 years later [1972]: increase in dosage, no overtly suicidal pattern—simply destruction—'dull the razor's edge.' "[66]

If the journals were meant for her eyes only, and in her interview with David Lazar she maintained that they were,[67] what was written there reveals feelings, attitudes, and weaknesses only hinted at in her work. "*Nobody* knows what I think I am. Therefore I must be/act/do as I feel right. Children never know *who* or *why*, until occasionally long after they are mature, i.e., I now understand my mother's nature better than I could have when we were alive together. Still, I'll never really know why she wept or smiled, nor why she was soft or firm or impatient. Occasionally there can be moments of near-fusion between people & animals. (Charles I [her cat] in St. Helena in empty house—) Usually, though, we can not know how another person will see what we do or say or write as a part of *us*."[68]

But by this time major articles by established writers and critics like Betty Fussell, Molly O'Neil, Ruth Reichl, and Patricia Storace were exploring more than M.F.K. Fisher's latest appearance or latest award; they were assessing her contribution to culinary literature and assessing what Laura Shapiro in *Newsweek* described as the essential distinction between the autobiography and the *author* of the autobiography. "Her literary agent has been urging her to name an official biographer—would-be scribes are at her heels constantly—but she refuses. 'There's nothing duller than an official biography,' she says.

Official or not, biographies may be redundant in her case; rarely has a life been so beautifully considered over the course of many years. Is there anything left to report? Is it all in the books? Her eyes flash. '*Nothing* is in the books,' she says firmly."[69]

Choosing to write a "collection of appreciations" and a record of her friendship with Mary Frances, Jeannette Ferrary published *Between Friends: M.F.K. Fisher and Me* in 1991. In lively language she recounted the stories that Mary Frances loved to tell, retell, and embellish while entertaining her guests at lunch or dinner at Last House. Rex's early role as a "goon of Colonel McCormick,"[70] her times as a "favored guest" at the Stanford Court, and her job as a gag writer for Paramount appear side by side with Ferrary's "nervous, ingenuous response to her subject."[71] Many of Mary Frances's longtime friends were offended by Ferrary's book, and Bouverie was the most straightforward. "I pray that your 'authorized biography' (and the impending film that you encouraged) will be above the shamefully low caliber of the recently published book about you. The body of your fine published work, written over a period of half a century, will evoke pleasure and adulation for very many generations to come. You need no low-grade endorsements. You have admirers everywhere, and it is hurtful for them to see your image sullied. Many many people in New York have spoken to me in those terms, and I have had letters from far and wide saying the same thing."[72] When asked by an interviewer if she liked the book, Mary Frances claimed that she had not read it, and she told friends that she had no idea that the book was being written.

By this time Mary Frances was taking a considerable number of prescribed medications to ease pain, control Parkinson's disease, and stabilize her moods. She sought relief in acupuncture at one time, massages at another. Attended by a rotating team of caregivers, Mary Frances worked until it was impossible to do so. Before Christmas 1991, Marsha wrote to Lescher thanking him in Mary Frances's name for the arrangements he had made with Pantheon[73] to publish Mary Frances's forthcoming books.

We are in the process of typing the manuscript for the first book we've been working on. We've been calling it *The Early*

Years,[74] but I don't know if Mary Frances will want to use that title . . . The second book is also ready to be typed. It includes mostly journal entries from MF's return from Europe with Al [Fisher], through her years with Timmy [Dillwyn Parrish], and a couple of journal entries after his death. It also includes about ten stories that have not been published[75] . . . I don't know if these books will be alright as they are, but they are the way Mary Frances wants them, and that seems important to me . . . Mary Frances is really not very well at all right now. She continues to get weaker and is now plagued with a urinary tract infection, which she refuses to take antibiotics for. She is really much weaker than when you were here and I am afraid that she may not be here much longer. The work on the books continues to keep her alive . . . I can hardly bear to think of what an empty space there will be in my life, and everyone's without her.[76]

In January of 1992, Anna visited her mother for the last time, and for the last time asked her to reveal the name of her father. Mary Frances turned away in refusal.[77] Back in Portland, Anna wrote, "We found you radiant. But there you are . . . definitely Dote."[78] Kennedy and Norah spent the night at Last House at least once a week. In April, Mary Frances authorized hospice care for her last days. Many of her friends brought a savory pâté or some other luscious dish, as a way of connecting with her. Others, like Maya Angelou, read a poem or hummed a tune to her, or simply held her hand.

Two days before her death, her nephew Sean visited on his way to his son's wedding in southern California. Kennedy said that Mary Frances had been looking forward to his visit, and when he left she seemed very much at peace. "That day was, for me, the beginning of the realization that Dote was dying," Kennedy later wrote to her cousin. "I did not know it then, but she had suddenly become much more distant . . . There is a part of me that wonders if she was waiting for you to come. You were the last of the family members whom she had not seen in awhile, and I think she may have held on to know that you were OK, and for you to know that she was, although dying, OK, too."[79] On June 22, 1992, ten days before her eighty-fourth birthday, with her nurses, and Marsha, Pat, Norah, and Kennedy present, Mary Frances died in her own bed as she had wished. Norah, Kennedy, and Marsha made "One Two Threes," placed one by her bedside, and raised their glasses in a final toast, but the moment of sharing was past.

Five days later, family, friends, and acquaintances gathered at Last House for a final tribute. The house was filled with roses, and champagne and strawberries were served. As a final goodbye to his RR (Resident Recluse), Bouverie tolled the bell in the tower, and a small group walked up the path winding away from the house into the dark cool woods. Mary Frances's grandchildren carried a rose-covered basket of her ashes that they scattered into the stream from a ledge under the waterfall. She had wanted it that way.

My whole reason for being lay ahead of me, on the lake near Vevey in the canton of Vaud, and I was hurrying there as irrevocably as an Arctic lemming hurries to the sea cliff, through poisoned fields and Fire and flood to what he longs for.[80]

Notes

Sources cited in the notes are abbreviated in the following way:

AAFG   *An Alphabet for Gourmets*
ACT   *A Considerable Town*
ACW   *A Cordiall Water*
AF   *Among Friends*
ALIL   *A Life in Letters*
ATW   *As They Were*
AWL   *A Welcoming Life: The M.F.K. Fisher Scrapbook*
CTO   *Consider the Oyster*
DH   *Dubious Honors*
FP   *Fine Preserving: M.F.K. Fisher's Annotated Edition of Catherine Plage-mann's Cookbook*
HLUF   *Here Let Us Feast*
HTCAW   *How to Cook a Wolf*
LAIF   *Long Ago in France*
LH   *Last House*
MFKF   M.F.K. Fisher
MOAT   *Map of Another Town*
NNBN   *Not Now But Now*
PC   MFKF Unpublished Journals and Papers, Private Collection of the Literary Trust u/w/o M.F.K. Fisher
SA   *Sister Age*
SIF   *Serve It Forth*
SL   Mary Frances Kennedy Fisher Papers, Unprocessed Collection, Arthur and Elizabeth Schlesinger Library, Radcliffe College, Cambridge, Mass.
SMOCM   *Stay Me, Oh Comfort Me*
SOTV   *Spirits of the Valley*
TAG   *Touch and Go*
TAOE   *The Art of Eating*
TBA   *To Begin Again*
TBD   *The Boss Dog*
TCOPF   *The Cooking of Provincial France*
TGM   *The Gastronomical Me*

TMOHP   *The Measure of Her Powers*
TPOT   *The Physiology of Taste* by Jean Anthelme Brillat-Savarin: A New Trans-
         lation by M.F.K. Fisher
TSOWIC   *The Story of Wine in California*
TTIP   *Two Towns in Provence*
WBKAF   *With Bold Knife and Fork*

PREFACE: WHO WAS THE WOMAN THAT WROTE THAT PAGE?

1. MFKF to Judith Jones, September 17, 1984, SL.
2. Kennedy Friede Golden, interview by author, tape recording, August 12, 1998.
3. Sean Kelly, interview by author, tape recording, June 14, 2003.
4. Jerry DiVecchio, interview by author, October 20, 2000.
5. Antonia Allegra, interview by author, April 26, 2001.
6. Elizabeth Hawes, "M.F.K. Fisher: A Profile," *Gourmet*, November 1983, p. 186.
7. Norah Barr, interview by author, tape recording, August 19, 1998.
8. Sean Kelly to Joan Reardon, October 3, 2002.

1: BORN ON THE THIRD OF JULY

1. MFKF, *TBA*, p. 4.
2. MFKF, *AF*, p. 21.
3. MFKF to Albert E. Peters, October 22, 1968, Albion Historical Society.
4. There is a discrepancy about the house Mary Frances was born in. When Rex
   and Edith arrived in Albion in 1908, they lived on the first floor of a two-storied
   house at 205 West Erie Street. Mary Frances writes about being born there in
   Among Friends and *To Begin Again*. In a letter to Frank Passic in Albion, Mary
   Frances wrote: "The only thing I know about the house I was born in is that Uncle Walter and Aunt Tim lived upstairs." MFKF to Frank Passic, December 17,
   1985, Albion Historical Society. The *Albion Evening Recorder* birth announcement lists the 202 Irwin Avenue address.
5. *Albion Evening Recorder*, July 3, 1908, p. 3. Also quoted in Frank Passic's "Mary
   Frances Kennedy Fisher Writes About Albion," *Journal of Albion*, January 4,
   1986.
6. Alma was a Presbyterian college and rival of the Methodist Albion College,
   where Walter Kennedy coached the football team. The sports rivalry between the
   two colleges frequently made the *Recorder*'s first page.
7. "Introduction" (unpublished), *WBKAF*, SL.
8. The Holbrook family was established in America in the early nineteenth century.
   At the beginning of the Civil War, MFKF's maternal grandfather, Bernard Holbrook (1836–1910), studied law at William and Mary and was commissioned by
   President Lincoln to help survey the Territory of Iowa. As the story goes, he carried his books in a small trunk along with him, and in time it became a strongbox
   for money and valuables that people entrusted to him when they sought his help
   in reading and signing documents. When he had traversed the Territory from east
   to west, he decided to settle in Onawa near the Nebraska border, and he became

the first banker in the western part of the state. Although he never liked the business of banking—he called it usury—it provided more than enough money for him to raise a family of successful, educated children.

MFKF's maternal grandmother, Mary Frances Oliver (1838–1920), came from an entirely different background. Allegedly because of the political indiscretions of her father, Henry William Oliver (1807–88), the family left County Tyrone in northern Ireland in 1845. The crossing was difficult, with the women, including Mary Frances, her mother, Margaret, and her baby brother James, in one part of the ship and her father Henry and brothers David and Henry in another. When they arrived in America, the Oliver family settled in Pittsburgh, and two more children were born. When Mary Frances met and married the banker Bernard David Holbrook is not known, but they had nine children together, four of whom died in infancy. MFKF's mother, Edith (March 27, 1880–May 9, 1949), was the youngest and only surviving daughter.

9. "Introduction" (unpublished), *WBKAF*, SL.

10. An apocryphal genealogical account of the Kennedy family begins with Ulric Kennedy, who in the twelfth century separated from the Ayrshire clan because of some transgression he committed and became accepted as a sept of the Cameron clan in Lochaber, Scotland. Subsequent Kennedys adopted the Cameron plaid as their tartan, and wore the Cameron motto *Avise la fin* (Consider the End) on their crest. They remained in Scotland for several generations before fleeing to Ireland and then much later journeying across the Atlantic to America, where the arrival of John Kennedy of Scotch-Irish descent on the East Coast and the marriage of his son, Alexander Kennedy (d. 1841), to Rachel Smith in southwestern Pennsylvania in 1820 is a matter of record.

A more fully documented history of the Kennedy family begins with Alexander's son, Benjamin Brownfield Kennedy (1824–92), who prepared for the Methodist Episcopal ministry in Ohio. Records of his early appointments in Pennsylvania, Ohio, and Illinois, his involvement in the Abolitionist movement, and his career as a circuit rider in Iowa were accurately preserved. His future bride, Patience Rosanna French (1824–1915), was born in western Virginia but raised in Ohio. When Benjamin and Rosanna married on August 5, 1847, they set up housekeeping in Benjamin's home county in Pennsylvania. After two years they moved to the Quaker town of Albany, Ohio, where the Underground Railroad flourished, and where their first son, Clarence Klaude (1849–1933), was born. After several appointments in western Illinois, Benjamin and his family, which now included Orin Aristo (1861–195?), settled in Carthage, Iowa, where their daughter, Leota (1865–1947), was born.

During their years in Illinois, Benjamin had acquired a 160-acre homestead in Lucas County, Iowa, by swapping his team of horses and his buggy. But it wasn't until 1867 that the family crossed the Mississippi River and claimed their property. While the Reverend Benjamin Kennedy and his son Clarence built the family's house, he maintained his travel circuit of nine appointments every Sunday. Clarence, who had attended Chariton Academy, began to teach at the school closest to the family farm before continuing his education at Simpson College in Indianola, Iowa. At Simpson he met Luella Green (1854–1933) from New York State, who was intent on studying to be a teacher.

At the end of her junior year, Luella married Clarence (CKK) on August 31, 1873, just weeks after his graduation, and they took up residence at the Kennedy family farm. After Luella and CKK's first son, Walter (1874–1954), was born, they moved back to Indianola and lived with Luella's mother, Clarence publishing the local *Recorder* and Luella completing her senior year at Simpson College. Ably assisted in caring for her child by her mother, Luella went on to study for a master's degree in science, interrupting her studies to give birth to MFKF's father, Rex Brenton Kennedy (1877–1953). She completed her degree the following year.

For the next twenty-five years, CKK and Luella published and edited the *Review* in Villisca, a thriving rural community in southwestern Iowa. They also increased their family by two more sons—Frederic (Ted) Green (1879–1970) and Burt E. (1883–1935).

11. Ted Kennedy to Etta Turner, September, n.d., in Ronald Kennedy, *My Glimpses of Family Past* (Rio Verde, Ariz.: Green Valley Publishing, 1989), p. 195.

12. *TBA*, p. 8; *AF*, p. 22.

13. *TBA*, p. 11.

14. Kennedy, *My Glimpses*, p. 243.

15. Benjamin F. Arnold and Artilissa Dorland Clark, *History of Whittier* (Whittier, Calif.: Whittier Printing Co., 1933).

16. Virginia Mathony, "Whittier's First Century," *Whittier Centennial Magazine*, 1987, pp. 4–8.

17. In 1888 George Parks, owner of Whittier's only saloon, shot an employee following an argument. In a rampage, the Quakers burned the saloon to the ground and prohibited the sale of intoxicating beverages in the town until 1940. Ibid., p. 7.

18. MFKF's description in the seventy-fifth-anniversary issue of the *Whittier News*, quoted in Ronald Kennedy, *Glimpses II: A Further Look into a Family Past* (Scottsdale, Ariz.: Green Desert Publishing, 1995), p. 43.

19. "The First Kitchen: Whittier, California," *The Cook's Room* (New York: Harper-Collins, 1991), p. 156.

20. Ibid.

21. "I don't know why I've always felt embarrassed when I have to admit that I'm not a native Californian. People tell me that I'm silly, and really I cannot say why I feel the way I do about this apparently delicate question of where I was born." "Native Truths," *TBA*, p. 7.

22. Ibid., p. 43.

23. Weare Holbrook to MFKF, July 21, 1982, SL. "I remember how in Whittier your mother proved that one doesn't have to be dead to 'lie in state' and how, when company was present she took pride in your obedience."

24. *AF*, p. 32.

25. Ibid., p. 47.

26. Ibid., p. 283.

27. Kennedy, *Glimpses II*, pp. 120, 128, 145.

28. Weare Holbrook to MFKF, July 21, 1982, SL.

29. MFKF to Weare Holbrook, August 2, 1982, SL.

30. Amy Wilson, "A House's Life," *Orange County Register*, November 29, 1998.

31. Campbellites were originally a Presbyterian sect, but in nineteenth-century America, under the leadership of Alexander Campbell, they became known as the Disciples of Christ.
32. *AF*, p. 283.
33. Ibid., p. 280.
34. Ibid., p. 291.
35. This incident appears in *AF*, p. 285; *TGM*, pp. 15–17; and "Q Is for Quantity," in *AAFG*, p. 121.
36. *AF*, p. 291.
37. *TBA*, p. 97.
38. *AF*, p. 7.
39. Sean Kelly to Joan Reardon, August 7, 2002.
40. Luella Kennedy to Ted Kennedy, May 27, 1919, in Kennedy, *Glimpses II*, p. 46.
41. MFKF to Weare Holbrook, August 3, 1984, SL.
42. *AF*, p. 305.
43. *TGM*, p. 18.
44. *TGM*, p. x.
45. Ibid.
46. *TBA*, p. 4.
47. *AF*, p. 160.
48. *TBA*, p. 13.

2: AN INTOLERABLE WAITING

1. Theodore Roethke, "I'm Here," in *Meditations of an Old Woman*.
2. *AF*, p. 168.
3. "Gracie," *TBA*, p. 106.
4. "The Broken Chain," *TBA*, pp. 114–19.
5. MFKF, "Loving Cooks, Beware!" *Journal of Gastronomy*, vol. 1 (summer 1984), p. 24.
6. "The Annual Edition," *Whittier News*, 1923.
7. "The Moon Maid," *The Whittier High School Yearbook*, 1923 ed., pp. 140–41.
8. *TBA*, p. 151.
9. *AF*, p. 174.
10. "G Is for Gluttony," *AAFG*, pp. 47–52; and "Young Hunger," *ATW*, pp. 31–36.
11. "The First Oyster," *TGM*, pp. 19–30.
12. Ibid., p. 30.
13. *The Well of Loneliness* was published in 1928. Since this incident occurred in 1925, MFKF either read another lesbian novel or fabricated the event.
14. "Ridicklus," *TBA*, pp. 144–46.
15. Ibid., p. 145.
16. Ibid.
17. MFKF to Eda Lord, November 18, 1959, PC.
18. Ibid.
19. "Poem," *El Miradero*, 1925, pp. 35–36.

Poem
Called the fairy to the limpid leaves,
"Why do you tremble?
Why do you shiver in the noon sun
And at dusk?"

"We are happy.
We whisper secrets of the breezes to each other.
And the bees tickle us with their wings."

"You should not shiver in your happiness.
Look! I dart
Like a tipsy butterfly, searching for flowers that are not.
I sing like a meadow-bird,
New-wedded.
I am a fairy, and cannot tremble.
Tell me why you do it ceaselessly."

"We soothe the frightened birdlets
With our sighing.
We make a dancing chorus for old Cricket
When he fiddles.
We tremble that the world may see our beauty."

"I calm wee birds, and dance to Crickets' music,
Even as you.
I long and long to tremble.
Tell me more, sweet leaves."
"We have no more to tell you.
You must try."

"I do
But when I try, all my body dances,
And I make lovely motions, like a sea-bird.
Swooping over silver fish.
Please tell me more."

"We tremble because of God.
Young fairy, why do you tremble?
And why weep?"

"Oh, green leaves, green leaves,
I know not!"

20. Norah Barr, interview by author, tape recording, August 10, 1998.
21. *El Miradero, 1926*, pp. 35–36.
22. MFKF to Naomi Pfeiffer, August 9, 1971, "Answers to MD Questionnaire," SL.

23. MFKF to Dr. Frumkes, November 2, 1953, SL; and *ALIL*, p. 122.

24. *TBA*, p. 153.

25. Ibid., p. 147.

26. Ibid., p. 149.

27. Ibid., pp. 153–55.

28. Norah Barr, interview by author, tape recording, October 2, 1997.

29. *TBA*, p. 161.

30. Ibid.

31. Ibid., p. 160.

32. Dismayed by the conditions under which workers and travelers had to eat, the English-born railroad worker Fred Harvey opened a clean dining room above the Topeka, Kansas, railroad station in 1876. The good food served in the dining room led to a chain of hotels, railroad restaurants, and dining cars by 1912, to Harvey diners in 1928, and in 1941 to Harvey House restaurants—all distinguished by cheerful waitresses who came to be known as "Harvey girls."

33. *TGM*, pp. 38–39.

34. *TBA*, p. 168.

35. Ibid., p. 165.

36. *TGM*, p. 38.

37. Ibid.

38. MFK to Family, December 11, 1927, PC.

39. January 30, 1928, Examination Book, Biology 9, SL; and *TBA*, p. 169.

40. MFKF to Eda Lord, November 18, 1959, sequence called "I Love You, Eda," PC.

41. Lawrence Powell, "Introduction" to Alfred Fisher's *Ghost in the Underblows*, cites Alfred as the oldest son, but Herbert H. Fisher, Jr., was the oldest of the Rev. Fisher's four children.

42. MFKF, "The Direct Approach," c. 1965, PC.

43. MFKF to Naomi Pfeiffer, August 9, 1971, SL.

44. "Reminiscences," insert in *Occidental College: Fifty Year Club News*. Winter, 1985–86.

45. Larry Bachmann, "M.F.K. Fisher: A Causerie," unpublished MS. written after MFKF's death in 1992.

46. Lawrence Powell, *Eucalyptus Fair*, p. 105.

47. Ibid.

48. *Tawney Kat*, Occidental College, 1928–29, pp. 17–18.

49. MFKF, Journal, 1929, PC.

50. Luella Kennedy to Ted Kennedy, October 7, 1929, in Kennedy, *Glimpses II*, p. 69.

3: THE FIRST INSOUCIANT SPELL

1. "Sea Change: 1929–1931," *TGM*, p. 42.

2. "N Is for Nautical," *AAFG*, pp. 93–94.

3. MFKF, Journal, 1929, PC.

4. Ibid.

5. A young circus performer described in *AF*, pp. 184–86.

6. "The Most Important Meal I Ever Ate," *Napa Valley Tables*, vol. 1 (spring/summer, 1990), p. 12.
7. "The Measure of My Powers: 1929–1930," *TGM*, p. 49.
8. Ibid., p. 51.
9. MFKF to David Kennedy, October 5, 1929, SL; and *ALIL*, p. 4.
10. MFKF, Journal, 1929, PC.
11. Ibid.
12. Ibid.
13. Ibid.
14. "Ollagnier" was the actual name of their landlords in Dijon. In *TGM* Fisher refers to them as the Biarnets, and in *LAIF* as the Ollangnier family.
15. *LAIF*, p. 15.
16. "Wine Is Life," *California Living Magazine*, October 28, 1984, p. 12.
17. *LAIF*, p. 47.
18. *TGM*, p. 65.
19. MFKF to Rex Kennedy, December 9, 1929, SL; and *ALIL*, p. 9.
20. MFKF to Edith Holbrook Kennedy, November 30, 1929, SL.
21. MFKF to Norah Kennedy, October 20, 1929, SL.
22. MFKF to Anne Kennedy, October 22, 1929, SL.
23. MFKF to Rex Kennedy, December 9, 1929, SL.
24. MFKF, Journal, January 10, 1931, PC.
25. Ibid.
26. "Noëls Provençaux," *LH*, p. 99.
27. "Afterword: The Way It Was, and Is," *DH*, p. 119.
28. MFKF, Journal, February 24, 1930, PC.
29. MFKF to Edith Holbrook Kennedy, February 15, 1930, SL.
30. MFKF, Journal, February 28, 1930, PC.
31. "Rigoulot" is the name of the family identified as successors to the Ollagniers in Lawrence Powell's letters and MFKF's *LAIF*. The name used in *TGM* is "Rigagnier."
32. *TGM*, p. 80.
33. *LAIF*, p. 129.
34. MFKF to Lawrence Powell, May 11, 1930, SL; and *ALIL*, pp. 15–19.
35. *LAIF*, p. 137.
36. Alfred Fisher quoted in Lawrence Powell's "Introduction," in Fisher, *The Ghost in the Underblows*, p. xvii.
37. See "The Georgian Sugar Shaker," *Art and Antiques*, February 1985, pp. 72–77.
38. Lawrence Powell, "La Belle Jeunesse," *Fortune and Friendship*, p. 32.
39. Ibid., p. 34.
40. MFKF to Norah Kennedy, June 20, 1930, SL.
41. Ibid.
42. Published in *SMOCM* (1993), the short story of the same name was written in 1937.
43. MFKF, Journal, 1931, PC.
44. Ibid.
45. Edmond Kelly was referred to as Ted Kelly by family and friends.
46. MFKF to Edith Holbrook Kennedy, April 3, 1931, SL. Although in *LAIF*, MFKF

maintained that she was not aware that she was to take Norah back to France until she was ready to leave Whittier, letters written in 1931 indicate that it was MFKF who suggested it before she departed from France to California.

47. *LAIF*, p. 74.
48. Powell, "Introduction," in Fisher, *The Ghost in the Underblows*, p. xiv.
49. Powell quoted in Kevin Starr, *Material Dreams*, p. 379.
50. Powell, *Fortune and Friendship*, p. 36.
51. *TGM*, pp. 45–46.
52. Norah Barr, "Introduction," in *SMOCM*, p. viii.
53. MFKF to Edith Holbrook Kennedy, October 12, 1931, SL.
54. Ibid.
55. The summary of Fisher's *cuisine personelle* appears in "The Measure of My Powers: 1931," *TGM*, p. 439; and also "From A to Z," *AAFG*, pp. 203–13.
56. Powell, *Fortune and Friendship*, p. 34. "She [Mary Frances] was beginning to write the pieces that were eventually to bring her fame as a writer on gastronomy and human foibles."
57. "Fifty Million Snails," *SIF*, pp. 40–46.
58. "Two Birds Without a Branch," *SIF*, pp. 95–98.
59. "The Pale Yellow Glove," *SIF*, pp. 99–105.
60. MFKF to Edith Holbrook Kennedy, January 23, 1932, SL.
61. "Borderland," *SIF*, pp. 30–32.
62. MFKF wrote about their months in Strasbourg in "The Measure of My Powers: 1931–32," *TGM*; and in "Borderland," *SIF*.
63. MFKF to Edith Holbrook Kennedy, March 21, 1932, SL.
64. Powell, *Fortune and Friendship*, p. 37.
65. Powell, "MF: A Reminiscence," *ALIL*, p. xv.
66. *TGM*, p. 118.

4. PAST AND PRESENT DEPARTURES

1. MFKF to June Eddy, February 8, 1966, SL.
2. *TGM*, p. 122.
3. Ibid., p. 118.
4. Kennedy, *Glimpses II*, p. 118.
5. Ibid., p. 119.
6. Ibid., p. 122.
7. Ibid., p. 123.
8. Ibid., p. 126.
9. "The Jackstraws," *TBA*, p. 136.
10. Kennedy, *Glimpses II*, pp. 128–29.
11. EOH Kennedy to Ted Kennedy, February 21, 1933, in Kennedy, *Glimpses II*, p. 128.
12. MFKF to Rex Kennedy, July 30, 1940, *SMOCM*, p. 227.
13. The Long Beach Earthquake measured between 6.2 and 6.4 on the Richter scale. http://neic.usgs.gov/neis/eqlists/USA/1933_03_11.
14. The illustrator and artist Maxfield Parrish was a cousin of Dillwyn and Anne Parrish. He painted both of them in murals like *The Pied Piper* and *Old King Cole*.

15. Anne Parrish's novels were "Harper's Finds." *Semi-Attached* and *The Perennial Bachelor* were the most financially successful.
16. Years later, not long after Dillwyn and Gigi met Mary Frances and Al, one of Dillwyn's testicles became tubercular and had to be removed, rendering him sterile.
17. Her name was Katherine (Katy), but her brother called her "Geegoo," which became Gigi.
18. Gigi Parrish, interview by author, tape recording, January 4, 1999.
19. "Laguna Journal," *SMOCM*, p. 4.
20. Ibid.
21. Ibid.
22. Ibid., p. 13.
23. Ibid., p. 20.
24. Ibid., p. 6.
25. A narrative of the relationships of these Occidental graduates, who had gone abroad to France and longed to establish some semblance of *la vie bohème* in southern California when they returned, was told by Larry Powell in his novel *Eucalyptus Fair*, written in 1943 but not published until the death of his wife Fay in 1990.
26. *SMOCM*, p. 35.
27. Ibid.
28. Ibid., p. 28.
29. Under the pseudonym Savarin St. Sure, Hanna edited a newsletter called *Bohemian Life*, monthly from 1948 to 1951 and bimonthly from October 1951 to 1954. Idwal Jones was a major contributor.
30. *ATW*, p. 61.
31. Ibid., pp. 60–61.
32. Ibid.
33. *SMOCM*, p. 48.
34. Ibid., p. 59.
35. Ibid., p. 60.
36. MFKF to Dr. George Frumkes, January 12, 1950, SL.
37. *DH*, p. 133.
38. MFKF to Dr. George Frumkes, January 12, 1950, SL.
39. Gigi Parrish, interview by author, tape recording, January 4, 1999.
40. Ibid.
41. MFKF, "The Direct Approach," c. 1965, PC.
42. *SMOCM*, p. 67.
43. Ibid., pp. 67–68.
44. Ibid., p. 66.
45. *Je m'en fiche* is translated as "I don't give a damn." Mary Frances used this colloquial French expression throughout her life to denote her detachment from difficult situations and hurts real or imaginary.
46. MFKF to Dr. George Frumkes, January 12, 1950, SL.
47. MFKF to Alfred Fisher, February 3, 1936, SL.
48. MFKF to Alfred Fisher, February 7, 1936, SL.
49. MFKF to Alfred Fisher, February 8, 1936, SL.
50. MFKF to Alfred Fisher, February 12, 1936, SL.

51. MFKF to Alfred Fisher, February 13, 1936, SL.
52. *TGM*, p. 129.
53. Ibid., p. 130.
54. MFKF to Alfred Fisher, February 21, 1936, SL.
55. MFKF to Alfred Fisher, March 5, 1936, SL.
56. MFKF to Alfred Fisher, March 10, 1936, SL.
57. "I Was Really Very Hungry," *The Atlantic Monthly*, June 1937; also as "Define This Word," *TGM*, 1943.
58. "The Standing and the Waiting," *SIF*, p. 68.
59. MFKF to Naomi Pfeiffer, August 9, 1971, SL.
60. *DH*, p. 134.
61. Nancy Milford, *Savage Beauty: The Life of Edna St. Vincent Millay* (New York: Random House, 2001), p. 387.
62. *TGM*, p. 133.
63. MFKF to Larry Powell, December 2, 1938 (unsent), *SMOCM*, p. 166.
64. "Sodom and the Potato Box," *SMOCM*, p. 73.
65. MFKF to Larry Powell, December 2, 1938, *SMOCM*, pp. 168–69.

5: VIN DE VEVEY

1. MFKF, Journal, November 9, 1954, PC.
2. "Vevey Journal, 1936–37," *SMOCM*, p. 76.
3. Ibid., p. 77.
4. MFKF, *TGM*, p. 150.
5. "Vevey Journal," *SMOCM*, pp. 84–85.
6. Rex Kennedy to Ted Kennedy, November 3, 1936, in Kennedy, *Glimpses II*, p. 142.
7. MFKF to Larry Powell, December 2, 1938, *SMOCM*, p. 169.
8. Alfred Fisher MS, SL.
9. Larry Powell to MFKF, November 1, 1938, SL.
10. In April, Rex had written to his brother Ted about his forthcoming trip to Europe to attend a Rotary convention in Nice because he was president of the Whittier chapter. He also told Ted about his and Edith's plan to visit Dote (Mary Francis) and Al in Switzerland and then tour England before returning to California: "We leave here April 20 [1937] and will be 24 days on the boat." Rex Kennedy to Ted Kennedy, April 15, 1937.
11. MFKF to Dr. George Frumkes, January 12, 1950, SL.
12. MFKF to Larry Powell, December 2, 1938, *SMOCM*, p. 170.
13. "Stay Me, Oh Comfort Me," *SMOCM*, p. 109.
14. Ibid., p. 110.
15. Ibid., p. 127.
16. MFKF to Larry Powell, January 25, 1944, SL; and *ALIL*, p. 62.
17. *SMOCM*, p. 134.
18. *AAFG*, pp. 665–66. The same incident appears in "The Measure of My Powers: 1936–1939," *TGM*.
19. MFKF to Larry Powell, August 12, 1937, SL; and *ALIL*, p. 131.
20. Rex Kennedy to MFKF, January 30, 1938, PC.

21. MFKF to Dr. George Frumkes, January 12, 1950, SL.
22. MFKF to Larry Powell, August 12, 1937, SL.
23. *The New York Times*, June 20, 1937.
24. Lucius Beebe, *New York Herald Tribune Books*, July 4, 1937.
25. Fanny Butcher, *Chicago Daily Tribune*, June 19, 1937.
26. Lewis Gannett, "Books and Things," *New York Herald Tribune*, June 15, 1937.
27. *The Times Literary Supplement* (London), July 24, 1937, p. 542.
28. MFKF to Naomi Pfeiffer, August 9, 1971, SL.
29. *SIF*, p. 4.
30. *TGM*, p. 152.
31. MFKF to Larry Powell, August 12, 1937, SL.
32. From *Northampton Sequence: 1937*, Smith College Archives.
33. Larry Powell to MFKF, November 1, 1938, SL.
34. MFKF to Larry Powell, October 5, 1937, SL; and *ALIL*, p. 32.
35. *Chexbres*, according to MFKF, is Old French for goat, and also the name of the village above Le Paquis. "It is pronounced Cheb, with just a little touch of the r, but no x and no s. It was an appropriate name because Dillwyn Parrish did look like an especially beautiful goat." MFKF to Margo, February 26, 1974, SL; and *ALIL*, p. 351. MFKF used it whenever she referred to Dillwyn Parrish in *TGM*. The family also used Tim or Timmy instead of Dillwyn.
36. *TGM*, p. 180.
37. Norah Barr, "Introduction" to *SMOCM*, p. ix.
38. Rex Kennedy to MFKF, January 30, 1938, PC.
39. *TGM*, p. 198.
40. MFKF to Jake Zeitlin, February 1, 1938, SL.
41. Ibid.
42. *SMOCM*, p. 136.
43. A bookseller named Peter Howard of Serendipity Books in Berkeley reports that he has seen a photocopy of a signed inscription in a copy of *TAG* in which MFKF says that she wrote the book entirely by herself and that Dillwyn had nothing to do with it.
44. *TAG*, p. 6.
45. MFKF to Larry Powell, February 28, 1939, SL; and *ALIL*, p. 45.
46. *TGM*, p. 168.
47. *SMOCM*, pp. 138–63.
48. MFKF, "Home for Christmas," *A New Christmas Treasury* (New York: Penguin, 1991), p. 163.
49. *TGM*, p. 185.
50. Charlotte Dean, "Fiction in a Lighter Vein," *The New York Times Book Review*, May 7, 1939, p. 17.
51. K.S., "The New Books," *Saturday Review of Literature*, May 13, 1939, p. 19.
52. MFKF to Larry Powell, May 2, 1939, SL; and *ALIL*, p. 45.
53. Edith Holbrook Kennedy to Ted Kennedy, November 25, 1938, in Kennedy, *Glimpses II*, p. 150.
54. *TGM*, pp. 187–88.
55. Ibid., p. 189.

6: BAREACRES

1. MFKF to Suzy Fisher, December 22, 1974, SL.
2. MFKF to Larry Powell, February 5, 1940, SL; and *ALIL*, pp. 46–47.
3. *SMOCM*, p. 181.
4. Eva to MFKF, January 20, 1940, SL.
5. Mme de Jonge to MFKF, January 16, 1940, SL.
6. "Bareacres Journal," *SMOCM*, p. 198.
7. Ibid., p. 182.
8. MFKF to Dr. George Frumkes, January 12, 1950, SL.
9. *SMOCM*, p. 205.
10. Anne Parrish to MFKF, February 3, 1940, SL.
11. MFKF to Larry Powell, February 15, 1940, SL; and ALIL, p. 47.
12. The notes gathered for this book were published as an article, "If This Were My Place," in *The Atlantic Monthly*, April 1950.
13. MFKF to Alexander Woollcott, February 8, 1940, SL.
14. MFKF, Unpublished Notes, "Restaurants . . . ," February 8, 1940, SL.
15. *The Atlantic Monthly*, April 1950.
16. MFKF to Edith Kennedy, January 30, 1940, SL.
17. MFKF to Mrs. Lewis Gannett, January 30, 1940, SL.
18. In addition to being MFKF's personal physician, Dr. Hal Bieler also treated many Hollywood stars and was known for prescribing very unusual and restrictive diets.
19. Gloria [Stuart] Sheekman to MFKF, February 18, 1940, SL.
20. Although MFKF used the phrase "come the substantials" in more than one article, an article thus entitled was never published.
21. Mary Leonard Pritchett to MFKF, February 13, 1940, SL.
22. This may have been published as "Three Swiss Inns" in *Gourmet*, September 1941.
23. Mrs. Pritchett placed the story in *The Saturday Evening Post*. Before it was actually published, war with Japan was declared, and because one of the main characters was Japanese, the editors pulled the article. The story did appear in the *Carleton Miscellany*, summer 1967.
24. MFKF to Edith Kennedy, August 7, 1940, *SMOCM*, p. 245.
25. Ibid., pp. 249–50.
26. Sean Kelly, interview by author, tape recording, June 14, 2003.
27. Sean Kelly, "Rex, Edith, and the Kennedy Ranch," in Kennedy, *Glimpses II*, p. 173.
28. *SMOCM*, p. 247.
29. Ibid., p. 248.
30. Ibid., p. 283.
31. Ibid., pp. 281–82.
32. Ibid., p. 292.
33. Ibid., p. 299.
34. MFKF to Rex Kennedy Family, January 10, 1941, SL; and *ALIL*, p. 52.
35. *Paintings & Drawings by Dillwyn Parrish* (Los Angeles: Ward Ritchie Press, 1941), UCLA Special Collections.

36. *SMOCM*, p. 319.
37. MFKF to Larry Powell, July 1, 1941, SL; and *ALIL*, p. 54.
38. MFKF to Leo Racicot, August 2, 1983, SL.
39. Norah Kennedy to MFKF, August 16, 1941, SL.
40. Norah Kennedy to Dillwyn Parrish, n.d. [late 1939], SL.
41. Sean Kelly, "Rex, Edith, and the Kennedy Ranch," p. 173.
42. In a summary of her clinical history (MFKF to Dr. Frumkes, January 12, 1950), MFKF wrote: "About two months after my husband Dillwyn's death I almost fainted from a sudden and very shocking desire to shoot myself . . . I had unpredictable returns of this feeling of frantic necessity to destroy for about a year."
43. *SMOCM*, p. 323.
44. Ibid.
45. *DH*, p. 135.
46. Patricia Storace, "The Art of MFK Fisher," *The New York Review of Books*, December 7, 1989, pp. 44–45.
47. E. L. Tinker, "Review," *The New York Times*, November 9, 1941, p. 38.
48. Clifton Fadiman, *The New Yorker*, September 23, 1941, pp. 56–58.
49. MFKF to Larry Powell, September 10, 1941, SL; and *ALIL*, p. 55.
50. *TGM*, p. 210.
51. MFKF to Norah Kennedy, October 14, 1941, SL; and *ALIL*, pp. 55–56.
52. *TGM*, p. 230.
53. Ibid.
54. Ibid., p. 242.
55. Ibid.
56. "The Measure of My Powers 1941" and "Feminine Ending," *TGM*.
57. Kennedy, *Glimpses II*, p. 174.
58. MFKF, "Blackout Lesson Drawn From Europe," *Whittier News*, December 24, 1941.
59. Rex Kennedy to Ted Kennedy, December [n.d.], 1941, in Kennedy, *Glimpses II*, p. 152.

7: HOLLYWOOD SCENARIOS

1. "To be happy, even to conceive happiness, you must be reasonable or (if Nietzsche prefers the word) you must be tamed. You must have taken the measure of your powers, tasted the fruits of your passions and learned your place in the world and what things in it can really serve you. To be happy you must be wise." George Santayana, *Egotism in German Philosophy* (New York: Charles Scribner's Sons, 1916), p. 152.
2. *DH*, p. 136.
3. "Conclusion," *HTCAW*, p. 350.
4. Reminiscing about *HTCAW* in *DH* in 1987, MFKF says she dictated it to her sister Norah, who typed it directly on the machine. "She was astonished by the smooth way it came out," Mary Frances writes. Norah has no recollection of helping with it and is sure that Mary Frances prepared the manuscript herself. Norah Barr, interview by author, August 14, 1998.
5. "Quintet," the working title of *The Blue Train*, by Larry Powell.

6. Presumably MFKF was revising or thinking about revising her first draft of the story "Stay Me, Oh Comfort Me" at this time.

7. MFKF to Larry Powell, March 17, 1942, SL; and *ALIL*, pp. 56–57.

8. In the twenties the Russian actress Alla Nazimova's mansion became a hotel, and bungalows were built around the swimming pool, which was shaped like the Black Sea. Among others, Robert Benchley, Humphrey Bogart, Errol Flynn, Kay Thompson, Artie Shaw, Clifford Odets, and Dorothy Parker stayed at the Garden of Allah, as did Groucho Marx.

9. Gloria Stuart Sheekman, interview by author, October 19, 1997.

10. *HTCAW*, p. 268.

11. Orville Prescott, *The New York Times*, June 28, 1942, p. 3.

12. Clifton Fadiman, *The New Yorker*, May 30, 1942.

13. *HTCAW*, p. 194.

14. Fadiman, *The New Yorker*, May 30, 1942.

15. Walter Kendricks, *The New York Times Book Review*, November 24, 1996, p. 35.

16. Paramount Archives, Academy Museum, Los Angeles.

17. Sean Kelly to Joan Reardon, July 6, 2002.

18. MFKF, "A Is for Dining Alone," *AAFG*, p. 7.

19. Ibid.

20. *Look*, July 28, 1942, pp. 24–26.

21. Ibid.

22. Ted Gill, *San Francisco Chronicle*, August 17, 1942.

23. Rex Kennedy to Ted Kennedy, July 18, 1942, in Kennedy, *Glimpses II*, pp. 156–57.

24. Sean Kelly to Joan Reardon, July 6, 2002.

25. MFKF to H. P. Austin, January 22, 1951, SL.

26. Rex Kennedy to Ted Kennedy, July 25, 1942, in Kennedy, *Glimpses II*, p. 157.

27. David Lazar, "Something of a Ghost," *Conversations with M.F.K. Fisher*, p. 147.

28. MFKF to Larry Powell, n.d. (unsent), SL.

29. "The Measure of My Powers, 1941," *TGM*, p. 545.

30. Notes MFKF prepared for her psychiatrist, Dr. George Frumkes, in 1950, SL.

31. MFKF, interview by author, tape recording, May 14, 1987.

32. Gloria Stuart Sheekman, interview by author, tape recording, October 19, 1997.

33. Sylvia Thompson, *Feasts and Friends* (San Francisco: North Point, 1988), p. 57.

34. *TGM*, pp. 9–10.

35. Gloria Stuart, *Gloria Stuart: I Just Keep Hoping*, p. 149.

36. MFKF to Larry Powell, January 18, 1943, SL; and *ALIL*, p. 57.

37. Although MFKF tried to publish her edition of the Cartwright autobiography many times, including offering it to North Point Press in the 1980s, it never appeared and remains in manuscript form in SL.

38. MFKF to Larry Powell, February 22, 1943, SL; and *ALIL*, p. 58.

39. Rex Kennedy to Ted Kennedy, n.d. [1943], in Kennedy, *Glimpses II*, p. 157.

40. MFKF to Larry Powell, June 15, 1943, SL.

41. Patricia Storace, *The New York Review of Books*, December 7, 1989, pp. 44–45.

42. MFKF to Larry Powell, June 15, 1943, SL.

43. "Foreword," *TGM*, [p. 1].

44. Ibid.

45. *TGM*, p. 75.
46. MFKF to Larry Powell, July 16, 1943, SL; and *ALIL*, p. 59.
47. Ibid.
48. Although Dr. Hal Bieler was well known for books like *Food Is Your Best Medicine*, he was also an advocate of natural childbirth without anesthesia or drugs.
49. When she began studying acting in New York City in 1961, Anne changed her name to Anna. She was also called Anneli by her family.
50. Sean Kelly to Joan Reardon, July 10, 2002.
51. MFKF to Eda Lord, May 2, 1952, SL.
52. MFKF to Larry Powell, November 3, 1943, SL; and *ALIL*, p. 61.
53. Stuart, *Gloria Stuart: I Just Keep Hoping*, p. 151.
54. MFKF to Marietta Voorhees, August 13, 1969, SL.
55. Larry Bachmann to MFKF, November 10, 1944, SL.
56. MFKF to Larry Powell, November 3, 1943, SL; and *ALIL*, p. 61.
57. In conversations much later in her life, MFKF always said that the only review that she ever read that pleased her was one of *SIF* by S. I. Hayakawa. But the book that Hayakawa reviewed in the November 28, 1943, issue of *Book Week* was *TGM*.
58. Sheila Hibben, *Weekly Book Review*, November 21, 1943, p. 8.
59. Clifton Fadiman, *The New Yorker*, November 20, 1943, p. 105.
60. Storace, *The New York Review of Books*, December 7, 1989, pp. 44–45.
61. Starr, *Material Dreams*, p. 380.
62. Larry Bachmann to MFKF, December 4, 1943, SL.
63. Larry Bachmann to MFKF, October 10, 1944, SL.
64. MFKF, "Napa and Sonoma," *Food and Wine*, August 1979, p. 32.
65. The episode that MFKF dubbed "Hollywood versus Fisher," along with the nature of her employment at Paramount, acquired more importance and exaggeration throughout her life. When fans and interviewers sought her out at Last House, the aged MFKF regaled them with stories about being a gag writer for the Hope and Crosby *Road* pictures. (Actually, two of the films predated MFKF's years at Paramount: *Road to Morocco* was released in 1942, and after a three-year pause in the series, *Road to Utopia* opened in 1945.) She also titillated her guests with stories about going on afternoon jaunts to Mexico with Ava Gardner, Greta Garbo, Joseph Cotton, and Mackinlay Kantor. Most often, however, she portrayed herself as a champion for the rights of writers to negotiate salaries and write for other studios.
66. MFKF, Journal, 1944, PC.
67. *LH*, p. 5.
68. MFKF to Harold Price, n.d. (marked Tuesday morning; unsent), PC.
69. MFKF to Larry Powell, March 30, 1944, SL; and *ALIL*, pp. 63–64.
70. *House Beautiful*, June 1944, p. 120.
71. "In Honor of Spring," *House Beautiful*, April 1945, p. 124.
72. MFKF, Journal, May 25, 1944, PC.
73. MFKF to Larry Powell, September 23, 1944, SL; and *ALIL*, p. 65.

8: THE REFUGEE

1. MFKF, Journal, January 1, 1952, PC.
2. Gloria Stuart Sheekman to MFKF, n.d. [1945], SL.
3. Ibid.
4. "H Is for Happy," AAFG, p. 54.
5. MFKF to Larry Powell, telegram, May 21, 1945, SL; and ALIL, p. 66.
6. MFKF to Larry Powell, May 28, 1945, SL; and ALIL, p. 66.
7. DH, p. 139.
8. MFKF to Larry Powell, May 28, 1945, SL.
9. DH, p. 138.
10. MFKF re-created her luncheon with Arnold Gingrich, substituting Donald Friede for Gingrich, in "H Is for Happy," AAFG, p. 54.
11. Arnold Gingrich, Toys of a Lifetime, pp. 198–208.
12. The precise nature of the case is not known, but Donald's brother was using the U.S. mail to send pornography and had listed Donald as a business partner. The suit against Donald was eventually settled.
13. Donald Friede to MFKF, July 8, 1945, SL.
14. MFKF to Donald Friede, July 15, 1945, SL.
15. "War," LH, p. 5.
16. MFKF to Dr. George Frumkes, January 12, 1950, SL.
17. "Afterword," NNBN, p. 260.
18. MFKF to Larry Powell, January 30, 1946, SL; and ALIL, p. 67.
19. "Kennedy Friede" appeared on the birth certificate, although MFKF, Donald, and the rest of the family called her Mary until she decided that she wanted to be called Kennedy in college. "Kennedy" is used throughout the text of this biography.
20. MFKF, Journal, July 3, 1946, PC.
21. Three years later when Donald Friede stayed at the Ranch with Rex for a short time, Rex told Donald that he was proud of the way Donald handled the situation, and Donald repeated the conversation to MFKF: "Suddenly he [Rex] started talking about little Anne and how happy he was to know that she *was* his grand-child . . . I only mention this to give you a clear picture of his whole attitude, and [he] went on to say how proud of you he was for your courage, and how sorry he was that you had kept it from him for so long, and particularly at the time itself when he wished he could have helped you. He told me of his admiration of you in general, and of what a grand child he had always thought Anne was, and of how he had for some time suspected the truth, and of how sure that your choice was soundly made. It was a wonderful thing coming from Rex." Donald Friede to MFKF, July 8, 1949, SL.
22. Donald Friede, "On Being Married to M.F.K. Fisher," PC.
23. MFKF, Journal, September 5, 1946, PC.
24. Ibid.
25. Ibid.
26. Ibid., September 6, 1946.
27. Ibid., September 14, 1946.
28. Ibid., September 7, 1946.

29. Ibid., September 21, 1946.
30. MFKF to Larry Powell, November 26, 1946, SL; and ALIL, p. 67.
31. *Kirkus Reviews*, October 1, 1946, p. 515.
32. Sheila Hibben, *Weekly Book Review*, December 22, 1946, p. 7.
33. MFKF, Journal, December 4, 1946, PC.
34. Ibid., November 21, 1946.
35. MFKF to Rex Kennedy, January 11, 1947 (unsent), SL.
36. MFKF, Journal, February 14, 1947, PC.
37. MFKF to Larry Powell, February 8, 1947, SL; and *ALIL*, p. 68.
38. "A Postscript from the Translator," *The Physiology of Taste*, 1971 ed., pp. 441–42.
39. "Translator's Glosses," *The Physiology of Taste*, p. 18.
40. "Aphorisms of the Professor," *The Physiology of Taste*, p. 3.
41. MFKF, Journal, February 14, 1947, PC.
42. MFKF to Larry Powell, March 26, 1947, SL.
43. "Tokay Jennie" was shortened, revised, and sold to *Town and Country*, June 1947.
44. John Farrelly, *The New Republic*, September 8, 1947, p. 30.
45. J. W. Chase, *The New York Times*, August 31, 1947, p. 7.
46. Hamilton Basso, *The New Yorker*, August 30, 1947, p. 64.
47. MFKF to Larry Powell, August 10, 1947, SL; and ALIL, p. 73.
48. MFKF, Journal, July 26, 1947, PC.
49. Sean Kelly to Joan Reardon, August 16, 2002: "MF later wrote that Donald Friede, who incidentally loathed my mother (and the feeling was mutual), pressured her into writing the novel which I will now reread . . . My copy of it is inscribed by MF 'For Sean K. Kelly—a short course in The Other Sex from MFK Fisher, devotedly.' "
50. MFKF to Larry Powell, July 15, 1947, SL.
51. MFKF, Journal, July 26, 1947, PC.
52. Rex Kennedy to MFKF, n.d. [1947], SL.
53. MFKF to Larry Powell, January 27, 1948, SL; and *ALIL*, p. 73.
54. MFKF to Pat Covici, September 14, 1948, SL.
55. MFKF to Larry Powell, August 17, 1948, SL; and *ALIL*, pp. 75–76.
56. Guggenheim Application, fall 1948, SL.
57. MFKF, Journal, October 1, 1948, PC.
58. MFKF to Pat Covici, June 28, 1949, SL.
59. MFKF to Larry Powell, February 18, 1949, SL; and *ALIL*, p. 77.
60. MFKF to Pat Covici, June 28, 1949, SL.
61. A reference to the charges brought against Donald Friede and his half brother Sidney in California in June 1945.
62. Donald Friede to MFKF, July 8, 1949, SL.
63. MFKF to Pat Covici, July 14, 1949, SL.
64. *Kirkus Reviews*, July 1, 1949, p. 365.
65. J. H. Jackson, *San Francisco Chronicle*, September 16, 1949, p. 20.
66. Rex Stout, *The New York Times*, October 9, 1949, p. 25.
67. Kappo Phelan, *Commonweal*, November 11, 1949, p. 165.
68. *The New Yorker*, December 24, 1949, p. 64.
69. MFKF to Dr. Tarjans, September 23, 1949, SL.
70. Gloria Stuart Sheekman, interview by author, October, 19, 1997.

71. MFKF to Donald Friede, October 17, 1949, SL.
72. MFKF to Donald Friede, November 7, 1949, SL.
73. Larry Powell, "MF: A Reminiscence," *ALIL*, p. xvi.
74. MFKF to Larry Powell, November 18, 1949, SL; and *ALIL*, p. 80.

9 : NOW AN ORPHAN

1. MFKF to Joan Reardon, September 3, 1987.
2. MFKF, Journal, May 16, 1952, PC.
3. Ibid.
4. MFKF to Donald Friede, November 7, 1949, SL.
5. MFKF to Donald Friede, November 23, 1949, SL.
6. MFKF to Donald Friede, January 7, 1950, SL.
7. Ibid.
8. Donald Friede to MFKF, November 28, 1949, SL.
9. MFKF to Donald Friede, December 7, 1949, SL.
10. *DH*, p. 139.
11. MFKF to Dr. George Frumkes, January 12, 1950, SL.
12. Ibid.
13. MFKF, Journal, February 19, 1950, PC.
14. MFKF to Pat Covici, March 8, 1950, SL.
15. Kennedy Friede Golden, interview by author, tape recording, August 25, 1997.
16. MFKF, Journal, February 19, 1950, PC.
17. MFKF to Pat Covici, March 3, 1950, SL.
18. MFKF to Pat Covici, July 8, 1950, SL.
19. *HTCAW* (rev. ed., 1951), p. 209.
20. Ibid., p. 322.
21. Ibid., p. 350.
22. MFKF to Dr. George Frumkes, June 1, 1950, SL.
23. MFKF to Dr. George Frumkes, June 6, 1950, SL.
24. MFKF, Journal, February 2, 1950, PC.
25. MFKF to Dr. George Frumkes, April 10, 1953, SL.
26. MFKF to Larry Powell, July 24, 1950, SL.
27. MFKF to Pat Covici, September 25, 1950, SL.
28. Ibid.
29. MFKF to Dr. George Frumkes, November 4, 1950, SL.
30. MFKF to Dr. George Frumkes, November 18, 1950, SL.
31. MFKF, "The Direct Approach," c. 1965, PC.
32. MFKF to Dr. George Frumkes, January 4, 1951, SL.
33. Ibid.
34. MFKF to Dr. George Frumkes, January 23, 1951, SL.
35. MFKF to Dr. George Frumkes, January 30, 1951, SL.
36. MFKF to Dr. George Frumkes, February 3, 1951, SL.
37. Eleanor Kask Friede, interview by author, tape recording, July 9, 2000. They were actually married in Reno when Donald's divorce became final in August 1951.
38. Donald Friede to MFKF, April 25, 1951, SL.

39. "Rex—I," 1950, *LH*, p. 12.
40. "Rex—II," 1951, *LH*, p. 17.
41. MFKF, Journal, July 10, 1950, PC.
42. MFKF to Dr. George Frumkes, July 12, 1951, SL.
43. "Legend of Love," *Ladies' Home Journal*, April 1952. p. 41.
44. Ibid.
45. Donald Friede to MFKF, November 3, 1951, SL.
46. MFKF to Donald Friede, November 5, 1951, SL.
47. MFKF to Norah Barr, March 23, 1951, SL.
48. *TGM*, p. 367.
49. MFKF to Dr. George Frumkes, October 19, 1951, SL.
50. MFKF to Dr. George Frumkes, September 20, 1951, SL.
51. MFKF to Dr. George Frumkes, October 19, 1951, SL.
52. MFKF to Dr. George Frumkes, October 20, 1951, SL.
53. Ibid.
54. Ibid.
55. MFKF to Dr. George Frumkes, March 25, 1952, SL.
56. Ibid.
57. MFKF, Journal, "Notes for Whittier Book," May 1952, PC.
58. MFKF to Norah Barr, April 12, 1952, SL.
59. Ted Kennedy to MFKF, December 1952, in Kennedy, *Glimpses II*, p. 187.
60. MFKF to Ted Kennedy, May 5, 1953, in Kennedy, *Glimpses II*, p. 188.
61. *Assembly Journal*, June 5, 1953.

10: CALIFORNIENNE

1. MFKF to Hal Durrell, October 12, 1957, SL.
2. "Another Love Story" appeared for the first time in *The New Yorker*, February 7, 1983, pp. 35–36, and was republished in *SA*, pp. 59–82.
3. *SA*, p. 77.
4. MFKF to Dr. George Frumkes, November 2, 1953, SL.
5. *SA*, p. 80.
6. MFKF to Pat Covici, November 9, 1953, SL.
7. MFKF, "Salt Lake Journal, June, 1953," PC.
8. MFKF to Dr. George Frumkes, November 2, 1953, SL.
9. Ted Kennedy to MFKF, August 1953, in Kennedy, *Glimpses II*, p. 192.
10. "Napa and Sonoma: The Best of Both Worlds," *Food and Wine*, August 1979, p. 43.
11. MFKF to Eda Lord, November 19, 1953, SL.
12. James E. Beard was a local printer and designer of wine labels. After M.F.K. Fisher met James A. Beard of cookbook fame, she referred to her St. Helena friend as "skinny Jim."
13. "Napa and Sonoma," p. 43.
14. Kennedy Friede Golden, interview by author, tape recording, August 1997.
15. "One Way to Give Thanks," *Antaeus*, spring 1992.
16. MFKF to Dr. George Frumkes, November 2, 1953, SL.
17. The amount each heir received was approximately $100,000.

18. MFKF to Larry Powell, February 15, 1954, SL; and *ALIL*, p. 124.

19. MFKF to Norah Barr, May 27, 1954, SL.

20. MFKF to Ted Kennedy, August 24, 1954, in Kennedy, *Glimpses II*, pp. 198–99.

21. *MOAT*, p. 34.

22. "Emmenée par des notables très fortement impliqués dans le mouvement touristique national, la Bourgogne épouse rapidement ces redéfinitions régionalistes et gastronomiques . . . En 1921, est créée la Foire Gastronomique de Dijon . . . pensée comme une vitrine de produits régionaux destinée à promouvoir la région; le régionalisme bourguignon se recentre autour de l'identité gastronomique avec l'invention de plats régionaux, la redéfinition de 'l'ethnotype bourguignon.' " From www.dijontourism.com.

23. "All the Foods and Wines Were There," *Holiday*, November 1957, pp. 27–29.

24. MFKF to Harold Price, November, n.d. [1954], SL.

25. *MOAT*, p. 75.

26. Ibid., p. 67.

27. MFKF to Larry Powell, February 15, 1954, SL.

28. J. T. Winterich, *New York Herald Tribune Book Review*, December 5, 1954, p. 32.

29. J. H. Jackson, *San Francisco Chronicle*, September 24, 1954, p. 15.

30. Alan Brien, *The Spectator*, September 24, 1965.

31. Clifton Fadiman, "Introduction," *TAOE*, p. vii.

32. MFKF to Ms. Jean Bennett, January 4, 1973, SL.

33. "Foreword," *TGM*, p. 353.

34. MFKF to Donald Friede, November 28, 1954, SL.

35. MFKF to Pat Covici, November 8, 1954, SL.

36. The exploits of this mongrel dog became the source of *The Boss Dog*. Fisher wrote the first draft of the book while in Aix in 1955.

37. MFKF, "Eaten Tree Journal," PC.

38. Small deep-fried fish eaten whole, a specialty dish in many Marseillaise restaurants.

39. MFKF, "Eaten Tree Journal," PC.

40. *ACT*, p. 136.

41. Ibid., p. 192.

42. "Preface" to "Wartwort," *ATW*, p. 114.

43. "Two Kitchens in Provence," *ATW*, p. 100.

44. MFKF to Norah Barr, May 16, 1955, SL; and *ALIL*, pp. 137–38.

45. MFKF to Donald Friede, November 11, 1955, SL.

46. MFKF to Barbara Marschutz, July 17, 1956, SL.

47. *ATW*, pp. 203–14.

48. MFKF to Donald Friede, November 11, 1955, SL.

49. Ibid.

50. Ibid.

51. MFKF, Journal, n.d., PC.

52. MFKF to Georges Connes, January 4, 1956, SL.

53. At this time television interviews of MFKF were limited to local Bay Area programs. An appearance on *Camera Three* in 1975 and one with Stephen Banker for *Tapes for Readers* in 1978 marked the beginning of many more TV interviews.

54. MFKF to Norah Barr, July 16, 1956 (unsent), SL.

55. MFKF, Journal, n.d., PC.
56. MFKF to Monique Wytenhove, September 7, 1956, SL.
57. *DH*, p. 142.

11: ONE VERSE OF A SONG

1. Erica Jong, *Sappho's Leap* (New York: W. W. Norton, 2003), p. 15.
2. *Architectural Digest*, July/August 1980.
3. Romie Gould, interview by author, tape recording, November 12, 1994.
4. "Napa and Sonoma," *Food and Wine*, August 1979, p. 43.
5. Ibid.
6. MFKF to Larry Bachmann, November 14, 1956, SL.
7. MFKF to Larry Powell, February 19, 1957, SL; and *ALIL*, p. 155.
8. Norah Barr, interview by author, tape recording, October 22, 2000. It is Norah Barr's opinion that Marietta Voorhees may have been born with a gender-identity disorder.
9. MFKF to Eda Lord, November 18, 1959, SL.
10. MFKF never identified the friend.
11. MFKF to Dr. George Frumkes, April 10, 1953, SL.
12. MFKF, Journal, 1957, PC.
13. MFKF to Larry Powell, April 7, 1957, SL.
14. MFKF to Larry Powell, May 30, 1957, SL.
15. MFKF to Hal Durrell, October 12, 1957, SL.
16. MFKF to Donald Friede, August 10, 1958, SL.
17. Ibid.
18. MFKF to Hal Durrell, October 12, 1957, SL.
19. MFKF, Journal, February 7, 1958, PC.
20. MFKF to Donald Friede, August 31, 1958, SL.
21. MFKF to Donald Friede, September 17, 1958, SL.
22. Ibid.
23. The house was sold in February 1962 because, as MFKF said, "I am too old to cope with it, many tangibles and intangibles." Journal, February 25, 1962, PC.
24. MFKF to Larry Powell, January 7, 1959, SL.
25. MFKF to Donald Friede, November 10, 1958, SL.
26. MFKF to Hal Durrell, October 12, 1957, SL.
27. MFKF to Donald and Eleanor Friede, August 9, 1959, SL; and *ALIL*, p. 163.
28. MFKF to Donald and Eleanor Friede, August 18, 1959, SL; and *ALIL*, p. 165.
29. MFKF to Eda Lord, November 18, 1959, SL.
30. Ibid.
31. Both MFKF and Eleanor kept them as souvenirs of Lugano. Because MFKF used to drink her special mixture of gin, vermouth, and Campari in one of them, she sometimes referred to it as a *boccalino*.
32. *MOAT*, p. 110.
33. MFKF to Larry Powell, February 18, 1960, SL; and *ALIL*, p. 167.
34. *MOAT*, p. 111.
35. "Two Kitchens in Provence," *ATW*, pp. 107–08.
36. "Journey," *LH*, pp. 180–81.

37. Every July since 1948 the city of Aix has hosted a major classical music and opera festival, called Festival International d'Art Lyrique et de Musique, in the Cathédrale St.-Saveur, its cloister, and the Théâtre de l'Archevêché.
38. Pat Covici to MFKF, October 27, 1960, SL.
39. MFKF to Larry Powell, August 31, 1960, SL; and *ALIL*, p. 172.

12: ILLNESS AND HEALING

1. *ACW*, p. 5.
2. MFKF, Journal, September 15, 1963, PC. The comment is made in the context of a discussion of prejudice toward blacks in the States; Mary Frances expresses pride that her daughters do not have racial prejudices. She did not elaborate on Anna's relationship with a young man from Madagascar.
3. *ACW*, p. 142.
4. MFKF to Larry Powell, August 31, 1960, SL; and *ALIL*, p. 172.
5. *MOAT*, p. 115.
6. "Preface," *ACW*, p. i.
7. MFKF, Journal, "Paris, 1960," PC.
8. Ibid.
9. MFKF, Journal, "Paris, 1960," PC.
10. MFKF, "Noël en Paris," *San Francisco Examiner*, 1987.
11. MFKF, "The Oldest Man," *The New Yorker*, December 5, 1964, pp. 62–66.
12. MFKF to Grace Holmes, March 15, 1961, SL; and *ALIL*, pp. 172–74.
13. MFKF to Donald and Eleanor Friede, May 24, 1961, SL; and *ALIL*, pp. 174–77.
14. Eleanor Friede to MFKF, March 2, 1962, SL.
15. *San Francisco Chronicle*, December 10, 1961, p. 45.
16. Fanny Butcher, *Chicago Sunday Tribune*, September 24, 1961, p. 3.
17. Elizabeth Janeway, *The New York Times Book Review*, November 12, 1961, p. 52.
18. *AAFG*, p. 680.
19. *ACW*, p. 105.
20. MFKF to Larry Powell, November 10, 1961, SL; and *ALIL*, pp. 177–78.
21. MFKF to Eleanor and Donald Friede, April 22, 1962, SL; and *ALIL*, p. 180.
22. MFKF to Kennedy Friede, January 13, 1962, SL.
23. MFKF to Kennedy Friede, March 12, 1962, SL.
24. MFKF to Eleanor and Donald Friede, May 14, 1962, SL; and *ALIL*, pp. 181–82.
25. Kennedy Friede Golden, interview by author, tape recording, August 4, 1998.
26. MFKF to Eleanor Friede, January 25, 1962, SL; and *ALIL*, p. 178.
27. Located next to the town's tavern, the general store that the Erskines purchased was in one of the oldest buildings in Genoa. It is now an antique shop.
28. MFKF to Eleanor and Donald Friede, April 22, 1962, SL; and *ALIL*, p. 180.
29. Ibid., p. 179.
30. Ibid.
31. MFKF, 1962 calendar, December 3, 1962, PC.
32. MFKF to Judith Jones, March 22, 1972, SL.
33. MFKF to Larry Powell, October 8, 1962, SL; and *ALIL*, p. 183.
34. Maynard Amerine, interview by author, October 25, 1994.

35. MFKF, Journal, November, 1962, PC.
36. MFKF, Journal, October 23, 1962, PC.
37. Ibid.
38. Ibid.
39. MFKF, Journal, March 3, 1963, PC.
40. MFKF, Journal, April 3, 1963, PC.
41. Ibid.
42. MFKF to Marian Gore, March 31, 1963, SL.
43. MFKF, Journal, August 15, 1963, PC.
44. MFKF to Henry Volkening, November 6, 1963, SL; and *ALIL*, p. 189.
45. MFKF, Journal, September 15, 1963, PC.
46. Ibid.
47. Ibid.
48. MFKF to June Eddy, January 18, 1964, SL.
49. Ibid.
50. Ibid.
51. MFKF, Journal, 1963, PC.

13: THE MOST ALONE

1. MFKF to Henry Volkening, March 22, 1964, SL.
2. Ibid.
3. Ibid.
4. MFKF to Grace Holmes, January 24, 1964, SL; and *ALIL*, p. 194.
5. Anne Kelly Erskine to MFKF, March 12, 1964, PC.
6. Anna Parrish Friede to MFKF, March 13, 1964, PC.
7. MFKF, "O Is for Old Age," MS, PC.
8. William Shawn (1907–92) was the illustrious editor of *The New Yorker* from 1952 to 1987.
9. MFKF to Grace Holmes, January 24, 1964, SL.
10. Ibid.
11. *MOAT*, p. 3.
12. Dorrie Pagones, *Saturday Review*, May 2, 1964, p. 33.
13. *The New Yorker*, July 11, 1964, p. 92.
14. MFKF to Marietta Voorhees, June 23, 1964, SL.
15. David Lance Goines, *The Free Speech Movement: Coming of Age in the 1960s* (Berkeley, Calif.: Ten Speed Press, 1993), p. 100.
16. Ibid.
17. MFKF to Elsine Ten Broeck, June 25, 1964, SL.
18. MFKF to Norah Barr, July 27, 1964, SL; and *ALIL*, p. 204.
19. MFKF to Norah and the Barrs, July 2, 1964, SL.
20. MFKF to Marietta Voorhees, June 28, 1964, SL.
21. MFKF to Norah Barr, July 27, 1964, SL.
22. MFKF to Chas Newton, October 25, 1964, SL.
23. MFKF to Georges Connes, July 11, 1965, SL.
24. MFKF to Sean Kelly, September 6, 1964, SL.
25. MFKF to Larry Powell, March 16, 1965, SL.

26. MFKF to Eleanor Friede, September 21, 1964, SL.
27. Ibid.
28. MFKF to June Eddy, November 30, 1964, SL.
29. MFKF to Georges Connes, July 11, 1965, SL.
30. MFKF to Marietta Voorhees, January 4, 1965, SL.
31. MFKF, "Genoa Journal," PC. MFKF never published her experiences at Piney Woods, but did tell the "story" to Charlotte Painter in *Gifts of Age: Portraits and Essays of 32 Remarkable Women*, pp. 55–60. "Birds of Passage" is a highly exaggerated account with many factual errors in which Piney Woods becomes the focal point of the search for the missing three civil rights workers, who were found dead at least 250 miles north and east of the school. This account does not correlate with the Piney Woods references in *ALIL*, pp. 199–210, or with manuscript material like lesson plans and notes in PC.
32. MFKF to Marietta Voorhees, January 4, 1965, SL.
33. MFKF, Journal, March 16, 1965, PC.
34. MFKF to Larry Powell, March 16, 1965, SL; and *ALIL*, p. 217.
35. MFKF, Journal, 1965, PC.
36. MFKF to Donald Friede, October 31, 1964, SL.
37. Ibid.
38. "The Full-Orbed Dinner," *The New Yorker*, June 5, 1965, pp. 145–50.
39. Ibid.
40. Ibid.
41. MFKF to Eleanor Friede, April 7, 1965, SL.
42. MFKF, Journal, April 7, 1965, PC.
43. Ibid.
44. MFKF, Journal, 1965, PC.
45. Ibid.
46. MFKF to Georges Connes, July 11, 1965, SL.
47. MFKF to Sean Kelly, August 27, 1965, SL.
48. MFKF to Eda Lord, October 15, 1965, SL; and *ALIL*, p. 225.
49. Eleanor Friede to MFKF, March 30, 1965, SL.
50. MFKF to Eleanor Kask Friede, April 7, 1965, SL.
51. MFKF, Journal, January 3, 1966, PC.

14: CARA MARIA FRANCESCA

1. MFKF to Arnold Gingrich, September 17, 1966, SL.
2. MFKF to Chuck Newton, February 3, 1966, SL.
3. MFKF to Kennedy Friede, March 5, 1966, SL.
4. *DH*, p. 143.
5. MFKF to William Targ, January 20, 1966, SL.
6. *WBKAF*, p. 100.
7. Claiborne gave Field's East Hampton restaurant one star in 1965: that was probably the beginning of their differences, which eventually escalated into a war of words over cookbook reviews, restaurant listings, and Claiborne's damaging review of *The Cooking of Provincial France*.
8. MFKF to Grace Holmes, May 17, 1966, SL. The contract with Time-Life Books

called for a flat fee of $10,000, but bonuses were offered for various reasons, like meeting deadlines.

9. Reprinted in *ATW*, pp. 215–26.
10. MFKF to Grace Holmes, May 17, 1966, SL.
11. In fact, Gingrich's wife Helen Mary had died.
12. MFKF to Arnold Gingrich, August 23, 1952, SL.
13. MFKF, "The Direct Approach," c. 1965, PC.
14. *Toys of a Lifetime* is a memoir about Gingrich's many homes, automobiles, violins, travels, pipes, and various other things and experiences that gave him pleasure.
15. Arnold Gingrich to MFKF, June 14, 1966, SL.
16. MFKF, Journals, "Paris-Aix, 1966," PC.
17. Brenda Wineapple, *Genet*, p. 5.
18. "Introduction to Alice Toklas Cookbook," *DH*, pp. 37–49.
19. Arnold Gingrich to John Gingrich, June 17, 1966, PC.
20. Arnold Gingrich to M. Charles Ritz, June 17, 1966, PC.
21. In MFKF's later accounts, Mme Lanes is named Mme Duval.
22. Simone Beck, coauthor of *Mastering the Art of French Cooking*, preferred to be called by her nickname Simca.
23. Simone Beck, *Food and Friends*, pp. 227–28.
24. MFKF, Journal, "Paris, 1966," PC.
25. Julia Child to MFKF, March 20, 1977, SL.
26. MFKF to Julia Child, August 21, 1966, SL.
27. MFKF to Arnold Gingrich, August 15, 1966, SL.
28. Ibid.
29. Ibid.
30. Ibid.
31. Arnold Gingrich to MFKF, October 12, 1966, SL.
32. MFKF to Arnold Gingrich, August 23, 1966, SL.
33. Ibid.
34. MFKF to Arnold Gingrich, September 4, 1966, SL.
35. Julia Child to MFKF, October 26, 1966, SL.
36. Julia Child to Dick Williams, October 24, 1966, SL.
37. MFKF to Arnold Gingrich, October 31, 1966, SL.
38. MFKF to Julia Child, October 21, 1966, SL.
39. MFKF to Arnold Gingrich, October 31, 1966, SL.
40. MFKF to Arnold Gingrich, November 5, 1966, SL; and *ALIL*, p. 242.
41. MFKF to Henry Volkening, January 16, 1968, SL.
42. Julia Child to MFKF, September 3, 1966, SL.
43. Julia Child to MFKF, September 23, 1966, SL.
44. Esther Aresty, *The Delectable Past: The Joys of the Table from Rome to the Renaissance from Elizabeth I to Mrs. Beeton* (New York: Macmillan, 1978).
45. Judith Jones to MFKF, November 16, 1966, SL.
46. MFKF to Paul and Julia Child, September 24, 1967, SL.
47. MFKF, Journal, February 28, 1967, PC.
48. MFKF, Journal, March 1, 1967, PC.
49. MFKF to Julia Child, March 24, 1967, SL.

50. MFKF, Journal, March 1967, PC.
51. MFKF to Kennedy Friede, April 5, 1967, PC.
52. MFKF to Arnold Gingrich, April 5, 1967, SL.
53. MFKF to Arnold Gingrich, May 8, 1967, SL; and *ALIL*, pp. 251–52.
54. Ibid.
55. Arnold Gingrich to MFKF, June 2, 1967, SL.
56. MFKF to Grace Holmes, June 15, 1967, SL.
57. MFKF, Calendar, 1967, PC.
58. MFKF to Grace Holmes, August 26, 1967, SL.
59. MFKF to Grace Holmes, July 1, 1967, SL.
60. MFKF, Journal, 1967, PC.

15: READING BETWEEN THE RECIPES

1. "Introduction" (unpublished), *WBKAF*, SL.
2. MFKF, Journal, January 22, 1969, PC.
3. Julia Child to MFKF, December 26, 1967, SL.
4. Craig Claiborne, "Debut for a Series of International Cookbooks," *The New York Times*, February 19, 1968, p. 46.
5. Ibid.
6. MFKF to Julia Child, April 24, 1968, SL.
7. MFKF wrote: "Serious French eaters—which means serious Frenchmen—often gauge the standards of almost any kitchen, whether great or modest, by its *terrine* (or *pâté*) *maison*, the special product of the house or restaurant." *TCOPF*, p. 62.
8. John L. Hess, "Time-Life Cookbook: It's Self-Roasting," *The New York Times*, April 15, 1969.
9. "A Gastronome's Revenge," *Newsweek*, April 28, 1969, p. 88.
10. Hess, "Time-Life Cookbook."
11. Nora Ephron, "Critics in the World of the Rising Soufflé (Or Is It the Rising Meringue?)," *New York*, October 1968, pp. 34–39.
12. Ibid.
13. Julia Child to MFKF, September 28, 1968, SL.
14. MFKF to Julia Child, October 24, 1968, SL.
15. MFKF to Julia Child, October 4, 1968, SL.
16. *WBKAF*, p. 115.
17. MFKF to Henry Volkening, September 20, 1968, SL.
18. Ibid.
19. MFKF to Julia Child, September 28, 1968, SL.
20. MFKF to Grace Holmes, September 29, 1968, SL.
21. MFKF to Georges Connes, February 15, 1969, SL.
22. MFKF to Dr. George Frumkes, February 20, 1968, SL.
23. MFKF to Grace Holmes, September 17, 1967, SL.
24. Kennedy Friede Golden, interview by author, tape recording, August 5, 1998.
25. MFKF to Dr. Hal Bieler, December 12, 1969, SL.
26. Kennedy Friede Golden, interview by author.
27. MFKF to Grace Holmes, May 20, 1968, SL.
28. MFKF to Grace Holmes, September 29, 1968, SL.

29. Rosamond Bernier, "Naturally Grand," *House & Garden*, July 1985, p. 176.
30. MFKF, Calendar, 1968, PC.
31. MFKF to David Pleydell-Bouverie, August 28, 1968, SL; and *ALIL*, p. 270.
32. MFKF to Georges Connes, February 15, 1969, SL.
33. MFKF to Weare Holbrook, June 24, 1969, SL.
34. MFKF to Arnold Gingrich, April 12, 1969 (unsent), SL.
35. Arnold Gingrich to MFKF, May 6, 1969, SL.
36. MFKF to Julia and Paul Child, July 13, 1969, SL.
37. MFKF to Georges Connes, March 22, 1970, SL.
38. Ibid.
39. MFKF to Dr. Hal Bieler, December 9, 1969, SL.
40. MFKF to Dear Family, October 7, 1969, SL.
41. MFKF to Arnold Gingrich, September 20, 1969, SL.
42. MFKF to Dr. Hal Bieler, December, 9, 1969, SL.
43. *WBKAF*, [p. 3].
44. Ibid., p. 103.
45. MFKF, "Introduction" (unpublished), *WBKAF*, SL.
46. Patricia Storace, *The New York Review of Books*, December 7, 1989, pp. 44–45.
47. MFKF, "Introduction" (unpublished), *WBKAF*, SL.
48. Ibid.
49. Frieda Gruenrock, *Booksellers*, November 15, 1969, p. 320.
50. Nika Hazelton, *The New York Times Book Review*, December 7, 1969, p. 18.
51. MFKF to June Eddy, December 14, 1969, SL.
52. MFKF to Anna Friede, December 8, 1969, SL.
53. Arnold Gingrich to MFKF, December 31, 1969, SL.
54. MFKF to Arnold Gingrich, December 28, 1969, SL.
55. MFKF to Norah Barr, December 26, 1969, SL.
56. MFKF to Marietta Voorhees, January 27, 1970, SL.
57. Arnold Gingrich to MFKF, December 31, 1969, SL.
58. MFKF to Arnold Gingrich, December 28, 1969, SL.
59. Eleanor Friede, interview by author, tape recording, July 5, 1998.
60. MFKF to Elizabeth Kirk Le Count, March 3, 1970, SL.
61. MFKF to Georges Connes, March 22, 1970, SL.
62. MFKF to Norah Barr, February 11, 1970, SL.
63. MFKF to Arnold Gingrich, March 16, 1970, SL.
64. Arnold Gingrich to MFKF, July 17, 1970, SL.
65. Arnold Gingrich to MFKF, June 4, 1970, SL.
66. MFKF, Journal, 1970, PC.
67. David Pleydell-Bouverie to MFKF, July 5, 1970, SL.
68. MFKF to Arnold Gingrich, July 16, 1970, SL.
69. MFKF to Arnold Gingrich, August 7, 1970, SL.
70. Ibid.
71. Arnold Gingrich to MFKF, August 19, 1970, SL.
72. MFKF to Arnold Gingrich, August 22, 1970, SL.
73. MFKF to David Pleydell-Bouverie, August 21, 1970, SL.
74. Sean Kelly to Joan Reardon, August 10, 2002.

16: ALIVE AGAIN

1. "A Common Danger," *ATW*, p. 136.
2. Richard Olney, *Reflexions*, p. 128.
3. MFKF to James Beard, in Evan Jones, *Epicurean Delight*, p. 285.
4. Olney, *Reflexions*, p. 130.
5. Ibid., p. 244.
6. Ibid.
7. In a letter that journalist Anthony Denney sent to David in 1986, he criticizes MFKF's *Two Towns in Provence*: "In the Aix section she describes proudly how she was able several times to resist being told and shown the preparation of *calissons d'Aix*: her own version then follows." David's biographer, Artemis Cooper, then adds, "For Elizabeth, who never turned down an opportunity to see how a local speciality was made, this about summed up the difference between herself and Mrs. Fisher." *Writing at the Kitchen Table*, p. 301.
8. MFKF to Julia Child, December 16, 1970, SL.
9. MFKF to Julia Child, January 6, 1971, SL.
10. MFKF to Arnold Gingrich, January 28, 1971, SL.
11. MFKF to Arnold Gingrich, February 6, 1971, SL.
12. James Beard, "Appreciation," *TAOE*, p. xvii.
13. MFKF to Julia Child, May 12, 1971, SL.
14. MFKF to Arnold Gingrich, May ?, 1971, SL.
15. MFKF, "New Orleans, Notes," PC.
16. MFKF to Arnold Gingrich, September 28, 1971, SL.
17. Ibid.
18. MFKF to Arnold Gingrich, September 12, 1971, SL.
19. *AF*, p. 278.
20. Ibid., p. 280.
21. Ibid.
22. Sean Kelly to Joan Reardon, September 3, 2002.
23. Jean Stafford, "Love Match of Pleasures," *Vogue*, January 1, 1972, p. 122.
24. M. M. Caffall, *Library Journal*, September 15, 1971, p. 2762.
25. MFKF to Norah Barr, December 17, 1971, SL.
26. MFKF to Dr. Hal Bieler, March 22, 1972, SL.
27. MFKF to Judith Jones, March 22, 1972, SL.
28. Mrs. Claude Kreider to MFKF, February 16, 1971, SL.
29. *AF*, p. 9.
30. Robert S. Pirie and Richard Sennett, *The New York Times Book Review*, February 6, 1972, p. 27.
31. Clifton Fadiman, *Saturday Review*, December 18, 1971, p. 42.
32. MFKF, Journal, 1971, PC.
33. Ibid.
34. MFKF to Arnold Gingrich, January 28, 1972, SL.
35. MFKF to Dr. Hal Bieler, March 13, 1972, SL.
36. Ibid.
37. MFKF to Arnold Gingrich, March 21, 1972, SL.
38. MFKF to Arnold Gingrich, May 11, 1972, SL.

39. MFKF to Arnold Gingrich, June 26, 1972, SL.
40. MFKF, "What I remember about Henry Volkening, after his earthly death," PC.
41. Ten cartons of manuscripts and personal papers were sent to the Schlesinger Library at Radcliffe College in November 1972.
42. MFKF to Norah Barr, November 7, 1972, SL.
43. *ATW*, pp. 89–90.
44. MFKF to Eleanor Friede, February 14, 1973, SL.
45. Norah never published the results of her research on Mary Magdalene.
46. MFKF to Arnold Gingrich, May 1, 1973, SL.

17: OTHER PLACES

1. MFKF, "Preface," *ATW*, p. 3.
2. MFKF, Journal, December 6, 1973, PC.
3. MFKF to Norah Barr, September 6, 1974, SL.
4. Ibid.
5. MFKF, Journal, 1974, PC.
6. See "Interviews—II," *LH*, pp. 118–23, for MFKF's account of her photography session with Annie Leibovitz.
7. MFKF to Arnold Gingrich, December 2, 1973, SL.
8. Nancy Scott, "The Grand Dame of Gastronomy," *San Francisco Chronicle*, May 22, 1977, pp. 20–26.
9. MFKF to Dr. Hal Bieler, October 4, 1972, SL.
10. MFKF, Journal, January 16, 1976, PC.
11. See Gloria Stuart, *Gloria Stuart: I Just Kept Hoping*, p. 153.
12. MFKF to Arnold Gingrich, February 17, 1975, SL.
13. MFKF to Mary Kiesling, December 18, 1974, SL.
14. MFKF to Norah Barr, January 20, 1976, SL.
15. Ibid.
16. MFKF to Arnold Gingrich, February 17, 1975, SL.
17. Jerry DiVecchio, interview by author, tape recording, October 20, 2000.
18. MFKF to Arnold Gingrich, February 17, 1975, SL.
19. Ibid.
20. *Esquire*, December 1975, pp 91–93.
21. MFKF to Norah Barr, May 30, 1973, SL.
22. MFKF, Journal, February 17, 1976, PC.
23. MFKF to Arnold Gingrich, March 30, 1976, SL.
24. MFKF, Journal, April 20, 1976, PC.
25. MFKF to Eleanor Friede, May 12, 1976, SL.
26. Judith Jones, interview by author, April 1, 2000.
27. MFKF to Anna [Parrish] and Kennedy [Wright], May 2, 1976, SL.
28. MFKF to Kennedy Wright, July 19, 1976, SL.
29. MFKF, Journal, July 30, 1976, PC.
30. MFKF to Rachel MacKenzie, December 1, 1976, SL.
31. Judith Jones, interview by author, April 1, 2000.
32. MFKF to Judith Jones, November 26, 1976, SL.
33. MFKF to Norah Barr, November 4, 1976, SL.

34. MFKF to Norah Barr, August 14, 1978, SL; and *ALIL*, p. 396.
35. See Frances Ring, "M.F.K. Fisher," *A Western Harvest: The Gatherings of an Editor* (Los Angeles: John Daniel & Company, 1991), pp. 107–13, for MFKF's correspondence with Frances Ring.
36. MFKF to Rachel MacKenzie, December 1, 1976, SL; and *ALIL*, p. 379.
37. *The New Yorker*, April 17, 1978.
38. *The New Yorker*, March 20, 1965.
39. *Ladies' Home Journal*, April 1952.
40. *ACT*, p. 139.
41. Fictionalized village in "The Lost, Strayed, Stolen," *SA*, pp. 111–41.
42. "Broadside," uncredited, written by MFKF for Standard Oil of California, 1946.
43. *ACT*, p. 147.
44. Ibid., p. 156.
45. Ibid., p. 5.
46. Jan Morris, "A Considerable Town," *The New York Times Book Review*, June 4, 1978, p. 10.
47. Anatole Broyard, "Books of the Times," *The New York Times*, May 10, 1978.
48. W. H. Auden, "Introduction to MFKF's" *TAOE* (London: Faber and Faber, 1963).
49. Broyard, "Books of the Times."
50. Rhoda Koenig, *Saturday Review*, June 24, 1978, p. 5.
51. MFKF to Eleanor Friede, December 20, 1977, SL.
52. MFKF to Julia Child, March 21, 1978, SL.
53. MFKF to Julia Child, June 17, 1978, SL.
54. MFKF to Julia Child, May 3, 1980, SL.
55. MFKF to Julia Child, August 10, 1979, SL.
56. MFKF to Norah Barr, April 21, 1980, SL.
57. Alice Waters, "Introduction" to MFKF's *Two Kitchens in Provence* (Covelo, Calif.: Yolla Bolly Press, 1999).
58. MFKF to Norah Barr, July 14, 1978, SL.
59. MFKF to Eleanor Friede, April 10, 1980, SL.
60. MFKF to Norah Barr, January 14, 1978, SL.
61. MFKF to Judith Jones, November 21, 1975, SL.
62. MFKF to James Beard, October 14, 1981, SL.
63. MFKF to Julia Child, May 4, 1982, SL.
64. MFKF, "Introduction" to Shizuo Tsuji's *Japanese Cooking: A Simple Art* (New York: Kodansha, 1980).
65. Ibid.
66. MFKF to Judith Jones, January 2, 1979, SL.
67. MFKF to Julia Child, December 11, 1978, SL.
68. MFKF to Judith Jones, January 2, 1979, SL.
69. MFKF to Norah Barr, November 30, 1978, SL.
70. Harvey Steiman, *San Francisco Sunday Examiner & Chronicle*, January 7, 1979, p. 5.
71. "Nowhere But Here," *ATW*, p. 251.

18: GARMENTS OF ADIEU

1. Theodore Roethke, *The Far Field*, IV, 1–5, quoted in MFKF, Journal, 1965, PC.
2. MFKF, Journal, September 28, 1980, PC.
3. MFKF to Judith Jones, September 3, 1980, SL.
4. MFKF, Journal, March 29, 1980, PC.
5. MFKF to William Turnbull, March 4, 1991, SL.
6. Clifton Fadiman, *Signature*, November 1981, p. 12.
7. Raymond Sokolov, *The New York Times Book Review*, June 6, 1982, p. 9.
8. John Updike, "Female Pilgrims," *The New Yorker*, August 16, 1982, p. 87.
9. Carolyn See, *Los Angeles Times*, June 14, 1982, V, p. 8.
10. MFKF to Bud Landreth, July 24, 1982, SL.
11. MFKF to Norah Barr, August 29, 1982, SL.
12. MFKF to James Beard, April 17, 1982, SL.
13. MFKF to Sam Davis, December 1, 1982, SL.
14. MFKF, "Afterword," *NNBN* (1982).
15. MFKF to Naomi Pfeiffer at *MD*, August 9, 1971, PC.
16. "Why We Need a Women's Party," *Newsweek*, February 11, 1980, p. 21.
17. Ruth Reichl, "M.F.K. Fisher: *How to Cook a Wolf* and Other Gastronomical Feats," *Ms.*, April 1981, pp. 90–92.
18. MFKF, Journal, August 29, 1980, PC.
19. "Why We Need a Women's Party," p. 21.
20. "Loving Cooks, Beware!" *Journal of Gastronomy*, summer 1984, p. 27.
21. MFKF to David Thomson, April 30, 1984, SL.
22. MFKF to Jeff Trachenberg, September 1, 1982, SL.
23. MFKF to Lawrence Clark Powell, April 18, 1982, SL.
24. Jacket blurb from *The Plain Dealer* (Cleveland). Quote used on *Sister Age* book jacket.
25. Michiko Kakutani, *The New York Times*, June 14, 1983, p. C13.
26. David Lehman, *Newsweek*, June 6, 1983.
27. Paula Weideger, "O Is Not for 'Onions,' but 'Ostentation,' " *The Guardian* (London), October 6, 1983, p. 13.
28. Cooper, *Writing at the Kitchen Table*, p. 319.
29. MFKF to Lawrence Clark Powell, September 16, 1983, SL.
30. MFKF to Harriet Jones, November 6, 1983, SL.
31. MFKF to David Pleydell-Bouverie, December 3, 1983, SL.
32. MFKF to Lawrence Clark Powell, October 24, 1984, SL.
33. MFKF to Judith Jones, September 17, 1984, SL.
34. Kennedy Friede Golden, interview by author, tape recording, August 10, 1998.
35. MFKF to Anna Parrish, March 24, 1984, SL.
36. MFKF to Norah Barr, Anna Parrish, and Mary Kennedy Wright, February 9, 1984, PC.
37. MFKF, *Napa Valley Wine Library Report*, spring 1985.
38. "Old Age: The Fires of Creativity Burn Undiminished," *The New York Times*, January 22, 1986.
39. MFKF to Dr. George Frumkes, March 10, 1968, SL.
40. Robert Lescher to MFKF, May 27, 1988, SL. By this time, Barbara Quick had

assembled a film crew, Jack Shoemaker had made a recommendation for a film, and Barbara Wornum was seeking a subsidy from the culinary community to make a video of MFKF.

41. Valerie Marrs, *Whittier Daily News*, December 12, 1987.

42. MFKF to Lil Bernstein, January 29, 1988, SL; and *ALIL*, p. 487.

43. MFKF to Norah Barr, March 25, 1988, SL; and *ALIL*, p. 489. Squeek was Eleanor Friede's nickname.

44. Ruth Reichl, "Savoring a Birthday with M.F.K. Fisher," *Los Angeles Times*, August 16, 1988, VI, p. 1.

45. Herb Caen, *San Francisco Chronicle*, October 10, 1988.

46. Jack Shoemaker to MFKF, September 21, 1988, SL.

47. Clifton Fadiman, *Reading I've Liked* (New York: Simon and Schuster, 1958); W. H. Auden, *Forewords and Afterwords* (New York: Random House, 1973).

48. Kathleen Hill, interview by author, tape recording, July 13, 1999.

49. MFKF to Anna Parrish, January 13, 1986, SL.

50. Anna Parrish to MFKF, January 25, 1992, SL.

51. MFKF to Eleanor Friede, September 21, 1988, SL.

52. Kathleen Hill, interview by author.

53. MFKF to Robert Lescher, September 7, 1989, SL.

54. Ibid. MFKF's account of this collaboration appears in "Frustration—II," *LH*, pp. 264–65.

55. Kathleen Hill, interview by author.

56. There are no letters to document this relationship, but several people—Kennedy Golden, Henrietta Humphries, Kathleen Hill, Marsha Moran—have all mentioned it, though with very little detail.

57. Kathleen Hill, interview by author.

58. Jan Morris, "Introduction," *LAIF*, p. x.

59. MFKF to Anna Parrish, May 8, 1989, SL.

60. *The New York Times*, February 26, 1991.

61. *The New York Times*, February 28, 1991.

62. Katherine Usher Henderson, "M.F.K. Fisher," *A Voice of One's Own: Conversations with America's Writing Women* (Boston: Houghton Mifflin, 1991).

63. MFKF to Judith Jones, September 17, 1984, SL.

64. MFKF, "Private Journal, 1973," PC.

65. MFKF, Journal, October 2, 1975, PC.

66. MFKF, Journal, November 2, 1972, PC.

67. David Lazar, "Something of a Ghost: Conversations with M.F.K. Fisher," *Conversations with M.F.K. Fisher*, p. 133.

68. MFKF, "Private Journal, 1983," PC.

69. Laura Shapiro, *Newsweek*, September 24, 1990.

70. Jeannette Ferrary, *Between Friends*, p. 109.

71. Victoria Glendinning, "The Gastronomical Her," *The New York Times Book Review*, June 9, 1991.

72. David Pleydell-Bouverie to MFKF, November 1991, SL.

73. With North Point's demise in 1991, Jack Shoemaker became West Coast editor for Pantheon.

74. *TBA* (Pantheon, 1992).

75. *SMOCM* (Pantheon, 1993).
76. Marsha Moran to Robert Lescher, December 21, 1991, SL.
77. Kathleen Hill, interview by author.
78. Anna Parrish to MFKF, January 25, 1992, SL.
79. Kennedy Friede Golden to Sean Kelly, October 10, 1992, PC.
80. *TGM*, p. 191.

Bibliography

BOOKS BY M.F.K. FISHER (FIRST EDITIONS)

Serve It Forth. New York, London: Harper, 1937.

Touch and Go. By Victoria Berne (pseudonym of M.F.K. Fisher and Dillwyn Parrish). New York and London: Harper, 1939.

Consider the Oyster. New York: Duell, Sloan and Pearce, 1941.

How to Cook a Wolf. New York: Duell, Sloan and Pearce, 1942.

The Gastronomical Me. New York: Duell, Sloan and Pearce, 1943.

Here Let Us Feast: A Book of Banquets. New York: Viking, 1946.

Not Now But Now. New York: Viking, 1947.

The Physiology of Taste, Or Meditations on Transcendent Gastronomy by Jean Anthelme Brillat-Savarin. A New Translation by M.F.K. Fisher with Preface and Annotations by the Translator and Illustrations by Sylvain Sauvage. New York: Limited Editions Club (George Macy), 1949.

An Alphabet for Gourmets. New York: Viking, 1949.

The Art of Eating. New York: Macmillan, 1954.

A Cordiall Water: A Garland of Odd & Old Receipts to Assuage the Ills of Man & Beast. Boston: Little, Brown, 1961.

The Story of Wine in California. Berkeley: University of California Press, 1962.

Map of Another Town: A Memoir of Provence. Boston: Little, Brown, 1964.

The Cooking of Provincial France. New York: Time-Life Books, 1968.

With Bold Knife and Fork. New York: Putnam (Perigree Books), 1969.

Among Friends. New York: Knopf, 1971.

A Considerable Town. New York: Knopf, 1978.

As They Were. New York: Knopf, 1982.

Two Towns in Provence. New York: Vintage, 1983.

Sister Age. New York: Knopf, 1983.

The Standing and the Waiting. Fallbrook, Calif.: Weather Bird Press, 1985.

Spirits of the Valley. New York: Targ Editions, 1985.

Fine Preserving: M.F.K. Fisher's Annotated Edition of Catherine Plagemann's Cookbook. Berkeley, Calif.: Aris Books, 1986.

Dubious Honors. San Francisco: North Point Press, 1988.

Answer in the Affirmative and The Oldest Living Man. Vineburg, Calif.: Engdahl Typography, Canto Bello Series, no. 3, 1989.

The Boss Dog: A Fable in Six Parts. Limited Edition. Covelo, Calif.: Yolla Bolly Press, 1990.

The Boss Dog: A Story of Provence. San Francisco: North Point Press, 1991.

Long Ago in France: The Years in Dijon. New York: Prentice-Hall, 1991.

To Begin Again: Stories and Memoirs, 1908–1929. New York: Pantheon, 1992.

Stay Me, Oh Comfort Me: Journals and Stories, 1933–1941. New York: Pantheon, 1993.

Last House: Reflections, Dreams, and Observations, 1943–1991. New York: Pantheon, 1995.

A Welcoming Life: The M.F.K. Fisher Scrapbook. Compiled and Annotated by Dominique Gioia. Washington, D.C.: Counterpoint, 1997.

M.F.K. Fisher: A Life in Letters. Selected and Compiled by Norah Barr, Marsha Moran, Patrick Moran. Washington, D.C.: Counterpoint, 1997.

Two Kitchens in Provence. Covelo, Calif.: Yolla Bolly Press, 1999.

The Measure of Her Powers: An M.F.K. Fisher Reader. Edited by Dominique Gioia. Washington, D.C.: Counterpoint, 1999.

From the Journals of M.F.K. Fisher. New York: Pantheon, 1999.

Home Cooking: An Excerpt from a Letter to Eleanor Friede. Pasadena, Calif.: Weatherbird Press, 2000.

UNPUBLISHED MANUSCRIPTS AND LETTERS

Mary Frances Kennedy Fisher Papers, 1929–1985. Unprocessed Collection 71, 58–87, M68. The Arthur and Elizabeth Schlesinger Library, Radcliffe College, Cambridge, Mass.

Journals and Papers. Private Collection of The Literary Trust u/w/o M.F.K. Fisher.

ABOUT M.F.K. FISHER

Ferrary, Jeannette. *Between Friends: M.F.K. Fisher and Me.* New York: Atlantic Monthly Press, 1991.

Fussell, Betty. *Masters of American Cookery.* New York: Times Books, 1983.

Lazar, David, ed. *Conversations with M.F.K. Fisher.* Jackson: University Press of Mississippi, 1992.

Painter, Charlotte. *Gifts of Age: Portraits and Essays of 32 Remarkable Women.* San Francisco: Chronicle Books, 1985.

Reardon, Joan. *M.F.K. Fisher, Julia Child, and Alice Waters: Celebrating the Pleasures of the Table.* New York: Harmony Books, 1994.

Tucher, Andie, ed. *Bill Moyers: A World of Ideas II.* "M.F.K. Fisher: Essayist." New York: Doubleday, 1990.

SELECTED BIBLIOGRAPHY

Bacon, Margaret Hope. *Mothers of Feminism: The Story of Quaker Women in America.* San Francisco: Harper and Row, 1986.

Banner, Lois W. *American Beauty.* Chicago: University of Chicago Press, 1983.

Beck, Simone. *Food and Friends: Recipes and Memoirs from Simca's Cuisine.* New York: Viking, 1991.

Bieler, Henry G. *Food Is Your Best Medicine.* New York: Ballantine, 1965.

Capra, Frank. *The Name Above the Title*. New York: Macmillan, 1971.

Chaney, Lisa. *Elizabeth David*. London: Macmillan, 1998.

Clark, Robert. *James Beard: A Biography*. New York: HarperCollins, 1993.

Cooper, Artemis. *Writing at the Kitchen Table: The Authorized Biography of Elizabeth David*. London: Michael Joseph, 1999.

Fisher, Alfred Young. *The Ghost in the Underblows*. Los Angeles: Ward Ritchie Press, 1940.

Friede, Donald. *Mechanical Angel*. New York: Knopf, 1949.

Gingrich, Arnold. *Toys of a Lifetime*. New York: Knopf, 1966.

Gould, Romilda Peri. *Con Brio: Romie & Paco*. Calistoga, Calif.: Illuminations Press, 1988.

———. *Whys & Sighs*. St. Helena, Calif.: Self-published, 1991.

———. *Paco! The World and Work of Francis Lewis Gould*. Calistoga, Calif.: Illuminations Press, 1992.

Jones, Evan. *Epicurean Delight: The Life and Times of James Beard*. New York: Knopf, 1990.

Kaplan, Louise J. *No Voice Is Ever Wholly Lost*. New York: Simon and Schuster, 1995.

Lord, Eda. *Childsplay*. New York: Simon and Schuster, 1961.

Mendelson, Anne. *Stand Facing the Stove: The Story of the Women Who Gave America "The Joy of Cooking."* New York: Henry Holt, 1996.

Mondavi, Robert, with Paul Chutkow. *Harvests of Joy: My Passion for Excellence*. New York: Harcourt, Brace, 1998.

Olney, Richard. *Reflexions*. New York: Brick Tower Press, 1999.

Powell, Lawrence Clark. *A Passion for Books*. Cleveland and New York: World Publishing Company, 1958.

———. *Fortune and Friendship: An Autobiography*. New York: Bowker, 1968.

———. *The Blue Train*. Santa Barbara, Calif.: Capra Press, 1977.

———. *The River Between*. Santa Barbara, Calif.: Capra Press, 1979.

———. *Eucalyptus Fair: A Memoir in the Form of a Novel*. Tucson, Ariz.: Books West Southwest, 1992.

———. *Looking Back at Sixty*. Recollections of Lawrence Clark Powell, interviewed by James V. Mink. Oral History Program, University of California, Los Angeles, 1973.

Reichl, Ruth. *Comfort Me with Apples: More Adventures at the Table*. New York: Random House, 2001.

Ritchie, Ward. *Printing and Publishing in Southern California*. Oral History Program, University of California, Los Angeles, 1969.

Smith, Sidonie. *A Poetics of Women's Autobiography: Marginality and the Fictions of Self-Representation*. Bloomington: Indiana University Press, 1987.

Spackman, W. M. *A Presence With Secrets*. New York: Dutton, 1982.

Starr, Kevin. *Americans and the California Dream: 1850–1915*. New York: Oxford University Press, 1973.

———. *Inventing the Dream: California Through the Progressive Era*. New York: Oxford University Press, 1985.

———. *Material Dreams: Southern California Through the 1920s*. New York: Oxford University Press, 1990.

Stuart, Gloria, with Sylvia Thompson. *Gloria Stuart: I Just Kept Hoping*. New York: Little, Brown, 1999.

Tebbel, John, and Mary Ellen Zucherman. *The Magazine in America: 1741–1990*. New York: Oxford University Press, 1991.

Wineapple, Brenda. *Genet: A Biography of Janet Flanner*. New York: Ticknor and Fields, 1989.

Acknowledgments

Writing a biography only a few years after the subject's death incurs a special debt. So I am grateful indeed that M.F.K. Fisher's sister Norah, daughters Kennedy and Anna, nephew Sean Kelly, and Eleanor Kask were truly generous with their time and revealed as much as they did about Mary Frances, a person who was so central to their lives and so loved.

Robert Lescher, M.F.K. Fisher's agent since 1978 and the trustee of the unpublished works of the M.F.K. Fisher Trust, has also been forthcoming and supportive of my efforts. Ever protective of his client, he has guided me and advised me. And in concurrence with the director of the Arthur and Elizabeth Schlesinger Library on the History of Women in America, Nancy F. Cott, and head of public services, Ellen M. Shea, he has granted me permission to publish material from the Mary Frances Kennedy Fisher Papers at the Schlesinger Library. Robert Lescher has also granted permission to publish manuscript material in the Private Collection currently in the possession of M.F.K. Fisher's heirs.

I wish to thank William Truslow of Ropes and Gray for permission to publish letters from the Julia McWilliams Child Papers, 1953–1980, in the Schlesinger Library Manuscript Collection. I would also like to acknowledge the kind permission to quote from the unpublished letters of Anna Parrish, Lawrence Paul Bachmann, Leslie R. Perry for David Pleydell-Bouverie, Judith Jones, Robert Lescher, Jack Shoemaker, Norah Barr for Rex Kennedy and Weare Holbrook, Marsha Moran, Gloria Stuart, Kennedy Friede Golden for Donald Friede and Eleanor Kask, Sean Kelly for Anne Kelly Erskine, Revan Miles for Alfred Fisher, and Michael Gingrich for Arnold Gingrich in the Schlesinger Library Manuscript Collection.

In addition to the wealth of material in the Schlesinger Library, the following libraries and historical societies have been rich sources for information: Albion Historical Society and Public Library, Laguna Beach Public Library, Whittier Historical Association, St. Helena Public Library and Napa Valley Wine Association Archives, Hemet Public Library, UCLA Library, Margaret Herrick Library, Smith College Library, The Bishop's School Archives, University of Chicago Records Office, Lake Forest College Library, and Lake Forest Public Library. The librarians at these institutions are too numerous to mention, but my sincere thanks go to all of them and, especially, to Kathy Jacob, curator of manuscripts at the Schlesinger Library, for their kindness and helpfulness.

John Updike's evocative description of M.F.K. Fisher as "a poet of the appetites" gave me the title of the book, and I thank him for his insight. I also want to thank Antonia Allegra, Maynard Amerine, Simone Beck, Julia Child (who passed on at the age of ninety-one as this book was going to press), Jerry DiVecchio, the recently deceased Richard Foorman, Jennifer Garden, Romie Gould, Kathleen Hill, Michael Hargraves, Henrietta Humphries, Judith Jones, Mary Jane Jones, Michelle Anna Jordan, Rosemary Manell, Marsha and Pat Moran, Joan Nathan, Barbara Quick, Rayford Redell, Gloria Stuart, Edith Taber, Liz Tamny, Maggie Waldren, Amy Wilson, Alice Waters, Gigi Parrish Weld, and countless others for sharing their expertise and memories with me. My special gratitude to Michael Hargraves, Richard Foorman, and Antonia Allegra for allowing me to photocopy their private collections of Fisher memorabilia. Kennedy Friede Golden has graciously put the family's collection of photographs at my disposal, and I want to thank Jill Krementz, Faith Echtermeyer, and Richard Foorman for permission to use their photographs. And in a class of his own, Donald Zealand, M.F.K. Fisher's bibliographer, has been more than generous in sharing his research with me. He is, indeed, a "completist," an ardent admirer of M.F.K. Fisher, and a resource nonpareil.

A thank-you must also be extended to all those who believed in this book so early and so continuously. From the beginning of our association, Doe Coover has been a true adviser, an astute critic, and a loyal friend, and her assistant, Mary Frances Kennedy, a source of encouragement. To the first editor of *Poet of the Appetites*, Elisabeth Dyssegaard, I owe my heartfelt thanks, and I am in debt to Rebecca Saletan for insisting that the biography have form, focus, and flavor. I also thank her successor, Linda Rosenberg, who has been a patient and wise guide to the finish line. Art director Susan Mitchell truly captured the spirit of Dillwyn Parrish's portrait of Fisher on the jacket, and Jonathan Lippincott has designed the book with style. The copyediting of Walter Havighurst has been sensitive and everything an author could hope for. And the wonderful marketing professionals at Farrar, Straus and Giroux have been extraordinarily helpful. Finally, my gratitude to Margo True is inestimable; without her intelligence, enthusiasm, and grace this past year, I would have written M.F.K. Fisher's biography, but it would not have been *this* biography. To her, and to all who encouraged this undertaking, I am grateful beyond measure.

Index

MFS

Spanish Sun